Mom

Mom

The Transformation of Motherhood in Modern America

REBECCA JO PLANT

The University of Chicago Press

Chicago and London

The University of Chicago Press, Chicago 60637
The University of Chicago Press, Ltd., London
© 2010 by The University of Chicago
All rights reserved. Published 2010.
Paperback edition 2012

Printed in the United States of America

21 20 19 18 17 16 15 14 13 12   2 3 4 5 6

ISBN-13: 978-0-226-67020-1 (cloth)
ISBN-10: 0-226-67020-1 (cloth)
ISBN-13: 978-0-226-67022-5 (paper)
ISBN-10: 0-226-67022-8 (paper)

Library of Congress Cataloging-in-Publication Data

Plant, Rebecca Jo, 1968–
    Mom : the transformation of motherhood in modern America / Rebecca Jo Plant.
        p. cm.
    Includes biographical references and index.
    ISBN-13: 978-0-226-67020-1 (cloth : alk. paper)
    ISBN-10: 0-226-67020-1 (cloth : alk. paper) 1. 307.76—United States. 2. Mother-
hood in popular culture—United States. 3. Wylie, Philip, 1902–1971—Criticism and
interpretation. 4. Friedan, Betty—Criticism and interpretation.   I. Title.
    HQ759.P564 2010
    306.874'3—dc22

                                                                        2009035339

♾ This paper meets the requirements of ANSI/NISO Z39.48-1992 (Permanence of
Paper).

To my parents, Allene Wenger Plant and Billy D. Plant

Contents

Acknowledgments

To come full circle, I want to thank two extraordinary teachers, Norman Dawson and Vicki Arndt-Helgesen, who first taught me how to think historically. My professors at Macalester College—Emily and Norman Rosenberg, Betsy Schmidt, James B. Stewart, and Peter Rachleff—encouraged my earliest attempts at historical scholarship and served as much admired role models. Without their example and support, I would never have embarked on my present course.

The History Department at the Johns Hopkins University funded my graduate studies and allowed me to work with some truly exceptional scholars. I am deeply grateful to Ruth Leys of the Humanities Center, who generously shared her vast knowledge of the history of psychiatry and psychoanalysis, and to Ronald Walters, who enriched my thinking about popular culture and served as mentor throughout my time at Hopkins. I especially want to thank my advisor, Dorothy Ross, on whose sage council I have continued to rely. My debts to her are simply immeasurable.

Friends and relatives sustained me throughout my lean graduate school years. My cousin Loree Schuster, her husband Stanley Todd, and their sons Jacob and Dustin welcomed me into their home in Philadelphia on numerous occasions. Michael Garral cheered me on and repeatedly restored my spirits. Dirk Bönker, Paul A. Kramer, Lynn Gorchov, Jeffrey Mullins, Bryan Callahan, Stefan Kühl, Stefan Ludwig-Hoffmann, and Till van Rahden all offered astute suggestions on early drafts. The members of my cherished writing group—Thomas Foster, Carolyn Eastman, and Frances Clarke—provided invaluable suggestions and encouragement. And thanks, too, to John Tambornino, who remained confident in my academic future even when the situation looked bleak.

Since then, various institutions and foundations have facilitated my research and writing. In 2002, I participated in a wonderful NEH-funded seminar, "Motherhood and the Nation State," led by Karen Offen and Marilyn Boxer, that helped me to begin to envision how to transform the dissertation into a book. A Library Research Grant from the Friends of the Princeton University Library funded a crucial research trip, and a fellowship from the American Association of University Women allowed me time to write. At the University of California, San Diego, grants from the Faculty Career Development Program and the Hellman Family's Faculty Fellowship Program provided additional support for teaching release and research. Finally, I was especially fortunate to spend 2005–6 as a fellow at the Radcliffe Institute for Advanced Studies—an experience that profoundly shaped the final version of this book. In particular, my interactions with Nancy Cott, Kathy Peiss, Andrew Cohen, and the members of the Tuesday writing group proved crucial in prompting me to rethink various aspects of my project.

Along the way, numerous librarians and archivists have assisted me in innumerable ways. Margaret Sherry Rich facilitated my research at the Firestone Library's Department of Rare Books and Special Collections, Susan Anderson inconvenienced herself so that I could have access to the unprocessed Edward Strecker collection at the Historic Library and Archives at Pennsylvania Hospital, and Diane Richardson shared her extensive knowledge of the collections at the Oskar Diethelm Library. I especially want to thank Ellen Shea of the Schlesinger Library and Nanci Young of the Sophia Smith Archives at Smith College, who guided me toward important materials that I would never have located on my own. Finally, I am grateful to a number of former undergraduate students who provided exceptionally capable research assistance: Catrin Lloyd-Bollard, Sarah Gaylin Heyward, Jacob Garrison, and Deidad Montoya.

Over the years, I have benefited immensely from exchanges with many colleagues and friends, including Caroline Winterer, Robert Moeller, Regina Morantz-Sanchez, Marian van der Klein, Arlene Tuchman, Helmut Walser Smith, Bill Caferro, Denis Flannery, Andrew Lakoff, Camille Forbes, and James Epstein. A special thanks to Sonya Michel, on whose work I have frequently drawn, and to two other historians of mother love and motherhood, Marga Vicedo and Jessica Weiss, who both have been extremely generous in sharing their work and ideas. Thanks also to Judith Coffin, who allowed me to read an early chapter draft from her book on Simone de Beauvoir's *The Second Sex*, and to Paula Michaels, who offered very valuable suggestions on chapter 4. Friends and colleagues Michael Henderson and Katherine Hijar arrived in San Diego just in time to be roped into reading the final chapters; I am grateful for their careful editing and thoughtful advice. Kudos also to my college friend and roommate Michelle Hovet, who read virtually the entire manuscript and shared her incisive, sardonic, and deeply humane vision of the joys and trials of contemporary motherhood.

Working with the University of Chicago Press has been a pleasure. I was blessed to have two external reviewers, Ellen Herman and Kathleen Jones, who read the manuscript with great care; their initial readers' reports served as the blueprint for the final version of this book. My editor, Robert Devens, has been a model of tolerance and good humor and provided many astute suggestions for improving the manuscript. I am also grateful to Susan Olin for her patience and meticulous copyediting.

Since 2002, I have been fortunate to be a member of the History Department at the University of California, San Diego. I particularly want to thank my colleagues Frank Biess, Tak Fujitani, and Judith Hughes for their helpful comments on various chapter drafts, as well as my department chair, John Marino, for his support over the past few years. Above all, I am deeply grateful to Rachel Klein, who has been a trusted mentor and friend since my arrival in San Diego. She read every chapter multiple times, and her astute comments improved the final product in ways large and small.

Three dear friends, all in the process of completing first books of their own, also deserve special mention. Since our auspicious meeting at the NEH summer seminar, I have often drawn sustenance from Darcy Buerkle's keen insights and integrity. As for Carolyn Eastman and Frances Clarke, I hardly know where to begin. From our time together in graduate school, they have contributed so much to this project that they seem to me an integral part of it. I treasure the gift of their friendship.

Finally, I want to thank my family. My brother-in-law Jim Boyden, and my sister, Alisa Plant, saw me through the very hardest part, and for that I will always remain grateful. Alisa has been engaged with this project from the very beginning. While I have benefited enormously from her editorial acumen, my debts to her are far more profound. Indeed, it is impossible to imagine having completed either my dissertation or this book without her. My husband, Rand Steiger, has enriched my life beyond measure and, quite literally, created the conditions that allowed me to bring the book to closure. Like others who know him well, I marvel at his ability to make the seemingly impossible possible. Then there is Sam, who arrived when the project was already well underway. Though I cannot say that he facilitated its completion, his presence did deepen the sense of urgency with which I approached it. My hope for him is the same impossible hope expressed by so many of the mothers in these pages—that he may always feel consoled and strengthened by my love, yet never burdened by it.

My deepest debts are to my parents, Bill and Allene Plant, who supported me in all the most important ways during my long and rocky transition to adulthood. Born and raised in rural settings, both succeeded in reconciling their formative experiences with the very different circumstances of their adult lives. If this sometimes proved a struggle—and surely it must have—they never wavered in their commitment to "the older generation." In some obscure way, this work is my expression of that same commitment, and thus a tribute to them.

Introduction

Mother love used to be regarded as one of the [most] beautiful things in the world. I do not believe in mother love. I think in nine times out of ten, mother love is self-love.

WILLIAM ALLAN NEILSON, 1937

On November 16, 1937, the Smith College Club of New York City held a dinner at the elegant Waldorf-Astoria in honor of the college's long-serving president, the charismatic and iconoclastic William Allan Neilson. Although the event drew nearly nine hundred alumnae, parents, and supporters of the prestigious women's college, it would hardly have been national news, save for some closing remarks made by President Neilson himself. Toward the end of a long speech in which he lavished praise on the school's trustees, faculty, and students, Neilson took satirical aim at the students' parents. Mothers in particular, he argued, undermined Smith's mission by clamoring for their daughters' company and valuing "social considerations" over "intellectual and spiritual development." "Mother love used to be regarded as one of the [most] beautiful things in the world," he proclaimed. "I do not believe in mother love. I think in nine times out of ten, mother love is self-love."[1] The well-heeled audience responded with uproarious laughter and applause.

Yet the humor did not carry the following morning, when Neilson found that his seemingly offhand remarks had ignited a heated debate about the role of mothers and attitudes toward motherhood in American society. Leading newspapers carried stories headlined "Dr. Neilson Finds Mother Love Is Only Self-Love" and "Dr. Neilson Warns on Mother Love," soon followed by articles about the ensuing conflict, such as one titled "Mother Love Talk Stirs Up a Storm."[2] Several dinner attendees rushed to Neilson's defense, arguing that his statements had been taken out of context. "The hundreds of alumnae present, many of whom were also parents, knew they were being spoofed, and loved it," explained one "alumna-parent" in a letter to the *New York Times*. "It was a happy family occasion, until outsiders viewed it with alarm."[3] Another woman explained that all those present had understood that Neilson's remarks should be viewed as "half truth and half chiding." "The truth they valued as the result of his long experience with parents," she wrote, "and the chiding they loved."[4] But most commentators who weighed in with their opinions—including psychologists and psychiatrists, well-known newspaper columnists, representatives of women's organizations, and ordinary readers—took the matter quite seriously. In the process, they gave voice to a cultural conflict that had taken shape in the 1920s, one that would ultimately lead to a major reformulation of the dominant maternal ideal in the United States.

The fact that Americans today rarely speak of "mother love" is one consequence of this change. Often written with a capital *M* and a capital *L*, the expression connoted a love so powerful, enduring, and selfless as to border on the divine. It evoked a maternal ideal dating back to antebellum times, when an emergent middle class had constructed a new model of sentimental domesticity that exalted the mother as the "angel of the house." As an iconic figure, the American Mother symbolized the virtuous nation; as a social type, her charge was to oversee her children's physical, intellectual, and spiritual development. This elaboration of the maternal role constrained middle-class women in countless ways, but it also elevated their status within the home and allowed them to exert greater control over their reproductive lives. Moreover, it provided middle-class women with a convincing rationale for engaging in a host of reform activities: in the name of protecting the home, they increasingly ventured beyond it. A rich body of historical scholarship has traced the rise of this domestic ideology, explored its relation to economic and political developments, and analyzed its class and racial dimensions.[5] But the demise of the moral mother remains less well understood.

This book traces the repudiation of moral motherhood and the rise of a new maternal ideal that both reflected and facilitated white, middle-class women's gradual incorporation into the political and economic order as individuals rather than as wives and mothers. It argues that the interwar period witnessed the emergence of an antimaternalist critique that ultimately helped to discredit four long-standing precepts that had defined late Victorian motherhood: the belief that the mother/homemaker role was a full-time, lifelong role, incompatible with the demands of wage earning; the notion that motherhood was not simply a private, familial role, but also the foundation of female citizenship; the conviction that mothers should bind their children (especially their boys) to the home with "silver cords" of love in order to ensure their proper moral development; and the assumption that motherhood entailed immense physical suffering and self-sacrifice. Of course, such ideas have not entirely lost currency in American culture today. In the early twentieth century, however, most middle-class Americans shared a conception of motherhood based on these principles; by the 1960s, most did not. Particularly after World War II, mainstream American culture ceased to represent motherhood as an all-encompassing identity rooted in notions of self-sacrifice and infused with powerful social and political meaning. Instead, motherhood came to be conceived as a deeply fulfilling but fundamentally private experience and a single (though still central) component of a more multifaceted self. *Mom: The Transformation of Motherhood in Modern America* attempts to explain this transformation and to explore its impact on women who possessed the material resources and demographic profile that allowed them to aspire to the dominant maternal ideal.

My first and most basic claim is that the ideology of moral motherhood endured longer than generally thought. Historians have tended to assume that the moral mother fell victim to the rise of "scientific motherhood" and the broader assault on Victorian gender ideals that began near the turn of the century and reached full swing by the 1920s. As numerous scholars have shown, reformers and experts increasingly challenged the adage "mother knows best" and asserted their authority over childrearing practices.[6] During the Progressive era, women reformers associated with the Children's Bureau played a major role in promoting scientific motherhood. These women held various cultural biases, and they often assumed a condescending stance in relation to poor, immigrant, and minority mothers. Still, they generally conveyed a basic respect for the mother as a person charged with an important and difficult task. In the 1920s, however, as male experts and professionally trained social workers began to supplant maternalist reformers, new and more psychologically oriented critiques of motherhood emerged, and mother-blaming expanded to encompass middle-class as well as poor mothers. Around the same time, as Ann Douglas has shown, modernist writers and intellectuals launched a full-scale assault on the "late-Victorian matriarch," deriding her sentimentality as insipid, her piety as hypocritical and repressive.[7] Male resentment over women's demands for political rights and social freedom lent animus to this assault: many men believed that women who wanted to vote, enter the workforce, and enjoy sexual freedom should cede the privileges and moral authority they had enjoyed in the past. In sum, by the end of the 1920s, the social, cultural, and political conditions that gave rise to the ideology of moral motherhood had shifted so radically that, by any logical measure, it should have been entirely defunct.

Yet when Neilson derided sentimental mother love in 1937, he was not simply beating a dead horse. Many people wrote letters protesting his remarks—missives that he privately mocked as "extremely amusing and not infrequently violent."[8] One woman vowed that her daughter would never attend Smith, "where the President throws mud at one of the most beautiful things in this world of ours—Mother Love—synonymous with Self-Sacrifice."[9] Another wrote, "To brand one of the most valuable and most beautiful of the primitive instincts . . . as you do—is almost unbelievable."[10] Yet another respondent attempted to shame the college president by reminding him of his own mother. "Can you remember back years the pair of loving hands that worked for you, and gave all to *try* to make a man out of you? Well that was mother," she chided. "Don't you keep her memory green?"[11] Male readers also found Neilson's assault on mother love offensive. One man, who described himself as "the son of one of the finest mothers that a son ever had," was so shocked that he wondered if there had been some mistake.[12] Another man angrily declared, "I hope the Board of Trustees kicks you out after your speech."[13]

For their part, Neilson's defenders saluted his debunking of mother love as a bold challenge to a veritable shibboleth. The famous advice columnist Dorothy Dix predicted that his comments would be denounced as "nothing less than sacrilege," since they struck at "the old tradition that when a woman bears a child she is automatically metamorphosed into an angel and filled with altruistic devotion to her offspring."[14] A former schoolteacher, who believed that "the idea that biological motherhood endows a woman with omniscience and unselfishness needs to be exploded," praised Neilson for airing "the truth about so-called mother love."[15] Similarly, the Nutcrackers Club—four men who decried "motheritis" as "the curse of American life"—applauded the college president and urged him to "stand up under the onslaught of 'American Motherhood.'"[16] Clearly, neither Neilson's detractors nor his defenders perceived the ideology of moral motherhood as anachronistic or irrelevant.

Because scholars have underestimated the persistence of the ideology of moral motherhood, they have lacked an adequate framework for interpreting the antimaternalist strain that emerged so prominently in American popular culture and psychological and social scientific literature in the wake of World War I. In general, they have regarded attacks on mothers as a form of antifeminism or "gender conservatism." This is especially true for works that focus on the 1940s and 1950s, when mother-blaming reached its zenith, as it did most memorably in the popular writer Philip Wylie's infamous "momism" critique, which accused middle-class, middle-aged "moms" of emasculating the nation.[17] Given the extraordinary misogyny that informed Wylie's screed and similar attacks on mothers, historians have tended to assume that they expressed men's profound resentment over changing gender roles and women's attempts to gain greater social, economic, and political power. There is some truth to this view: mother-blaming was deeply irrational, and the same anxieties and rage that fueled attacks on the "modern woman" could easily mutate into attacks on mothers and homemakers. But such interpretations have obscured the fact that critics like Wylie were lambasting a long-standing set of beliefs about motherhood—beliefs they viewed as simultaneously outmoded and still pervasive.[18] The most severe critics of American motherhood, as historian Ruth Feldstein has convincingly shown, were not conservatives or traditionalists but liberals who espoused progressive views on race, social welfare, and other issues.[19] (Neilson, for instance, was left-leaning in his political views; the right-wing ideologue Elizabeth Dilling had even deemed him worthy of an entry in her infamous 1935 publication, *The Red Network*.)[20] In turn, the most passionate defenders of American motherhood tended to be social conservatives who believed that critics like Neilson and Wylie devalued women's domestic roles.

Throughout the 1920s and 1930s, traditional and modern conceptions of motherhood vied for dominance within mainstream American culture. Traditionalists did not think of motherhood as a job that women performed or a role that they assumed, but rather as a sacred estate that they entered—a calling that would demand their attention and energy throughout their adult lives. Mother love, they believed, had the capacity to transform and redeem: it could turn a shallow and vapid woman into a noble character; it could recall a wayward son or daughter to the path of virtue; it could mold a poor and scrawny boy into a great and powerful leader. When traditionalists spoke of "American motherhood," they meant something beyond a familial identity shared by many American women: they meant an *institution*—a fundamental pillar of the nation's social and political order. Maria Leonard, dean of women at the University of Illinois, articulated this view when she rebuked Neilson for his "breathtaking" remarks. A few "irritating and exasperating mothers," she wrote, should never be allowed to overshadow "that great army of mothers, past and present, who have stood as the symbol of the purest love and deepest sacrifice known to mankind. When motherhood goes to the gates of death to give life, perhaps it is too much to ask that any father understand sacrifice and courage, walking alone through 'the valley of the shadow.'"[21] Leonard and like-minded Americans could refer to "motherhood" as an active, collective entity because they actually perceived it as such; to them, "American motherhood" was almost like a branch of government, charged with reproducing the populace and upholding the nation's guiding principles. Phrases like "that great army of mothers" rolled readily off their tongues, because they assumed that mothers performed a noble civic duty that entailed courage and self-sacrifice. Indeed, from their perspective, the male counterpart to the mother was not the father but the soldier, who similarly risked his life for the greater good of the nation.

Modernists envisioned motherhood in far less exalted terms. Mothers, they insisted, were simply female individuals—some admirable, some not— who had been through a certain biological experience. Although modernists granted that motherhood might consume a woman's full energies for a certain period of her life, they believed that women should pursue interests and activities beyond the home as their children grew older. Receptive to contemporary psychological theories, they viewed sentimental mother love and assumptions about female moral superiority as psychologically destructive. A recent graduate of Smith College gave voice to this perspective when she defended Neilson's remarks in a letter to *The New York Times*:

> Of late years there have been some particularly helpful discussions on the subject, either set forth by psychologists . . . or by novelists who have traced the sometimes irreparable emotional damage done to a human being who was taught that "Mother knows best; you must love her best in the world"—and motherhood in itself endows a woman with indisputable wisdom and the inalienable right to lifelong—and exclusive—respect and devotion.
>
> Fortunately, this mother-taught brand of sentimentality is fast passing and has, by the mothers of today, many of them the victims of it, been good-naturedly condemned. The modern young mother cultivates interests besides her family and disdains to wear a halo or carry a sceptre as symbols of her biological office.[22]

This young woman welcomed the efforts of psychological experts and modernist writers to expose sentimental mother love as an unnatural and unhealthy emotional stance. Eschewing the role of "angel of the house," she preferred to conceptualize motherhood as a "biological office," devoid of intrinsic moral purpose or meaning.

This book explores how the conflict between these two views played out during the interwar period and World War II, and how the assault on moral motherhood abetted the rise of a new maternal ideal that achieved dominance in the postwar period. Throughout, I use the terms "maternalism" and "antimaternalism." Scholars first began employing "maternalism" to designate an ideology espoused by women reformers who played a critical role in shaping the early welfare state in the late nineteenth and early twentieth century. "Maternalism," as historians Seth Koven and Sonya Michel first defined it, "exalted women's capacity to mother and extended to society as a whole the values they attached to that role: care, nurturance and morality. . . . it extolled the private virtues of domesticity while simultaneously legitimizing women's public relationships to politics and the state, to community, workplace and marketplace."[23] The term offered a preferable alternative to "social feminism" in that it allowed historians to more clearly differentiate progressive reformers from equal rights feminists, who staked their claims on the grounds of liberal individualism.[24] However, "maternalism" has since been used in a wide array of other contexts, to describe virtually any type of political activity in which women have emphasized their roles as mothers. For example, Christine Erickson coined the phrase "patriotic maternalism" to characterize the activities of right-wing women's organizations in the interwar period, while Laura McEnaney has characterized the Cold War civilian defense program as a "militarist-maternalist" movement.[25] In what follows, I stretch the term even further, to encompass not only a gender ideology that legitimized certain political activities but also a sensibility that affected cultural representations, maternal subjectivity, and interpersonal relationships.[26] As I employ it, "maternalism" refers to an outlook that defined motherhood as both a familial and a civic act; enabled white, middle-class women to exert a morally charged influence within the public and private realms; and allowed mothers to claim the largest share of their children's gratitude and affection.[27]

A possible objection to such a broad definition is that it ends up lumping together women who were in fact political adversaries. Yet this is precisely why I find the term is helpful, because it transgresses and complicates standard political categories. One of the key shifts this book seeks to illuminate is how motherhood came to figure less centrally as a component of white, middle-class women's civic identities—a development that cannot be characterized as wholly "progressive" or "conservative" in its political implications. In the 1920s and 1930s, progressive maternalism declined, while patriotic maternalism gained strength, but "conservative" and "maternalist" never aligned in a complete or tidy fashion. Indeed, many left-leaning women, especially peace advocates, retained a maternalist orientation in the 1930s and 1940s and even thereafter. Thus, when Congress debated whether to draft women during World War II, an unlikely coalition of far-right women and pacifists opposed the legislation; although each group raised additional, very different objections, both argued against it on the grounds that women were already making a vital contribution to the national cause as mothers and homemakers.[28] I use the term "maternalism" to signal this gendered conception of citizenship rather than support for a certain political agenda or set of policy proposals.

In turn, I use the term "antimaternalism" to refer to the belief that motherhood had become too freighted with political meaning and too laden with sentiment, and that it should instead be construed in a more limited and rational manner—as a biologically based familial role. "Antimaternalism" does not imply a particular set of beliefs about women's proper social role; it could signal a commitment to feminism, although usually it did not. Broadly speaking, three kinds of people articulated antimaternalist arguments: critics who railed against sentimentality, hypocrisy, and sexual repression; social scientists and psychologists who sought to extend their professional expertise; and women (especially young women) who disliked the Victorian construction of motherhood, with its associations of self-sacrifice and suffering. Some commentators debunked old gender ideals in order to promote new ones, but many others were simply disillusioned with contemporary women and nostalgic for gender ideals rendered anachronistic by modernity, which lent their critiques a reactionary character. But in either case—whether they consciously rejected the ideal of the self-sacrificing mother as a worthy goal, or lashed out at modern mothers for falling short of it—antimaternalist critics helped to undermine the image of American mothers as morally superior and politically disinterested.

Although anxiety over the effeminizing influence of mothers dated back to the late nineteenth century, a thoroughgoing assault on the ideology of moral motherhood emerged only in the aftermath of World War I. Initially, the attacks on American motherhood emanated primarily from psychological professionals and the cultural avant-garde. By the 1940s, however, antimaternalism had gone mainstream. Critics argued that what appeared like self-sacrificing mother love could in fact be narcissistic, possessive, and pathogenic. They claimed that medical advances had dramatically reduced the suffering and mortality associated with childbirth, rendering the age-old analogy between mothers and soldiers obsolete. They pointed to laborsaving devices in the home, lower birth rates, and longer life spans, arguing that many women had become idle or even parasitic. And they cynically mocked suffragists' earlier predictions that women, acting as virtuous mothers, would purify politics once they attained the vote. Again, some critics who advanced these claims hoped to push women in the direction of liberal individualism, while others simply wanted to undermine the old model of female moral authority. What must be stressed is that their critiques could sound strikingly similar, even when fueled by radically different motives and political visions.

The demystification of mother love should be seen as part of a much broader transformation of gender ideology and sexual relations. Victorians had postulated a world divided into separate, yet complementary spheres: whereas women relied upon men for economic support and physical protection, men depended on women to nurture their bodies and guard their souls. Idealized notions of womanhood dictated middle-class women's exclusion

from the corrupt commercial and political realms, and this presumed exclusion in turn helped to make the idealization of womanhood convincing.
Beginning in the 1890s, the rise of sexual liberalism and women's increasing forays into male-dominated realms undermined these convictions. On
the one hand, the New Woman who demanded a career, the vote, and even
sexual satisfaction directly challenged accepted notions of female nature.[29]
On the other hand, women who advanced their agendas in the "traditional"
language of motherhood subverted Victorian gender ideals in a less direct
but not necessarily less daunting manner. The "organized mother-love"
championed by late nineteenth-century maternal reformers represented a
significant departure from the mother love espoused in antebellum domestic
tracts; once women began to lobby the government, instead of appealing to
the individual male conscience, their moral authority increasingly came to be
associated with the coercive powers of the state.[30]

The growing skepticism of mother love also reflected fundamental
changes in conceptions of sexuality and sexual identity. In the nineteenth
and early twentieth centuries, a certain fluidity characterized expressions of
love, for the sharp line cordoning off romantic, heterosexual desire as entirely distinct from other types of longing had yet to be drawn. Middle-class
women and men spoke and wrote openly of their deep feelings for friends
of the same sex, unconstrained by the fear of being labeled homosexual that
would lead to greater restraint and self-policing in the twentieth century.[31]
Similarly, mothers and children (especially sons) expressed their desire for
one another in romantic terms that would later come to be seen as decidedly
pathological. A mother might unself-consciously call her son "Lover Boy,"
while a son could refer to his mother as "my best girl" without fear of mockery.[32] In the 1920s, however, psychologists such as the behaviorist John B.
Watson depicted "mother love" as "a sex-seeking response" and shrilly denounced mothers who cultivated passionate relationships with their sons.[33]
As such ideas filtered into the broader culture, prolonged mother-son intimacy increasingly came to signal male effeminacy, homosexuality, and even
political subversion.[34]

The counterpoint to the assault on mother love was thus an anxious appeal for greater paternal involvement, which emerged in the late nineteenth
century and persisted as a constant refrain in the twentieth.[35] In the Victorian
era, when masculine and feminine natures were held to be fundamentally
different and male and female pursuits more sharply diverged, mother-son
intimacy had not constituted grounds for alarm. Quite the reverse. Victorians
viewed mother love as the substance from which men were forged, for they
believed that manliness followed naturally once discipline and self-restraint

had been acquired.[36] However, in the late nineteenth century, middle-class Americans increasingly came to view "masculinity" as a coveted trait in its own right. This new ideal of masculinity placed greater emphasis on physical vigor and, as Arnaldo Testi has noted, tended to be defined in opposition to "a radical other" (femininity) rather than an earlier phase of life (youth).[37] According to its logic, women could play little if any role in cultivating manhood, except in the negative sense of knowing when to snip the apron strings. Unlike their Victorian forefathers, modern American men would learn to construct their masculine identity largely in opposition to, rather than in concert with, their mothers.

The rise of antimaternalism proceeded apace with another major cultural trend that had profoundly ambiguous political effects—the rise of a therapeutic culture and the expansion of the psychological professions.[38] In this regard, too, the Neilson controversy is instructive, for it exposed a serious fault line between psychological professionals and their numerous critics. Speaking to the *New York Times*, the left-wing social psychologist Goodwin Watson claimed that clinical experience bore out the truth of Neilson's claims. "If society employed everyone at interesting work, mothers could love children without getting in their way," he argued. "Bridge clubs are a pathetic substitute for something else to do."[39] The prominent psychiatrist Karl Menninger also seconded Neilson's views; he forwarded the college president a newspaper story that linked the two men, commenting wryly, "I was proud to be associated, even in persecution, with yourself."[40] In contrast, many of Neilson's critics condemned the growing influence of the psychological professions and the therapeutic approach to selfhood they promoted. "It is well that we mothers do not take the psychologists and educators too seriously," wrote a woman in a letter to the *New York Times*. "There is a higher law than the psychologist or the educator can fathom which guides a mother's love or whatever you wish to call it. Instinct is a better word."[41] Although this woman stressed that the "intelligent mother" was "ever alert to hear and learn for the benefit of her children," she believed that "maternal instinct" would ultimately prove more trustworthy than whatever guidance a psychologist or educator might offer. This basic conflict—between experts who questioned maternal wisdom, and mothers who questioned psychological expertise—would persist in ensuing decades, with experts increasingly, but by no means completely, gaining the upper hand.

If psychological experts played a critical role in legitimizing the attacks on sentimental mother love, they had very accommodating allies in the publishing industry. Sensationally titled stories and articles, such as "What's Wrong with American Mothers?" or "Are American Moms a Menace?" provoked controversy and debate, which in turn helped to sell newspapers and magazines. Thus, though Neilson made only a few fleeting comments about mother love at the end of a long speech, the *Times* chose to run with the headline, "Dr. Neilson Warns on Mother Love." Soon thereafter, various individuals from the publishing world stepped forward, eager to fan the flames of controversy. A literary agent offered Neilson his services; a journalist from *Physical Culture* magazine requested an authorized interview; the managing editor of *Scribner's* inquired if he would be interested in writing an article for their publication. "We would like to have you handle the subject completely without gloves as we are not afraid of offending anyone," she assured him. "In fact, we enjoy it very much."[42] Although Neilson apparently declined these overtures, many experts who shared his views on mother love acceded to similar requests or sought out public forums on their own initiative. By joining forces to warn Americans of the dangers of maternal pathology, the popular press and psychological experts together forged a mutually beneficial alliance.

The transformation of mother love unfolded in two overlapping stages. For most of the interwar period, commentators and experts remained preoccupied with dismantling the ideology of moral motherhood, and their critiques retained much of the flavor of the 1920s rebellion against Victorianism. When criticizing mothers, they also frequently attacked stringent moral prohibitions on sexuality, sentimental expressivity in popular culture, and sometimes even xenophobia and knee-jerk patriotism—all of which they associated with white, middle-class matrons. Such attacks generally went hand-in-hand with calls for women to cultivate a more rational sensibility in regard to their maternal role. Until the late 1930s, most childrearing experts sought to restrain maternal affectivity by urging women to adopt strict "scientific" schedules that would serve to regulate the child's biological needs, while also mitigating the emotional intensity of the mother-child relationship.

During and especially after World War II, however, the preoccupations surrounding motherhood shifted, and the antimaternalism of the interwar period gave way to a more narrow, psychologically focused form of mother-blaming. Attacks on middle-aged mothers who exerted maternal influence in both the home and the broader culture receded, for the battle against them had largely been won. Experts continued to rail against maternal overprotection, but they now increasingly fretted about maternal deprivation and rejection as well. (Indeed, some experts suggested that maternal overprotection often served as a form of compensation, masking a more fundamental attitude of maternal rejection.) At the same time, the prewar ideal of the modern, "scientific" mother, who gave birth under full anesthesia and raised her babies by the book, yielded to a celebration of "natural motherhood." Condemning the overly rational and scientific approaches of the interwar period, experts reversed course and promoted a "permissive" approach that included plenty of warm, physical contact. In the process, they revived the concept of maternal instinct as a mother's most trustworthy guide during her child's first few years.[43]

At first glance, the postwar maternal ideal appears almost like a return of the Victorian glorification of motherhood. The insistent calls for mother-child bonding, the pronatalist cultural climate, and even the fashions of the day—the billowing skirts and accentuated bosoms—all seem to point to a revival of older ideals. But a closer look suggests that the similarities between Victorian and postwar ideals of motherhood were largely superficial.[44] In the late nineteenth and early twentieth centuries, motherhood had been conceived as an all-encompassing identity that shaped a woman's entire adult life. In popular culture "Mother" was typically portrayed as a middle-aged or elderly lady, her kindly face etched with age, gray hair drawn back in a bun. By the post–World War II period, American popular culture primarily celebrated young, fertile women: the most glowing representations of motherhood tended to feature beautiful young women with babies or toddlers. Even the way that white, middle-class Americans referred to mothers changed, as the Victorian "Mother" gradually yielded to the twentieth-century "mom," acquiring a possessive qualifier along the way.[45] People spoke of "my mom" rather than "Mother," because motherhood had become a more informal and exclusively familial role. Of course, many postwar Americans still believed that mothers made crucial contributions to the nation's civic and political life, as remains the case today. But after the 1930s, politicians rarely spoke of childbearing and childrearing as services rendered unto the state, and fewer women envisioned their maternal role as the source of their civic identity. In all these ways, motherhood became more compatible with liberal individualism and the cultivation of a sense of self distinct from familial obligations and relationships.

Above all, the profound wariness with which so many experts and commentators came to regard maternal influence reveals the chasm that separated the nineteenth from the mid-twentieth century. Whereas Victorian commentators never tired of declaring their faith in the redemptive powers of Mother Love, postwar experts often seemed almost phobic in their attitude toward maternal affectivity. To be sure, they emphasized the necessity of intensive maternal care in infancy and early childhood to a greater extent than ever before. But they also reduced the period in which maternal influence represented an unmitigated good to the first few years of life, and they

demoted Mother Love, with its lofty spiritual connotations, to maternal instinct—a psychobiological drive. Moreover, despite their tendency to portray
maternal instinct in biological terms, experts betrayed profound doubts about
middle-class women's "natural" capacities as nurturers. This is particularly
evident in two postwar diagnoses, the "refrigerator mother" and the "schizophrenogenic mother," which attributed childhood autism and schizophrenia
to frigid and inconsistent mothers.[46] Such egregious formulations, which no
doubt resulted in untold heartache to countless women already facing severe
life challenges, could only have gained credibility in a culture characterized
by both a deep suspicion of maternal influence and a high level of deference
toward psychiatric and psychoanalytic authority.

    This book should not be viewed as a history of American mothers. It is,
first, a history of how the ideology of moral motherhood came to be largely
discredited in favor of a more narrow, psychological and biological conception of the maternal role. Second, it is a history of how that shift influenced
the ways in which white, middle-class women conceptualized and experienced their maternal role. Although I refer to nonwhite and working-class
mothers at various points throughout, I do so primarily to highlight the class-
and race-based assumptions that informed the dominant maternal ideal. As
numerous historians have demonstrated, cultural representations and experts' perceptions of nonwhite and working-class mothers strongly reflected
prevailing prejudices and assumptions. (For instance, psychiatrists virtually
never diagnosed black or other minority women as "refrigerator mothers,"
even when their children displayed classic signs of autism, for they believed
only well-educated whites capable of this particular form of maternal rejection.)[47] In addition, immigrant and ethnic mothers, African- and Mexican-
American mothers, and poor and working-class mothers have often defined
and experienced motherhood in ways that diverged markedly from mainstream American culture.[48] I ultimately found that the vast diversity of maternal ideologies and experiences exceeded the parameters of a single study.

    This book does, however, discuss important shifts in the racial construc-
tion of the dominant maternal ideal. In the nineteenth and early twentieth
century, the racialization of American motherhood occurred in fairly predictable ways: the modern, white, American mother tended to be defined in
opposition to the superstitious or unhygienic ethnic or black mother. But in
the interwar era, the dichotomy between so-called civilized American mothers and their class or racial "others" gradually became less stark. Mother-
blaming continued to be racially coded, as Ruth Feldstein, Gwendolyn Mink,
and other scholars have shown. Beginning in the 1930s, social scientists and
psychologists articulated a powerful critique of unwed black "matriarchs" that

would ultimately play a major role in fueling the backlash against welfare.[49] Yet by the 1940s and 1950s, many experts also suggested that women of color who allegedly relied more on their maternal "instincts"—aged "mammies," or mothers in developing countries who carried their babies in slings and fed them on demand—actually did a better job of caring for very young children than did educated white women. Of course, this new discourse reproduced the distinction between middle-class white and "other" mothers, and it was by no means free of pernicious racial assumptions. (Indeed, the fiction that nonwhite women were "naturally" more maternal would prove highly reassuring in subsequent decades, as growing numbers of affluent parents began hiring such women as nannies.) The point here is that, whereas mother-blaming in the past had often reinforced the cultural authority of middle-class mothers at the expense of poor or nonwhite women, mother-blaming after World War I tended to lower the status of mothers across the board.[50]

Although many of the developments traced here can be viewed as part of a larger, trans-Atlantic history concerning the evolution of motherhood, this study is very much a nation-based history. Other countries have experienced the same basic trends—such as declining birth rates, dramatic improvements in maternal and infant health, the introduction of new household technologies, and the influx of mothers into the workforce—that helped to transform the experience and cultural ideal of motherhood within the United States. For instance, historian Ann Taylor Allen has shown how the significance of motherhood in Western Europe also contracted over the course of the twentieth century, as what was once a "life-long status" gradually came to be redefined as "a role—a flexible and optional activity that could be chosen, combined with other identities, or refused."[51] But if large-scale forces that diminished or decentered the maternal role spanned the industrializing world, the particular manner in which any given society experienced this shift reflected its own unique economic, cultural, and social circumstances.

In the United States, the transformation of motherhood was unusual, perhaps even exceptional, to the extent that it was fueled by an assault on the figure of the moral mother. No other Western nation witnessed such intense and concerted attacks on middle-class matrons; the charge of "momism" did not translate into other cultural contexts, even English-speaking ones. This reflects the fact that in no other nation had middle-class women succeeded in exerting a comparable degree of cultural and political influence. "Although 'maternalist' ideas about social welfare spread across the industrializing world in the late nineteenth and early twentieth centuries," Theda Skocpol has observed, "they loomed politically largest in the United States."[52] There are many reasons why the United States proved so conducive to maternalism: the strength of Protestant religiosity; the relative weakness of the labor movement; anxieties generated by a diverse ethnic and racial population—all these factors helped to explain the power of a racialized ideal of "American motherhood." What is indisputable is that virtually all commentators believed that American mothers (and American women more broadly) had achieved a position of cultural, political, and familial influence unrivaled by women elsewhere in the world. As the émigré psychoanalyst Frieda Fromm-Reichmann casually asserted in 1940, "We all know how different things are in this country. . . . In the family group American women are very often the leaders, and men wait on them as wives wait on their husbands in European families."[53] I attempt to explore this cultural construction of the "American Mother" and the "American mom" as mythical figures, while simultaneously attending to the social and political realities that led so many people to embrace an exceptionalist view of gender roles in the United States.

One goal of this book is to provide an overarching interpretation that will help readers to synthesize the vast literature on motherhood that has appeared in recent years. Historians and other scholars have analyzed maternalist politics, childrearing advice literature, cultural representations of mothers, and the medicalization of childbirth in the twentieth century.[54] Yet there is currently no study that seeks to illuminate the connections between these discrete areas.[55] I aim to show that it was not coincidental that maternalism lost much of its viability as a political strategy around the same time that numerous experts began to portray sentimental mother love as a cause of widespread psychopathology, or that sentimental images of middle-aged mothers began to lose resonance in popular culture around the same time that maternal mortality rates dropped precipitously. For all these trends were constitutive of a broader shift, in which the notion of motherhood as a role that entailed self-sacrifice—and therefore warranted public recognition— yielded to a conception of motherhood as a private experience that promised women deep personal fulfillment.

By offering a new interpretation of the decline of social motherhood, I also hope to contribute to the ongoing debate regarding postwar domesticity and the origins of second-wave feminism. Since the 1990s, a new body of revisionist scholarship has convincingly challenged what had been a vastly oversimplified view of the postwar era—a view first advanced by Betty Friedan in *The Feminine Mystique*. "Fulfillment as a woman had only one definition for American women after 1949—the housewife-mother," Friedan asserted. "As swiftly as in a dream, the image of the American woman as a changing, growing individual in a changing world was shattered."[56] After conducting her own survey of postwar magazines, Joanne Meyerowitz concluded that postwar gender ideology was in fact much less hegemonic than Friedan suggested, with domestic ideals coexisting "in ongoing tension with an ethos of individual achievement that celebrated non-domestic activity, individual striving, public service, and public success."[57] Subsequently, historians Jessica Weiss and Susan Hartmann demonstrated how postwar experts and commentators, far from insisting that women restrict themselves to the home, actually encouraged them to reenter the workforce once their children reached a certain age.[58] Increasingly, the trend in historical scholarship has been toward emphasizing the contradictory nature of the messages that women received and the myriad ways in which their lives deviated from the dominant cultural ideal.

There is no denying that women received contradictory messages in the postwar period or that their life experiences frequently stood in tension with mainstream gender ideology. But, at times, this new scholarship threatens to eclipse what Friedan and early women's historians got right about the period. In my view, the postwar era was in many respects a nadir for white, middle-class American women, for reasons that were indeed difficult to name at the time. In the wake of World War II, politicians and the press continually reminded "the American woman" of her enviable status—her relative affluence, her freedom from arduous labor, her ability to exercise political rights, and her access to modern obstetrical care. Yet even those women for whom such claims were actually true often did not feel particularly empowered as individuals or even as mothers. Friedan provided a partial explanation: she captured suburban women's feelings of discontent and their desire to participate in the nation's broader social, economic, and political life. She also astutely analyzed how "femininity"—the very essence of a woman's gender identity—had been transformed into a quality that women felt pressured to prove or display. But Friedan missed—indeed, she contributed to—the frustrations many women felt due to a cultural climate that constantly criticized and denigrated mothers and homemakers. The "problem with no name" was really twofold, for women not only felt oppressed by a feminine mystique that hindered their ability to define themselves as individuals, they also felt devalued within their traditional, gender-specific roles.

In the postwar era, white, middle-class American mothers found themselves betwixt and between. By stigmatizing "idle" housewives, deriding female voluntary efforts, and pathologizing prolonged mother love, numerous commentators in the 1940s and 1950s undercut the ability of such women to construct a satisfying identity based on motherhood and homemaking. To a certain degree, they actually pushed women in the direction of liberal individualism. Yet virtually no one suggested that women and men ought to share the responsibilities of homemaking and childrearing equally or otherwise acknowledged the severe obstacles that prevented women from achieving meaningful equality. Moreover, psychological experts routinely pressured women to conform to the dictates of domesticity by portraying marriage and motherhood as crucial evidence of a woman's femininity and basic mental health. To appreciate the complexity of postwar gender ideology, it is thus necessary to view antimaternalism and pronatalism as paradoxically collaborative forces. While antimaternalist critiques at times helped to promote a more gender-neutral understanding of women's roles and capabilities, postwar pronatalism contained the revolutionary implications of this shift by recasting maternity as the ultimate source of "feminine fulfillment." In other words, during the postwar era, middle-class women continued to be defined primarily in relation to their familial roles, and they continued to face pervasive discrimination in the public realm, even as society repealed many of the privileges and compensations that prior generations had claimed as wives and mothers.

Finally, this book attempts to explore the elusive emotional history of motherhood—to capture something of what it felt like to bear and raise children after the Victorian faith in mother love had fallen away. In 1991, historian Joan Scott cautioned historians against privileging first-person accounts of experience over other forms of evidence, since all "experience" is itself discursively constructed. She criticized the tendency, prevalent among those who studied women and other marginalized groups, to view personal narratives as if they were unmediated by culture and thus capable of providing access to a more authentic past.[59] While I appreciate Scott's call for a more critical approach, in the process of researching and writing this book I nevertheless came to view women's letters as different from other types of evidence. To put it simply, I found them more surprising and compelling than most published sources; they challenged my presuppositions and expectations to a greater extent and led me to conclusions that I would not otherwise have reached. This is by no means to suggest that women employed language in a manner that somehow escaped or transcended the constraints of their time. On the contrary, one of the lessons of this history is how deeply it mattered that a term like "sexism" did not exist prior to the 1960s, and how much its absence restricted women's abilities to challenge antimaternalist critiques. I do, however, seek to affirm the simple fact that many ordinary women managed to articulate their thoughts, feelings, and experiences in a manner that conveyed something of the particularities of their lives and personalities. They drew on stock phrases and narrative conventions—as do we all—but certain passages or turns of phrase still leap out as unexpected and revealing.

The effect, however, is not always uplifting. For while some letters demonstrate women's capacity to resist or creatively appropriate antimaternalism, others simply expose its emotional toll. Consider the following letter, from a mother living in Nashville, Tennessee. In 1937, she implored Neilson to send her a copy of his full speech and to share his "constructive ideas" about childrearing—ideas that would "help mothers instead of discouraging them." As she explained:

> I know mother love isn't enough. . . . It lacks many things, and I haven't yet found out what they are. I should like to know exactly what you believe is wrong with mother love, and what you think mothers can do about it. That is, if you were speaking seriously. You were, weren't you? I hope so; if it were a jest, it is too cruel.[60]

This woman clearly hoped to discover what she was doing wrong as a mother, and how she might correct her errors. What makes her appeal so pathetic is that she turned to Neilson—an imposing figure of male authority—even though she correctly sensed that he was not really "speaking seriously." For whether or not Neilson truly believed that mother love threatened American youth, he spoke at least partially "in jest," knowing full well that his audience would relish the chance to display its sophistication by laughing off his rebuke. The mother in Nashville, however, did not have the luxury of irony. She understood that mother love was not all it had been cracked up to be, but she still had to contend with the pressing needs and vexing behavior of four young children. She was worried; she did not want to fail them; she needed support and sympathetic advice. Unfortunately, as the twentieth century progressed, many women like her would find such advice in short supply.

Debunking the All-American Mom:
Philip Wylie's Momism Critique

I don't know whether I ought to be writing to you or not, being confused as to whose
side I am on now.

A mother to Philip Wylie, 1945

Neither Philip Wylie nor his editors, John Farrar and Stanley Rinehart, had
high hopes for *Generation of Vipers* when the first run of 4,000 copies appeared in December 1942. Rinehart had sought to delay publication, arguing
that the book contained "so many changes of pace, from objective thinking
to shrill hysteria," that the end result was "confusion."[1] For his part, Wylie insisted that the book contained "by far the best stretch of writing that
has come from this cerebrum," but he frankly conceded that it might not
"hit a jackpot."[2] Yet hit a jackpot it did. As of 1945, the book had sold more
than 75,000 copies, and the rate of sales was still rising.[3] By 1955, when Wylie
published an annotated edition of *Generation of Vipers* to commemorate its
twentieth printing, the number of hardback copies purchased had topped
180,000, and the American Library Association had named it one of the most
important nonfiction works of the first half of the twentieth century.[4]

No single message can account for this unexpected success. Both substan-
tively and stylistically, the book is a truly bizarre hodgepodge. *Time* described
it as a "raging and sometimes very funny set of lay sermons," while Malcolm
Cowley of the *New Yorker* deemed it a "tub-thumping diatribe against American customs."[5] Throughout its pages, Wylie decried a host of national failings, but he especially railed against Americans' blind faith in science, rampant materialism, and hypocritical attitudes toward sex. He also lampooned
a series of national "archetypes," including doctors, businessmen, politicians, professors, and military men. In the final chapter, Wylie interpreted
Jesus Christ's message to humanity ("know thyself") as equivalent to that of
psychoanalysis, while in the conclusion, he presented a futuristic promised
land—complete with air-conditioned streets—that Americans could one day
inhabit if only they redeemed their ways. The book alternately reads like a

Menckenesque satire, a hellfire sermon, a primer in Jungian psychology, a work of wartime propaganda, an autobiography, a lurid novel, and a science fiction fantasy.

But the section that earned Wylie lasting fame and infamy was the tenth chapter, entitled "Common Women." Here he depicted middle-aged and middle-class American moms as domestic tyrants, voracious consumers, and tiresome meddlers in social and political affairs. To capture the insidious power that such women wielded, he coined his provocative neologism, "momism." At first, there was little indication that Wylie's ruminations on moms would come to be considered the most compelling part of *Generation of Vipers*, let alone the author's most significant legacy. In 1945, when Wylie wrote a brief postscript describing readers' responses to the book, he did not even mention reactions to the momism critique.[6] But that same year, *Look* magazine ran an excerpt of the momism chapter, and psychiatrists and other social scientists began to appropriate and expand on the concept in works of their own, lending it a semblance of scientific credibility.[7] Thereafter, Wylie increasingly found himself identified as the momism critique's original exponent.

While priding himself for having "broken a path" that "the stateliest psychiatrists" had followed, Wylie regretted the tendency to focus exclusively on the momism chapter and complained that people often failed to discern his humorous intent.[8] He repeatedly tried to set the record straight, as in this 1954 interview with the *New York Times*:

> Look here, in *Generation of Vipers* there were nineteen pages about that. Nineteen, that's all. In the middle of it, I said the whole thing was a gag. I thought it was hilariously funny.
>
> When I was writing it, I'd come downstairs and read it to Ricky [Frederica Ballard, his second wife] and we'd laugh 'til our sides hurt. I didn't expect to become known for the rest of my life as a woman hater. That's the first thing they'll put in my obituary—a woman hater. Me.[9]

When Wylie died in 1971, his obituaries memorialized him just as he had bitterly predicted they would: the *Washington Post* headlined its story, "Philip Wylie Dies; Assailed 'Momism,'" and the *New York Times* announced, "Philip Wylie, Author, Dies; Noted for 'Mom' Attack."[10] Since then, scholars have sustained the author's reputation as (in his own self-pitying terms) "the all-out, all-time, high-scoring world champion misogynist."[11] The standard interpretative line goes something like this: "The late 1940s and 1950s were rife with an explicit antifeminism that made this period especially inhospitable for those women who aspired to life beyond the confines of their suburban dream houses. This antifeminism was typified by such books as Philip Wylie's *Generation of Vipers*."[12]

It is easy to dismiss Wylie's disclaimers, for the misogyny in *Generation of Vipers* is truly breathtaking. Nevertheless, I argue in this chapter that scholarly interpretations have generally failed to grasp the significance that the momism critique held for contemporaries. This stems in part from a tendency to reduce the critique to an attack on cloying or domineering mothers.[13] In the postwar era, this was indeed how the term "momism" came to be understood and codified in dictionaries; the *Oxford English Dictionary*, for instance, defines "momism" as "Excessive attachment to, or domination by, the mother."[14] However, maternal behavior toward children was by no means Wylie's sole concern, for he also railed against women's purported habits of consumption and the social and political activities that they pursued, often in the name of motherhood. He hoped to curb not only mothers' influence over their sons but also their power as consumers, their demands to be indulged by husbands and honored by the state, and, finally, the censorious and sentimentalizing force they exerted in American culture. At base, Wylie challenged the idea that women should be regarded as morally superior beings, entitled to special prerogatives and deserving of influence simply because of their sex or their status as mothers.

Scholars have also frequently portrayed the momism critique as fueled by, and reflective of, issues only secondarily related to motherhood or maternal influence, such as the threat of fascism and communism, resentment toward Rosie the Riveter, or anxieties concerning the alleged rise in male homosexuality.[15] However, while the momism critique certainly expressed a wide range of fears and fantasies, it was still fundamentally about a certain cohort of white, middle-aged, middle-class American women. Because Wylie displayed such extraordinary misogyny, and because he used such overblown rhetoric, scholars have underestimated the extent to which his text spoke to social realities, even as it appealed to psychological fears. The clubwoman in her floral hat, the matron who referred to her adult son as "my boy," the self-important Daughters of the American Revolution (DAR) member—for many readers in the 1940s and early 1950s, these were not simply demonic images that conveyed anxieties arising from other sources; they were convincing caricatures of real women who elicited emotions ranging from venomous resentment to bemused exasperation. It was precisely Wylie's ability to evoke a figure that people instantly recognized, and then to infuse that figure with sinister meaning, that made his text so powerful.[16]

Finally, whereas many scholars have viewed the momism chapter as a prescient work that anticipated the rise of Cold War culture, it is in fact highly derivative of a certain strain of interwar cultural criticism.[17] Many of the specific phenomena that Wylie railed against—Mother's Day, radio soap operas, the DAR—had long been favorite targets of satirists associated with cultural venues such as the *American Mercury* and *Esquire*. Even Wylie's loquacious and acerbic style—a style perfected by H. L. Mencken in the 1920s—already struck some readers in the 1940s as quite dated. To be sure, Wylie's critique would endure and acquire new meanings in the 1950s and even into the 1960s. But to comprehend why *Generation of Vipers* created such a sensation in the first place, it must be viewed as what it initially was: an explicitly retrospective wartime jeremiad. By condemning the folly of the interwar period, Wylie hoped to spur a national renewal that would generate the steely resolve necessary for waging war.

This chapter presents Wylie's momism critique not as an antifeminist screed that anticipated cold war anxieties but as the culminating expression of an interwar assault on what Ann Douglas has called "the late-Victorian matriarch."[18] Instead of denouncing women who embraced modern ideas about sexual equality, Wylie took aim at those who espoused a traditional ideal of womanhood and motherhood, despite recent changes that had granted women greater social and political equality. He attacked clubwomen who expressed their civic identities not as individuals but as mothers, wives, and daughters; homemakers who expected to be economically supported by men; women who embraced highly sentimental forms of popular culture; and mothers who ignored the admonitions of modern psychologists and cultivated overly intimate bonds with their sons. In the process, he challenged virtually all the fundamental precepts and cultural traditions that had informed the ideology of moral motherhood. Convinced that many women were trying to have their cake and eat it too—demanding full equal rights while still expecting special privileges and indulgences—Wylie attempted to deliver a final blow to the battered, yet remarkably enduring, ideology of moral motherhood.

When one views the momism critique as an attack on the ideology of moral motherhood, it becomes somewhat easier to grasp why many readers saw it as daringly subversive, even "un-American." This comes through clearly in the flood of correspondence that Wylie received in response to *Generation of Vipers*, which includes more than a thousand letters written during the years 1943 through 1946 alone.[19] Although men wrote slightly more than 60 percent of these letters, women constituted the majority of respondents who referred to the momism chapter: they were more than twice as likely as men to address that particular component of the book. (Thirty-two percent of female respondents, compared to 14 percent of male respondents, referred to the momism critique.)[20] Some respondents heatedly condemned Wylie for attacking American mothers, but a large majority praised the momism chapter, even when articulating important caveats and qualifications. This should not, however, be taken to mean that most Americans would have endorsed Wylie's critique, for his correspondents were not representative of the American populace as a whole.[21] In general, they were white, middle-class, and relatively well-educated individuals, many of whom criticized what they saw as the prevailing values of mainstream American society. *Generation of Vipers* held particular appeal for disaffected youth, who rightly viewed it as an indictment of their parents' generation.[22] Drawing on these letters, I try to recapture what the momism critique meant to its contemporaries and, more broadly, to analyze what its resonance suggests about changing attitudes toward motherhood in the 1940s and 1950s.

Archival materials also provide ample support for a psychoanalytic reading of the momism critique—a line of analysis this chapter does not pursue. Six years after *Generation of Vipers* appeared, Wylie suddenly recalled previously repressed memories of having been sexually abused by his mother, who died in childbirth when he was only five years old. In a letter to his friend, the psychoanalyst and popular author Robert Lindner, he even speculated that his rage toward moms stemmed from the repressed hostility that he harbored toward his own mother. "If they deserved it, intellectually and on the grounds I chose," he mused, "my own motives may still have been more complex, eh?"[23] In another unpublished document, titled "Notes on Alcoholism," which appears to have been an attempt to record insights that he had reached in psychoanalysis, Wylie described his anxious preoccupation with homosexuality and—more unexpectedly—his suspicion that his own body was somehow sexually indeterminate. His childhood experiences, he wrote, had resulted in "institutionalized anal eroticism," "disidentification with males," and "wishing or wondering if I were not a hermaphrodite with, perhaps a sealed vagina that might someday open up and be iseable [*sic*]; ultimate total confusion and identity loss."[24] Such sources would seem to go a long way toward explaining the momism chapter's most disturbing passages, which portray menopausal or postmenopausal women as monstrous and masculinized beings; too venomous to masquerade as satire, these passages are simply hateful, like racist screeds that demonize the "other" as physically repulsive or degenerate. What Wylie's personal papers suggest is that his misogyny sprang from profound self-loathing over the perceived insufficiency and sexual indeterminacy of his own body—a loathing that he projected onto middle-aged moms.[25]

Yet if a psychoanalytic approach is indispensable for understanding Wylie's animosity toward moms, it is ultimately of limited use in explaining the text's broader resonance and effects. Wylie certainly received his fair share of overwrought letters from unapologetic misogynists—a veteran infuriated by his mother's Pollyannaish bromides, an ex-husband who bitterly resented having to pay alimony, a "confirmed woman-hater" who described himself as "beset with homosexual tendencies."[26] Even leaving aside those letters that seemed to mirror the author's own rage and anxiety, there is no question but that readers' reactions to *Generation of Vipers* were colored by personal experiences and emotional conflicts of which they themselves may have been only dimly aware. Still, the fact that the majority of responses cannot be classified as misogynist diatribes points to the insufficiency of a psychoanalytic interpretation, for most readers who applauded the momism critique did so for reasons that went beyond the purely emotive. The central question this chapter seeks to answer is why so many seemingly reasonable people did *not* dismiss the momism critique as a hysterical rant. In other words, I hope to explain why, despite Wylie's misogynist hyperbole, numerous readers—including many women and even some feminists—conceded that Wylie had a valid point when he decried the influence of a certain type of American woman.

One could simply argue that readers have a remarkable capacity for appropriating texts according to their own needs and desires, but then one would miss the larger historical dynamic at work.[27] For the letters that Wylie received also underscore the fact that the assault on mother love was a complex phenomenon driven by very different constituencies: misogynists who resented any type of female power or influence, to be sure, but also progressive women who wanted to be viewed as individuals rather than simply as wives and mothers, psychologists and social scientists who sought to further extend their professional authority, and many ordinary Americans fed up with hypocrisy and sentimentality. These people may have shared little else, but all had a powerful interest in eradicating the vestiges of sentimental motherhood and Victorian morality from the nation's cultural, political, and familial life.

The Politics of the Momism Critique

Mom is organization-minded. . . . With her clubs (a solid term!), mom causes bus lines to run where they are convenient for her rather than for workers, plants flowers in sordid spots that would do better with sanitation, snaps independent men out of office and replaces them with clammy castrates, throws prodigious fairs and parties for charity and gives the proceeds, usually about eight dollars, to the janitor to buy the committee some beer for its headache on the morning after, and builds clubhouses for the entertainment of soldiers where she succeeds in persuading thousands of them that they are momsick and would rather talk to her than take Betty into the shrubs. All this, of course, is considered social service, charity, care of the poor, civic reform, patriotism, and self-sacrifice.[28]

Historians have often described the momism critique as antifeminist, but "antimaternalist" is a more apt (if still imperfect) characterization. Although Wylie reviled feminists, the momism chapter targeted less politically minded women—the great mass of middle-class matrons who joined women's clubs and voluntary associations.[29] During the Progressive Era and interwar period, some of these groups pursued liberal goals, such as public health reforms. (In the momism chapter, Wylie referred to his efforts to enlist Miami clubwomen in support of milk pasteurization.)[30] Others focused primarily on moral issues, such as eradicating vice. (Here Wylie specifically mentioned women's attempts to ban prostitution.)[31] Progressives and moralists alike, however, often presented themselves as politically disinterested mother-citizens, acting on behalf of the larger public good.[32] When Wylie portrayed women's groups as nothing more than fronts that members used to pursue their own selfish goals and desires, he in effect attacked this maternalist conception of female citizenship.

Wylie's respondents clearly grasped the thrust of his critique. For instance, the director of a home for unwed mothers, who wrote to Wylie in 1948, believed that his caricature perfectly fit the moralistic board members with whom she had to contend. "If any group of women belong to the vipers class it is certainly the class that make up the Boards of these Homes! They still think these girls should be placed in a pillory on the public highway."[33] Another fan, writing in 1945, commented wryly, "Were conditions permitting, every Ladies Aid Society and Association for The Upliftment of Bent Over Petunias would have a copy [of your book], for my two bits worth."[34] In turn, readers who took umbrage at the momism critique often defended the value and integrity of women's voluntary efforts. For instance, when *Look* reprinted an excerpt of the momism chapter in 1945, it also ran a rebuttal that lauded "the good work women's organizations have accomplished in every section of our country." The writer pointed specifically to women's attempts to reduce infant mortality, improve public schools, and "break the grip of the saloonkeepers and brothel proprietors in our cities."[35] In sum, supporters and critics alike interpreted the momism critique as an assault on the broader phenomenon of organized womanhood, rather than an attack on feminism per se.

Scholars have also typically portrayed Wylie's momism critique as a reactionary ideology closely associated with anticommunism, but this, too, is problematic.[36] In fact, Wylie reserved his greatest ire for the most politically

conservative branch of organized womanhood—patriotic women's groups
that had themselves crusaded against communism during the interwar
period. He dwelled at length on women who called themselves "a Daughter
of this historic war or that," which readers generally interpreted to mean
the Daughters of the American Revolution.[37] He also referred briefly to war
mothers' organizations, like the Gold Star Mothers—a subject addressed in
the following chapter. Both types of organizations promoted a highly traditional vision of female citizenship, in which women defined their relationship to the nation not as individuals but as mothers or daughters of male
citizen-soldiers.[38] Moreover, both DAR members and Gold Star Mothers had
been widely criticized in the interwar period for promoting a nativist and
racist conception of American identity that, by 1942, stood at odds with the
wartime celebration of a pluralist democracy.

By the time *Generation of Vipers* appeared, the DAR in particular had
emerged as a favorite target of both progressive reformers and male satirists.
Beginning in the mid-1920s, feminists and pacifists like Carrie Chapman Catt
challenged the group's reactionary agenda and condemned its red-baiting tactics.[39] At the same time, numerous writers lampooned the DAR for their for-
mulaic patriotism and social pretensions. In his acerbic 1936 book, *The Influence of Women and Its Cure*, the literary critic John Erskine argued that women
who joined "societies which call themselves Daughters of something or other"
evinced no comprehension of the Constitution's revolutionary character and
rushed to defend it "with the same mentality with which the Tories opposed
the Revolution and the southern planters opposed emancipation."[40] The
painter Grant Wood conveyed the same basic idea in his 1932 painting *Daughters of Revolution*, which features three middle-aged "Tory gals," one primly
holding a teacup, seated before a reproduction of *Washington Crossing the
Delaware*. The women's pursed lips, narrowed eyes, and Victorian dress signal
the antiquarian and elitist nature of their "patriotism."[41] Wood's arresting image came to be widely known, even abroad; in 1947, Carl Jung suggested that
Wylie have the image reproduced in future editions of *Generation of Vipers*.[42]

Wylie's references to patriotic Daughters would likely also have brought to
mind a national controversy that had erupted only three years before *Generation of Vipers* appeared, when the DAR barred the famous African-American
contralto, Marian Anderson, from performing at Constitution Hall.[43] The
Daughters' display of bigotry prompted Eleanor Roosevelt to resign from
the organization and led the NAACP to arrange for Anderson's momentous
Easter Day performance at the Lincoln Memorial.[44] The "freedom concert,"
which drew a crowd of 75,000 and was broadcast nationally over the radio,
has long been regarded as a landmark in African-Americans' struggle for civil

rights. But it is also notable for the way in which it juxtaposed two radically different images of American womanhood: a hereditary organization that claimed to be honoring the nation's Revolutionary heritage while enforcing segregation, pitted against an immensely accomplished black woman, standing alone on the steps of the Lincoln Memorial. Secretary of the Interior Harold Ickes, who introduced Anderson at the concert, may well have been recollecting the episode when he wrote to Wylie in 1943, stating, "I wish that I could have written such a book. You have said frankly, even bluntly, what has needed to be said for some time."[45]

In light of these recent events, criticism of the DAR could easily have been assumed to imply a critique of segregation or racism. But in fact, Wylie did not develop this line of argument.[46] Rather than condemning patriotic women's groups for their racism or reactionary politics, he drew on fantastic similes to accuse the Daughters of usurping and corrupting a legacy of male civic sacrifice. "By becoming a Daughter of this historic war or that," he argued, "a woman makes herself into a sort of madam who fills the coffers of her ego with the prestige that has accrued to the doings of others."[47] As if these charges were not sufficiently hyperbolic, he then proceeded to compare DAR members to Hitler and his followers:

> In the matter of her affiliation of herself with the Daughters of some war the Hitler analogue especially holds, because these sororities of the sword often constitute her Party—her shirtism. . . . But mom's reverence for her bold fore-bears . . . instructs her in nothing. She is peremptory about historical truth, mandates, customs, fact, and point. She brushes aside the ideals and concepts for which her forebears perished fighting, as if they were the crumbs of melba toast. Instead, she attributes to the noble dead her own immediate and selfish attitudes.[48]

The Daughters, Wylie insisted, did not really care about historical truth or the heroic men whom they pretended to venerate: they sought veneration only for themselves. At base, his critique expressed anger and anxiety over women's cultural authority rather than outrage over elitism or racial discrimination. Yet because criticism of the DAR (and patriotic women's groups more generally) had become so strongly associated with racial liberalism, readers tended to impute a more progressive agenda to Wylie than his book actually implied.

Another reason why the momism critique is difficult to classify politically stems from the complex relationship between cultural rebellion and left-wing politics. Many youthful readers viewed *Generation of Vipers* as "radical" because Wylie passionately condemned conventional morality and orthodox religiosity. An ensign in the U.S. Naval Reserves, who wrote to Wylie in 1945, attributed his enthusiasm for *Generation of Vipers* to the fact that he had experienced "an over exposure to the strictest of Protestantism and all too much Ladies Aid momism."[49] Similarly, a young woman read the momism chapter as validating her decision to defy her widowed mother by working as a showgirl in Europe rather than attending college. As she explained in a 1945 letter to Wylie:

> My mother is a "good woman". . . . She doesn't drink, smoke, or swear. She is a regular "church goer." She reads her bible. Sex is only a word to her. She has never shot craps, nor has she ever pushed her grandmother down a flight of stairs, or robbed pennies from blind men. Nevertheless, I am heartily in accord with your observation and personal views of "Moms." More than once, I have dared to express similar views on the same subject, only to receive horrified exclamations or frigid stares. I am a freak! A traitor to my sex![50]

These young adults perceived Wylie's book as a defiant repudiation of Protestant orthodoxy and Victorian sexual repression, both of which they associated with the cultural idealization of motherhood. But whether their rebellious attitudes translated into progressive political views is not at all clear.

Some of Wylie's fans, however, praised his critique of sexual repression and hypocritical morality in more explicitly political terms.[51] For instance, Philip Stoughton, a chemist who had developed a contraceptive foam powder in the 1930s, wrote to Wylie in June 1943, just days after a newspaper columnist reported—falsely, it turned out—that the War Department would be issuing contraceptives and prophylactics to all members of the Women's Auxiliary Army Corps (WAAC). The article had produced a public outcry, which would ultimately lead to Congressional hearings; as Stoughton characterized the uproar, "the representatives of what you call 'Mom' in American life" had "erupted into a storm in defense of the 'purity of American Womanhood.'" Disgusted by the military's institutionalization of the sexual double standard, Stoughton pointed out that no one invoked the "Purity of American Manhood" as a reason for denying servicemen prophylactics.[52] To a scientist who believed that antiquated Victorian ideals prevented a rational and responsible approach to the issue of sexuality, Wylie sounded like a voice of reason above a din of overwrought moral pronouncements.[53]

For similar reasons, Albert and Mary Lasker, leading philanthropists who supported the birth control movement, avidly embraced *Generation of Vipers*. Albert bought numerous copies of the book to distribute to friends and acquaintances, believing it to be "the most thought-compelling writing on the current home and world scene yet produced."[54] His wife Mary, who served as secretary of Planned Parenthood, wrote separately that she had just received a letter from Margaret Sanger, the nation's foremost birth control advocate, in which Sanger described *Generation of Vipers* as "'one of the most profound, and caustic books I have ever read!'"[55] Of course, support for the birth control movement did not necessarily imply a commitment to progressive politics or feminism: some birth control advocates hoped to limit the reproduction of minority groups and those deemed eugenically unfit, while others appeared far more concerned with freeing men from sexual constraints than empowering women.[56] Nevertheless, such responses further illustrate why "antifeminist" is not the most accurate or helpful description of Wylie's critique.

Even on the issue of homosexuality, *Generation of Vipers* is more politically complex than historical accounts have suggested. Wylie's homophobia, like his misogyny, is undeniable. Indeed, he presciently articulated the very fears and prejudices that, eight years later, would fuel attempts to drive gays and lesbians from positions in the federal government. In a chapter called "Statesmen," he denounced the "sisterhood in our State Department" and complained that the United States was often represented by "a nance" in diplomatic situations that called for "a man of iron." He even asserted that, if the war effort had the effect of purging the State Department of effeminate men, it would be "one of the rare purifying acts for which we can thank the Nazis."[57] Yet elsewhere in the book, Wylie condemned violent acts against homosexuals and the criminalization of homosexuality. He argued, as did most liberals at the time, that homosexuality should be treated neither as a sin nor a crime but rather as a manifestation of "private neurosis," asserting, "To treat it as a fiendish manifestation, like ax-murdering, is silly."[58] The point is that, within the context of the 1940s and 1950s, Wylie's views on homosexuality could be interpreted as either profoundly reactionary or moderately progressive, depending on which passages one emphasized.[59]

This is by no means to say that the momism critique appealed only to liberals, or that liberals unequivocally endorsed *Generation of Vipers*. According to Wylie, when Farrar and Rinehart sent the manuscript to the writer and New Dealer Steven Benét for his evaluation, Benét denounced it as "fascist" and argued that it should not be published.[60] Wylie did in fact receive fan mail from some right-wing extremists—including a few letters that expressed open admiration for Nazism. These respondents saw, or at least believed they saw, their own anxieties about modernity and biological degeneration reflected in Wylie's tirades. For instance, a man who applauded the Nazis' "statutory euthanasia and positive and negative practice of eugenics" praised Wylie's momism critique by comparing it to the work of fascist ideologue Ewald Banse.[61] Another man echoed the rhetoric of Nazi racial hygiene when he asserted that, because of the "enervating" conditions of contemporary urban life, the "modern woman" had "lost nearly all her biological vigor and capacities for motherhood—both physically and mentally."[62] More traditional, religiously oriented conservatives, however, tended to view the momism chapter as loutish and unpatriotic. One seventy-year-old man reminded Wylie that Christ had been "gentle and kind to children and very understanding with women."[63] For similar reasons, as chapter 3 will detail, the cold warrior Ronald Reagan would speak out against the momism critique in the 1950s.

All of this helps make the appeal of *Generation of Vipers* to some left-leaning women a bit less perplexing. Feminists today are generally so appalled by the book that they cannot conceive of its progressive resonance for some women in the 1940s and 1950s. Yet some of their predecessors appeared remarkably unfazed by Wylie's misogyny, for they read his work not as an attack on women per se but as an attack on women who defended paternalism and sexual inequality.[64] Simone de Beauvoir quoted from *Generation of Vipers* at length, referring to it in wholly favorable terms in *America Day by Day* and *The Second Sex*, which appeared in 1948 and 1949 respectively.[65] Likewise, though Betty Friedan did not mention Wylie by name in her 1963 classic, *The Feminine Mystique*, she cited psychiatric appropriations of the momism critique, as chapter 5 will detail.[66] From the perspective of these iconic feminists, the momism critique read less like a misogynist diatribe than an exposé of the psychological and cultural toll of sexual inequality, which forced women to seek power within the domestic realm.

Most women readers, however, displayed greater ambivalence in their responses to Wylie, as they struggled to reconcile enthusiasm for certain aspects of his critique with the feelings of anger it evoked. For instance, a mother who recommended *Generation of Vipers* to her three sons, all serving in the Army, assured Wylie that, "there are a million [middle-aged women] like me, who will read your book with understanding and intelligence even tho [*sic*] on personal contact we might knock your block off." In one breath, she effusively praised Wylie, declaring, "If only there were a million 'you' [*sic*] to hammer truth into the minds of the bewildered boys and girls of the world." But in the next, she criticized Wylie's misogynist "slurs" against the journalist Dorothy Thompson, insisting that Thompson was "articulate and has a brain which she is sincerely trying to do something with"—which, she pointedly added, was "what you seem to advocate we women do."[67] She also pointed to the example of her congresswoman, Frances Bolton, who "by tradition and wealth" had been "fitted to play the grand dame," but had nevertheless chosen to shoulder the responsibilities of leadership. "I am not a joiner or a doer and hang no blue stars in my window," she wrote in closing, "for I have been too long heartsick over the mess our generation has handed to all the grand boys in the world, and I do mean Grand." While this woman's feelings of guilt and indebtedness toward the younger generation clearly conditioned her response, she embraced *Generation of Vipers* at least in part because she interpreted it as urging women to contribute to the political process directly (like Representative Bolton) rather than in more traditional and derivative ways (like the Blue Star Mothers).[68]

Similarly, a journalist at the *Charlotte Observer*, who described herself as a fan of the feminist historian Mary Beard, wrote in 1947 that she was "glad" Wylie had written *Generation of Vipers*, even though the book made her "angry." American women, she believed, needed "to be stung and goaded into action" so they would finally "leave the beauty shops and dress shops and bridge clubs like the children in Hamlin and go somewhere!" Yet she also penned a sweeping feminist rejoinder to Wylie's arguments about female dominance:

> Philip Wylie—it's not easy being a woman—a woman with a college education, energy, and a fair amount of brains. . . . Men made the war—and now they're fumbling with atom bombs instead of making peace. (How many women in the U.N.? About 10 to 500 men?) They control business (even tho' women hold more of the wealth). They control the courts. . . . Laws in our courts often favor women, yes—but the men *make* the laws. Women have privilege, yes—but men have the power.[69]

As this respondent well understood, the feminine privileges that so infuriated Wylie did not amount to real power: any educated woman in the 1940s who hoped to apply her "energy" and "brains" to serious pursuits beyond the home faced an uphill battle. Still, though clearly cognizant of Wylie's blindness to gender discrimination, she nevertheless deemed his attack on conventional womanhood convincing and potentially useful.

In contrast, Mary Beard shared none of her younger fan's ambivalence: she repudiated the momism critique outright, even as she relied on some of the same negative tropes that Wylie employed to characterize American women. Writing to Woman's Bureau director Frieda Miller in 1946, the seventy-year-old historian bemoaned the fact that homemakers had taken to "playing bridge, running to the movies, taking guests to the theater or opera or night clubs" instead of serving, as they had historically, as "a force in lifting thought to new creative levels." Like Wylie, Beard depicted a large pool of idle, middle-aged women who indulged in mass culture as a potentially dangerous and reactionary political force. Yet whereas Wylie saw female idleness as a sign of women's increasing dominance, Beard viewed it as evidence of homemakers' declining prestige. "If [the homemaker] does not regain her own sense of . . . her inherited power, she will be the kind of material on which Hitler and other dictators of our age have preyed for their designs," she warned, adding, "And in our society we allow a man like Philip Wylie to make 'Mom' just a 'jerk.'"[70] It is telling that Beard, who had come of age during the Progressive Era and participated in maternalist reform movements, interpreted *Generation of Vipers* as a fundamentally antifeminist work. Because her understanding of feminism incorporated a maternalist perspective, she saw little distinction between antifeminism and antimaternalism: to her mind, any book that so viciously attacked the influence of "home women" could only be antithetical to the cause of women's rights (and democracy more broadly). But many younger women, who regarded domesticity as a source of oppression rather than potential empowerment, did not share this view.

To be clear, my point is not to redeem Wylie as a misunderstood feminist, for this he certainly was not. Ultimately, for Wylie, the problem was less the ideology of moral motherhood than the chasm between the ideology and contemporary realities. In a society that acknowledged female sexuality, granted women the vote, and assiduously catered to their consumer desires, Wylie believed that the ideal of the self-sacrificing Mother could only be met with derision. He wanted to strip middle-class women of the influence they wielded as moral mothers, without positing alternative ways through which they might construct their identities or exercise authority. Too much of a jaded modernist to advocate a restoration of the old ways, he was also too much of a misogynist to advocate true equality. But that did not stop some women from extracting a feminist message from his critique.

The Critique of Female Idleness and Consumerism

Woman, whose hands for tens of thousands of years never stopped tending babies, feeding fires, twirling flax, and pushing broom-handles, are idle, at last, by the million. If the machine age had emancipated those hands for some less trifling tasks, there would be no reason for this book and there would be no war. But the machine age merely cut off the hands. War is restoring some of those hands. If I were a labor leader, I would think hard about that. But, most likely, after the war the ladies will go back to their clattering cipherdom.[71]

The most fundamental misreading of the momism critique is that it served as "an instrument in the battle to return [women] to the home" after World War II. Several scholars have advanced this interpretation, portraying *Gen-*

eration of Vipers as contributing to a postwar backlash against female employment and the war's disruptive influence on gender roles more broadly.[72] But not only did Wylie write the book prior to the large influx of women into the workforce, he actually seemed to welcome the prospect of increased female employment. Moreover, readers hardly ever interpreted the chapter as a negative commentary on women's growing presence or influence within the workplace. (Indeed, some working women seemed to relish Wylie's attack on homemakers; as one woman wrote, "I didn't just produce a cheeild [*sic*] and then figure the world . . . owed me a living.")[73] Rather than venting hostility toward working women, the momism critique expressed antagonism toward women who pursued a life of ease by capitalizing on their relationships with men.[74]

By caricaturing mom as lazy and parasitical, Wylie sought to dispel the image of the virtuous homemaker who labored tirelessly and managed the family budget with painstaking care, meeting everyone's needs (save her own) through hard work, thrift, and ingenuity. In the past, he granted, American women had kept busy "raising a large family, keeping house, doing the chores, and fabricating everything in every home except the floor and the walls." But as the birthrate fell, longevity increased, and new laborsaving devices eased the difficulties of housekeeping, the nation's industrious mothers had devolved into idle and profligate moms.[75] Still worse, the very same economic processes that relieved women of hard labor and granted them new power as consumers had served to diminish the status of American men, stripping them of autonomy as workers and burdening them with greater demands as breadwinners. "The male is an attachment to the female in our civilization," Wylie pronounced. "He does most of what he does—eighty per cent, statistically—to supply whatever women have defined as their necessities, comforts, and luxuries."[76] Though men still ran the nation's corporations and controlled its government, what did it signify when all their efforts focused on divining and satisfying the desires of the "little woman" at home?

During the 1920s and 1930s, numerous male commentators, of varying political persuasions, argued that modern economic developments had shifted the balance of power between the sexes in favor of women. Those who decried the feminization of culture most insistently tended to be men, like the writer Sherwood Anderson, whose occupational identities led them to fear association with the feminine masses. Anderson, who worked for many years in advertising, constantly ruminated about the decline of a male producer ethic and the corrupting influence of commercial culture, as historian T. J. Jackson Lears has shown.[77] Like Wylie, he connected men's diminishing power as productive workers to women's growing influence as consumers:

the new America, he wrote in 1931, was "a woman's world," in which the
nation's industrial capacities had been harnessed to satisfy female needs and
desires, and in which newspapers, magazines, and stores were all "run for
women." Anderson and Wylie even drew upon similar images and tropes;
for instance, both highlighted the pathetic figure of the male department
store clerk, reduced to waiting upon a largely female clientele.[78] Noting that
his own stint as a department store clerk had equipped him with much of
his insight into "this matter of moms," Wylie bitterly observed, "Clerks are
wallpaper to moms."[79] Similarly, Anderson argued that girls who worked
alongside male clerks did not regard their coworkers as potential mates, since
"No woman really wants a man who feels defeated, crushed by life."[80]

But if Wylie's tirade about female idleness and consumption voiced masculine angst and resentment, it also resonated in curious ways which a long-
standing feminist critique of female "parasitism." In the late nineteenth and
early twentieth centuries, Charlotte Perkins Gilman and the South African
Oliver Schreiner developed extensive economic assessments of female idleness; both insisted that middle-class women needed to share the burdens of
labor if they hoped to be released from their state of abject dependency.[81]
A younger generation of feminists made similar arguments in the interwar
period. In her study, *Women and Leisure: A Study of Social Waste*, Lorine
Pruette argued that many American women deluded themselves into believing that "the care of a small household is a full-sized job" and were "going
soft" in both body and mind as a result. "From an individual standpoint
they form a pathetic picture . . . but from the social standpoint they form
an actual menace," she warned.[82] In 1942, Dorothy Canfield Fisher, who had
been writing about the dilemmas of dissatisfied and insufficiently occupied
homemakers for decades, expressed her hope that the wartime crisis would
finally catapult well-educated women into a more useful and meaningful existence. "I believed that work for women is an old, not a new thing, and they
have been deprived of much of it by having far fewer children than formerly
and by many other developments of modern life that have taken much of
the preparation of food and clothing as well as education of the young out of
their homes," she wrote.[83] Of course, feminists departed dramatically from
Wylie in regard to the solutions they proposed, but their historical understanding of the problem of female idleness strongly resembled his own.

Finally, Wylie's portrait of unoccupied, middle-aged moms also had much
in common with more dispassionate assessments advanced by social scientists and psychologists. The same year that *Generation of Vipers* appeared,
the sociologist Talcott Parsons argued that "the feminine role" had become
"a conspicuous focus of the strains inherent in our social structure" as the

homemaker's job declined in importance and prestige. Instead of seizing the opportunity for "genuine independence," he wrote, too many middle-class women either fell prey to "neurotic illness or compulsive domesticity" or threw themselves into "community or club activities" with a level of seriousness "out of proportion to the intrinsic importance of the task."[84] Likewise, the psychologist Anna Wolf asserted in 1941 that middle-class American women were going through "a transition period" in which they had been "evicted" from their traditional role in society. "With essential work removed from her hands," she argued, the middle-aged homemaker had become "overwhelmingly busy with nonessentials." Although Wolf assumed that men would continue to serve as the primary breadwinners, she argued that American women now needed to accept that they had "two jobs in life, not one."[85]

During the 1930s, resentment over alleged female idleness had rarely translated into support for married women working outside the home. Though Depression-era popular culture celebrated the plucky, self-supporting single woman, the large majority of Americans (more than 80 percent) believed that wives should not hold paying jobs unless necessity made it absolutely imperative.[86] But the situation changed drastically during World War II, when unemployment evaporated and the demand for labor power soared. Remarkably, assumptions about widespread female idleness had become so pervasive that the Office of War Information felt it necessary to remind Americans that women were, in fact, capable of labor. "Women can stand a lot, and actually they are workers by tradition," declared one agency bulletin. "It is only in recent years, and mostly in the United States, that women have been allowed to fall into habits of extraordinary leisure."[87] In the wartime context, the idle woman came to be represented as unpatriotic, even subversive: her negative characteristics—materialism, dependency, immaturity—signified the failings of the nation as a whole.

By the time *Generation of Vipers* appeared in December 1942, the U.S. economy had absorbed virtually all able-bodied male workers and most single women as well. "This leaves, as the next potential source of industrial workers, the housewives," *Fortune* magazine observed in February 1943.[88] That same month, Congressmen James W. Wadsworth and Warren Austin introduced the Austin-Wadsworth Bill (or National Service Act), the first conscription measure in U.S. history to encompass both men and women. The bill would have required all women between the ages of eighteen and fifty (and all men between the ages of eighteen and sixty-five) to register for the draft, though women who were pregnant, raising children under eighteen, or caring for sick or elderly dependents were to be granted exemptions.[89] In the end, Congress did not pass the measure, nor any other legislation that would have drafted women. But the debate over conscription did force Americans to consider whether or not homemakers with grown children still performed "essential" work, and to what extent women's wartime duties should extend beyond the home.

To the extent that Wylie's momism critique figured in this broader debate, it served as a means of rebuking middle-aged women who believed that their status as homemakers exempted them from contributing to the war effort in more substantive ways. This is readily apparent in a *Life* editorial that appeared in January 1945, shortly after President Roosevelt had called for a bill allowing nurses to be drafted in his State of the Union Address.[90] The editorial, written in support of Roosevelt's proposal, quoted at length from *Generation of Vipers*. American women, the (anonymous) writer argued, were simply not pulling their weight: despite the dire need for nurses and industrial workers, "the movies are full of so-called housewives all day long, and there is scarcely a woman's club where the war is not discussed solely in terms of the servant problem—over the bridge table." This shameful evasion of duty revealed that "American women, as a class . . . have a lot to learn about the responsibilities of all-around citizenship and their role in the modern world."[91] The editorial is difficult to classify politically, for it simultaneously looked backward to a pioneer past (when women had shared life's burdens with their menfolk) and forward to a future when full equality would presumably be achieved. What seems clear, however, is that the writer viewed the momism critique as lending support to the case for universal conscription.

The *Life* editorial generated an outpouring of responses that suggest how other Americans, beyond Wylie's correspondents, might have viewed his wartime critique of female idleness. Of the published twenty letters to the editor, roughly half condemned the editorial. Not surprisingly, the most heated responses came from middle-aged women.[92] "My face is red, but the shame is on you," wrote a woman who signed herself "Mom":

> Who do you suppose is caring for the young mothers, wives, sweethearts and babies of the servicemen in servantless homes all over this broad land? And who is supposed through it all to look young, gay, amused and nonchalant while her son is going through hell and she cannot help him in any other way than by trying to be the same old Mom when he comes, if he comes, back?
>
> Draft us for war work if you like! We're in the front trenches now![93]

This woman argued that America's middle-aged mothers sustained the homefront in crucial ways: bereft young women, left to bear and raise babies without their husbands' support, needed mothering themselves, while ser-vicemen deserved to know that a loving mother awaited their return. Middle-aged women who provided such practical and emotional support to the younger generation, she argued, were performing an essential, though largely unrecognized, wartime service.

Similarly, a woman from Oklahoma City fired off an indignant reply to *Look* when the magazine excerpted Wylie's momism chapter in December 1945. Describing herself as the mother of six children, one of whom had died in the war, she pronounced Wylie's article "an unforgivable [*sic*] crime against humanity":

> You talk of old fat women with nothing to do I wish you could just follow me thru one week you would probably be helpless for the rest of your life. I not only cook, sew, wash, iron, sweep, and clean but find time for church ac-tivities and Red Cross work also cookies for U.S.O. and keep a sleeping room available for the U.S.O. Travelers Aid for service men wives or mothers. I have 2 sons in High School and I for one should not have to defend the mothers of this generation who have not only given of their time and energy in the cause of war and peace but have given their sons and their very hearts.[94]

Enumerating the myriad tasks that she performed, this correspondent sought to demonstrate that middle-aged women could be highly productive work-ers without ever entering the labor force. Indeed, to her mind, the fact that she had freely given her time and energy made her exertions on the nation's behalf all the more laudable.

Predictably, women who read *Generation of Vipers* were less likely to pen outraged defenses of American womanhood than those who encountered Wylie's ideas in truncated forms in popular magazines. Most respondents who wrote directly to Wylie granted the basic validity of his depiction of idle women, even as they sought to amend or moderate his critique. For instance, a woman who wrote in 1943 wondered whether he had "seen the change in women" since the United States had entered the war. "So many of the para-sites, widows with plenty of money to live 'nice' are working in our defense plants, taking it day after day, and liking it, feeling they are being useful once again," she wrote. "I see club women, women I have detested for their very uselessness, blossom out into defense workers, and proud of it."[95] In 1947, a woman who allowed that she had observed many "horrid examples" of mom-ism offered "a word of explanation" as to the root cause of the problem. For some two decades, she asserted, most middle-class women lived in a state of "virtual domestic slavery." Though laborsaving devices had indeed lightened their load, no machine had been invented to "feed the baby" so that a woman could "take the afternoon off to listen to a lecture on Democracy or Women's Rights." Given the severe constraints that most mothers faced, she argued, it was hardly surprising that they did "wasteful and foolish things" once they finally managed to escape the incessant demands of homemaking. "If you want to *do sumpin'* for Mom, work up some practical plans for getting her help and a little leisure while raising a family," she urged. "More nursery schools, or more glamour in baby-sitting, or something! Don't stop half-way with condemning the poor woman!"[96] But of course, Wylie did stop halfway with condemning women.

Fears about female idleness did not disappear when the wartime demand for womanpower evaporated. Even as the domestic mystique took hold, pressuring young women to relinquish jobs and career aspirations, commentators and the popular press continued to voice anxieties about idle, middle-aged women. For instance, a 1947 *Life* feature on "the American Woman" quoted the "successful mother and historian" Margaret Perry Burton, who cautioned, "If the young mothers were better trained to understand that they must be constantly building their bridges out into the community, then, instead of being confronted in their forties with relative unemployment and the loneliness, frustration and suffering which go with it, they would be more ready to use their experience and talents outside the home."[97] The article went on to note that approximately 20 million women, constituting nearly half of the adult female population, were "essentially idle": "They do not have children under 18, they are not members of the labor force, they do not work on farms, nor are they aged or infirm. With not nearly enough to do, many of them are bored stiff."[98] Such concerns were still being aired in 1960, as when the *Saturday Evening Post* sternly warned, "With early weddings and extending longevity, marriage is now a part-time career for women and unless they prepare now for the freer years, this period will be a loss. American society will hardly accept millions of ladies of leisure—female drones—in their 40's."[99]

At least some women took these messages to heart and tried to plan their lives accordingly. In 1950, one twenty-three-year-old mother explained to Wylie how she envisioned her future. "When the children attend school all day, I hope to do part time work, not to bring in money principally but so I will not become stagnant and dowdy and most of all, complacent, like some many older mothers I've met," she wrote. "Complacency doesn't belong in the world today." This woman's letter was by no means free of dissent: she went on to challenge Wylie's depiction of mechanized homemaking as a complete snap, and she protested that American mothers and homemakers performed a difficult and important job, despite being subjected to widespread condescension and scorn. Still, her remarks indicate that she had absorbed one of the momism critique's central lessons, for she accepted the notion that her homemaking duties would soon no longer amount to a full-time occupation, and that she was at risk of becoming "stagnant and dowdy."[100]

The momism critique did indeed contribute to the establishment of a new gender order in the postwar period, but not, as many have suggested, by pressuring women to return to the home. Rather, by stigmatizing female "idleness" and questioning women's right to complete, lifelong economic dependency, it helped to legitimize the emerging trend in female employment, in which women returned to the workforce once their children reached a certain age. This helps to explain what has long been considered one of the central "paradoxes" of postwar women's history—the fact that, despite the pervasive celebration of motherhood and domesticity, the rate of women in the workforce steadily rose throughout the 1950s.[101] Although historians Jessica Weiss and Susan Hartmann have convincingly argued otherwise, this marked rise in female employment is still widely viewed as a trend at odds with the prevailing gender ideology.[102] But in fact, not only was there significant support for the idea of middle-aged women reentering the workforce; from some quarters, there was even a certain amount of pressure to do so. During the postwar era, the message directed toward middle-class women was twofold: the home should remain their primary concern, but homemaking could no longer be considered a full-time, lifetime job.

Momism and the Feminization of Culture

The radio is mom's final tool, for it stamps everybody who listens with its matriarchal brand—its superstitions, prejudices, devotional rules, taboos, musts, and all other qualifications needful to its maintenance. Just as Goebbels has revealed what can be done with such a mass-stamping of the public psyche in his nation, so our land is a living representation of the same fact worked out in matriarchal sentimentality, goo, slop, hidden cruelty, and the foreshadow of national death.[103]

Just as Wylie challenged the image of the typical American homemaker as industrious and frugal, so he mocked the notion that she helped to refine and civilize American society. On the contrary, he argued, mom exerted a profoundly negative force on the nation's cultural life. Though she had been respectably educated and enjoyed a solidly middle-class standing, her pedestrian taste revealed her to be utterly common.[104] (Hence the chapter's title, "Common Women.") Instead of acting as a force of uplift, she dragged the whole society down to her own abysmal level.[105]

Here again, the momism critique should be seen as a repudiation of older gender ideals and traditions—in this case, the long-standing tradition whereby middle-class American women acted as cultural guardians and disseminators. Beginning in the antebellum era, domestic writers like Catherine Beecher argued that, because American men were so preoccupied with the business of conquering the continent and developing its resources, it fell to the nation's educated women to fill the cultural void by acting as agents of civilization.[106] At the same time, as historian Rachel Klein has shown, many writers began to associate a refined sensibility with moral virtue and to identify women as natural repositories of aesthetic taste.[107] These cultural discourses both reflected and reinforced American women's increasing engagement with educational and cultural pursuits. Over the course of the nineteenth century, elementary school teaching (and librarianship as well) became thoroughly feminized—"a feat," Ann Douglas has noted, that women "accomplished in no other country, and one which was to cause immense uneasiness in men involved in American education by the turn of the twentieth century."[108] In addition, middle-class clubwomen organized numerous campaigns to ban obscenity and promote cultural "purity."[109] These efforts were not relegated to a distant Victorian past; they persisted well into the 1930s and would therefore have been familiar to many of Wylie's readers.

By portraying mom as a vulgar and prurient consumer of low-brow mass culture, Wylie derided this image of American women as agents of moral and cultural uplift. His diatribe against women's cultural consumption reached its climax in a lengthy peroration about daytime serials, or radio soap operas, which were broadcast weekdays in fifteen-minute installments from the 1930s through the 1950s. Sponsored by companies that sold products designed to assist women in their domestic labors, daytime serials specifically targeted women who did not work outside the home.[110] Over the course of the 1930s, the new genre became phenomenally popular and profitable; by the time Wylie penned his withering critique, over half of all American housewives listened daily to at least one soap opera (out of some fifty broadcast nationally).[111] Constituting more than half of all weekday radio programming, daytime serials were "the most financially profitable radio programs of the radio age," according to historian Kathy M. Newman, and "in effect subsidized much of the other programming" heard on the air.[112]

Lampooned by satirists, studied by social scientists, scorned by countless ordinary Americans, radio soap operas drew an enormous amount of scrutiny and commentary. In March 1942, just four months before Wylie began writing *Generation of Vipers*, a psychiatrist named Louis Berg published the first of two widely publicized pamphlets denouncing daytime serials as a potential threat to listeners' mental health.[113] His second report, released in September 1942, dramatically declared, "To use the hearts and minds of millions of women without regard to their mental or emotional welfare to sell a product is little short of treason in a nation at war."[114] Berg's "methodology" was soon exposed as laughably unscientific—in essence, he had listened to fifteen episodes of two different serials and tested his own physiological responses, along with those of an assistant.[115] Nevertheless, according to James Thurber, who wrote about soap operas for the *New Yorker*, Berg's allegations resulted in "pandemonium" within the industry.[116] Radio executives scurried to commission a panel of medical experts to examine the issue, which obligingly issued an exculpatory report.[117]

In retrospect, the debate over radio soap operas seems absurd in its gravity, like the uproar over comic books in the 1950s. But many ordinary listeners in 1930s and 1940s appeared genuinely incensed by the genre. According to a journalist writing in 1940, "letter files of the radio companies are shot through with complaints and threats of boycott" from housewives who viewed the serials as "a shocking affront to their intelligence" and "a fearful waste of a mighty medium."[118] In late 1939, some forty women's clubs in Westchester County, New York, even united to form an "I'm Not Listening" campaign that tried—unsuccessfully—to pressure radio executives to air more intelligent programming.[119] Many of Wylie's fans would have applauded such efforts. "For years I've wanted to purge the sound waves of those damnable soap-operas—have felt they were an insult to American intelligence, but then decided I've just been over-rating that intelligence," one woman wrote in 1945. "Women must like them or they wouldn't listen."[120] Another woman closed her letter with the following postscript: "If you are *ever* able to do anything about getting those damned soap operas off the air and some good day-time programs on, don't forget to call on me. *There* is a Cause!"[121]

Why were so many people up in arms about something as seemingly trifling as radio soap operas? It was certainly not because the shows challenged traditional gender roles or threatened to undermine conventional morality, charges that cultural conservatives often leveled at Hollywood films. Daytime serials adhered to their own stringent code of "daytime morality," and their content almost always reinforced the notion that mothers belonged in the home.[122] Indeed, even after the Office of War Information began urging cultural producers to support its Womanpower campaign (which sought to draw women into the workforce), serial writers seemed reluctant to depict female characters in ways that challenged the primacy of their domestic commitments.[123] No leading female character on a radio soap opera joined the military, and only a few took jobs in defense industries, according to historian Susan Hartmann. "Written for the woman who was at home, not work," she notes, daytime serials strove to reassure the homemaker of "the importance of her situation."[124]

The intense reactions that radio soap operas engendered therefore must be understood as reflective of hostility and anxiety surrounding the homemaker role and the cultural traditions associated with it. Unabashedly sentimental, many radio soap operas celebrated a distinctly "old-fashioned" conception of motherhood: they featured middle-aged or even elderly women who stood at the moral center of their families and communities, dispensing love and homely wisdom to all in need of compassion or correction.[125] For instance, one of the most successful and long-running serials, *Ma Perkins*, starred "America's mother on the air"—a benevolent widow in her sixties who owned and ran a lumberyard in a fictitious small town. Another show, *The Story of Mary Marlin*, featured a U.S. president who leaned heavily on his aged mother for advice—a storyline that particularly exasperated critics like Thurber.[126] These and other serials merged narratives of maternal sacrifice and redemption with sensational and highly implausible plot lines. (Kidnapping and amnesia were favored devices.) To their critics, they revealed the utter bankruptcy of the feminine literary tradition; no longer a force of uplift, sentimentalism now sought refuge in the lowest of lowbrow genres.

Thus, when the *American Mercury* writer Whitfield Cook described his first encounter with radio soap operas in 1940, he sounded like a disillusioned suitor who had just learned the rude truth about the woman he idolized. "I had no idea that my favorite radio stations were two-faced," he wrote, "that at night, and particularly on Sunday, they dressed in good taste, while six days a week they were ordinary and incredibly dull." Cook made his unwelcome discovery after tuning in to hear a male friend perform his part on a daytime serial. "I heard my friend portray the finest, most upstanding, wisdom-spouting young lover it has ever been my misfortune to encounter," he wrote. "He was not a character; he was the audible embodiment of ancient tear-jerking sentimentality." Angered to witness his friend's unmanning, Cook acidly inquired, "Does the modern housewife, busy with her electric gadgets, crave these orgies with Life as—forgive the word—entertainment? If so, I'll take a girl of an older vintage."[127] In this manner, he reminded readers that men, after all, were the ultimate "consumers," and that women who forgot that fact might well be left on the shelf.[128]

In *Generation of Vipers*, Wylie drew upon such masculinist critiques, while also obliquely echoing more academic studies of mass culture, such as those associated with the Frankfurt School. Like Cook, Wylie denounced the image of American manhood that soap operas projected, complaining that, "The most oafish cluck the radio executives can find, with a voice like a damp pillow—a mother-lover of the most degraded sort—is given to America as the ideal young husband." At the same time, he blamed the radio for drawing "a whole nation of people" into a state of "eternal fugue." Instead of engaging in serious contemplation of the conflicts that plagued their psyches and the world around them, he charged, Americans had retreated into an isolationist fantasyland, utterly removed from pressing personal and political dilemmas. Whereas radio should be limited to "music, intelligent discourse and news—all other uses being dangerous," mom would not allow for it: "Rather than study herself and her environment with the necessary honesty, she will fight for this poisoned syrup to the last. Rather than take up her democratic responsibility in this mighty and tottering republic, she will bring it crashing down." In Wylie's formulation, propagandists in Nazi Germany exploited the power of radio for nefarious political ends, while in America, the commercial interests that had seized control of the new medium catered only to Mom and her pocketbook.[129] For Wylie, radio soap operas represented a kind of American fascism: they dulled critical thinking and preempted dissent by luring citizens into a state of captivated passivity.[130]

Of course, the sentimental literary tradition had always attracted a certain amount of derision. But in the 1930s and 1940s, several factors—the sheer pervasiveness of consumer culture, its increasingly blatant commercialization, and rising concerns about the threat of fascism—led many to view mass-produced sentimentalism in increasingly alarmist terms. One of Wylie's fans, for instance, linked the consumer rituals surrounding Mother's Day to totalitarian-like mind control. Adopting Wylie's sardonic tone, he wrote in 1945:

> Of all the sickening signs of our disintegration into a race of soft-brained guinea pigs our tolerance of the swooningly sentimental commercialization of Mother's Day is the most nauseous. . . . Most of us love our mothers but if the purchase of a potted plant on a specific day is necessary to remind us of that fact, it is a sad commentary on both the quality and the constancy of our affection. . . .
>
> I suppose our Lilliputian minds are so saturated with the sickly drivel of planned emotions and so accustomed to unreasoning obedience to organized sales propaganda that most of us went home, on the eve of Mother's Day, with a bunch of flowers.[131]

To this reader, the hoopla surrounding Mother's Day suggested more than just consumer manipulation—it exposed the public's suggestible character, and hence raised the specter of totalitarianism.

Most of Wylie's readers, however, did not discuss the issue of women's relationship to culture in such extreme terms; instead, they challenged the older view of women as agents of cultural uplift. For instance, numerous respondents expressed impatience with female cultural arbiters by mocking "prim and prissy" librarians who kept *Generation of Vipers* "concealed under the counter."[132] One woman related her encounter with a "disapproving librarian" who informed her "'it is a dreadful book'" and pressed upon her "a recently published religious book which she, no doubt, felt would exorcise the evil in yours."[133] Another reported that her interaction with the librarian—"who doesn't like you nor your book"—had been "amusing": "I happened to be the first to ask for it and she hadn't put it on the shelf!"[134] These and other respondents clearly evoked a familiar stereotype—that of the repressed and bespectacled spinster librarian—to signal their receptivity to Wylie's book. Yet it would be wrong to dismiss their reports, for they still may have been accurately reporting what occurred at the circulation desk. It is entirely plausible—in fact, even likely—that some women librarians would have tried to suppress *Generation of Vipers*.

In the 1940s and 1950s, many women readers who disliked sentimental culture, or who wanted to show that they were not humorless, naive, moralistic, or obsessed with romance, ended up embracing masculinist literature, in part simply for a lack of better options. This appears to have been the case for a book club, composed of six mothers, that devoted an entire year to reading and discussing *Generation of Vipers*. As they explained to Wylie in 1945:

> We're six women in our thirties, living in a small Ohio town. We're neither wealthy nor poor, we're excellent cooks and housekeepers, fond mothers, delightful wives, tepid church-goers, delinquent members of the Woman's Club, College Club and bridge clubs. We're awfully nice. And sometimes that *ain't enough.*
>
> *Every* two weeks for a year one of us read 'Generation of Vipers' aloud and the rest darned socks and argued and fumed, agreed and disagreed, and laughed like mad over the Mom chapter. We were all set to write you a sizzling letter when the last chapter fell like a benediction and left us cursing softly, 'He's O.K. He's on the beam. *If* we write him now, it will have to be as Admirers....
>
> Six women approaching middle age, all, no doubt, incipient Moms; six women, apparently contented Book-of-the-Monthers. We're pleasant, polite, well-groomed, engrossed in our children, our husbands, our houses. Some of

us doing outside work: Red Cross, social welfare, art classes, salesmanship. . . .
We read the Satevepost [Saturday Evening Post] and quote the Readers' Di-
gest. You know us. You've met us often and probably discounted us. *Don't*.
Because we, of all people, are YOUR ADMIRERS.

"The Vipers"[135]

For these women, reading and discussing Wylie's book constituted a
mildly rebellious activity—one that they explicitly contrasted to their conscientious housekeeping, obligatory participation in women's clubs, and routine consumption of middlebrow culture. Embracing *Generation of Vipers*,
they positioned themselves, if only temporarily, beyond the confines of the
culture that so thoroughly defined them and through which (as they self-
mockingly acknowledged) they usually defined themselves. Their ability to
use Wylie's book to assuage their dissatisfaction as suburban homemakers
is surely a testament to their resourcefulness. Yet how should we interpret
the fact that, in order to distance themselves from those aspects of "women's
culture" they found oppressive or tedious, they felt compelled to reach for
Generation of Vipers? One can appreciate the element of resistance that characterized such appropriations while still regretting the poverty of popular
literature that prompted "the Vipers" and other women to seek meaning in a
fundamentally misogynist work.[136]

Women's attraction to *Generation of Vipers* should be understood as reflecting the cultural component of a much broader realignment, as American
society gradually shifted from a world characterized by high degree of sexual
segregation to one characterized by a high degree of sexual integration. Just
as many well-educated women rejected separatist or maternalist politics, so
they rejected feminine and sentimental literature. Yet in their enthusiasm to
distance themselves from women's culture, readers like "the Vipers" often
quelled the anger or misgivings that a work like *Generation of Vipers* aroused.
Instead of writing a "sizzling letter" that threatened to mark them as censorious moralizers—the very role they hoped to disown—they settled for
reminding male debunkers that even seemingly contented housewives might
long to escape the confines of mainstream American culture.

Exposing "Mother Love"

"Her boy," having been "protected" by her love, and carefully, even shud-
deringly, shielded from his logical development through his barbaric period,
or childhood . . . is cushioned against any major step in his progress toward
maturity. Mom steals from the generation of woman behind her (which she

has, as a still further defense, also sterilized of integrity and courage) that part
of her boy's personality which should have become the love of a female contemporary. Mom transmutes it into sentimentality for herself.[137]

Wylie's denunciation of cloying and overbearing mother love would prove
to be the most consequential component of his momism critique. According
to Wylie, what looked like self-sacrificing mother love was in truth a selfish
and manipulative strategy designed to keep sons trapped in emotional bond-
age. By monopolizing their son's affections and surreptitiously undermining
paternal authority, he alleged, moms rendered boys incapable of developing
into healthy men who could form mature heterosexual relationships.

As a number of historians have shown, Wylie's critique of pathological
mother love represented an extreme articulation of arguments advanced
by psychoanalysts, psychiatrists, and other psychological and social scientific experts during the 1940s and 1950s.[138] However, what has not been adequately understood is that the momism critique was also a repudiation of
a conception of maternal affectivity that had previously enjoyed widespread
acceptance within mainstream American culture—the notion that mothers
should strive to bind sons to the home with "silver cords" of love. Insisting that overly possessive mothers produced effeminate sons who weakened
the nation, Wylie urged Americans to reassess certain maternal attitudes and
behaviors, deeming what had once seemed natural and laudable as deviant
and pathological. By discrediting an older maternal style that was already fast
becoming anachronistic, the momism critique helped to narrow the limits
within which maternal influence could be unequivocally celebrated.[139]

The pretherapeutic conception of mother love that so enraged Wylie is evident in a small number of letters that he received from women who presented
themselves as unreconstructed moral mothers. In 1946, a sixty-four-year-old
woman, who admitted that she had "many Victorian inhibitions" and described herself as "very ignorant," grew pensive after completing *Generation
of Vipers*. "Being the mother of a large family of sons, I have always fancied
myself as a sort of modern 'Cornelia with her Jewels,' " she confessed. A heroic
Roman mother, widowed when quite young, Cornelia had refused to remarry
so that she could fully devote herself to her children—a self-denying stance
that could only be regarded as unhealthy in a post-Freudian age. Moreover,
after equipping her sons with a sense of duty and a desire for glory, Cornelia
came to regard them as her "jewels"—precious objects that bestowed stature
upon their "owner." Of course, Wylie rejected all the messages about motherhood that followed from the Roman matron's story—the notion that motherhood required immense self-denial, the idea that mothers should derive

their identity and self-worth from their children, and the belief that a man's civic virtue or battlefield prowess reflected on his mother. Reading his attack on moms, the letter writer apparently grew self-conscious and self-critical of a maternal stance she had long assumed. "I, truly, am not guilty of many of the superficial faults you regale us with, however, in the more fundamental aspect I seem to have a spiritual awareness of guilt and great humility," she wrote. "Perhaps under those circumstances there is some chance for growth. (?)"[140]

In contrast, another mother, whose two sons were currently serving in the military, passionately defended "the tradition of gloried mother-hood" in a letter sent to Wylie in 1945:

> We mothers didn't ask for this War—And we gave our sons gladly to the cause. . . .
>
> I shall use my self to write poetry, Sonnets, shall pray like never before; that the halo over all mothers shall glow more brightly—who does he [Wylie] think he is to dare clarify so loudly in print, to assert to us "mothers" whether we're the doting kind or not? "Is he a Mother??" It's like a person who never bore a child . . . how to "rear it," they go about telling. I say for all mothers, the word Viper or Jerk is hardly good upright Christian form.[141]

First, the writer depicted motherhood as a sacred entity to be revered in prayers and extolled in sentimental poetry. Second, she argued that, because mothers bear and raise children, they should be considered the ultimate authorities on childrearing. And finally, she implied that mothers were entitled to assume a possessive stance toward their children: they could rightfully speak of "giving" their sons to the nation, for children truly were their lifework, their most valued possessions. Here, in a nutshell, was the ideal of mother love that Wylie hoped to pathologize.

If Wylie's most outraged critics voiced a highly sentimental and religious view of motherhood, many of his fans self-consciously embraced a more psychologically oriented perspective. In describing their views, they articulated some of the basic assumptions that informed therapeutic culture—that the husband-wife relationship should trump the mother-son relationship, that maternal affection and romantic love ought should be entirely distinct emotions, that repression of healthy sexual desires could lead to crippling neuroses, and that mother love needed to be modulated, lest it become pathogenic. Given that experts had been articulating these precepts since the early twentieth century, it may seem surprising that respondents still felt compelled to articulate and defend them in the 1940s and 1950s. What Wylie's correspondence suggests is that emotional norms changed unevenly and slowly, and that such shifts often came to be experienced most powerfully in the form of intergenerational conflict.

In fact, several respondents who lauded Wylie's momism critique explicitly contrasted their own, more psychologically astute approach to childrearing with the mothering they themselves had endured as children. "I had an American mom myself and as a result had to spend large chunks of a secretary salary in getting myself psychoanalyzed, so I took warning [from the momism critique]," explained a woman who read *Generation of Vipers* after giving birth to her first child in 1944.[142] Another woman, who described herself as "the product (or victim) of a 'Mom,' " wrote, "The advantage [of having had a Mom] lies solely in my awareness of its evils as regards the welfare of my own children. The disadvantages are legion, among them being the struggle to pay my analyst—even at once a week visits, which are woefully inadequate."[143] Blaming their emotional conflicts on their mothers, these women sought out therapy and embraced more psychologically oriented approaches to childrearing in hopes of avoiding the pitfalls of momism.

As historian Mari Jo Buhle has argued, Wylie's book "undoubtedly derived at least part of its commercial energy from its ability to tap into the resurgence of psychoanalysis as a popular discourse."[144] Many of Wylie's respondents described how reading *Generation of Vipers* had piqued their interest in psychoanalysis and strengthened their resolve to pursue self-knowledge. Yet the book appealed not only to ordinary Americans who had grown "fascinated at what psychology and psychiatry can do for this goofy world," as one fan put it, but to many psychiatrists and physicians as well.[145] It circulated widely within psychiatric circles and won accolades from two of the most prominent American-born psychiatrists and psychoanalysts, O. Spurgeon English and Karl Menninger. These men shared both Wylie's concerns about pernicious maternal influence and his interest in reaching a broad readership. English, a leading figure in psychosomatic medicine who would later coauthor a popular book called *Fathers Are Parents, Too*, sent Wylie a lengthy letter after reading *Generation of Vipers* during his trip to the annual meeting of the American Psychiatric Association.[146] Menninger, perhaps the nation's most famous psychiatrist, compared Wylie's book to his own recently published bestseller, *Love against Hate*, also published in 1942. "There are some themes in your book which are very close to my own thinking," he wrote to Wylie in March 1943. "I believe you might get some of the same narcissistic satisfaction that I got from reading my views expressed by you if you will read my recent book . . . and see your views expressed by me."[147]

The striking parallels between *Love against Hate* and *Generation of Vipers* point to the close relationship between antimaternalism and the popularization of psychiatry and psychoanalysis. Though Menninger called himself a Freudian, whereas Wylie promoted Jungian psychology, both men were in truth eclectic popularizers whose attempts to reconcile psychoanalysis with Protestant religiosity tended to baffle their European-born counterparts.[148] Like Wylie, Menninger regarded female dominance and male passivity as the central problems that plagued the American family (and hence American democracy). "The American boy too often does not turn his interest to girls in any deep, enduring way," he wrote, "but remains unconsciously and sometimes quite consciously attached in a passive way to his father or his mother."[149] This dependent attachment made the typical American man a weak and sexually unsatisfactory mate, which led his wife to turn her affective energies toward their children (particularly sons)—a phenomenon that Menninger dubbed "the vicious cycle." To break the cycle, he urged Americans to adopt a more sensible and realistic attitude toward motherhood. "It is customary to pay [mothers] homage and to exalt their sacrifices, and in doing so to ignore their status as human beings," he wrote. "Women have long recognized that the tendency of men to put them on pedestals and to idealize them has great disadvantages and penalties, and some of them have properly rebelled against it, preferring understanding and recognition of their individual needs."[150] Though Menninger, again like Wylie, actually had a quite reductive view of sexual difference, these passages suggests how anxieties about maternal influence and male effeminacy could easily translate into something that sounded like a call for women's emancipation.

This helps to explain why some women appeared receptive to critiques of maternal pathology.[151] Several of Wylie's respondents even seem to have read *Generation of Vipers* as if it were an advice book, one that might sit comfortably next to Benjamin Spock's *The Commonsense Book of Baby and Child Care.* The mother of three teenage daughters, who wrote in 1958, added in a postscript, "I forgot to say the 'Generation of Vipers' has occupied a place of honor on our bookshelves for many years and that we have found its precepts very helpful in bringing up our children."[152] Another woman wrote, "Young mothers and fathers of extremely young children were not, I hope, the generation you were indicting, but you've given us a lot to search for, and a great deal to avoid."[153] Many other women responded to the momism chapter by seeking to ascertain whether, or to what extent, Wylie's critique applied to them. Some exonerated themselves fully. "'Mom' touched a sore spot— but when I tore the chapter apart, and searched myself for resemblance to the mom you berated I gave myself a clean bill," wrote one woman. "I just don't belong in that category."[154] Others acknowledged that they had seen aspects of themselves reflected in Wylie's caricature. One mother, for instance, reported that Wylie's book had given her pause, "which was all to the good, since I have three sons. I hope your diatribe against 'Moms' kept me from smothering them entirely."[155] Anxious to dissociate themselves from such an unflattering caricature, and fearful of damaging their children, these respondents vowed to be more self-reflective and self-policing in fulfilling their maternal role.

Not surprisingly, women who applauded Wylie's critique of maternal pathology often took pains to disavow any investment in the notion of motherhood as a transformative experience that elevated womankind. "I believe that motherhood does NOT automatically enoble [sic] a woman, and, what is more, I believe that every woman knows this," wrote one woman. "Whatever kind of judgment, love and goodness went into a girls [sic] upbringing is the basis for whatever quality of nobleness and goodness she may rise to as a woman, and as a mother."[156] Some women went so far as to dispute the assumption that mothers were guaranteed a special place in their children's hearts by virtue of their unique relationship. "I'm trying to give my children a better deal all the way around. I figure that they had nothing to do with me being their mother," wrote one young mother. "Therefore it is up to me to earn their love and respect."[157] These women disliked the notion that the mother-child relationship should be structured according to prescribed roles that reflected a generic view of maternal duties and children's needs. Rather than expecting love and affection as a matter of course, they stressed their determination to win their children over through their personal attributes and actions.

Still other respondents embraced Wylie's attack on the mainstream, middle-class American Mom because it seemed to validate their own, more marginal status. In 1945, an unmarried white woman whose child was part Mexican wrote, "I am a mother and really enjoyed your chapter on Moms! You certainly hit the bulls-eye on every count."[158] Another woman, who found "all this palaver about 'Mother Love'" nauseating, described how she had been "criticized and talked about" by her neighbors, one of whom had even threatened to have her children "taken away." As she explained, "I've tried to live and develop into the kind of woman who would be respected and liked for herself and not because she happened to be someone's mother. Do you know that . . . your book is the first actual encouragement I've ever had from a grown person?"[159] This reader, who wanted motherhood to be considered incidental to her more basic identity, viewed Wylie as taking aim at spurious maternal standards that she had been deemed incapable of meeting; from her encounter with *Generation of Vipers*, she derived a sense of validation and "encouragement."

Yet even women who adopted Wylie's critique as a way of affirming their own maternal attitudes and practices could find themselves accused of momism, as one middle-aged mother discovered to her chagrin. Writing to Wylie in 1945, she explained:

> You really started a battle in this home two years ago between my son and my-self. I don't know whether I ought to be writing to you or not, being confused as to whose side I am on now. Having been a deadly hater of "Momism" all my life, my head whirled when Bud (my renegade son's name) turned on me and accused me of all those loathsome things. I could not pat his head, nor cook his favorite dish without taunts of "Momism" being hurled at me. I went on strike, saying nothing, which puzzled him, and then came the blarney, and the dawn for him. "Go 'way," I said, "with your 'sonism.'"

In this case, a son appropriated the momism critique as a way of expressing his desire to distance himself, both emotionally and physically, from his dot-ing mother; the epithet provided him with a blunt but highly effective tool for conveying his impatience. (It is unclear whether he spoke in a tone of gentle mockery or one of full-blown hostility, though his mother's reference to their "battle" suggests perhaps the latter.) But the respondent went on to narrate an even more complicated story of familial tensions and emotional needs, for while she chafed at her son's accusation, she leveled the very same charge at her mother-in-law. Indeed, over the course of her letter, it becomes clear that anger toward her mother-in-law is what prompted her to write to Wylie in the first place:

> Right now I am in a state of fury because his [her son's] dear Papa is at my mother-in-law's toadying to one of the greatest exponents of the art [of mo-mism] that one could meet. She is almost illiterate but has me in a constant daze at her cleverness (almost wrote "wiliness" but remembered your name). I married a wonderful son but I wait daily for a miracle to happen that would turn him into a husband. No wonder "Momism" continues, and 'tis the lonely woman who seeks to break the chain. However, I shalln't get morbid. . . . Thanks for listening, if you have.[160]

This woman accepted Wylie's portrait of pathogenic mother love and there-fore sought to restrain herself when dealing with her son. But she felt that she had been deprived of her rightful compensation—a loving and attentive hus-band—because her mother-in-law did not abide by the same standards. Her bitter observation—"'tis the lonely woman who seeks to break the chain"—can be read as a commentary on the plight of women of her generation, who found themselves emotionally shortchanged by a shift in the cultural norms that governed relations between mothers and their children.

In the end, many mothers felt the full force of the momism critique only as their children grew more independent and they themselves began approaching middle age. As their lives progressed, some women who had heartily endorsed Wylie's critique in their youth, often in rebellion against their own mothers, found themselves having second thoughts. In 1958, one such woman sent Wylie an unpublished essay, entitled "What Philip Wylie Really Thinks about Women," recounting how her views had evolved since 1942, when she first encountered *Generation of Vipers*. At the time, she related, she had been "single and childless, a young woman just graduated from the Smith School of Psychiatric Social Work, full of professional jargon, in the midst of my own analysis." Her job at the Children's Bureau, where she counseled "disturbed" and "inadequate" mothers seeking child guidance and foster home placement, combined with her "hostility" toward her own mother, "which is always present in the midst of one's own analysis," had made her particularly receptive to Wylie's critique: "I embraced Mr. Wylie's philosophy regarding our cannibalistic matriarchy avidly, in my youthful unsophistication taking all that he said as a literal condemnation of motherhood in its entirety." But after she married, gave up her career, bore four children, and found most of her contacts "limited to other moms," she found herself resenting "the ever increasing hostility towards American mothers exhibited by most males" and reassessing her own antimaternalist views. Ultimately, she concluded that her own coming-of-age conflicts, combined with her immersion in psychiatry and psychoanalysis, had led her to adopt a stance that, in retrospect, seemed unjustifiably harsh.

Still, despite her evident intelligence and literary skill, this woman faltered in her attempt to defend American mothers. Although she contacted the editors of a national magazine, who encouraged her to pursue her idea for an article entitled "In Defense of American Women," she could not bring herself to finish the piece. Instead, she did a remarkable and self-defeating thing: she turned her material over to the very man whose ideas she hoped to challenge. "Mr. Wylie started the thing, I thought. He had the reputation, the experience, the male point of view," she wrote in the essay that she forwarded to Wylie. "People listen to him and care what he thinks." Her defense of American womanhood thus collapsed into an appeal for exoneration, as she implored Wylie to assure her cohort of mothers that they had succeeded where their own mothers had failed: "I had to see for myself what a man of his great literary gifts and powers of perception really thinks about American women as a whole. Are we to him a lost cause?"[161] Sadly, this woman seemed unable to challenge Wylie's "expert" authority, even though *she* possessed the professional accreditation that he sorely lacked.

Her capitulation is instructive, for it suggests the difficulty that women like her experienced in countering the momism critique. Because the assault on moral motherhood was so strongly associated with the repudiation of sentimentality and repressive moralism, those who embraced the tenets of the dominant therapeutic culture hesitated to articulate their objections to the momism critique, even when it left them feeling deeply discomfited. The fact that Wylie seemed happy to oblige such women by reassuring them that *they* were not "moms" did little to diminish the pernicious influence that his critique continued to exert through the 1950s and into the 1960s.

By the early 1960s, American culture had begun to change in ways that would make it hard to perceive what had once seemed trenchant and even liberating about Wylie's momism critique. Anxieties about female idleness did not totally disappear, but they lost salience as more middle-aged women entered the workforce. Patriotic women's groups persisted, but no longer as major players on the national stage. The last radio soap opera went off the air in 1960, and television shows typically featured youngish suburban mothers (like June Cleaver or Donna Reed) or middle-aged mothers who evoked nostalgia for an ethnic past (like Molly Goldberg or Mama Hansen), rather than the archetypical all-American Mom.[162] Though more difficult to gauge, people's behavior changed as well. Most middle-class mothers appeared somewhat less intent on molding their children's characters and more casual in relating to their children than had mothers of prior generations. As the particular references and cultural patterns that had informed readers' responses to Wylie's momism critique in the 1940s slowly fell away, what remained powerful was its virulent, now naked, misogyny.

Thus, when a minister reread *Generation of Vipers* in 1962, he found himself in greater accord with Wylie's views than he had been the first time around, nearly two decades before. "Especially about Momism," he explained. "The rise of juvenile delinquency is concurrent with the rise of 'freedom' of the American woman, and her assumption of the pants. If I were a dictator of the U.S., I'd force all married women who work for the hell of it to return to their homes, doff the pants, re-don their panties, and take care of the kids."[163] Here, at last, is the kind of favorable response that most historical accounts of the momism critique would lead one to expect—a straightforward assertion of male dominance, based on the conviction that married women should be relegated to the home. But as we have seen, it is not representative of how most readers, apparently including the minister himself, reacted to the critique in the 1940s and 1950s. Then, Wylie's screed had read more like a damning indictment of traditional gender roles than a call to resurrect them.

By the early 1960s, white, middle-class American homemakers had lost much of their prior prestige, and women's presence in the workplace had increased considerably. Assumptions about where women derived power shifted accordingly. The middle-aged matron no longer seemed both laughable and formidable; she just seemed laughable. Thus, when people read *Generation of Vipers* in the 1960s and thereafter, they often simply assumed that working women or feminists must have been the real targets of Wylie's wrath. For as the years passed, and the cultural authority and influence of middle-aged matrons receded, the notion that "traditional" moms could have elicited such vehement anger and masculine angst grew less and less comprehensible. Increasingly, misogynist sentiments would affix to women who competed with men directly, rather than to those who claimed special privileges based on their status as women and mothers. Yet even as the reactionary core of the momism critique became more starkly evident, its emancipatory potential had still not been wholly spent. In 1963, Betty Friedan—a forty-two-year-old mother of three, who had read Wylie's book in the 1940s when she was fresh out of college—appropriated his ideas as part of her own sweeping assessment of the American mother and housewife. As the final chapter of this book will show, this time the critique would come with a feminist proposal to redress the problem.

Mothers of the Nation:
Patriotic Maternalism and Its Critics

Have you gentlemen stopped to think consider what America would have done if it had not been for these mothers? Not alone the gold star mothers, but the mothers who gave their sons to serve their country. It was the mothers who suffered to bring these boys into the world, who cared for them in sickness and in health, and it was our flesh and blood that enriched the foreign soil.

MATHILDA BURLING, testifying before the House
Committee on Military Affairs, January 27, 1928

There was a lot to say about how courageous and fine nearly everyone was. But in answer to a question about the Japanese population problem in the Islands, I remarked that some American soldiers had raped Jap girls on the plantations after the attack. Shades of "Momism," you should have been there. I had telephone calls and anonymous letters about my depravity in hinting any such thing. One woman, a ringer for your arch-type Mom, told me that I probably didn't understand that many of the women in my audience had sons in the Army and that a statement like mine was insulting to them.

A woman who had been at Pearl Harbor, describing to Philip Wylie
her experiences as a speaker at a women's club meeting, August 26, 1943

When Philip Wylie had completed about half of the manuscript for *Generation of Vipers*, he attended a party at which the writer Hervey Allen expressed "a fine and funny fury" over a recently viewed newsreel. The offending film portrayed an infantry division of American soldiers spelling, in formation, the word "MOM" as a tribute to Mother's Day—a spectacle that prompted Allen to conclude, "There is too much Mom in America." Although Wylie already planned to include "a treatise on Matriarchy" in his forthcoming book, Allen's anecdote provided his hook. As he later explained, "'Mom' was the word I needed and 'Mom' spelled out by ten or fifteen thousand soldiers was the proper scale: 'Momism' was a natural derivative to describe the unconscious and abnormal piety of the popular mind."[1]

Wylie's moment of inspiration reveals much about the political context that helped to distinguish his critique from earlier attacks on sentimental mothers. Viewed from above, each soldier seemed reduced to a mere speck, as if the act of honoring motherhood required male identities to be blurred and submerged. This vision spoke to Wylie so strongly of something gone amiss that he needed a new word to describe it. "Matriarchy"—an expression frequently used in the 1920s and 1930s—did not fit the bill, for it failed to convey the threat of ideological hegemony and lockstep mass behavior. By tacking a sinister "ism" onto "mom"—a modern American colloquialism—Wylie succeeded in uniting antagonism toward mothers with the political fears of the moment.

That a group of GIs honored mothers in such a fashion, and that their doing so provided fodder for cynical party conversation, also says much about both the persistence of and the growing resistance to patriotic maternalism within American culture. In prior military conflicts, images of mothers dominated patriotic iconography; the soldier's virtuous devotion to his mother had signaled his willingness to sacrifice for the national cause.[2] During World War I, for example, General Pershing urged American soldiers to write home to their mothers on Mother's Day, proclaiming that such letters would "carry back our courage and our affection to the patriotic women whose love and prayers inspire us and cheer us to victory."[3] In contrast, during World War II, the youthful and glamorous "pin-up" girl usurped the maternal figure as the primary representative of American femininity.[4] And to the extent that the all-American mom remained a potent icon, critics increasingly perceived the public's reverential attitude toward mothers as evidence of a serious national failing.

Why did the American mother lose her privileged place within the national iconography? Why did numerous critics begin to view political rhetoric that vaunted the "glorious sacrifices of American mothers" as incompatible with democracy? This chapter argues that the decline of the iconic mother reflected a fundamental transformation of the gendered structure of American political culture. According to the long-standing paradigm of Republican motherhood, women tempered the conflict inherent in partisan politics by acting on behalf of the public good. This tendency to view white, middle-class women as morally pure and politically disinterested allowed women to wield influence in the public realm while also serving as convincing symbols of the nation itself. The roots of this tradition can be traced to the Revolutionary era, when American women first began to emphasize their maternal role as a means of laying claim to a new, albeit derivative, political identity. Excluded from formal politics and barred from performing various civic duties, women attempted to achieve influence by stressing their importance as mothers of the Republic who educated their children to be virtuous citizens.[5] These arguments assumed a more religious cast in the antebellum era as large numbers of middle-class women joined church-affiliated voluntary associations, justifying their activities by drawing on evangelical notions that deified maternal impulses.[6] In the post–Civil War years, the women's club movement emerged as the most extensive manifestation of female voluntarism.[7] Initially focused on self-improvement, the club movement became more politicized—and more visible on both a local and a national level—in the 1880s and 1890s.[8] Casting themselves as upholders of civic virtue and the moral order, clubwomen battled vices ranging from municipal corruption to prostitution and drunkenness, often with considerable success.[9] In the Progressive Era, reformers capitalized on maternalist ideologies to make even bolder forays into the political realm, lobbying for legislation that would acknowledge and protect the role mothers fulfilled by rearing citizens and workers.[10]

Until recently, historians tended to date the demise of a separate women's political culture at around 1920. They have pointed to a variety of developments—including the suffrage victory, the rise of professional social work, and the growing emphasis on class-based politics in the 1930s—as factors that made gender a less salient basis for political mobilization. For example, in a groundbreaking article, Estelle Freedman attributed the decline of feminism following World War I to the dissolution of "female separatism in social and political life."[11] Likewise, in an influential work on the gendered structure of American politics, Paula Baker argued that the suffrage amendment "represented the endpoint of nineteenth-century womanhood and woman's political culture. . . . No longer treated as a political class, women ceased to act as one."[12] But in fact, even after attaining the vote, American women held fast to the rhetoric of domesticity and motherhood and continued to band together in voluntary organizations.[13] Although the notion of a cohesive "woman's bloc" had been discredited by the late 1920s, the tradition of female voluntarism continued to thrive throughout the interwar era.[14] Indeed, according to Nancy Cott, "It is highly probable that the greatest extent of associational activity in the whole history of American women" occurred between the two world wars, "after women became voters and before a great proportion of them entered the labor force."[15] To explain this phenomenon, some scholars have pointed to women's frustration with party politics. Others have argued that, despite dramatic cultural change, women's identities remained largely rooted in the home.[16] What seems clear is that suffrage did not, at least in any immediate sense, lead the majority of middle-class women to reconceptualize their civic identities in fundamental ways. On the contrary, most continued to perceive their relationship to the state and the political process in highly gendered terms.[17]

Yet if middle-class women employed traditional organizational and rhetorical strategies, they did so in an altered context that increasingly eroded the foundation for a separate women's political culture. First, the basic fact that women could vote undermined their ability to cast themselves as disinterested citizens. And, second, as different groups of women appropriated maternalist rhetoric for widely divergent ends, it lost all coherence as a political ideology. In the late nineteenth and early twentieth centuries, maternalist rhetoric had generally signified support for social legislation to protect women and children as well as a commitment to eradicating such moral vices as alcohol consumption and obscenity.[18] But in the 1920s and 1930s, women who lobbied for the *repeal* of prohibition adopted the language of "home protection"; militarists and peace activists alike framed their appeals as mothers; and fascist nations developed their own varieties of maternalism. This fragmentation of meaning rendered maternalists vulnerable to critics who depicted them as mere opportunists or, even worse, protofascists. Although women would continue to employ maternalist rhetoric in various circumstances during and after World War II, the emphasis on protecting the nation's mothers and children would never again be such a central and unifying focus for women activists and reformers. Nor would the image of the all-American mother be such an effective symbol of the values and virtues of the republic itself.

The Campaign for Gold Star Mothers' Pilgrimages

The continued viability of maternalism in the late 1920s and the reasons for its subsequent decline can be better understood by analyzing a largely forgotten episode in American history, the gold star mothers' pilgrimages of 1930 to 1933.[19] The legislation that provided for these government-run pilgrimages, enacted in March 1929—an era noted for its fiscal conservatism and limited conception of government—stands out as a remarkable departure. It allowed more than 6,600[20] women to travel to Europe, during the worst years of the Depression, to witness the graves of loved ones who had perished in World War I. Housed in first-class hotels, the pilgrims spent a full two weeks in Europe, shepherded through detailed itineraries that included sightseeing and shopping excursions as well as trips to cemeteries and battlefields.[21] Although unmarried widows also participated in the program, mothers constituted the overwhelming majority of pilgrims, and policymakers justified the trips almost exclusively in maternalist terms. Both the campaign for the pilgrimages and the government's conduct of them reveal the enduring potency of a highly sentimental and nationalistic conception of motherhood the late 1920s and early 1930s. Yet the program also drew criticism as it progressed over time and indeed long after its conclusion. Because the pilgrimages so dramatically exemplified a certain strain of maternalism, they provoked some

Americans to question the beliefs and assumptions that lent motherhood its political and symbolic capital. To that extent, the pilgrimage program also became an agent of change, helping to discredit the very ideas and images it sought to reaffirm.

The success of the pilgrimage legislation suggests that the 1920s did not witness the demise of maternalism per se, but rather that "progressive maternalism" came to be challenged, and to some extent supplanted, by "patriotic maternalism."[22] In June 1929, less than three months after passing the pilgrimage bill, Congress effectively killed the Maternity and Infancy Protection Act (otherwise known as the Sheppard-Towner Act), the first federal program designed to improve maternal and infant health. Passed by a wide margin in 1921, the legislation had initially enjoyed the support of nearly all women's groups, including the Daughters of the Americans Revolution. Yet by 1926, in a shift that reflected the growing polarization of organized womanhood, the DAR and other conservative women had joined the American Medical Association in calling for its termination. Women's historians have therefore rightly linked the Sheppard-Towner Act's repeal to the splintering of the broad-based coalition of women's groups that had previously lent support to maternalist initiatives. Yet they have not discussed the near simultaneous passage of the pilgrimage bill, which established a federal program, designed explicitly for mothers, that required roughly the same level of annual expenditure over a period of four years.[23] Even as progressive maternalists encountered bitter defeats, conservative women succeeded in shaping public policy by emphasizing the civic dimensions of motherhood.

Like progressive reformers, the organized war mothers who lobbied for the pilgrimages held that motherhood was not simply a private, familial role: mothers who raised soldier-sons, they claimed, fulfilled a civic duty as crucial as soldiering itself. And like their progressive counterparts, they cast the state in the role of a benevolent caretaker, insisting that war mothers deserved consolation (in the form of pilgrimages) and, if needed, material compensation (in the form of pensions). Moreover, both groups embraced an ethnocentric conception of "American motherhood," though progressive reformers typically advocated "scientific motherhood" as a path to Americanization, whereas patriotic women's groups tended to be frankly exclusionary. The two constituencies differed fundamentally, however, in their use of motherhood as a political platform. Whereas progressive maternalists argued that all mothers made a civic contribution by rearing citizens, organized war mothers emphasized the fact that they had reared and sacrificed soldier-sons. And whereas progressive maternalists strove to improve material conditions for poor, working-class, and rural mothers, patriotic maternalists stressed the emotional and symbolic aspects of motherhood by privileging a select group of elderly women who were no longer actively engaged in maternal work. In 1929, when Congress passed the pilgrimage legislation and yet refused to renew funding for the Sheppard-Towner Act, it signaled that the psychological needs of bereaved war mothers had gained precedence over the material needs of younger mothers.

When "maternalism" is defined broadly enough to encompass conservative and patriotic women, its downfall must be dated later and attributed in part to its growing association with a host of controversial political positions. As criticism of the pilgrimage program reveals, in the minds of many politically liberal Americans, paeans to American motherhood came to connote not only retrograde gender roles, but also narrow-minded bigotry, disregard for social and economic inequality, and lockstep patriotism and militarism. Commentators wary of the type of nationalism that had prevailed during World War I increasingly perceived maternalist rhetoric as incompatible with modern democracy—a notion that appeared borne out in 1939, when a sprawling coalition of reactionary mothers' groups, some overtly fascist, emerged to protest U.S. intervention in World War II.[24] To be sure, the history of maternalist politics cannot be viewed as simple story of its appropriation by the far right, for some progressive women, most notably peace activists, continued to employ maternalist arguments and rhetoric in the interwar period and beyond.[25] But to a significant extent, patriotic and conservative women's groups usurped maternalism, making it more difficult to employ for progressive aims.

The organized war mothers who lobbied for the pilgrimages embraced a sentimental ideal of motherhood, dating from the early nineteenth century, while also appropriating the Progressive Era view of motherhood as a direct form of service to the nation state. Nothing in their congressional testimony acknowledged the notable change in women's political status that had occurred nearly a decade before, when women gained the right to vote. These mothers did not present themselves as representatives of a politically empowered constituency but as grieving women who spoke on behalf of other, less economically privileged, bereaved mothers. Moreover, they addressed congressmen less as political representatives than as gentlemen who held the power to grant them a special favor. Yet even as they held tight to a Victorian ideal of motherhood, the pilgrimage advocates pursued public recognition of that ideal in a manner that their forebears would probably neither have recognized nor condoned.

Prior to World War I, the term "war mother" was not widely used, nor did American women claim the identity as grounds for mobilization. The mother celebrated in Civil War literature, poetry, and songs bore her suffering in solitude and silence, never calling attention to her sacrifices and pain. She appeared less frequently as a subject in her own right than as an object of contemplation, as when soldiers sang, "Just Before the Battle, Mother, I Am Thinking Most of You."[26] The most famous reference to a mother from the Civil War era appears in a letter attributed (perhaps erroneously) to Abraham Lincoln:

> I have been shown in the files of the War Department . . . that you are the mother of five sons who have died gloriously on the field of battle. I feel how weak and fruitless must be any words of mine which should attempt to beguile you from the grief of a loss so overwhelming. But I cannot refrain from tendering to you the consolation that may be found in the thanks of the Republic they died to save. I pray that our heavenly Father may assuage the anguish of your bereavement, and leave you only the cherished memory of the loved and lost, and the solemn pride that must be yours to have laid so costly a sacrifice upon the altar of freedom.[27]

Here, the war mother appears only in a dim outline, as the object of Lincoln's tender feelings and noble sentiments. She did not come forward to proclaim her own loss and grief; her case was brought to Lincoln's attention by a third party. This self-effacing passivity was no minor detail but rather part of what made her worthy of presidential consolation.

The organizations for war mothers that emerged in the interwar period present a striking contrast to this image of the isolated and apolitical grieving mother. War mothers first came together locally and informally, but they eventually established two major national organizations, the American War Mothers, founded in 1919, and the American Gold Star Mothers, founded in 1928.[28] Open to any mother with a son or daughter who had served in World War I, the American War Mothers had a predominantly Anglo-Saxon constituency, with a small number of Jewish and African-American members. The American Gold Star Mothers, composed of women whose sons or daughters had perished in World War I, admitted only women of the "Caucasian race." Though ostensibly nonpolitical, the American War Mothers and the American Gold Star Mothers advocated military preparedness and consistently aligned with the forces of antiradicalism, as G. Kurt Piehler has noted.[29] Their emergence should be viewed as part of a larger trend, the rise of the nation's first broad-based conservative women's movement. Historians have been slow to appreciate the scale and import of this movement, but, as Christine Erickson and Kirstin Delegard have demonstrated, it played a crucial role in fracturing the coalition that had supported maternalist initiatives prior to the war.[30] In 1925, a group of right-wing women, determined to counter the influence of the Women's League for International Peace and Freedom, established the Women's Patriotic Conference for National Defense, an umbrella organization that aimed to coordinate the activities of conservative and patriotic women. By the late 1920s, as many as one million women, associated with some forty organizations, had coalesced under the WPCND's rubric.[31]

The history of the pilgrimage legislation, which unfolded over a ten-year period beginning in 1919, reflects the growing influence of conservative and patriotic women's groups in general, and war mothers' organizations in particular. The idea of government-funded pilgrimages to European gravesites did not, in fact, originate with war mothers, nor did the initial proposal privilege maternal grief. In 1919, the decorated war veteran and congressman Fiorello LaGuardia devised a bill that would have subsidized trips for fathers, mothers, or widows, so long as the family consented to having the body interred in one of the eight American military cemeteries scheduled to be built in Europe. But the bill failed to receive a hearing; as LaGuardia subsequently explained, "Everything was concentrated on getting those bodies back." (In the end, roughly 70 percent of family members exercised their right to have the bodies of their loved ones repatriated.)[32] Organized war mothers subsequently began to call upon the government to provide trips for mothers who had allowed the bodies of their sons to remain in Europe and could not afford to travel there to witness the gravesite. In 1924, Congress held hearings on such a bill, but it floundered due to disagreements over logistical issues. The third bill, introduced in September 1927 and enacted in March 1929, succeeded primarily because organized war mothers persistently lobbied Congress, supported after October 1928 by the powerful American Legion. By restricting eligibility to those who had not previously visited their loved one's grave, the legislation retained the basic idea of a needs-based program, but government officials waived this provision once the pilgrimages got underway.[33] As will become clear, what began as a proposal to serve poor war mothers ultimately evolved into a program that showcased American wealth and governmental munificence.

The women who led the campaign for the pilgrimages differentiated themselves from special interest groups by emphasizing that they were not paid lobbyists seeking government handouts but rather helpless ladies urging a benevolent government to do a noble deed. "We have no paid lobbyists," proclaimed Mathilda Burling, national representative of the Gold Star Mothers, proclaimed. "We have but ourselves and our hearts to crave a favor our country should grant. Surely the great Senate must see this case through our eyes. Surely it must know what it means to us who bore the loss."[34] This stance of deferential supplicant, however, concealed a strong sense of entitlement. When the congressmen failed to live up to the chivalric role imputed to them, the mothers did not attempt to hide their frustration. At the end of a hearing in which some objections had been raised, Burling scolded the congressmen for delaying the bill. "May I ask you gentlemen why all of this discussion . . . ?" she demanded. "It is something that we mothers should not be pleading for."[35] In an ideal world, she implied, the congressmen would have already taken it upon themselves to enact the appropriate legislation. A properly grateful son, after all, did not require prodding to attend to his mother's needs and desires.

These women's feelings of entitlement derived from their view of motherhood as an experience rooted in physical suffering and self-sacrifice that produced a unique bond between mother and child. Emphasizing the pain they had endured in childbirth and the care they had expended in raising their sons to adulthood, they presented their losses in a highly possessive manner: the bodies that fell in Europe were *their* bodies—the bodies that they had produced and sustained. "It is a part of [the mother's] body that is lying over there," Mrs. Effie Vedder asserted. "She spent 20 years . . . in bringing up that boy; she gave her time, both day and night."[36] Ethel Nock urged the congressmen to remember that the "body under the little white cross was once a part of the mother's own heart, nourished by her in her own body."[37] "It was the mothers who suffered to bring these boys into the world, who cared for them in sickness and health, and it was our flesh and blood that enriched the foreign soil," declared Burling.[38] Men could never understand the pain of maternal loss, the mothers argued, because they never experienced such intense feelings of identification and attachment to another human being. As Vedder stated baldly at the outset of her testimony in 1924, "I want to begin by telling you that you are all men and you have not and cannot feel the way a mother feels. . . . none of you can realize what a mother's loss is."[39] Such rhetoric not only privileged maternal suffering to the exclusion of wives and fathers but also blurred the boundary between mother and son, virtually equating the mother's sacrifice with that of her fallen son.

A few of the mothers, believing that the husband-wife relationship paled in significance to that between mother and son, went so far as to suggest that the trips should exclude all widows. The bill debated in 1928 included only those widows who had not remarried, thereby ensuring that the pilgrimages would honor women's undying devotion. Yet these parameters did not satisfy Ethel Nock, who warned that including widows might transform the sacred pilgrimage into a "junket" or "pleasure trip." "You must remember," she testified, "that many of these widows are girls whom the boys would never have met had it not been for the contingency of camp life. . . . Many of these widows are not worthy." When pressed by a senator, she turned the question back to him, asking if he knew of any wife to whom the words of Rudyard Kipling's poem "Mother o' Mine" could apply.[40] (The senator conceded that he did not.) No wife, Nock insisted, could love a man as much as his mother: "I think that mother love is greater than anything in the world. The widows, those who have not married again, perhaps it is the result of circumstances and not of wish. The mother lets no one take the place of that boy, and we mothers are carrying on, but there are times in the night when it is hard, when we think we ought to have him back."[41] Mrs. Charles Haas, New York state president of the War Mother's Association, seconded Nock's position, claiming, "We have also a great many mothers who object very much to the widows going over. . . . We have in our own city a great many wives of soldiers who are divorced, and a great many of those who have remarried a short time after the boy was gone."[42] These women felt that the mother alone should be entitled to make the pilgrimage, because only she could be trusted to remain true to "her boy."

As for fathers, the legislation excluded them entirely.[43] Fatherhood lacked the civic dimensions and emotional intensity attributed to motherhood, which meant that paternal claims carried less weight.[44] Fathers very rarely spoke of "giving" their sons to the nation, in part because men did not typically define their relationship to the state through their paternal role, and in part because cultural norms barred fathers from adopting such a possessive stance toward their sons. Although several people testified on behalf of gold star fathers, even those who argued for their inclusion in the pilgrimages readily acknowledged the superiority of maternal claims. For example, the Veterans of Foreign Wars proposed an amendment that would have allowed gold star fathers to make the journey to Europe, but only in cases in which no mother or wife survived. The father "probably feels not quite, but almost as keenly the situation as the mother," the VFW representative noted, hastening to add that his organization would not want to press for the amendment if it in any way imperiled the legislation for the mothers.[45] Similarly, a father from Bridgeport, Connecticut, argued that the government should fund trips for fathers, but he did so on the grounds that their inclusion would facilitate the trips for the mothers, since "a great majority of them are not used to travel [sic] alone." Only then did he issue his own appeal as a father, describing how he had encouraged his younger son to enlist even after his firstborn had been killed, mildly concluding, "It seems that gold star fathers deserve some consideration."[46] The restrained character of his appeal suggests the powerful role that gender norms played in determining how men and women understood and expressed their losses. As one gold star father explained to a reporter, "We prefer to stay at home, let our losses remain memories, and our grief under cover of our daily lives."[47]

In marked contrast, the mothers publicly proclaimed their suffering and justified the pilgrimages as a salve that promised emotional and psychological restoration. Most of the women who testified at the hearings had already visited their sons' graves, some on multiple occasions, and they spoke passionately about how such trips had revived them to health. In a 1924 hearing, Jennie Walsh described the palliative effects of a pilgrimage she had made in 1921: "I think that it helped cure me; it gave me a little solace, and I feel certain if you send over the poor mothers who cannot afford to pay their own way, you will save the minds of a great many of them."[48] Ethel Nock related a similar story to the Senate subcommittee in 1929. "During the nine years intervening between my son's death in 1918 and my pilgrimage in 1927, I was a broken, grief-stricken woman, avoiding all contacts outside my home and wrapped in a great sorrow," she testified. "I have tried to show you, through my own experience, how greatly a mother may be improved mentally and physically by the pilgrimage."[49] According to Nock, statistics gathered by the American War Mothers indicated that gold star mothers were dying at twice the rate of those women whose sons had returned home uninjured.[50] Only the experience of witnessing the actual gravesite, she argued, would help to restore the mothers' debilitated bodies and minds.

In the face of these emotional appeals, the pilgrimage bill proved "impossible to resist politically," as G. Kurt Piehler has noted: the House of Representatives paid homage to the mothers by passing the bill without debate and without a single dissenting vote.[51] Maternalist claims not only served as the pilgrimages' primary justification but also stood essentially unchallenged, even by those who opposed the bill's passage. Indeed, the only notable group of dissenters were those who believed that the funds would be better spent caring for living, disabled veterans—or *their* mothers and wives. "What's the idea of giving the gold-star mothers a trip to Paris and doing absolutely nothing for the mothers of the disabled soldier...?" demanded one woman who wrote to Senator Hiram Bingham to protest the proposed legislation. "They had to witness those promising lads, the fruit of their life's work, returned wrecks."[52] But in the flush times that prevailed in 1928, most Americans, and virtually all politicians, seemed disinclined to weigh the mothers' claims of worthiness against those of others who had suffered because of the war.

This seeming unanimity, however, masked significant differences of opinion as to the fundamental meaning of the pilgrimage program and the form that it ought to assume. Most leading war mothers viewed the pilgrimages as a social provision designed to meet the special needs of a uniquely deserving group of citizens. But some of the women, along with a number of congressmen, also imagined the pilgrimages as a grand commemorative gesture, akin to the 1921 entombing of the Unknown Soldier.[53] Although pilgrimage advocates rarely perceived these two visions as incompatible, in fact they entailed strikingly divergent conceptions of the program and indeed of the pilgrims themselves. Defined as a form of compensation, the pilgrimages cast each war mother as an individual beneficiary, and the emphasis fell on the emotional catharsis that she would experience at her son's gravesite. Defined as an act of commemoration, the pilgrimages cast the war mothers as American icons, and the emphasis fell on the pathos and patriotism that they would evoke in a national audience.[54] In the end, the pilgrimage program reflected elements of both models, never resolving the contradictions between them. Yet whereas an emphasis on compensation predominated during the congressional hearings, the idea of a grand patriotic gesture ultimately proved more crucial in determining how the pilgrimages unfolded. In particular, three important decisions—to have the War Department oversee the pilgrimages, to portray the program as an unprecedented and exceptional form of social spending, and to segregate the black gold star mothers—served to further the government's nationalist aims.

The War Department's oversight of the program represented a significant victory for those who believed that the pilgrimages should affirm an alliance between the military and the nation's mothers. Reflecting the pervasive antiwar and antimilitarist sentiments of the 1920s and 1930s, a number of congressmen had initially promoted a very different vision of the program, construing it as an internationalist gesture that would promote the cause of world peace. Representative Thomas Butler, who introduced the 1927 pilgrimage bill, claimed that the gold star mothers would "do more to promote the peace of our country and the peace of the world than marching armies."[55] Representative LaGuardia concurred, declaring, "When these American mothers arrive in France, they will come in contact with the Gold Star Mothers of France, and they will create a common understanding that will be far more lasting than any peace treaty that we can negotiate."[56] In keeping with this view, Butler believed that the program should be run by the American Red Cross, an organization long associated with the relief of wartime suffering.[57] Such "missions of mercy . . . can be better attended by keeping the soldiery out of it," he argued, adding emphatically, "These people are not to be taken on a parade."[58] But a number of war mothers objected to this proposal, insisting that the program should fall under the auspices of the War Department. "My hope is that the mothers will [go] over as a sacred pilgrimage," Ethel Nock stated, "and if our Quartermaster Department conducts it I am sure that is the way the crusade will be accomplished." War mothers like Nock probably also wanted to avoid association with pacifist initiatives, such as the Peace Pilgrimage to London organized by the Women's International League for Peace and Freedom in 1926, that had been framed in similar terms. In keeping with the war mothers' wishes, responsibility for the pilgrimages ultimately fell to the Quartermaster Corps, which conducted the pilgrimages as quasi-military ventures, steeped in patriotic ritual. For instance, at the ceremony marking the first group's departure, brass bands played old wartime favorites like "Over There," and dozens of Navy fighting planes roared overhead as the ship disembarked.[59] Just as Butler had feared, the gold star mothers found themselves in the spotlight of a highly choreographed nationalist spectacle. The conduct of the program thus reinforced rather than challenged the alliance between the military and the nation's mothers.

In the end, the pilgrimage program also came to be represented as an incomparable and sacred undertaking—one that should be exempt from standard political vetting and fiscal concerns. Here again, this particular approach was by no means inevitable, and in fact represented a significant departure from ideas articulated in the 1924 hearings. When Representative Samuel Dickstein first introduced his bill, he compared it to measures on behalf of disabled veterans and to the World War Adjusted Compensation Act (the Soldiers' Bonus Act), enacted by Congress that same year.[60] Likewise, the mothers who testified requested brief, no-frills "tours" for women who could not afford to pay their own way; they had yet to adopt the lofty language of "pilgrimage." Effie Vedder stated that the women would need to spend only four nights in France, explaining that they did not "care about the fine things of Europe," and Mathilda Burling suggested that the government could use one of its own ships that would otherwise be standing idle, assuring the congressmen, "We are not asking to be sent across as a pleasure trip."[61] But this emphasis on economizing appeared more muted in the 1928-29 hearings and all but vanished in the publicity leading up to the first pilgrimage. Instead, congressmen and journalists extolled the lavish accommodations that the pilgrims would enjoy as "guests" of the U.S. government. An article in the Quartermaster Corps' official publication, for instance, promised that each pilgrim would feel "as though some 'influential' friend, with 'means,' had

invited her to take a trip to Europe, which is exactly the case."[62] Rather than
running the pilgrimages like a social program for poor women, the government seemed determined to treat the gold star pilgrims in a grand style.

Critics of the Pilgrimages

Unless, that is, the women were black. Proponents of the pilgrimages had
championed them as a manifestation of the nation's democratic spirit, in
which poor and rich alike would be accorded equal honors, but in March
1930 the War Department announced that African-American gold star mothers and widows would be required to travel separately. In response, fifty-five
black mothers and wives (out of 219 who had indicated their intent to participate in the pilgrimages) heeded a call by the NAACP and declared that they
would refuse the trips unless the government reversed its decision. "Twelve
years after the Armistice, the high principles of 1918 seem to have been forgotten," they wrote in a letter to President Herbert Hoover. "We who gave and
who are colored are insulted by the implication that we are not fit persons to
travel with other bereaved ones."[63] But Hoover refused to address the matter,
and the War Department released a disingenuous statement asserting that
segregation was in "the interests of the pilgrims themselves" and promising
that all would receive "equal accommodations, care and consideration."[64] In
fact, the accommodations for the black women who ultimately participated
in the program differed significantly: whereas the white pilgrims stayed at
first-class Manhattan hotels and traveled on luxury liners, the black pilgrims
stayed at the Harlem YWCA and sailed on second-tier passenger ships.[65] In
France, however, the black women enjoyed first-class accommodations and
received an especially warm public welcome from Parisians and African-
American expatriates.[66]

The decision to impose segregation reflected the institutionalized racism
of the day, but it can also be viewed as the government's awkward attempt
to fulfill its two mutually incompatible goals. When viewed as an act of commemoration, what seems remarkable about the pilgrimage program is that
it included black women at all, considering the extent to which they were
either excluded or demeaned in the national iconography of the time. Only
a few years before enacting the pilgrimage legislation, the Senate passed a
bill (spearheaded by the United Daughters of the Confederacy) that would
have resulted in the erection of a national monument, on the Washington mall, designed to commemorate the "faithful colored mammies of the
South."[67] Although the legislation ultimately stalled in the House, its popularity in Congress provides a rough indication of how resistant most white

Americans would have been to honoring black women as war mothers. As a national icon, the caricature of mammy, who showered unconditional love on her white charges, could not have differed more from the dignified "race mother," who reared proud African-American soldiers. When the pilgrimages are viewed as a form of compensation, however, the black pilgrims' inclusion appears less surprising, for in the realm of social provisions there was at least some precedent for recognizing black women's civic status. During the war, despite intense opposition from southern elites, black servicemen's wives received allotments, monies that many used to free themselves from the very jobs the mythical mammy so cheerfully performed.[68] But, of course, unlike allotments, the pilgrimages were designed to be patriotic spectacles. Thus, the government tried to compensate the pilgrims while simultaneously upholding the racial construction of the all-American war mother—an utterly contradictory undertaking.

In segregating the black pilgrims, the government not only denied them the equal rights to which they were entitled as citizen-mothers but also withheld from them the special privileges they deserved as honorable "ladies." Long after suffrage, as Linda Kerber has shown, white women's rights as citizens tended to be subordinated to, or even defined as, the "right" to enjoy special privileges (especially exemption from certain onerous civic duties).[69] The pilgrimage program's emphasis on providing "first-class" accommodations reflected this gendered conception of citizenship, just as the segregation of its black participants exposed its racial limitations. By imposing segregation, the government signaled its reluctance to assume the role of chivalrous host and to treat the black pilgrims as ladies—a status it enthusiastically accorded the white pilgrims, regardless of their class or ethnicity. Stories in the black press repeatedly described the government's policy as an "insult" to the black pilgrims. For example, the *Chicago Defender* pointedly reported that a white woman arrested for selling liquor would be allowed to sail with the other mothers (though she had clearly forfeited any right to call herself a lady), whereas law-abiding and virtuous black pilgrims would be forced to travel separately.[70] Indeed, it is impossible to say which outraged the black community more—the violation of the women's rights or the social slight against them, for the gendered construction of citizenship made the two offenses indistinguishable. Thus, black participants tried to defend their decision to sail to the broader community by demonstrating that they had, in fact, been treated as ladies. "Uncle Sam is doing his best for us," Mrs. Bascomb Johnson of Pittsburgh told the *Afro-American*. "Why, I had a private French maid all to myself on the ship. Nothing more could be done for us unless they presented us with a sack of gold."[71] By emphasizing the extravagant manner in which they had been treated, the black pilgrims argued that, despite segregation, their civic status had been honored in the same gendered manner as that of their white counterparts.

The government's policy confronted African-American war mothers and wives with a wrenching dilemma, forcing them to weigh their commitment to racial justice against their most cherished personal attachments. Many could not reconcile themselves to the high cost of standing on principle, for the government-funded pilgrimages represented the only chance that they would likely ever have to witness the graves of their loved ones. "Ever since I lost my son in 1918 I have been wanting to come," one pilgrim explained. "I would have come over on a cattle-boat. I would have swam over if possible. I love my race as strongly as any other but when I heard that the United States was going to send us over I could not refuse."[72] In this woman's mind, there was no question but that mother love trumped racial solidarity. Her feelings for her race were strong, but comparatively impersonal: she loved her race "as strongly as any other." But she loved her son as did *no* other. To drive home the point, she asserted that she would have submitted to far worse indignities than segregated accommodations in order to witness his grave. In the minds of those who organized and supported the boycott, however, acquiescence to segregation could never be justified by appeals to mother love, because it violated the principles for which black soldier-sons had sacrificed their lives.

The charges that critics leveled against the black pilgrims reflected African-American appropriations of maternalism, which held black mothers responsible for instilling and cultivating racial pride.[73] Writers and activists viewed the pilgrims' capitulation to segregation as a *maternal* failure, which helps to explain the strikingly harsh manner in which they condemned the women.[74] "Surely the dead will rise again to undo the wrongs of these mothers who accepted the morsel of the honor due a mother of one who died for his country," the *Chicago Defender* thundered when the first group of black gold star mothers and wives sailed for Europe in July 1930. The editors went so far as to list the names and hometowns of all the pilgrims, prefaced with the stinging rebuke: "Their Sons Died for Segregation."[75] In the same issue, the celebrated sportswriter Frank A. Young accused the mothers of having "set back" the entire black race. He singled out the Atlanta educator Willie D. Rush, arguing that if her son could "look down from above and communicate with her," he would insist "that the principle at stake was worth more than one look at the marble slab at the head of his grave."[76] Another leading black paper, the Baltimore *Afro-American*, emphasized the valor of those women who elected to remain at home, recognizing that "there are some factors in human feelings which outweigh even mother love."[77] A caption for a photograph that portrayed the pilgrims holding small American flags noted derisively: "War Mothers Waving the Flag which Allows Them To Be Jim Crowed."[78] Having failed to measure up to the ideal of the proud "race mother," the pilgrims found themselves accused of complicity with a racist state and all but blamed for the perpetuation of Jim Crow.

White liberals also denounced the segregation of the black pilgrims, but their critiques sometimes seemed inspired less by outrage over institutionalized racism than by antagonism toward the American Gold Star Mothers and other patriotic women's groups. Thus, whereas African-American critics focused their attacks on those who had the power to reverse the decision—President Hoover and the War Department—their white counterparts appeared equally intent on deriding organized war mothers as hypocritical and self-righteous prigs. An editorial in the *Nation*, for example, argued that those women "so delicately constituted that they could not endure to travel on the same ship with a black woman whose son or husband were killed in France" should have cancelled their passages.[79] This tendency to view racism as a form of feminine snobbery gained strength over the course of the decade, as evidenced by the uproar that ensued when the DAR barred Marian Anderson from performing in Constitution Hall in 1939. According to a Gallup poll, most Americans supported Eleanor Roosevelt's decision to rebuke the organization by resigning her membership, but this result surely revealed more about the depths of populist scorn for the DAR than it did about the strength of white Americans' commitment to ending segregation.[80] Similarly, although the controversy surrounding the black pilgrims reinforced negative perceptions of organized war mothers as small-minded and undemocratic, such sentiments did not reliably translate into a principled stance on racial issues.

If relatively few whites criticized the pilgrimages for perpetuating racism, however, a growing number did denounce the program as an unjustifiable use of federal resources. The idea of sending war mothers on "first-class" European pilgrimages, without any regard for cost, had attracted little dissent in 1928, but the Depression prompted closer scrutiny of the program in light of competing claims for government assistance. In March 1930, a New York woman, herself a gold star mother, wrote to President Hoover that she opposed government spending on "free excursions" when "our reconstruction work goes so slowly" and "shattered men . . . suffer so desperately still."[81] A few months later, a disabled veteran's wife, exhausted from pounding the pavement in search of work, exploded with fury upon reading a newspaper account about the pilgrimages to France. "Think what all that money could have done for the men who were disabled for life and who cannot, even on their knees, get the sum of $50 a month for all the horror they went through overseas," she wrote in a letter that appeared in the *Los Angeles Record*. Enraged at the government's refusal to honor what she saw as its obligations to her husband and herself, she vowed never to play the part of the patriotic war mother: "I would kill a son of mine with my own hands rather than let the government ruin him for life, then turn him loose like a whipped cur to beg, steal, or commit murder in order to live."[82]

The belief that the government had failed to meet its obligations to World War I veterans seemed dramatically confirmed in the spring and summer of 1932, when thousands of destitute veterans converged on the nation's capital in what came to be known as the Bonus March. The veterans demanded immediate payment of bonuses that, according to legislation enacted in 1924 (over President Coolidge's veto), would be disbursed to them in 1945. The amount of money due to each veteran differed according to the particularities of his service, but the certificates' average value would have been around $1,000 in 1945; by way of comparison, the government was spending an average of $850 on each of the gold star pilgrims.[83] After Congress defeated the so-called Bonus Bill on June 17, some eight thousand men refused to leave their shantytown in Anacostia Flats, and tensions mounted. On July 28 violence broke out, culminating in General Douglas MacArthur's notorious destruction of the veterans' makeshift dwellings—a shameful display of force that seemed to epitomize the government's imperviousness to the prevailing desperation.[84] That very same day, representatives from the Quartermaster Corps ferried a contingent of gold star pilgrims about on sight-seeing excursions outside Paris.[85]

It requires no leap of imagination to understand why the pilgrimage program, which proponents had championed as above all financial consideration, might have aroused popular resentment. Still, the fact that veterans often directed their anger toward the pilgrims, rather than the congressmen who had enacted the pilgrimage legislation, suggests that they were not simply critiquing government policy. Just as African-Americans lashed out at black pilgrims because they compromised the ideal of the proud "race mother," veterans criticized the pilgrims on the grounds that they failed to embody the ideal that the program allegedly honored. "Many of us are actually hungry, and insufficiently clothed; yet, through taxes, we are compelled to pay for these expensive trips to European countries," complained one man in January 1933. "It does not seem human, or even possible, that these 'War Mothers' would expect or could enjoy this visit to the graves of their loved ones which would add to the burden of suffering in a country for which their boys gave all."[86] Another man expressed amazement that the gold star mothers could even "think of accepting a trip abroad, increasing the expense from an already depleted Treasury" and thereby "lessening their sons' sacrifice." "Cannot they see," he wondered, "that giving them the trip abroad was simply a gesture of politicians who were not at all patriotic but simply thought a scheme like that would draw votes for them at the next election?"[87] This man expected politicians to be self-serving and insincere, but he seemed incredulous that war mothers would actually fall prey to their tactics. Any truly patriotic war mother, he believed, would have considered the nation's plight and selflessly declined the government's offer.

Similar criticism emanated from peace advocates, who tended to view the pilgrimage program as a publicity stunt designed to silence criticism of the government's wartime activities. As numerous Americans retrospectively questioned the nation's participation in the war, patriotic displays like the pilgrimages became targets of mounting anti-militarist sentiment. The publisher George Palmer Putnam, for instance, claimed that the War Department employed the ruse of "protecting" gold star mothers in order to censor materials that would expose the true nature of modern warfare. He quoted an official who, upon denying his request for graphic wartime images, had instructed him to "Think of the Gold Star mothers" who "carried home in their minds beautiful pictures of . . . well-kept resting places."[88] Other commentators portrayed the gold star pilgrims as unwitting accomplices in the government's attempts to whitewash the war. The *San Francisco Examiner*, for instance, ran an anti-interventionist editorial in 1938 that derisively characterized the pilgrims as "a pathetic little band of American mothers" who had "shed futile tears . . . over little white crosses."[89] Although these critics stopped short of denouncing the gold star pilgrims themselves, they strongly implied that the women had been duped, and that the government had cynically used them as props and decoys in order to pursue its militarist agenda.

The reaction to one renegade student group in the mid-1930s illustrates the tendency to associate criticism of the gold star pilgrims with support for the broad-based peace movement. In 1936, after Congress finally passed a Bonus Bill (over President Roosevelt's veto), some cheeky Princeton undergraduates expressed their dissent by founding an organization called the Veterans of *Future* Wars. Students at Vassar College joined the hoax by establishing a women's auxiliary, the Association of Gold Star Mothers of the Veterans of Future Wars. Striking a pose of dead seriousness, the students demanded $1000 bonuses for every man under age thirty-six who expected to be drafted, along with government-financed trips to Europe for every woman in the same age bracket. The soldiers of the next war, they reasoned, ought to be given money before they met their "sudden and complete demise," just as

future mothers should be granted the opportunity to visit their future sons'
burial grounds before war ravaged the landscape.[90] Staunchly conservative in
their political views, the students did not set out to make an antiwar statement but rather to ridicule veterans and war mothers who used lofty patriotic
rhetoric to demand government "handouts."[91] (Their salute was the fascist
salute, but with the palm turned upward.) However, as Veterans of Future
Wars chapters sprang up on colleges and universities across the nation, along
with Gold Star Mothers of Veterans of Future Wars auxiliaries, the organization assumed the character of an antiwar movement, attracting supporters
like the well-known pacifist and advocate for racial justice, Oswald Garrison
Villard.[92] In an editorial in the *Nation*, Villard mocked those veterans and
war mothers who rose to the students' bait. "Do the Gold Star Mothers wish
to reserve for themselves the precious patriotic experience that is theirs of
having given their sons at their country's behest in the most futile of wars,
or are they willing to have others ennobled by this experience?" he acidly
inquired.[93] Assuming that only confirmed leftists would debunk the nation's
veterans and gold star mothers, Villard and others misread the students' ir-
reverent cultural style as signaling a radical political outlook, which was not
the case at all.

From the students' perspective, Villard's unwelcome defense no doubt
confirmed what they had already been forced to concede: that, for the vast
majority of Americans, a satirical attack on gold star mothers simply went
beyond the pale. Even as they continued to goad irate veterans—"National
Commander" Lewis Gorin proudly reported that one veteran had taken a
swing at him, only to miss—they shrank from confrontation with the Gold
Star Mothers and sought to make amends by renaming the women's auxiliary.[94] (They settled on the nondescript "Home Fires Division," which,
Gorin privately conceded to a female friend, was "not so good as the former
name.")[95] Speaking to the *New York Times*, Gorin claimed, rather implau-
sibly, that he and his conspirators had never intended to satirize gold star
mothers. But he acknowledged that they had badly misjudged "the general
feeling throughout the country" and found themselves "accused of trampling
sacred sentiments."[96] Writing to his friend at Vassar, where the college president had forced a chapter to disband, Gorin reflected more frankly, "I suppose the name Future Gold Star Mothers was responsible [for the uproar].
That name turned out to be a little too bitter a satire for sensitive people
to stand."[97] The lesson seemed clear: a satirical attack on veterans aroused
passions but was deemed permissible and even daring on the playing field
of American politics. A similar attack on gold star mothers was judged an
egregious foul.

Thus, by the mid-1930s, the gold star pilgrims had been attacked by disgruntled citizens on numerous grounds—for their discriminatory practices, uncritical patriotism, and consumption of scarce national resources in a time of economic crisis. Yet none of this criticism directly engaged their central claim—the notion that, as war mothers, they had performed a civic duty co-equal to that of their soldier sons for which they deserved recognition and compensation. Nor did most of these critics directly challenge the iconic status of the all-American war mother. But that which remained largely proscribed in political discourse surfaced in popular culture. In the 1930s and 1940s, a number of popular authors produced highly unflattering depictions of gold star mothers that betrayed a profound suspicion of mother love and intense anxiety about male psychological autonomy. For instance, in 1933, the final year of the pilgrimage program, Hollywood released a major picture about a ruthless war mother who ultimately finds redemption during her pilgrimage. Directed by John Ford, *Pilgrimage* centers on Hannah Jessop, a pious farmwoman who sends her son Jim to war rather than accept his love for a local girl.[98] "I know her kind," she carps. "She'd take you away from me. She'd poison your mind against me." In a later scene, Hannah hunts down the girlfriend and warns her to stay away from Jim, declaring, "I'd rather see him dead than married to you." True to her word, when the young lovers still refuse to part, Hannah instructs the local Army recruiter to draft Jim, and soon thereafter he is killed overseas. On the pilgrimage, Hannah repents her fatal misdeeds and deeply mourns her loss, returning home to embrace Jim's former girlfriend and illegitimate son. Still, the film's emotional climax, in which Hannah begs forgiveness at Jim's grave, does not efface the powerful image of a mother bent on either possessing or destroying her son.[99]

Still more monstrous images of gold star pilgrims appeared in satirical works that conflated fears of maternal aggression, masculine vulnerability, and the power of the modern state. In 1935, the new men's magazine *Esquire* published a biting piece—subtitled a "monologue in the true spirit of sacrifice by one who proudly gave her sons to the slaughter"—written in the voice of a pilgrim who describes her experiences to a gathering of women.[100] To emphasize the docile and dim-witted character of the assembly, the writer depicted the women as cows (Mrs. Holstein, Mrs. Jersey, and so on). The speaker is portrayed as both ignorant (she makes many grammatical errors) and bigoted (she disdains the "great black cow," Mrs. Guernsey). Above all, she comes off as a vacuous stooge who mouths platitudes about the "Spirit of Sacrifice" and revels in her status as a gold star mother. Recalling the mechanized killing of "Our Dear Boys," she exclaims: "They never stopped, but only whimpered a little for their mothers, and marched straight head of them, their eyes open, to make the Supreme Sacrifice before their Maker. And when the twenty-pound sledge fell and their front legs collapsed and the blood spurted I thought: How morvelous! [*sic*]." While elements of this dark satire—the debunking of racial bigotry and patriotic ritual—echoed earlier critiques, *Esquire* writer Philip Stevenson presented a new and truly nightmarish vision: war mothers who gladly supported the state's attempt to sanitize the deaths of their own sons.[101]

A similarly hostile and satiric view of gold star pilgrims surfaced in Philip Wylie's *Generation of Vipers*, even as a new generation of American mothers confronted heartbreaking losses. Indeed, the pilgrimages must have made a strong impression on Wylie, for nearly a decade after the program's conclusion, he referred to it with undiminished outrage:

> I have seen the unmistakable evidence in a blue star mom of envy of a gold star mom: and I have a firsthand account by a woman of unimpeachable integrity, of the doings of a shipload of these supermoms-of-the-gold-star, en route at government expense to France to visit the graves of their sons, which I forbear to set down here, because it is a document of such naked awfulness that, by publishing it, I would be inciting to riot, and the printed thing might even rouse the dead soldiers and set them tramping like Dunsany's idol all the way from Flanders to hunt and haunt their archenemy progenitrices—who loved them—to death.[102]

Like Stevenson, Wylie accused war mothers of reveling in the accolades and prestige that their sons' deaths afforded them. Being Wylie, he went even further, implying that the gold star mothers had somehow murdered their own sons. No longer the self-sacrificing figure soldiers fought to defend, the American war mother had become the self-aggrandizing figure from whom they needed defending.

During World War II, few (if any) large-circulation magazines would have been willing to print such a slur against gold star mothers. But letters written to Wylie suggest that his sensationalist attack struck a chord with readers who had come to view self-identified war mothers with deep skepticism. In 1943, an "ex-soldier" declared that he was "most grateful to see a capable writer . . . fan the hell out of the self-pitying gratification found in the current momism of the blue and gold star cult."[103] Another reader reported that she had been "ranting for years . . . against Gold Star mothers who 'give' their sons to their country."[104] Even a correspondent who took issue with Wylie's momism critique seemed prepared to make an exception in the case of gold star mothers: "I don't know about the gold star mothers. I can't understand anyone ever claiming to be one."[105] War mothers' claims had not rankled so much during World War I, when issued within a cultural context that still assumed a harmonious mutuality between mothers and sons, and a political context in which women's exclusion from power had been more formal and complete. But by the 1940s, the rhetoric of patriotic maternalism resonated differently. Those Americans who recoiled from organized war mothers did so in part because they felt the identity of "war mother" implied an overly possessive stance, and in part because they had grown uneasy with the long-standing tradition of Republican motherhood, at least in its most undiluted form. Once women began to vote and even serve in the military, war mothers who continued to define their civic identities and wartime contributions in exclusively derivative and relational terms began to strike some observers as anachronistic, if not parasitic.

American women continued to identify as war mothers and to join war mothers' associations during and after World War II, but they would not be honored on a national scale in a manner comparable to that of their pre-decessors. In the 1920s, organized war mothers succeeded in promoting the pilgrimage program because they could draw upon a long-standing, senti-mental ideal of motherhood, and because many Americans were receptive to the notion that mothers performed a civic duty that should be duly recog-nized by the state. But by the end of World War II, the assault on pathological mother love and the discrediting of patriotic maternalism had rendered an undertaking like the pilgrimage program virtually inconceivable. Too closely associated with a possessive maternal stance now deemed pathological, with ethnocentric and racist views increasingly attacked as antidemocratic, and with ritualized forms of patriotism that struck many as foolish or even sinis-ter, the American war mother had been diminished as a symbol of national unity.[106] Though women would still be lauded for raising citizen-soldiers, they would no longer be viewed as "mothers of the nation" whose sacrifice and suffering equaled that of their sons, entitling them to compensation and acclaim.

Competing Images of War Mothers during World War II

During World War II, patriotism and sentimental maternalism remained close allies in mainstream American culture. Yet numerous commenta-tors began to portray "mother worship" as overly emotional and irrational. Attachment to one's mother or to the abstract ideal of motherhood, they argued, was no substitute for a rational commitment to democratic prin-ciples. To these critics, the appropriation of maternalist rhetoric by fascists abroad and right-wing extremists at home exposed the dangers of combining motherhood and politics. Though maternalist and antimaternalist impulses coexisted and competed throughout the war years, World War II would pave the way for a more decisive repudiation of the iconic middle-aged mother in the cold war era.

It is highly fitting that the incident that provoked Wylie to coin the word "momism" was a Mother's Day event at a military base. Such celebrations united sentimental maternalism and patriotic ritual to evoke a sense of mutual obligation between servicemen and the homefront. Especially during the early phase of American participation in World War II, Mother's Day commemorations assumed a markedly florid quality. In 1942, a *Life* feature covering celebrations at two military bases documented precisely the type of activity that Wylie's friend Hervey Allen had mocked. At Langley Field, Virginia, a group of servicemen gathered in a heart-shaped formation to salute Mrs. Blanche Carr, who stood in the heart's center, holding her son's hand.[107] On the accompanying page, pictures portrayed a wrinkled and bespectacled old woman, Mrs. Covington, riding in a military jeep to a ceremony at Camp Forrest, Tennessee, where she was crowned "Dear Mom." A large photograph of Covington at her coronation, flanked by military men and smiling young women, looks to us like a high school homecoming gone horribly awry.[108]

Such rituals were not simply southern phenomena; New Yorkers, for example, regaled the nation's mothers in a similarly effusive manner. Speaking to a crowd of 2,500 gathered in Central Park on Mother's Day in 1942, a lieutenant colonel proclaimed that "the names of America's war mothers should be inscribed in the nation's hall of fame along with its military heroes." Meanwhile, U.S.O. clubs featured "adopt-a-mother" celebrations that brought together mothers whose sons were serving abroad with servicemen separated from their own mothers. As the *New York Times* reported, across the midtown area, "gray-haired women, proudly leaning on the arms of uniformed sons, crowded entertainment places in celebration of their reunions or strolled along enjoying the bright, sunshiny day."[109]

This blend of patriotism and public visibility characterized Mother's Day celebrations throughout the war, with mothers of servicemen predictably drawing the greatest accolades. "Pastors will preach sermons on 'Mother,'" the *New York Times* reported in 1943. "Everywhere special prayers will be offered for the mothers of men in our armed forces, and tribute will be paid to mothers whose sons have made the supreme sacrifice."[110] Mothers of decorated soldiers and high-ranking officers were accorded special praise. In 1942, the mother of John D. Bulkely, a lieutenant famed for his heroic exploits in the Philippines, headed a Mother's Day parade in Queens accompanied by her son.[111] That same year, Mary P. MacArthur, mother of General Douglas MacArthur, received the following message from the residents of the Brooklyn Hebrew Home and Hospital for the Aged: "Love from all 389 mothers in our home to a mother endowed with kindliness, patience, and courage, who has given to the world a hero to free men the world over."[112] Honors were also bestowed on women who had a large number of children in the service. For example, in 1944, the Mother's Day Commemorative League selected Emma Van Coutren, "a mother who has given eleven of her twelve children to the armed services," as the outstanding Mother of the Year.[113] Like their World War I predecessors, the war mothers of World War II could expect to gain recognition based on their sons' deeds and sacrifices.

Of all American mothers, the woman who attained the terrible pinnacle of maternal sacrifice was Aletta Sullivan, the "champion gold star mother of World War II."[114] The Sullivans, an Irish-American family from Waterloo, Iowa, lost all five of their sons in November 1942 when the cruiser *Juneau* went down in a naval battle off the Solomon Islands. (Defying Navy policy, the Sullivan boys had insisted that they be allowed to serve together on the same ship.)[115] After receiving confirmation of their sons' deaths, the parents agreed to a request by the Industrial Incentive Division of the Navy to tour defense plants in order to help speed production.[116] According to Mrs. Sullivan, her husband Thomas was initially "a little shaky" about the idea and reluctant to leave his railroad job. But they soon embarked on a nationwide speaking tour that involved as many as ten stops a day. "The Navy told us that every time we appeared at a defense plant," Aletta Sullivan later wrote, "the production record of the plant went surging magically upward."[117]

The Sullivan tragedy captivated the nation, leading to an outpouring of sympathy and sustained press coverage. Accounts of this episode, however, tended to focus more on Mrs. Sullivan than her husband, reinforcing the primacy of maternal sacrifice. The *New York Times*, for example, reported on the Sullivans' visit to the Todd Eerie Basin shipyards in Brooklyn, New York, where the couple had urged speed-ups so that "many more sons will come home to their mothers." Speaking "in a voice that at times threatened to break," Mrs. Sullivan appealed to workers "as a mother who lost five sons." "Now we have more sons in action," she implored. "We must give them everything they need." The article then noted that her husband—"a slight man with graying hair"—had also issued a "brief plea."[118] This tendency to efface Thomas Sullivan is even more pronounced in the layout that accompanied a story Aletta Sullivan wrote for *American Magazine*. Entitled "I Lost

Five Sons," the article featured a photograph of the handsome, beaming Sullivan boys in Navy uniforms, along with an insert of their mother. The family patriarch did not appear.[119]

The maternal figure also predominated in *The Fighting Sullivans*, a movie about the family released in 1944.[120] The film focuses almost entirely on the boys' childhood and teenage years, presenting the band of brothers as a high-spirited and cooperative democratic unit. The father appears as the typical bumbling American Dad, forever losing his hat to the clothesline as he trudges off to work. Yet he is also shown to possess a volatile Irish temper that could lead to abusive behavior toward his sons. Ultimately, it is the mother—called "darling" by her doting boys—who serves as the family's stable, guiding force.

Images of patriotic war mothers surfaced in a number of other wartime movies, including the 1943 release, *So Proudly We Hail!* In this film, "Ma" McGregor—a middle-aged "battle ax," widowed while pregnant during World War I—serves as a commanding nurse in Bataan. Her grown son has followed in his father's footsteps by enlisting in the military. Near the film's end, he is badly injured; after having both legs amputated, he dies in his mother's arms. "I bore a son and he's dead," the grief-stricken McGregor cries. "I bore a son, a healthy, muscular child who was a good son. It used to break my heart just to look at him, he was so beautiful. The handsomest son in the world. But now I have no heart to break." Her mother's lament, however, quickly transmutes into an affirmation of the national cause. "Like his father, he died for what he knew was right. He was right, my son and his father. And this time, if we don't make it right, my son and his father and all our dead will rise up and destroy us." In this stilted fashion, *So Proudly We Hail!* attempted to reinforce the public's commitment to the war effort by dramatizing the theme of maternal sacrifice.[121]

Though highly successful at the box office, several reviewers criticized *So Proudly We Hail!* as overwrought and mawkish. James Agee cleverly alluded to the film's excesses while praising the sober realism of British war documentaries; he entitled his review of the movie for the *Nation* "So Proudly We Fail." Hollywood productions, Agee insisted, indicated that Americans "remain untouched, virginal, prenatal, while every other considerable population on earth comes of age."[122] This tendency to link sentimentality to political and psychological immaturity became increasingly pronounced as the war progressed. To critics wary of emotionalism, the nation's reverential attitude toward motherhood demonstrated that Americans were ill prepared to assume the responsibilities of international leadership.

Preston Sturges's uproarious 1944 comedy, *Hail, the Conquering Hero*, suggests the extent to which skepticism regarding the all-American mom could achieve articulation within the dominant culture, or at least within wartime Hollywood. When the film opens, a narrow-shouldered young man burdened with the preposterous name "Woodrow Lafayette Pershing Truesmith" sits despondently at a bar while a vocalist sings "Home to the Arms of Mother." The son of a decorated World War I marine who was killed on the day of his birth, Woodrow had long dreamed of joining the U.S. Marine Corps. But after only a month in the service, he was discharged due to chronic hay fever. Ashamed to return home, he is hiding out and working in a shipyard, while a friend stationed overseas posts his letters to his mother.

After relaying his sorry tale to six Marines who stumble into the bar, Woodrow finds himself suited up in a decorated uniform and forcibly restored to his hometown. (The driving force behind the charade is a mother-obsessed Marine who sternly reprimands Woodrow, "You shouldn't do that to your mother. . . . That's a terrible thing to do to your mother!") The rest of the film chronicles the mass hysteria that ensues as the townspeople welcome their local "hero" and draft him to run for mayor. Eventually, Woodrow summons up the courage to reveal the truth, at which point he prepares to exile himself from the community. But the upstanding "Doc" Bissell intervenes to redeem his reputation, proclaiming, "If to act out a little lie to save one's mother humiliation was a fault . . . in other words, if tenderness toward, and consideration of, one's mother was a fault, it was a fault any man might be proud of." The townspeople then rush to reclaim Woodrow as their chosen leader. [123]

On the surface, *Hail, the Conquering Hero* promotes a sentimental and populist vision of small-town America, in which a devoted son and his loving mother ultimately prevail over the unsavory local elite. But the film also portrays maternal influence as an irrational force capable of disrupting both individual lives and the sociopolitical order. Although Mrs. Truesmith emerges as a sympathetic character, her naive patriotism and unreasonable expectations are what compel her son to follow a course of deception. It is Woodrow's protective attitude toward his mother—and his inability to confront her with disappointing realities—that initiates the chain reaction culminating in hysterical mob behavior. The film thus draws the same association between sentimental mothers and democratic fragility that Wylie advanced in *Generation of Vipers*.

If the nation's penchant for mother-worship could provide comic relief to some, others viewed the situation more seriously. The sociologist Robert

Merton, for example, developed a highly critical analysis of the political impact of maternalist and sentimental rhetoric in his 1946 study, *Mass Persuasion*. Merton conducted interviews with radio listeners who had tuned in to a war bond drive led by the singer and radio personality Kate Smith on September 21, 1943.[124] Famed for her debut of Irving Berlin's "God Bless America," Smith enjoyed immense popularity in the late 1930s and early 1940s.[125] (Indeed, one poll indicated that she was among the three most admired women in America, along with Eleanor Roosevelt and Helen Hayes).[126] Although single and childless, Smith's stout frame and folksy ways allowed her to be widely perceived as a maternal figure.[127] She was also known to be an earnest patriot as well as a tireless promoter of various charitable efforts.

Mass Persuasion sits squarely within the genre of social scientific literature, yet it parallels *Generation of Vipers* in important respects. Echoing Wylie's jaundiced view of the all-American mom, Merton expressed a deep suspicion of Smith's persona. His writing is characterized by a muted but persistent strain of debunking; acerbic descriptions of Smith as "a flag-wrapped symbol" and a "patriot nonpareil" punctuate the staid presentation of data.[128] The singer's celebrated "sincerity," according to Merton, was difficult to reconcile with her commercial sponsorship of various products, and her self-effacement was contrived to call attention to her own "sacrifice." (For the bond drive, Smith stayed on the air a full twenty-four hours). Above all, Merton sharply criticized Smith and her scriptwriters for turning the purchasing of war bonds into a "sacred act" by appealing to "pathos-laden sentiments"—an approach that "found its most typical and complete expression in portraying the desperate fears and glorious sacrifices of American mothers." According to Merton, because Smith neglected to explain how war bonds helped to control inflation, relying instead on "large, delusive statements," she deprived the public of an "opportunity for education in vital present-day economics." "For a manipulated public opinion in a fascist state, where only immediate results need to be taken into account, this might be of little consequence," he dryly concluded, "but in a democracy the quality of public understanding is not irrelevant."[129] In other words, Merton suggested that Smith's rhetorical tactics and general outlook were more befitting a fascist regime than a democratic state.

Critics who believed that potentially fascistic impulses lurked under the guise of sentimental maternalism did not have to take on a superpatriot like Kate Smith to draw their point. Instead, they could readily point to a coalition of ultraconservative mothers' groups that emerged between 1939 and 1941 to lobby against U.S. involvement in the war. Concentrated in the Midwest, the roughly 150 groups that comprised this movement boasted names like "We, the Mothers Mobilize for America," "Mothers of the U.S.A.," and "Mothers and Sons Forum." According to Laura McEnaney, their constituencies were consistently "white, middle class, and middle-aged." Employing maternalist rhetoric charged with nativism and fundamentalist religiosity, these women staged sensational protests against the Lend-Lease Act in early 1941. Intervention in the European conflict, they argued, would disrupt families and strengthen the intrusive power of the state, thereby undermining "good old-fashioned Americanism."[130]

Even after Pearl Harbor, some of these women continued to oppose the war, fueling fears that dogmatic mothers might undermine the war effort. Elizabeth Dilling, a well-known anticommunist, anti-Semitic demagogue who had spearheaded a "Mothers' Crusade to Defeat H.R. 1776" (the Lend-Lease Act), was even charged with sedition.[131] Although self-identified fascists constituted a minor fraction of the right-wing mothers' movement, the media seized on the notion of a feminine "fifth column." In a July 1944 article called "The Menace of the 'Mothers,'" Liberty urged American mothers to beware that "certain 'mothers' groups" were seeking "to exploit their wartime worry and grief to foment racial strife and disunity."[132] Similarly, an article in Women's Home Companion lamented, "The word mother has always stood for goodness, tenderness, dignity and charity, but today this sacred name is being exploited by some who would make it a national epithet for intolerance and hate."[133]

Those who attempted to alert the public to the danger posed by certain mother's organizations took pains to distinguish between bad, disloyal mothers and good, democratic ones. For example, the author of the Liberty article consistently used quotation marks around "mothers" when referring to the reactionary women, as if to shield the word from negative connotations. "Perhaps the challenge of these 'mothers' groups," the authors concluded, "will be answered by organizations of intelligent and loyal women like the Gold Star Mothers and the General Federation of Women's Clubs."[134] Likewise, when Women's Home Companion exposed "The Mother Racket," the editors included a sidebar story entitled "Mothers: The American Way" that praised groups like the Blue Star Mothers of America and MOMS (Mothers of Men in Service).[135]

Yet even as commentators attempted to redeem democratic motherhood from its usurpers, they also suggested that sentimentality and emotionalism made all mothers vulnerable to subversion. For example, the journalist John Roy Carlson, who wrote about the right-wing mothers' movement in his 1943 exposé Under Cover, emphasized the disparity between the women's benign maternal appearance and the seemingly hysterical behavior in which they engaged. Reporting on one of their rallies, he noted, "As I took leave of the thundering herd, I looked for the last time on the decent, kindly mothers transformed into screaming fish wives and trying desperately to remain respectable under the wild leadership of their herd leader."[136] Adorned with floral hats and pocketbooks, the reactionary mothers who stormed congressional offices and saluted Hitler looked like Everyman's Mother, prompting observers to wonder: Did the all-American mom harbor irrational inclinations that, if exploited by a skillful demagogue, could be transformed into a truly dangerous political force? In 1944, Harvard English professor Howard Mumford Jones argued that American mothers were "in a fine position to lose the war" should they begin demanding their sons' immediate return. Recalling the recent episodes in which "certain subversive groups dressed up like mother and went to Washington," he declared "organized motherhood" to be a potentially "ominous force." His more pressing fear, however, was that "real" American mothers might prove just as dangerous as their imposters. "If a vast tidal wave of mother love and mother longing should sweep the country," he warned, mothers might "march to the polls" without pausing "to distinguish between a statesman and a demagogue." According to Mumford, when maternal sentiment fueled political behavior, the result could mean capitulation to antidemocratic forces.[137]

The growing skepticism about mother love as a political force did much to undermine the already waning tradition of organized womanhood and to decenter maternalist rhetoric within middle-class women's associations. Historian Sylvie Murray, who has explored suburban women's activism in Queens during the postwar period, found her subjects' "self-identification as political actors and citizens" to be "characterized by an uneasy relationship to their culturally prescribed gender roles." Though "undoubtedly conscious of the power that their maternal role could yield politically," these women "chose to downplay their feminine identity when entering the public and political arena" by presenting themselves as "'rational' citizens, therefore operating on the basis of objective knowledge as opposed to maternal instinct."[138] Historian Jennifer Stevens has reached strikingly similar conclusions about women who engaged in environmental activism in Western cities in the decades following World War II. These white, middle-class women managed to exert substantial influence over development and development policies, but they typically entered the public sphere "without reference to their domestic roles as housewives and mothers." Indeed, Stevens found that their references to children and motherhood were so rare as to be "a glaringly conspicuous absence."[139]

Of course, maternalist rhetoric never disappeared from the political landscape. But from 1950s through the 1980s, those women most likely to frame their political demands in the language of motherhood tended to be situated on the far ends of the political spectrum. On the one hand, as Michelle Nickerson has shown, conservative women associated with the Republican Party continued to emphasize their roles as housewives and mothers. Portraying themselves as the party's industrious "housekeepers," they argued that mothers had "moral and spiritual responsibility . . . to protect their families and communities from godless Communism."[140] On the other hand, in the late 1960s and 1970s, poor and minority women who spearheaded the welfare rights movement sought to legitimize their demands by emphasizing their labor and civic contributions as mothers and housewives.[141] Yet the very constituency that had previously represented the bulwark of maternalist reform efforts—white, middle-class women who saw themselves as moderately liberal or nonpartisan—increasingly left the politics of motherhood behind.[142] Compared to their predecessors, these women were far less likely to view their maternal and civic roles as inextricably intertwined. The decline of maternalism, however, would be accompanied by strident claims about the centrality of motherhood to women's private identities—the subject to which we now turn.

Pathologizing Mother Love:
Mental Health and Maternal Affectivity

Oh, the unselfishness of it! And then the patience and long-suffering of it. There is nothing quite like it in this world of ours—nothing so morally beautiful: a self-fed, self-sustaining love, yet, under any circumstances, chiefly a sorrow-bearing love, of which the joys are cares, the duties are inflictions of pain upon itself, the pride is nourished to be bestowed elsewhere, and the fondest gain is the sorest loss. About every true mother there is a sanctity of martyrdom—and when she is no more in body, her children see her with the ring of light around her head.

Godey's Lady's Book, 1867

Self-made martyrs are unnecessary, tiresome people. And their exaggerated opinion of what their children owe them does untold harm to everybody concerned.

ELIZABETH COOK, *American Home,* 1935

In 1957, Mrs. O. of Napa, California, wrote a letter to Philip Wylie in which she recollected the thoughts that had passed through her mind nearly two decades before, after she had given birth on her own twenty-fifth birthday:

I remember lying in the hospital bed and thinking what a terrible responsibility that was. Projecting myself forward, I saw myself at forty: one of those white haired, charming, terrible octopus women in a smart lilac colored suit, violets, and immaculate gloves. I was sitting in a fashionable restaurant with a handsome young man, and we were celebrating "our" birthday. That vision frightened me. I saw how easily I could forge a chain out of the accident of these simultaneous birthdays. I imagined how he could be summoned from school, from his job, and later from his own family, because it was "our birthday, and we have always celebrated it together." And I made a quiet vow there and then that where ever else I succeeded or failed in motherhood, this was one tragedy I would not bring about.[1]

Contemplating her new role, Mrs. O. had immediately envisioned an image of the type of mother that she did *not* want to become. That image was vivid in details: a middle-aged woman who relied on the accessories of respectable femininity—violets and white gloves—to conceal her "terrible octopus" nature. Such a woman would regard her handsome young son as but another accessory, and she would exploit the fact that they shared a birthday to strengthen her hold over him. To be a truly good mother, as opposed to the type of mother lauded by society, Mrs. O. believed she would need to resist the temptation to cultivate an intimate relationship that might prove satisfying for her, but only at the expense of her son.

Why would a new mother in the late 1930s have been haunted by the fear that her love for her helpless newborn might one day prove detrimental? Or, granting the fickle character of memory, why did a middle-aged mother in the late 1950s recall having had such ominous postpartum reflections? The historically specific nature of her anxiety appears in sharp focus when her account is compared with that of Sarah Huntington, a middle-class Bostonian who recorded the following diary entry in 1820, after giving birth to her first child: "Deeply impressed with a sense of the vast importance of a mother's duties, and the lasting effect of youthful impressions, I this day resolve to endeavor, at all times, by my precepts and my example, to inspire my children with just notions of right and wrong, of what is to be avoided and what pursued, of what is sacredly to be deserved and what unreservedly depreciated."[2] Although both women experienced an overwhelming sense of responsibility on becoming mothers, their fears as to how they might fail their children could scarcely have differed more. Sarah Huntington, fearful that she would not be mother enough, pledged to follow a course of self-vigilance and intervention, molding her newborn and future children into virtuous adults. Mrs. O., fearful that she would mother too much, vowed to practice self-restraint, lest she stymie her son's ability to function as an unfettered and autonomous adult.

The difference between these two women's reflections points to a transformation in the cultural construction of maternal affectivity that significantly influenced middle-class mothers' behavior and emotional lives.[3] In the twentieth century, the ideal of mother love that had taken root in Sarah Huntington's day came under vigorous assault. Cultural critics and psychological experts rejected three of its tenets with particular vehemence: the conviction that mother love was the purest of all human sentiments, entirely unrelated to sexual desire; the notion that motherhood entailed tremendous self-sacrifice, and that children owed a debt to their mothers that could never be repaid; and the belief that mothers should forge emotionally intense relationships with their children, especially their sons, to keep them on the path of virtue. By the 1950s, psychological experts and their popular exponents had all but inverted these views. Portraying motherhood as the pinnacle of feminine fulfillment, they jettisoned the concept of maternal self-sacrifice and reversed the trajectory of indebtedness between mother and child. They warned that maternal attachment could be narcissistic and that women's unmet sexual desires could easily—and disastrously—become misdirected toward their children, especially their sons. And finally, they insisted that, after a period of intense attachment during the child's first few years, mothers should restrain their maternal impulses and work to encourage emotional separation and independence. Particularly in the decade that followed World War II, commentators and experts expressed a wariness of mothers and maternal influence that Victorian Americans could scarcely have fathomed.

It is difficult to reconcile the extent and intensity of postwar mother-blaming with standard views of the era as one that glorified motherhood and suburban domesticity. Scholars have often suggested that, in the wake of World War II, motherhood came to be conceptualized as an all-consuming role, akin to the nineteenth-century ideal of moral motherhood.[4] But the type of mother-child relationship that experts prescribed in the 1940s and 1950s—and that many women embraced—is in fact much closer to contemporary views than to nineteenth-century conceptions of maternal obligation. Victorians idealized "Mother" because she sacrificed herself for the good of her children and because her moral guidance was deemed so indispensable to proper character formation. In contrast, postwar psychological experts of various schools portrayed motherhood as the pinnacle of feminine fulfillment and construed the benefits of mother love in narrower and more psychological terms. The mother's most crucial task, most argued, was to equip her children with a sense of "security" by following her "natural instincts" and providing warm and loving care during infancy and early childhood. As Nancy Pottisham Weiss has noted, this new permissive childrearing ideology—articulated most effectively by the phenomenally popular Benjamin Spock—actually intensified maternal obligations, for it tethered mothers more closely to young children and heightened their responsibility for emotional as well as physical well-being.[5] What has not been widely recognized, however, is that the same prescriptions simultaneously delimited the maternal role. By portraying the need for intensive maternal care as concentrated in the earliest years of life, and by stigmatizing prolonged mother-child (especially mother-son) intimacy as pathological, postwar experts urged women to adopt a more self-conscious and wary view of their maternal emotions.[6] Rather than ushering in a resurrection of the Victorian ideal of Mother Love, the 1940s and 1950s witnessed its demise in mainstream American culture.

Pathologizing Mother Love

In 1928, a longtime member of the Mother's Club of Cambridge, Massachusetts, reflected on the ways in which motherhood had been transformed by the rise of the psychological professions. Speaking at the club's fiftieth anniversary celebration, Mrs. Crothers noted that, although motherhood had been more "laborious" in her own day, she considered herself fortunate to have raised children in an era when "our attention was focused on physical and moral defects." Her own generation, she explained, had experienced "no haunting doubts as to the desirability of the job and not many as to our ability to do it." Instead, their "doubts or misgivings" had "largely centered on the children. It was the children who were difficult." Crothers pitied contemporary young mothers, who seemed to her poised before the "bottomless pit of the Subconscious":

> If the present-day mother is conscientious and not too busy, she dips into Freud, or even goes on to Watson on behaviorism or Ternan [sic] on mental tests. After that we advise her to "come up for air," for not only will "the child" seem an insoluble mystery, but she will find that the non-matured ego of the parent is a greater threat than the tubercle bacillus, and not as easily recognized. We escaped all that. We did not know that our ego was immature; we thought we were quite grown-up, and so did the children; and I can not help feeling that the children's misplaced confidence helped to mature their inadequate parents.[7]

Crothers' observations capture something essential about the changing emphasis and tenor of childrearing literature. Whereas Progressive Era experts had concentrated primarily on maternal practices (what mothers actually did), after World War I, they increasingly focused on maternal attitudes and emotions. What mothers felt, and how they manifested those feelings, became a subject of intense preoccupation.

In the Victorian era, mother love had been lauded as the purest of human emotions—a benevolent force that constructed the moral self. As Michael Rogin has expressed it, "The domestic mother created moral character by giving and withholding love. She entered the self, formed it, understood its feelings, and thereby at once produced it and protected it from corruption."[8] Victorian ideals of motherhood did not encourage mothers to foster autonomy and emotional independence in their children. On the contrary, as Mary Ryan has demonstrated, a "tight, indeed controlling bond between mother and male child was at the very core of the cult of domesticity." A mother's duties were "time-consuming and exhausting": she was required to maintain a "constant moral vigilance" over her children until that hazardous moment when they left the parental home.[9] Even then, the importance of maternal influence did not diminish, for affective ties to the mother served as a rudder, guiding the adult throughout his or her life course. To be powerless in the face of mother love did not imply a loss of self but rather a recall to the values and relationships that anchored the self and gave it meaning.

This view of mother love remained potent in the early twentieth century. Consider the following exchange between Douglas MacArthur and his mother, "Pinky," in 1901, when young Douglas had been called to testify before Congress about the hazing of cadets at West Point. Shortly before he took the stand, Pinky slipped him a piece of paper, on which she had copied the final stanzas of the following late nineteenth-century poem, "Like Mother, Like Son":

> Do you know that your soul is of my soul such a part,
> That you seem to be fibre and core of my heart?
> None other can pain me as you, dear, can do,
> None other can please me or praise me as you.
> Remember the world will be quick with its blame
> If shadow or strain ever darken your name.
> "Like mother, like son" is a saying so true
> The world will judge largely the "mother" by you.
> Be yours then the task, if task it shall be,
> To force the proud world to do homage to me.
> Be sure it will say, when its verdict you've won,
> "She reaped as she sowed.
> Lo! This is her son."[10]

Asserting a unity between mother and son, the poem admonishes the son to behave honorably, since his actions will both deeply affect his mother and be viewed as a reflection upon her. Moreover, it urges the son to act as the mother's emissary and defender in the public world from which is she is largely excluded: although she lacks power, he will force the powerful to pay her homage. By the 1920s, this type of maternal glorification—so ubiquitous in the late nineteenth and early twentieth centuries—would appear not merely old-fashioned but downright sinister. "There is no female in the world more dreadful than the determined mother who has ambitions for her son or daughter. There is no greater social menace," the journalist Burton Rascoe declared in 1935. "Iron-willed, frustrated, self-sacrificing mothers, trying to live a dream life through their progeny, have wrecked more lives than has syphilis."[11]

Similarly, romanticized depictions of mother-son relationships that had earlier seemed innocuous or laudable would be regarded as disturbing and unnatural by the mid-twentieth century. For instance, it is hard to imagine a military newspaper during World War II publishing the following poem, "The Little Mother," which appeared in the *Stars and Stripes* in 1918:

> I am writing this little poem
> To the mother I left behind,

And it tells of my longing for her
  Over here in the daily grind. . . .
How I long for your smiles of gladness
  That are haunting my mem'ry still,
And the love in your eyes beseeching
  Even now makes my pulses thrill.
How you held me with hands so gentle,
  Closely pressed to your throbbing breast;
In that last fond embrace I promised
  To live true through the crucial test.
The caress of your hair, soft silver,
  On my cheek how I fain would feel,
And from lips that are soft as roses,
  A sweet kiss I would like to steal.
Little mother, for you there's burning
  A deep love that will never die,
Spurring on the fight before us
  Where the Angel of Death doth fly.[12]

This soldier pines for his mother in a manner that would later seem appropriate only when directed toward a female contemporary. He dreams of stealing a "sweet kiss" from her lips and longs to feel the "caress" of her soft hair against his cheek; the very memory of her causes his pulse to race. The poet could frankly express this desire for physical contact with his mother only because he retained a pre-Freudian sensibility, in which the expression of passionate and romantic desires had a purview beyond the heterosexual couple. But in the 1920s and 1930s, commentators and experts recast such expressions of mother love as decidedly pathological. For instance, in 1938, a writer for the *American Mercury* sarcastically provided mothers with a blueprint of "How to Make Your Son a Misfit," in which he facetiously encouraged them to refer to their sons "Mother's Lover," "Mother's Little Lamb," or "Sweetie Pie," and to "act in public as though the boy were really your lover. Slobber his face with kisses; pat him as though he were a lamb; teach him to be the Model Little Gentleman who treats his mother with that consideration which a young man bestows upon his best girl." The mother who faithfully followed these instructions, he promised, would reap her just reward: a son who refused to face "unpleasant realities" and "avoided responsibility."[13]

While it is difficult to gauge the degree to which such cultural representations reflected or influenced individuals' actual behavior and emotional lives, at least some mothers and sons in the early twentieth century did fashion their relationships in highly romantic terms. For instance, as a young man

in the 1910s, Supreme Court justice Frank Murphy routinely opened his letters home with the salutation "Darling Mama" and concluded them with a
string of x's. In one letter, written shortly before he returned from serving
overseas during World War I, he pined, "I will be home with you in a few
days and we will walk and talk just like the lovers we are," while in another,
he wrote, "Tonight if I could sit near you or brush your hair or stroke your
forehead or just feel your presence I would be in paradise."[14] Similarly, in her
1925 memoir, Annie Kilmer depicted her rivalry with her daughter-in-law,
Aline, in remarkably forthright terms. Describing the emotional departure
scene before her son went off to war, she wrote, "Before I got in the car I said,
'Aline, you may kiss him last,' though had I known it was to be the last time
his dear lips would touch mine, I doubt if I could have been brave enough
to have said it. He kissed me . . . , first on the mouth and then on the left
cheek—always that cheek! Then I got in the car. He kissed Aline, and she got
in beside me. . . . His dear brown eyes looked so steadily in mine—then at his
wife—but last, at me, thank God!"[15] Though one might wonder whether her
son, Joyce Kilmer, would have described the scene in similar terms, he clearly
did not recoil from his mother's attentions. In what would turn out to be his
final letter to her, Joyce requested an additional copy of a photograph that
he had cropped to fit in his wallet. "All the rest of the fellows have pictures
of their mothers," he confided, "but none of them so good looking as mine."
The coveted photograph depicted Annie gazing at a framed photograph of
Joyce: in other words, the image that Joyce cherished was an image of his
mother cherishing him.[16]

   Though historians and other scholars have commented extensively on
mother-blaming in popular and psychological literature, few have noted that
the experts who railed against sentimental mother love were repudiating a set
of attitudes and behaviors with some basis in social reality.[17] In other words,
experts and commentators were not only scapegoating mothers (though they
were certainly doing that as well), they were also attempting to alter Americans'
perceptions of acceptable maternal affect and behavior.[18] For instance, in the
nineteenth century, domestic literature urged mothers to use the "silver cord"
of love—the emotional bond between mother and child—as a kind of disciplinary tool: a good mother taught her children the difference between right
and wrong, but she relied on her emotional power over them to ensure that
they would internalize her lessons. She sought to raise an adult son who would
strive to be "the man my mother thinks I am"—a son who would not hurt
or disappoint her. But in the twentieth century, childrearing techniques that
had once been praised as proper and Christian came to be regarded as manipulative and pathogenic. The internalization of the moral mother no longer

appeared to be a way of helping the child to achieve proper self-governance but rather seemed like a threat to the child's developing sense of self.

Indeed, if nineteenth-century Americans "seem never to have dreamed that a mother's love might be a source of ill," by the 1920s experts had begun to display a reflexive suspicion of maternal influence as the primary obstacle to self-realization.[19] Psychoanalysts and behaviorists alike developed a "stinging critique of American motherhood" during the interwar period that was readily embraced by practitioners within child guidance clinics.[20] Experts routinely indicted a certain type of woman: the "overprotective" or possessive mother who stymied her son's psychological development while relegating her husband to the sidelines.[21] According to behaviorists, who dominated childrearing advice in the 1920s and early 1930s, the solution resided in strict "scientific" schedules and limited physical contact.[22] In the best-known childrearing manual of the era, *Psychological Care of Infant and Child*, the behaviorist John Watson railed against "The Dangers of Too Much Mother Love,"[23] and offered the following advice: "Treat [children] as though they were young adults. . . . Never hug and kiss them, never let them sit in your lap."[24] To Watson and others, a stance of detached objectivity offered the best defense against maternal pathology, because it introduced an element of distance and rationality into the mother-child relationship. As the psychologist and early childhood educator Ada Hart Artlitt put it, the home should be governed not by "mother love," but rather by the "kitchen time-piece."[25]

Still, even as interwar experts routinely condemned sentimental mother love as a potentially pathological force, it continued to figure prominently in American popular culture throughout the interwar era. Indeed, it is impossible to comprehend their tirades without appreciating the ubiquity of sentimental paeans to motherhood. For instance, in *Life Begins*, a popular 1932 Hollywood film set in a maternity ward, a Miss Layette—an unwed sophisticate—asks the other women on the ward if they are interested in the "psychological conditioning of infants." She then reads a passage from Watson's book that excoriates mothers who "pet" their children. Mrs. West, the oldest and most traditional of the bunch, indignantly protests, "Of all the ridiculous nonsense!" to which Miss Layette replies, "It's not ridiculous nonsense. Of course women have got to get over this slobbering over their babies." But once she gives birth, Miss Layette forgets all about Watson's admonitions; fawning and cooing over her infant, she wholly capitulates to the lure of mother love. The woman in the next bed, Florette, a hard-drinking showgirl who plans to sell her newborn twins, mocks her sudden conversion: "Oh, scientific Rosie, getting slushy over the joys of motherhood." But of course, Florette soon undergoes her own conversion. When the would-be adoptive mother arrives to take the babies and talks of placing the less robust one in an orphanage, Florette's maternal instincts are finally aroused. After shooing the woman away, she picks up the ailing baby for the first time and begins to fret over its shallow breathing. "You can't depend on anyone but yourself. It's love the little one needs," advises Miss Layette, revealing how fully she has discarded the precepts of scientific motherhood. Utterly enamored, Florette can only gush, "Oh gee, I feel like I got religion or something." If *Life Begins* dramatizes the rise of new sexual mores and psychological expertise, it nevertheless portrays mother love as a redemptive force lurking within the hearts of modern women—a force capable of transforming a cool devotee of science into a fount of maternal wisdom and a hard-living floozy into a fiercely protective, anxiously doting mother.[26]

Or take the 1938 film, *Of Human Hearts*, which an acerbic reviewer for *Time* derided as "dedicated to the proposition that a boy's best friend is his mother."[27] Set in the antebellum and Civil War years, the film stars a young Jimmy Stewart as Jason Wilkins, the ungrateful only child of a forbidding minister and a doting, angelic mother (played by Beulah Bondi). After his family struggles to send him to medical school, Wilkins joins the Union forces and wins renown for his compassion and skill. Yet for a full two years, he neglects to write his now widowed and impoverished mother. Assuming the worst, she contacts the White House for assistance in locating her son's grave. Her plea animates the sympathies of President Lincoln himself, who summons the wayward young surgeon to the Oval Office and commands him to sit down at once and write a letter to his mother. The president then warns Wilkins that he will be court-martialed if he fails to write to his mother at least once a week for the remainder of his service. The movie ends with the chastened doctor rushing home to atone for his neglect. To the modern viewer, the reunion scene is downright shocking, for mother and son lock in a passionate embrace, kissing one another on the lips. Perhaps the filmmaker felt able to depict the mother-son bond in this manner because the film was set in the nineteenth century: after all, Bondi played a true, self-sacrificing Victorian mother, not a pampered and cloying "modern" mother. But after World War II, Hollywood films would never feature such a kiss between a mother and her son, unless the intent was to underscore the deeply pathological nature of their attachment, as in the horrifying incestuous kiss between Angela Lansbury and Laurence Harvey in the 1964 film, *The Manchurian Candidate*.

The growing skepticism of mother love is evident in changing attitudes toward women who reared children without men, whether as widows, adoptive single mothers, or unwed mothers. In the interwar period, psychological experts and popular commentators increasingly argued or implied that a woman could not be a good mother outside of a sexually satisfying marriage, for they regarded unmitigated mother love as a burdensome force, tinged with repressed sexual desire. Thus, whereas the young widow who declined to remarry so that she could devote herself fully to her children had been viewed as admirable in the nineteenth century, she more frequently appeared as a pathogenic figure by the 1920s. As the psychiatrist William A. White warned in 1919, a young widow raising an only son was apt to lavish on him "love which is not just a mother's love . . . but in addition a love which should have had an adult form of expression." Boys raised under such circumstances, he argued, tended to be "ill-adapted to withstand the hard knocks of reality" and frequently never married.[28] Similarly, the psychologist Lorine Pruette asserted in 1932 that widows who chose not to remarry were acting out of "a mistaken sense of duty." Such women would be better mothers if they led "a normal, adult life with other objects than children for love," she insisted, adding, "No child should have to bear the full burden of an adult's love."[29] This shifting view of young, widowed mothers—from admirable martyrs to unhealthy neurotics—reflected not only a new emphasis on fathers' contributions to child development but also the mounting suspicion that, in the absence of a paternal figure, mother love could mutate into a dangerous force.

The 1949 film, *A Holiday Affair*, conveyed these messages quite clearly. The film focuses on the emotional journey of Connie Ennis, a young war widow and mother of an eight-year-old son, Timmy, as she struggles to relinquish the past. Although Connie is depicted as a conscientious and loving mother, the film also intimates that her protective and possessive tendencies will cause problems for Timmy in the absence of a new paternal figure. The climactic scene occurs on New Year's Eve: Connie has broken off an amicable but passionless engagement while also rebuffing the attentions of Steve Mason, the man she truly loves. As she sits before a mirror applying make-up, Timmy begins talking of how he will someday marry and perhaps move to another city. Stunned to realize how quickly he is growing up and jolted by the idea that another woman will one day claim her son's affections, Connie races to the train station (with Timmy in tow) to catch Steve before he departs. The audience is given to understand that, by yielding to her desire for Steve and allowing him to disrupt her exclusive relationship with Timmy, she is saving both herself and her son from the dangers of maternal pathology.[30]

This belief that children needed more than mother love also influenced attitudes toward adoption, as historian Julie Berebitsky has shown. In the early twentieth century, before adoption had become a widely accepted practice, reformers who promoted "child rescue" often viewed mature single women as ideal adoptive parents, for they assumed that such women possessed a surfeit of unexpended mother love. But in the 1920s, professional experts, newly convinced that children needed to be protected from such pent-up maternal desires, began to reject single women as potential adoptive parents. Berebitsky rightly attributes this shift to the growing preoccupation with lesbianism and the increasing emphasis on fathers as agents of gender socialization.[31] One might add that it also reflected a waning belief in mother love as a benevolent force that lurked within the hearts all virtuous women, whether or not they birthed children of their own.

The notion that an unmarried woman could not be a successful mother (even if she had already proven herself the most "maternal" of women) also informs the 1941 film *Blossoms in the Dust*, one of MGM's top-grossing releases of the year. The film dramatized the true story of Edna Gladney, founder of the Texas Children's Home and Aid Society in Fort Worth, Texas. After Edna and her husband lose their only son in an accident, she eventually founds an orphanage. Among her first charges is Tony, a very ill and crippled baby whom she nurses back to health and comes to love as her own. Several years pass, during which time her husband dies. At the film's end, her trusted friend and adviser, who is also the children's doctor, tells Edna that he has located a new home for Tony. At first, Edna refuses to relinquish the boy, ar-guing, "But I gave him his life." The doctor, however, insists that Tony needs a father and argues that Edna should continue to champion the cause of all children rather than devoting herself to a single child. Although the orphan-age is as homelike as any institution could possibly be, and although Edna has already established a deep emotional connection with Tony, she must ultimately accept that she cannot provide him with the home life he needs.[32]

This new tendency to view unmarried women as inherently inadequate as mothers can also be seen in shifting policies governing maternity homes. As historian Regina Kunzel has shown, evangelical women who established and ran maternity homes in the late nineteenth and early twentieth centuries went to great lengths to keep mothers and babies together, for they viewed motherhood as a "rehabilitative force" that could redeem the fallen. "There is a God implanted instinct of motherhood in every woman's heart," explained Katherine Barrett, founder of the Florence Crittenton Mission, "that needs only to be aroused to be one of the strongest incentives to best living." Yet by the 1940s, a younger generation of social workers, who gradually usurped the authority of evangelical women, had begun to promote adoption as a prefer-able alternative for white women's babies. Influenced by the growing prestige of psychiatry and especially psychoanalysis, caseworkers came to view white unwed mothers as "neurotic" young girls, wholly lacking in maternal capaci-ties and credentials.[33] Thus, whereas young white women who gave birth in maternity homes prior to the 1940s had been heavily pressured to assume the responsibilities of motherhood, those who did so after World War II were all but denied the option of mothering their babies.[34]

In sum, as the assault on sentimental mother love gained steam during the 1920s and 1930s, it contributed to new childrearing prescriptions and new approaches to social issues such as adoption and unwed motherhood. Yet throughout the interwar period, highly sentimental depictions of middle-aged mothers continued to surface in Hollywood films and other cultural venues. As late as the 1940s, popular culture frequently idealized a sentimental style of maternal affect that psychological professionals had uniformly condemned since the 1920s. At the same time, public and patriotic events like the gold star mothers' pilgrimages and Mother's Day celebrations reinforced a pathos-filled image of the self-sacrificing, all-American mother. But during World War II, as the United States battled an enemy that made a cult of hypermasculinity, an increasing number of critics would portray Americans' attitudes toward mothers as the nation's Achilles' heel—a disturbing weakness that threatened to undermine the struggle to defeat fascism and defend the American "way of life."[35]

Combat Exhaustion and Mother-blaming

In early 1947, the wife of a World War II veteran sat down at a typewriter and pounded out a letter to Philip Wylie in which she vented her frustration and disappointment. The nation's former war wives, she believed, had been "let down" by husbands who, upon their return, had failed to measure up as strong household heads and capable providers. To make matters worse, she and other young women had to contend with experts who dispensed maddeningly contradictory advice:

> As one of the millions of war wives I am told repeatedly that my husband has just been through a terrible ordeal . . . that he is nervous and confused and it will take time and infinite patience and understanding from me to help him return to normal. Then again I am told as a wife and mother that our service men suffered from a new disease called "Momism" and it is up to we mothers to teach our children to be independent—to help them stand on their own feet and think for themselves. Those two attitudes contradict each other.[36]

This woman landed upon two key themes that any peruser of the popular press would likely have encountered in the mid-1940s: first, the claim that pathological mothering had contributed to the high incidence of neuropsychiatric casualties among American troops; and, second, the notion that

returning veterans needed supportive mates to help them regain their emotional equilibrium. Whereas the former chastised women for imperiling the
mental health of American men by nurturing too much, the latter urged
women to help restore the mental health of American men by nurturing
more. Yet these messages were in fact not as contradictory as they first appeared, for they targeted two different generations of women—middle-aged
mothers and young wives—perceived as having very different roles to play in
relation to servicemen and returning veterans.

In extensive discussions concerning the mental health of servicemen and
veterans, experts and popular commentators articulated the new emotional
norms, or "feeling rules," that would help to structure affective relations between middle-class mothers and their adult sons during the postwar era.[37]
Typically, advice writers depicted servicemen's and veterans' attachments to
their mothers as neurotic and regressive, while portraying their relationships
with loyal girlfriends and wives as healthy and mature. From a contemporary
perspective, this might seem unremarkable, but it had not always been so.
During both the Civil War and World War I, popular culture had lauded the
soldier's emotional bond with his mother even above that which he shared
with his wife, and his homecoming had often been represented as a tender
mother-son reunion.[38] In contrast, during and after World War II, experts
and cultural producers frequently identified excessive mother-son attachment as the root cause of maladjustment and prescribed heterosexual romance and marriage as its therapeutic antidote.[39] Thus, even as middle-aged
mothers found themselves castigated as "moms," young women won praise
for guiding boyfriends and husbands to "maturity."[40]

World War II heightened the concerns about American manhood that
had surfaced during the interwar period by exposing what appeared to be a
veritable epidemic of mental illness among the nation's young men. Over the
course of the war, Selective Service examiners rejected some 1,846,000 men—
amounting to 12 percent of all recruits—from induction into the Armed Services on neuropsychiatric grounds. Yet despite these screening measures,
more than half a million servicemen received an "NP" or neuropsychiatric
discharge—a number that accounted for an astonishing 49 percent of all
medical discharges.[41] Because of censorship restrictions, the magnitude of
the problem was not fully publicized until the war's end.[42] But well before
then, commentators who sought to explain the problem had begun to reproduce the arguments about maternal pathology that had become so firmly
entrenched in Americn popular culture and psychological thought.

Repeatedly, psychiatrists traced servicemen's emotional difficulties to
mothers who consciously or unconsciously attempted to maintain a bond

of mutual dependency with their sons. For instance, a 1943 article in *Mental Hygiene* detailed the case of "Private L.," an eighteen-year-old soldier, still in training, who appeared "emotionally distressed" and "cried frequently." A psychiatric interview revealed that he had never previously been away from home and remained "excessively attached" to his ailing mother, who wrote to him almost daily, "complaining of her 'sufferings' and of her difficulty in adjusting to his absence." In psychotherapy, Private L. gained "insight into the neurotic nature of his relationship to his mother." The psychiatrist also sent "a sympathetic, but frank" letter to the private's mother, "eliciting and securing her cooperation." By redirecting Private L.'s emotional attachment toward his company, while restraining his emotionally demanding mother, the psychiatrist and company adviser together strove to transform Private L. into a "'good soldier,' as well as a mature man."[43]

Similarly, after studying two hundred neuropsychiatric patients at an Army hospital in the South Pacific, medical officers J. L. Henderson and Merrill Moore concluded that war neuroses were "made in America"—particularly by the nation's mothers.[44] In their 1944 study, published in the prestigious *New England Journal of Medicine*, they argued that the single most important factor predisposing servicemen to psychological breakdown was not traumatic combat experience but rather "distorted" familial relations. "In nearly every case, a mutually dependent neurotic relation existed between mother and child," they claimed, sketching the typical background of a psychoneurotic soldier:

> The mother was found to stand out. She was usually a "nervous woman" and had often had a nervous breakdown but was rarely hospitalized for it. . . . She tended to worry, particularly about her children, and to be overly concerned about them. For example, most of the mothers had waited up for their boys to come in at night up to the time that they entered the service. The father seemed to be in the background. . . . From these observations the following interpretation is made: The mother is an immature person who feels herself insecure and in her marriage tends to establish a childish, dependent relation to her husband.[45]

Significantly, Henderson and Moore traced the problem of neuropsychiatric breakdown to maternal weakness: if the mother herself remained "childish" and "dependent," her son could not develop into a mature and capable adult.[46]

Other psychiatrists interpreted the very symptoms that predominated among neuropsychiatric casualties as evidence that too many American men could not control their dependent longings. Roy Grinker and John Spiegel, psychoanalysts who served as medical officers during the Tunisian campaign, were initially puzzled by the low incidence of cardiac symptoms (which had been rife among shell-shocked soldiers during World War I) and the comparatively high incidence of gastrointestinal problems. In a classified military report that would become a groundbreaking work on the diagnosis and treatment of war trauma, they attempted to decode the psychological meaning of gastrointestinal symptoms. Because of the stomach's association with "passive reception" of food, they argued, it served as "the organ for expressing passive intaking trends."[47] In other words, servicemen's gastrointestinal problems could not be understood simply as somatic reactions to stressful situations, for they also reflected a deep longing to remain protected and dependent.[48] Elaborating on their findings in 1945, Grinker and Spiegel suggested that the discovery of pronounced passive trends "among so large a portion" of the nation's young men called into question Americans' conception of themselves as a self-reliant people. Instead of fostering rugged individualism, various aspects of modern-day American life, including the "increasing feminine dominance of family life" tended to prolong dependency "beyond its usual biological duration." "We have been struck," they noted, "by the different ways, some subtle, some forthright, in which parents, especially mothers, attempt to bind the boys to the family bosom."[49]

Given the pervasiveness of mother-blaming within midcentury psychiatry, it was perhaps inevitable that Wylie's momism critique would come to figure in discussions of traumatized servicemen and veterans. Indeed, a few readers of *Generation of Vipers* drew this connection on their own. "We have just completed . . . a war in Europe where the greatest objective was to get back home to 'Mom' and her pies," an embittered Information Education Officer who worked for the Army Air Force wrote in 1945. "Of course you are aware of the staggering mental casualties suffered overseas and in this country. Surely 'mom' killed as many men as a thousand German machine guns."[50] In more temperate language, a medical resident in psychiatry at Winter General Army Hospital in Topeka, Kansas, explained in 1946 that his experience treating veterans had alerted him to the pervasiveness of momism. He had "taken too many histories, seen too many cases," he wrote, to dismiss Wylie's charges lightly.[51] Because Wylie leveled his attack on moms just as commentators began to voice concerns about the mental stamina of American draftees and servicemen, these and other respondents readily linked the two issues.

The man most responsible for injecting the term "momism" into discussions of neuropsychiatric casualties was Edward Strecker, chair of the Department of Psychiatry at the University of Pennsylvania and one of the nation's leading psychiatrists. During World War II, Strecker served as a consultant to the Surgeons General of the Army, Army Air Forces, and Navy, as well as an advisor to the Secretary of War, so he well understood the concerns of military psychiatrists and medical officers.[52] In November 1944, he delivered a speech in which he speculated that the high numbers of neuropsychiatric rejections and casualites could be traced to "defects in childhood training." However, nothing in his talk, or in any of his previous work, suggested that he regarded maternal influence as uniquely problematic.[53] But on April 27, 1945, just a few days before V-E Day, Strecker confidently claimed to have located the primary culprit underlying the rash of neuropsychiatric rejections and casualties: American moms. In a lecture entitled "Psychiatry Speaks to Democracy," delivered before some two hundred medical students and physicians at the New York University College of Medicine, he asserted that a significant portion of neuropsychiatric casualties had never endured the grueling ordeal of combat but had instead succumbed to the minor strains of military life. "Now I am on dangerous terrain," he forewarned his audience, "because . . . I am about to indict a certain considerable number of American mothers, part of a time-honored and revered national institution and popularly and collectively known as 'Mom.'" Predictably, Strecker's speech caused quite a stir, generating interest that extended far beyond the medical community; the *New York Times* reported on it under the headline "'Moms' Denounced as Peril to Nation."[54]

Strecker no doubt relished the *Times* coverage, for he actively pursued connections in the publishing industry that would allow him to disseminate his message to a broad popular audience. Prior to his lecture, he had written to Ellis Bacon, an editor at Lippincott, informing him of the event and suggesting that his remarks could be developed into a book.[55] Bacon attended the talk with his junior colleague Lynn Carrick, a former Marine who immediately sensed the market potential of Strecker's attack on moms. Carrick encouraged the psychiatrist to regard his "general thesis" as one of "great value and significance" that should have "as wide a circulation as possible." "In this instance," he added, "I'm able to speak not only as an editor but as an ex-Marine who has returned from service in the Pacific."[56] Within a matter of weeks, Strecker had contracted with Lippincott to produce a book geared toward a popular audience.[57] He then approached the popular science writer Greer Williams about the possibility of previewing an excerpt in the *Saturday Evening Post*. Williams reported back that a mere "three minutes' conversation" was enough to convince his superior that the *Post* should publish Strecker's "declaration of war on moms." The article, "What's Wrong with American Mothers?" appeared in October; the book, *Their Mothers' Sons: The Psychiatrist Examines an American Problem*, followed in December and became an instant bestseller.[58] Assisted by writers and publishers eager to capitalize on the public's increasing fascination with psychiatry, Strecker transformed himself into a nationally recognized expert who enjoyed a broad readership.[59] Having appropriated a concept from popular culture, he proceeded to recycle his own version back into the popular press, with the added endorsement of psychiatric authority.

While Strecker openly acknowledged his debt to *Generation of Vipers*, he sought to distinguish himself as a dispassionate professional by criticizing Wylie's approach as "too vindictive . . . to satisfy a trained psychiatrist."[60] In truth, *Their Mothers' Sons* was also extremely vitriolic. But Strecker's indictment of American mothers departed from Wylie's in a number of ways. He differentiated between two, equally destructive types of moms—the "sweet, doting, 'self-sacrificing'" mom and "the stern, capable, self-contained, domineering" mom—as well as a variety of subtypes. He also acknowledged the existence of "mom surrogates" and admitted that, paradoxically, "sometimes 'pop' is 'mom.'"[61] Moreover, unlike Wylie, Strecker portrayed moms themselves as victims of "a social system veering towards matriarchy in which each individual mom plays only a small part."[62] And finally, whereas Wylie used the phrase "maturity" only in passing, Strecker discussed the concept in great detail—as did many of his postwar contemporaries.[63] "Why did the desire for self-preservation defeat one group of men, to their discredit, and not the other?" he asked. "The answer in ninety percent of the cases can be given in one word, IMMATURITY."[64] The mature democratic character, Strecker argued, was established in infancy and childhood through the give-and-take of the mother-child relationship. All mothers confronted the dilemma of meeting children's needs while simultaneously steering them toward independence, yet too many American mothers kept their children in a state of abject dependency, bound by a "silver cord." To promote greater maturity among the nation's citizens, Strecker urged Americans to combat momism just as they had sought to eradicate diseases like tuberculosis, by launching a "three-fold program—talking about [moms] freely, presenting the cold hard facts for all to see, and continuous unrelenting public education."[65]

Despite its popular success, critical reception of *Their Mothers' Sons* was mixed. A reviewer for *Mental Hygiene* noted that the only thing new about Strecker's book was the severity of his charges: "The smothering mother was pretty thoroughly exploited during the first ten years of the child-guidance movement, though I can't remember any statement of that period that is as devastating . . . as this."[66] E. B. Garside of the *New York Times* conceded that Strecker had "performed a genuine service by striking with all his authority at the root of a social ill," but he found it "regrettable" that the psychiatrist had resorted to a "vehement, even contemptuous, style that hardly becomes a healer of psyches."[67] The most damning review, however, was written by none other than Philip Wylie. Wylie agreed that the high rates of neuropsychiatric disorders had proven that "momism is the deadliest disease of the nation," and he claimed to welcome Strecker's "quasi-official sanctioning" of his terminology. But in contrast to those who found the book's language intemperate, Wylie dismissed Strecker's approach—and Strecker himself—as "very mild and inadequate." "Indeed, the farther one gets into *Their Mothers' Sons*," he wrote, "the more clearly one perceives that Dr. Strecker is trying to analyze Moms and Momism without saying a word that would violate the ruinous tabus of a single Mom."[68]

Despite the criticism it garnered, *Their Mothers' Sons* had a lasting impact. By linking the problem of maternal influence even more firmly to the question of national security, Strecker helped to transform the momism critique from a raucous satire into a quasi-diagnosis taken seriously by a battery of experts. Even an article designed to counter those who "rant against 'momism'" bowed before the psychiatrist's authority, conceding, "Still, you can't laugh it off. . . . Not when Dr. Edward A. Strecker . . . points to the 2½ million men rejected or discharged from the services for neuro-psychiatric reasons and says they're Mom's handiwork."[69] Well into the postwar period, commentators continued to refer to draftees' and servicemen's psychological problems as evidence of pervasive maternal pathology and faltering masculinity. A 1956 article in *Life* noted that "the increasing emotional immaturity of the American male was borne home . . . most strongly during the war" and cited statistics of neuropsychiatric casualties to support its point.[70]

Yet while the popular media latched onto Strecker's findings, some observers remained skeptical of the notion that American mothers had eroded the nation's masculine fortitude. The actor and consummate cold warrior Ronald Reagan expressed his reservations in 1952 when speaking before the graduating class of William Woods College for Women in Missouri. "During World War II a new word was coined . . . the term 'momism,'" he recounted, and, soon thereafter, numerous articles began to appear in popular magazines "deploring the influence of the American female on the men of this man's world." Reagan declined to "take issue" with psychiatrists who held mothers responsible for servicemen's psychological difficulties. But he did reason that, if momism was to blame for men who had failed the test, then momism must also be credited with the successes of those who had served valiantly. To illustrate the point, he told a story of heroic self-sacrifice by an Air Force pilot whose plane had been hit during World War II. After ordering his crew to bail out, the pilot chose to stay with his gunner, who remained trapped in the ball turret. As the others parachuted out, and the young man grew increasingly desperate over his predicament, the pilot took his hand and calmly reassured him, "Never mind, son. We'll ride it out together." By becoming a selfless mother to a helpless and terrified boy, the pilot exemplified the very highest of martial values; Reagan concluded the story by stating, "Congressional Medal of Honor posthumously awarded."[71] The lesson for the women graduates was clear: the pilot could behave so nobly only because his mother had once bestowed such selfless devotion upon him. Clearly, Ronald Reagan did not believe that sentimental mother love threatened American manhood, leaving the nation vulnerable to communism; on the contrary, he retained an older notion of internalized mother love as the force that made men moral.

The tendency to blame American mothers for U.S. servicemen's alleged psychopathology resurfaced during the Korean War when, in 1953, twenty-one released POWs chose to defect to North Korea. A number of commentators alighted upon maternal failure and homosexuality as key factors that helped to explain the POWs' treasonous behavior. In contrast, a California chapter of the American Legion proposed that the POWs' mothers be flown to Korea to persuade the men to return.[72] The legionnaires apparently assumed that if anyone could recall the defectors to their sense of duty and true values, it would surely be the men's own mothers. Here again, the episode is revealing: not only does it belie the assumption that mother-blaming and conservative politics went hand-in-hand, it also reminds us that, even in the early 1950s, when psychological authority was arguably at its most powerful, some Americans preserved an older, more idealized conception of maternal influence.

Veterans, Mothers, and Wives

As in the national discussion of neuropsychiatric casualties, psychiatrists' concerns about maternal influence played a central role in the debates about returning veterans. Well before the war ended, a vast array of books and articles on veteran readjustment began to appear. While such works varied widely, nearly all portrayed readjustment in psychological terms, as an emotionally fraught process that could result in serious difficulties if mishandled.[73] The effect of this literature, as historian David Gerber has noted, was "to cast doubt on the mental stability of every demobilized man. . . . Every veteran was a potential 'mental case,' even if he showed no symptoms."[74] Numerous writers, including veterans themselves, deplored this tendency to construct a "veteran problem." (The columnist William Lynch, for instance, lambasted "those half-baked popularizers of psychology who are responsible for the hundreds of articles and lectures that would have us believe that every veteran will return hateful, maladjusted and resentful.")[75] Yet the therapeutic framework proved so pervasive that even dissenters had trouble conceptualizing the issue of veteran readjustment in alternative ways.[76]

According to prescriptive literature and popular dramatizations, the veteran's best hope for recovery resided in a girlfriend or wife who could steer him toward greater self-reliance, if necessary by acting as a buffer between him and his mother. Should the wife herself need guidance, experts urged her to turn not to an older, more experienced woman, but to the veteran's psychiatrist or doctor, who embodied the paternal authority deemed so sorely lacking in the typical American home.[77] Together, the wife and the doctor formed a therapeutic team, supplanting the sentimental mother who had tended to the veteran in previous eras. To them fell the duty of restoring men who had suffered not only the trauma of war but also the effects of pathological familial relationships.

Successful readjustment, as portrayed in the advice literature and popular culture, entailed several steps: leaving the security of the hospital or the parental home; finding a job or enrolling in school; and assuming or reassuming the role of husband and father. Experts stressed that it was especially imperative for married veterans to attain emotional and financial independence from their parents. According to a professor at New York University, the less young couples depended on their elders, the better their chances for a successful marriage: "Above all, parents should not subsidize their children. The further geographically removed the young and old generations are, the better."[78] Similarly, Charles Brown, chief of the New York Mental Hygiene Service, decried the acute housing shortage—which forced many young couples to reside at least temporarily with parents—as "one of the biggest factors in making many veterans mentally sick."[79] Even if the decision to live with parents seemed freely chosen, experts took exception. The psychiatrist George Pratt, for example, warned of two types of cases: those in which a young war wife felt unable to assume "independent living away from . . . her mother," and those in which a married veteran, who remained "immature and dependent on *his* mother," wanted to move back to his childhood home. Such couples, Pratt insisted, needed to strike out on their own.[80]

In case histories and dramatizations, the veteran's decision to leave his parents, especially his mother, often figured as a critical step on his road to recovery. For instance, an article about psychodramatic theater, a new technique being employed with returning neuropsychiatric casualties, related how a serviceman named Bill struggled to break free from his possessive

mother. "How can I get loose from mamma?" he asked, enacting his dilemma before an audience of patients and hospital staff. "She wants me to
stay home forever when I get out of the Navy. . . . I'm afraid to hurt her, but
I've got a job waiting for me in Texas that I want to take." When Bill then
attempted to rebut his mother's protests, he came across as timid and uncon-
vincing, prompting a fellow patient to remind him, "There's not much place
for a mamma's boy in the Navy or in Texas." Finally, after reenacting the
same scene over the course of three months, Bill acquired the psychological
strength to defy his mother and accept the job—a decision that culminated
with his discharge from the hospital.[81]

A veteran who wrote to Philip Wylie in 1947 portrayed his decision to
leave his widowed mother's home in very similar terms, suggesting how individuals drew upon the dominant therapeutic discourse to comprehend
and alter their own circumstances. Realizing that he needed "to be weaned,
mature, face it," he braved his mother's tears and his relatives' disapproval
and moved into an apartment of his own. Though he lived only some ten to
twelve blocks away, it felt to him like "a million miles." "I might never have
known my predicament had I not seen a close friend go through all this with
much more suffering," he confided to Wylie. "Much to his mother's sorrow . . . he is getting along fine, marrying a wonderful girl in a few weeks."
The writer further noted that he had acquired "insight into the whole situation" by observing the plight of "two other fellows . . . who had the same
trouble—they left, but I guess it was too late—they are both homosexual—
terrific persons, both of them." Echoing countless postwar experts, this young
man suggested that separation from the mother could foster healthy hetero-
sexuality, whereas prolonged mother-son attachment might lead to homosexuality. Depicting his own separation in therapeutic terms, he boasted, "I
have never felt better, my school work is easier to cope with and, in general,
I'm living a normal existence."[82]

In cases of veterans who suffered from serious physical illnesses or injuries, experts tended to be particularly wary of anxious mothers who might
undermine the efforts of health care professionals. *A Psychiatric Primer for
the Veteran's Family and Friends* described the disruptive behavior of one
"distraught mother": "When she came to visit her son, she walked on tiptoe,
shushed everybody in sight, peered nervously around the door before entering the room, and . . . cautioned and questioned until the doctor began to
wonder whether it wasn't she who should be in the hospital instead of her
son."[83] The psychiatrist George Pratt related a similar dynamic involving a
veteran, Arthur, who had suffered severe facial disfigurement. After working
with a psychiatrist to conquer "his oversensitiveness and morbid preoccu-

pation" with his scars, he returned home, only to contend with his family's "artificial Pollyanna-like treatment":

> It annoyed him beyond words to have Mother tiptoe about the house, shush-
> ing everyone who talked loudly, to have her fuss over him and to see the tears
> of silent pity course down her cheeks as she begged him to 'rest' on the couch
> in the living room. . . . He strove manfully to stifle his exasperation when his
> mother insisted on his reciting over and over again the intimate details of
> his wounding; how it happened; when it happened; did it hurt much; did he
> lose quantities of blood . . . until her well-meaning interrogations into these
> personal matters hurt worse than the surgeon's probing for embedded mortar
> fragments.[84]

Arthur's mother erred in numerous ways, according to Pratt: she failed to contain her own grief over his injury; she attempted to nurture him in in-appropriate ways; and, worst of all, she violated his privacy by insisting that he revisit the scene of the trauma. When she urged her son to recall and ar-ticulate his traumatic experiences, the result was neither catharsis nor greater insight but regression and loss of initiative. In contrast to a psychiatrist, who could help a young man come to terms with his past, a mother presumably could not absorb the "intimate details" of wartime trauma without absorbing the man himself.

Case histories like these implied that the veteran's mother should follow a highly constrained course of action—a view that sociologist Willard Waller voiced explicitly in his 1945 *Ladies' Home Journal* article, "What You Can Do to Help the Returning Veteran." Though Waller allowed that returning veterans might need maternal "warmth and tenderness," he urged mothers to be circumspect. If a son wanted to talk, the mother should be available to listen; if he preferred to remain silent, she should not pry. Yet Waller deemed even this modest role appropriate only for mothers of unmarried sons. The mother of a married veteran, he counseled, faced "a much more complex sit-uation" that demanded "great self-restraint." "There is only one bit of advice that one can honestly give to such a mother, and that is: Let the young people alone! . . . Every generation has the right to make its own mistakes. . . . You will meddle but to mar. Let the young people alone!" As Waller's emphatic refrain made clear, mothers of married veterans could do little if anything to assist their sons, except in the negative sense of making themselves scarce.[85]

In contrast, Waller prescribed a far more active role for young wives. He urged the wife of a returning veteran to engage in "serious study of the vet-eran and his psychology" by forming reading groups to discuss the literature of World War I as well as articles and manuals on veteran psychology. She should then scrutinize her husband "in the light of what she has learned," striving "to understand his particular case." In essence, Waller urged the wife to assume the stance of a therapist, regarding her husband with the requisite detachment to assess his "case" and determine a proper course of action. He was quick to add, however, that the well-informed wife would "realize when she needs professional help" and take the lead in convincing her husband to seek mental health care. Thus, whereas Waller found it necessary to restrain or even banish servicemen's mothers during the delicate phase of readjustment, he believed that young wives, backed by mental health care specialists, could act in a therapeutic capacity.[86]

Numerous postwar films dramatized this basic idea by portraying veterans and their young wives (or girlfriends) who overcome the effects of parental failure by turning to one another. In the somber 1949 film *Not Wanted*, for example, a veteran with a prosthetic leg encounters a pregnant, unmarried girl who eventually gives her child up for adoption. The film portrays the girl's mother as a frightful nag and household drudge; in fact, the audience is given to understand that the mother, by creating such an unpleasant home environment, is actually responsible for her daughter's moral lapse. The veteran has no family at all. *Not Wanted* endorses marriage as the only solution for these two lost souls. At the film's end, they literally save one another: the girl's grief over her child is so unbearable that she rushes to a bridge to commit suicide; the veteran attempts to stop her, but his physical disability prevents him and he winds up prostrate on the bridge, pounding his fists in frustration. It is his raw display of neediness—more than his evident love—that finally makes her stop, turn toward him, and choose life. She will nurture him; he will take the place of her relinquished baby. Yet the final image of the film, in which she cradles him on the bridge, suggests how desperate and wounded both individuals are, and how isolated they are from other sources of emotional support. *Not Wanted* thus holds out marriage as the answer, but it does so in strikingly unromantic terms, with the promise of sexual gratification downplayed in favor of safety and emotional security.[87]

The 1945 film *The Enchanted Cottage* also depicts a healing union between an emotionally wounded young woman and a physically wounded veteran. An Air Corps pilot returns home with a lame arm and a disfigured face, only to have his fiancée recoil in horror when confronted with his injuries. Seeking refuge, he flees to the remote cottage that they had intended to rent after their marriage. Here he meets a homely young woman, Laura, who provides him with constant reassurance and physical care. Ultimately, the two marry, but both suspect that the marriage is a farce: he fears that he has selfishly saddled her with a broken man, whereas she fears that he can never truly love her, nor know how much she loves him. The tension is resolved through a miraculous transformation on their wedding night, a none-too-subtle allusion to the powers of the nuptial bed: she becomes beautiful, and he is made whole. Their newfound happiness, however, is shattered when the veteran's mother and stepfather arrive for a visit, and the mother's insensitive reaction reveals that their transformation is illusory. (When the camera portrays them from one another's perspective, they appear whole and beautiful, but when portrayed from the mother's perspective, they appear as before.) *The Enchanted Cottage* thus drives home quite conventional themes: love can heal; beauty is in the eye of the beholder. Yet at the same time, it alludes to the fragility of the marital union, which could blossom only in a remote location, far from meddling relatives who threatened to break the spell that binds the two in mutual happiness.[88]

Wherever young couples looked—in popular magazines, Hollywood films, or professional literature—they found their desires for autonomy validated and their ambivalence and antagonism toward their parents, especially their mothers, legitimized. Of course, many veterans scorned literature that depicted them as a social problem, and women could be highly skeptical of expert advice and idealized portraits of wifehood and motherhood. Still, though impossible to measure, the discussion surrounding returning veterans had important consequences. By lauding the therapeutic capabilities of girlfriends and wives, it helped to validate the trend toward youthful marriage and inward-looking nuclear families that characterized the postwar era. And by reinforcing the critique of American "moms" as overly involved in their children's lives, it condoned attitudes and behavior toward mothers ranging from the dismissive to the contemptuous.

Initially, a mutual disdain for middle-aged mothers could fuel a couple's sense of independence and solidarity. But such a stance could not easily be sustained over time, particularly if the couple became parents themselves. Consider the following account of a veteran's wife, who wrote to Philip Wylie in 1947. As she explained, her husband had spent more than three years in the Army, and his denunciations of "mom" made Wylie's own acerbic critique "seem almost kindly":

> For he fully believes that most of the disgraceful acts of the American soldier were due to too much coddling and not enough discipline from dear old you know who, that the outrageous behavior of our occupation troops was traceable to mom, that she preferred to feed, feed [sic] her own ego rather than instill the true attributes of manliness in her son. And the Veterans psychiatric wards are full of the boys who couldn't take it thanks to Mom's depleting influence.

> My son is only four months old, but I intend, instead of using the more
> orthodox books on child rearing, to keep "Generation of Vipers" close at
> hand. And my husband has a very successful method of controlling me. He
> merely says, "Don't be a mom."[89]

One can only wonder how this couple dealt with the difficulties of readjustment, and whether or not the specter of wartime horrors haunted their relationship. What seems clear is that the husband's fervent antimaternalism
profoundly affected his wife's views, feelings, and behavior. Yet even though
the wife pledged to avoid the dangers of momism, shunning any sense of
identification with the women of her mother's generation, she still had to
suffer her husband's corrective jabs. In prescriptive literature and popular
depictions of veteran readjustment, antimaternalist sentiment generally centered on middle-aged mothers, but in private life, young wives and mothers
found themselves targeted as well.

Raising a New Generation

In 1949, the child psychoanalyst Sibylle Escalona commented on the "remarkable change in cultural attitudes toward specific child-rearing practices" that
had occurred in the prior decade. It seemed incredible to her that, less than
ten years before, psychological authorities and "public opinion" still favored
strict schedules and limited physical contact during early childhood. "From
the vantage point of the present," she mused, "it is difficult to recapture the
feelings and expectations on which such convictions about child-rearing
practices were based." According to Escalona, the emphatic rejection of behaviorist principles reflected a more general disillusionment with the notion
that science and technology could "solve the problems of human existence."
In the new atomic age, she observed, "scientists and everyone else" had come
to view "the unconscious, or whatever it is that determines human behavior"
as "the main source of threat to future security and well being."[90]

The political upheavals of the 1940s dramatically influenced attitudes toward mothering. Intent on curbing human aggression and irrationality, numerous experts came to view the mother-child relationship as the cornerstone
of a peaceful and democratic order. Although their anxieties about clinging
and overprotective mothers did not diminish, they increasingly turned their
attention to the problems of maternal deprivation and rejection. Influenced
by Anna Freud's wartime studies of orphans, which were widely publicized
in the United States, experts and commentators began to emphasize young
children's presumed need for intensive, uninterrupted maternal care.[91] The
withholding of maternal solicitude in infancy, previously regarded as a sound

approach to the irrational impulses of mother and child alike, came to be perceived as a denial of legitimate need—a denial that actually produced the dependent tendencies that it sought to prevent. More broadly, the behaviorist view of infants as blank slates to be molded by all-powerful parents ceased to appear as a positive good—an opportunity to engineer a modern society free of the inhibitions that had marred prior generations. Instead, psychiatrists and psychologists of varying theoretical persuasions invested their hopes for the future in a more favorable view of the infant as a nascent individual who would naturally develop into a reasonable, democratic citizen, provided that he or she received loving and physically indulgent maternal care during the earliest phase of life.

Thus, during the 1940s, as a newer set of concerns about mothering augmented the old, the anxiety surrounding motherhood grew even more high-pitched. The dilemma that presented itself was this: How could experts prescribe a style of mothering that allowed for infantile bonding, without reverting to a sentimental and moralistic notion of mother love? For most experts, the solution resided in a notion of maternal instinct that stripped mother love of its broader cultural dimensions and demoted it to a manifestation of psychological and biological drives. In fact, many abandoned the expression "mother love" altogether, no doubt because it was so freighted with older meanings. On those occasions when experts did refer to "mother love" in a nonderisive sense, they tended to present it as something so elemental that it was practically secreted from the maternal body.

This valorization of maternal instinct is also apparent in experts' tendency to reduce mother love to a physical substance by comparing it to nutrients—an analogy that had rarely surfaced in earlier eras. As Margaret Ribble wrote in 1943, "Mother love is a good deal like food. It has to be expressed regularly so that the child expects it; a little at a time, and frequently, is the emotional formula."[92] Or, as Benjamin Spock patiently explained, "Every baby needs to be smiled at, talked to, played with, fondled—gently and lovingly—just as much as he needs vitamins and calories."[93] The British psychoanalyst John Bowlby drew the same analogy in 1951 when he complained that governments, social agencies, and the public still failed to appreciate that "mother-love in infancy and childhood is as important for mental health as are vitamins and proteins for physical health."[94] Only a physically intimate, nourishing relationship to the mother, nearly all postwar experts agreed, produced the necessary emotional "security" that allowed a child to develop into a well-balanced adult.

Indeed, many childrearing experts in the 1940s and 1950s defined their role as helping women to *recover* their true maternal "instincts." This of course distinguished them from prewar advocates of "scientific motherhood," who tended to regard the very notion of "maternal instinct" as an old-fashioned myth that perpetuated dangerously misguided practices.[95] The psychoanalyst Margaret Ribble, for instance, bemoaned the fact that contemporary women, after decades of being subjected to heavy-handed expert advice, had come to distrust their own maternal impulses. "Our highly impersonal civilization has insidiously damaged woman's instinctual nature and has blinded her to one of her most natural rights," she wrote in 1943, "that of teaching the small baby to love, by loving it consistently through the period of helpless infancy."[96] Likewise, a psychiatrist quoted in *Collier's* in 1947 described how he handled cases in which the mother became so intent on studying advice literature and visiting psychiatrists that her child developed a neurosis. "As soon as she has unlearned her collection of fancy and conflicting theories and learned what nature is reputed to teach most mothers via instinct," he explained with dripping condescension, "she is discharged and returned to her family."[97] These and other experts praised the rise of permissive parenting in large part because they believed that it would help to restore motherhood to a more "natural" basis.

A similar (though ultimately more complex) view of maternal nurturance informed the experimental psychologist Harry Harlow's 1958 presidential address to the American Psychological Association, "The Nature of Love," in which he discussed his widely publicized experiments with rhesus monkeys. Separating babies from their mothers soon after birth, Harlow provided the young monkeys with two types of surrogates. The first consisted of a wooden block covered with rubber and terry cloth and equipped with a "uni-breast" that held a bottle; a light bulb warmed the "mother" from behind. The second surrogate, made of bare wire mesh and also equipped with bottle, differed only in its inability to provide "contact comfort." Harlow and his researchers found that, when given a choice, a baby monkey would spend nearly all its time with the cloth surrogate, even if it could receive milk only from the wire surrogate. They therefore concluded that babies cling to their mothers not only because they need food but also because they crave warm, physical contact: infants, in other words, needed "love" as well as food.[98] Both at the time and later in historical account, Harlow's experiments have been viewed as reinforcing the cultural idealization of mother love. But, as historian Marga Vicedo has shown, his conclusions suggested that any warm and reliable caregiver—including a father—could meet an infant's needs equally as well as his or her biological mother.[99] In fact, Harlow actually implied that an inanimate object, entirely devoid of personality, could be a successful mother—indeed, an ideal mother—since the infant's primary emotional need was for a warm, soft, ever-present entity. If other psychological experts demystified mother love by portraying it as an instinctual drive, Harlow went even further by detaching it from female biology: his "mother love" dispensed with the mother altogether. In this respect, however, Harlow was rather unique, for most postwar experts celebrated the physicality of motherhood and maternal care.

The growing emphasis on the importance of warm, physical care led some commentators and experts to advance a new set of claims about the relationship between race, class, and maternal capacities. In the early twentieth century, when infant mortality rates remained high, reformers who championed "scientific motherhood" frequently denigrated the maternal traditions of immigrant and African-American women. Although cultural producers often romanticized the loyal and nurturing mammy, they rarely did so in a manner that called white women's maternal capacities into question. In the 1940s and 1950s, however, a number of experts who denounced the excesses of "scientific motherhood" unfavorably compared affluent white mothers to black mammies or immigrant nursemaids. Ribble, for example, suggested that old-school "Negro mammies of the South" had a better understanding of babies' needs than well-educated white women.[100] Likewise, the writer Della Cyrus speculated that the "superstitions and vulgarities" of the "much maligned 'dumb' nursemaid" might have been "far less dangerous than the overanxious, impatient expectations of the intelligent and discontented mother." Of course, such claims did not reflect a genuine appreciation of contemporary African American or immigrant mothers; after all, both writers invoked stereotypical figures from the past. Rather, this tendency to romanticize "other" mothers' nurturing capacities underscores the fear that "modern" women had become alienated from their instinctual selves and thus could not provide the indulgent love that the experts now prescribed.

Yet even as psychological experts placed greater emphasis on the need for intensive maternal care during the very earliest years, they continued to warn against the dangers of momism. Typically, they counseled mothers to provide intensive care in infancy, while consciously striving to lessen children's emotional dependency as they grew. For instance, in 1955 the psychologist Elizabeth Hurlock exhorted readers of *Health* that "Mothering Does Not Mean Smothering." The newborn baby, she wrote, "is helpless and needs and demands your constant attention. . . . [b]ut nature does not permit this state of helplessness to last for long." The mother who thwarted her child's early attempts at self-reliance should not be surprised if he later demanded "unnecessary help," for she had effectively "made him a helpless dependent, a victim of 'Momism.'" Likewise, Representative Katharine St. George, a longtime proponent of the Equal Rights Amendment, offered the following advice to women students at George Washington University in 1949: "If we sacrifice our children's infant years to any career, no matter how successful and useful, we are doing them and ourselves an irreparable injustice. However, in a very few short years this part of our lives is over and we must have the courage and intelligence to untie the apron strings to let these children of ours stand on their own feet and to strike out and have lives and careers of their own." Warning that "momism" was "one of the curses of life in the United States," St. George suggested that mothers and children alike would benefit from greater emotional autonomy and self-reliance.[101]

The extent to which good mothering came to be defined as the ability to refrain from intervening is well illustrated by a passage from Ferdinand Lundberg and Marynia Farnham's 1947 bestseller, *Modern Woman: The Lost Sex*, an antifeminist polemic that presented motherhood as the pinnacle of female fulfillment. Although women's historians have often cited this book as a classic articulation of the postwar "feminine mystique," they have not noted how radically the maternal ideal that its authors advocated departed from prior conceptions. Consider, for instance, how Farnham and Lundberg described the ideal, truly "feminine mother":

> Is she so very wise? No, hers is not wisdom in the sense of intellectual knowledge. She just likes her children. . . . Being in balance, she feels no need to inquire into every detail of their lives, to dominate them. Instead, she watches with somewhat detached interest to see what each one takes. . . . She can tell, without reading books on child care, what to do for the children by waiting for them to indicate their need. This method is infallible. She does not fuss over them. If they are too cold, too hot, too wet, hungry or lonesome, they let her know it and she meets the need. Otherwise she leaves them pretty much to their own devices, although keeping a watchful eye on them.[102]

Here, the mother emerges as a curiously affectless figure, the very antithesis of the Victorian matron who sought to bind her children with a "silver cord" to better scrutinize the state of their souls. In fact, Farnham and Lundberg seemed determined to avoid all reference to maternal "love": their ideal mother merely "liked" her children and offered them "reassuring support" in infancy and early childhood, thereafter viewing them with greater emotional detachment. In essence, these and other experts urged mothers to refrain from attempting to mold their children and instead to serve as a loving yet blank background against which children could define themselves.

The notion that the woman who mothered least mothered best surfaced even in an article designed to counter the hostile attacks on American mothers. Published in *Better Homes & Gardens* in 1947, "You Can't Talk That Way about Mother!" featured seventy-two-year-old Janette Murray, a "kindly but unsentimental" woman who had raised five successful children while contributing to a wide array of reform movements. Murray, the writer approvingly noted, "never had time to bind her children in emotional coils." Instead, she won praise for serving as a constant but unobtrusive presence; in her daughters' words, she was "always there, in the background, to help out in an emergency, to greet our friends, or to set out breakfast for the school friend who stayed overnight." Describing the Murrays' childrearing philosophy, the writer succinctly expressed what one astute contemporary observer dubbed the new "fun morality."[103] "They shared their lives with their children in whatever they did. It was no sacrifice. It was just more fun." One of the few passages that quotes Murray directly, however, struck a quite different note. "Love your children and share your life with them, and they'll come out all right," she advised. "Share the work, the sacrifices, the burdens and the joys—everything—and you won't have to worry." Though Murray herself spoke an older language that recognized "sacrifices" and "burdens" as an inevitable part of motherhood and family life, the article tried to transform her into an exemplar of the new childrearing ideology, one in which notions of maternal self-sacrifice had no place.[104]

Indeed, contrary to popular views of the era, experts in the 1940s and 1950s repeatedly condemned "self-sacrificing" mothers who concentrated all of their energies on their children. "The mother who devotes herself exclusively to her child may have the satisfaction of playing the martyr, but she may dangerously handicap her offspring," warned the psychiatrist David Levy. "Mothers have the difficult job of restraining onrushing, embracing, helping impulses; they must learn that 'they also serve who only stand and wait.'"[105] Edward Strecker cautioned that mothers lauded by the community should be regarded with skepticism; though they were "spoken of as 'giving their lives' for their children," in truth they demanded "full payment in the emotional lives of their children."[106] The psychiatrist Herman Bundesen singled out one such mother—a woman "known as an unselfish, devoted parent" of a maladjusted nine-year-old boy, whose neighbors would frequently comment, "She gives her whole life to that boy!" In truth, Bundesen argued in a 1950 *Ladies' Home Journal* article, the mother's self-sacrificing behavior lay at the root of her son's problems.[107] These experts regarded maternal self-sacrifice with such deep skepticism because they did not view it as genuinely selfless: what appeared like maternal selflessness, they argued, was often an attempt to fulfill a self-centered desire.

Mothers in the 1940s and 1950s also heard from many sources that they should *not* focus solely on their children and their homes. Psychological experts often urged women to cultivate identities beyond that of "mother," while popular culture for the first time began to condone mothers' employment outside the home on the grounds that it benefited children.[108] Psychologist Anna Wolf argued in 1941 that the woman with a "strong" personality needed "larger worlds to conquer than her home and family," if only because "her energies need deflection."[109] Similarly, Zuma Steele, writing for *Good Housekeeping* in 1945, alerted readers to the dangers of focusing exclusively on home and family. "The woman who gives up everything for her home is doing herself and her home a disservice," she stressed. "Variety of interest gives a rounded viewpoint and a sense of balance indispensable to a happy home."[110] In 1956, a psychoanalyst quoted in *American Weekly* went so far as to argue, "If staying home is depressing [the mother] and failing to stimulate her creatively, then I believe her husband and children are better off if she gets herself a job outside the home for eight hours a day. She can't try to please friends, neighbors or relatives. She has to please herself *first*, then try to please others."[111]

Such sources should not, however, be read as evidence that the postwar cultural climate was actually more favorable for women than feminists and scholars have previously suggested. Rather, what they suggest is that the widespread discontent among middle-class women cannot be attributed solely to a "feminine mystique" that exiled women to the domestic realm. The dilemma that such women confronted is better understood as a vicious double bind. Still largely barred from constructing their identities as autonomous individuals, and still prevented from competing on equal terms with men in the workplace and the broader public realm, they were now also discouraged from constructing their identities as selfless nurturers, whose sacrifices entitled them to certain emotional rewards. Instead, experts and popular culture promoted the dominant therapeutic ethos by insisting, somewhat paradoxically, that truly "feminine" women achieved fulfillment as *individuals* through motherhood. Thus, when *Life* celebrated the "American Woman" in 1947, the magazine praised the outlook of a young mother by emphasizing the personal satisfaction that she derived from homemaking: "Because as an individual she likes the job that she does, she has no problem right now. Like most busy housewives, however, she gives little thought to the future—to satisfactory ways of spending the important years after her children have grown up and left home."[112] No longer a sacred calling and duty, motherhood and homemaking came to be construed as an emotionally fulfilling "job"— one that would ultimately end. The problem with this model, of course, is that unremunerated homemaking and childrearing did not fit easily into a therapeutic model that privileged individual self-realization: the demands of caring for a family frequently often did require women to subordinate their own interests and desires, yet they were increasingly prohibited from seeking recognition for their sacrifices, or even from viewing them as such.

When the historian Anne Kuhn published a book about motherhood and education in antebellum New England in 1947, she closed by drawing a sharp contrast between her own era and her period of study. Though Kuhn applauded the expansion of women's rights and opportunities in the twentieth century, she suggested that those gains had been accompanied by a devaluing of the maternal role. During the antebellum era, when "every slightest mood and gesture of the mother was thought to be influential in the formation of child character" and her "incessant activity and vigilance . . . was believed essential to the carrying out of democratic purposes," middle-class mothers had entertained few doubts as to the importance of their task. In contrast, contemporary American mothers, charged with fomenting all manner of psychological and social ills, seemed to her to have adopted a "defeatist attitude" that distinguished them markedly from their predecessors. Though Kuhn had no desire to resurrect antebellum gender ideals, she closed by venturing, "One thing the mid-nineteenth century can surely offer the mid-twentieth is to suggest ways in which maternal self-confidence may be restored."[113]

The "feminine mystique" that flourished after World War II was indeed a far cry from the Victorian idealization of moral motherhood. For although experts and producers of popular culture repeatedly reminded mothers of the crucial role that they played in sustaining democracy, a deep suspicion of maternal influence underlay their exhortations. By the 1940s and 1950s, the fear of pathological "mother love" had grown so pronounced that the ideal mother tended to be defined negatively, with the emphasis falling on her ability to refrain from objectionable behaviors: she did not undermine her husband's authority, guilt-trip her children, pry into their personal lives, or look to them to meet her emotional or physical needs. As a result, even the mother who managed to raise successful, "mature," and well-adjusted children might be left with little sense of personal accomplishment. For if she believed the experts, once she had equipped her children with a sense of "security" during their very earliest years, her most important contribution had been to stay out of their way.

4

Banishing the Suffering Mother:
The Quest for Painless Childbirth

My friend once said to me . . . "My dear since last I saw you, you have been through the valley of the shadow of death. That is where we women go to get our children." And she was quite right. That is where we all go—that path our feet must tread. We enter upon it with high hearts, happily . . . but even with the most loving care, even with the most scientific aid, some of us never return. . . . Let us . . . take away the stain from our flag and hold out a hand of love and feeling and understanding to all the women who must tread that lonely path that so many of us here have trod.

MRS. THEODORE ROOSEVELT, speaking at a Mother's Day
luncheon hosted by the Maternity Centre Association, 1931

Wherever women are gathered together and the subject of childbirth arises, the general trend of the remarks is that childbirth is a martyrdom which, though probably best forgotten, is satisfactorily recalled with obvious pride.

GRANTLY DICK-READ, obstetrician and natural childbirth advocate, 1944

In her 1959 book, *Thank You, Dr. Lamaze*, Marjorie Karmel recounted her struggle to find an obstetrician willing to deliver her baby without anesthetics, and with her husband in attendance as her labor coach. Karmel had previously given birth in Paris using the Lamaze method, and she wanted to ensure that her second birth would be a similarly positive experience. Finally, she located an "elderly and distinguished" obstetrician in New York who agreed to her conditions. But when she and her husband sat down with him, they soon realized how radically his notion of "natural childbirth" differed from their own. As he reflected on how his practice had changed since the 1920s, when he had routinely delivered babies without recourse to medication, the doctor explained:

That's the way we were in my day. We believed in letting nature take its course. No pampering. . . . Women knew they had to suffer to bring forth and that was that. You shall bring forth in pain. No one tried to dodge the issue. Childbirth *is* painful. Now we know how to alleviate suffering somewhat. But is it really worth it? . . . Out of a woman's suffering springs her mother love.

The young couple nodded politely and fled as quickly as possible, dissolving into laughter once they reached the street. The next day, Karmel phoned the

doctor's office with a concocted excuse as to why they would not be employing his services after all. For in light of his "philosophical convictions of forty
years standing," she felt it would be futile to attempt to explain that her own,
more recently acquired convictions allowed her to anticipate a delivery that
would be at once "natural" and *painless*.[1]

The chasm in perspective that separated Karmel from the elderly obstetrician reflected seismic shifts in the experience and representation of
childbearing in twentieth-century America. In truth, very few doctors in the
1950s (or even the 1920s) would have asserted that mother love sprang from
childbirth suffering. But until the 1940s, childbirth continued to be widely regarded as an intensely painful, debilitating, and potentially life-threatening
ordeal. Some obstetricians promoted this perspective for reasons at least
partially self-serving, as it helped to justify their interventions and enhance
their professional prestige.[2] But the association between childbearing and
suffering also reflected long-standing cultural traditions and demographic
realities. Until maternal death rates began to decline precipitously in the mid
to late 1930s, childbirth retained its aura of sacrifice, as evidenced by the religious language and martial analogies used to characterize the experience. Just
as the soldier risked life and limb for his country, so the childbearing woman
bravely descended into "the valley of the shadow of death" to bring forth the
nation's future citizens.

By the late 1930s, however, a growing number of obstetricians, writers, and
mothers themselves had begun to challenge this view of childbirth by depicting it as a wholly "normal" and "natural" event. While fascists like Mussolini
continued to proclaim that "war is to man what maternity is to woman,"
Americans increasingly adopted the view of British obstetrician and natural
birth advocate Grantly Dick-Read, who argued that "pregnancy should be as
normal for a woman as wage-earning is for a man."[3] Especially after World
War II, experts and popular writers assured women that modern medicine,
equipped with its arsenal of safe and effective anesthetic techniques, had made
giving birth almost as routine as a trip to the dentist. More radically still, a
small but influential group of childbirth reformers joined Read in asserting
that *without* anesthesia, childbirth could be the most pleasurable experience
of a woman's life. In either case, whether medicalized or naturalized, childbearing ceased to be viewed as an act of painful self-sacrifice, and birthing
women lost their status as pitiable yet courageous martyrs.

The normalization of childbirth in the 1940s and 1950s helped to fuel,
but was also fueled by, the broad cultural shifts this book has traced. As the
previous chapter illustrated, postwar childrearing experts largely repudiated the ideal of maternal self-sacrifice by recasting maternal obligations as

sources of feminine fulfillment. But for motherhood to be truly modernized, with the emphasis shifted from self-sacrifice toward self-realization, child-birth itself had to be transformed from a dangerous and dreaded ordeal into an exhilarating experience. The decline in maternal deaths was no doubt a necessary precondition for such a reorientation. Yet even as medical developments helped to render the figure of the suffering mother anachronistic, so the widespread repudiation of that ideal influenced medical thinking and practice. The cultural assault on the moral mother can be detected not only in mainstream obstetrics, with its heavy reliance on anesthesia and analgesia, but also in the postwar natural childbirth movement that arose to challenge standard obstetrical procedures. For in both cases, physicians and childbearing women themselves pledged to banish not only pain and suffering but also maternal martyrdom and the burdens of guilt and indebtedness that it implied.

Pain and Suffering: Childbearing before the 1940s

The history of American childbirth prior to the 1940s is one of enormous change and surprising continuity. Over the course of two centuries, as Judith Walzer Leavitt and other historians have detailed, childbearing evolved from a bodily and spiritual trial overseen by women into a medical procedure controlled by men.[4] This transformation originated in the mid-eighteenth century, when a few elite women began enlisting male physicians instead of midwives to attend their births. By 1930, physicians attended roughly 85 percent of all births, with midwifery persisting only in the rural South and Southwest and within some urban immigrant communities.[5] Yet medicine's triumph over childbirth was still far from complete. As late as the mid-1930s, more than half of all births occurred in private homes, and high maternal mortality rates continued to shame the medical profession. In fact, the rise in hospital births did not initially lead to fewer maternal deaths; if anything, women who gave birth in hospitals during the 1920s and early 1930s faced *greater* risks than those who delivered at home.[6] "To every nubile woman," *Time* magazine observed in 1936, childbirth "still evokes the Lord's words to sinful Eve: 'I will greatly multiply thy sorrow and thy conception. In sorrow thou shall bring forth children.'"[7] Thus, despite the dramatic changes wrought by medicalization, childbearing continued to conjure up images of suffering, debilitation, and even death well into the twentieth century.

Basic assumptions about the essential nature of childbirth also endured, even as anesthesia, first introduced in obstetrics in 1847, altered the childbearing experiences of many middle-class women. Euro-Americans had long indulged in racial fantasies about Native American and slave women who gave birth with ease, and some antebellum health reformers disputed the notion that labor pain was natural or inevitable.[8] But most nineteenth-century Americans simply assumed that childbirth entailed severe pain. Some physicians and moralists continued to insist that childbed suffering was the price women paid for Eve's transgression. For instance, when the social scientist Lorine Pruette's mother gave birth in Tennessee in 1876, the doctor withheld chloroform on the grounds that childbearing women ought to suffer.[9] More typically, physicians viewed excruciating labor pain as a consequence of advancing "civilization," which they believed had caused affluent white women to become more sensitive and delicate. In either case, childbirth and suffering remained inextricably linked, even in the language of the times; as Martin Pernick has noted, nineteenth-century Americans used the same word—"pains"—to describe both labor contractions and the distressing physical sensations that accompanied them.[10]

Yet if assumptions about the painful nature of childbearing held constant, the meanings attributed to childbirth suffering evolved considerably over course of the nineteenth century. Victorian culture tended to accentuate the experience of childbirth suffering in ways that reflected the new ideal of refined "true womanhood" and the growing intensity of the mother-child bond. The term that colonial Americans used for labor—"travail"—"connoted not simply pain but effort, especially strenuous or self-sacrificing effort," according to historian Laurel Thatch Ulrich.[11] Yet by the 1830s, many elite and middle-class women had begun to refer to labor as a time of "sickness" or "illness," suggesting that they saw themselves more as victims of a pathological process.[12] Rather than a punishment to be endured, childbirth pain increasingly came to be construed as a torment that sanctified the sufferer, like Christ's trial on the cross. Both women and men described labor as an unparalleled form of suffering, and both portrayed it as the crucible from which "mother love" emerged.[13] Indeed, some doctors and clergymen went so far as to oppose the use of anesthesia in childbirth, claiming that it might diminish maternal devotion. As one physician expressed it, "The very suffering which a woman undergoes in labor is one of the strongest elements in the love she bears her offspring."[14]

Although middle- and upper-class women objected to this glorification of maternal pain, insisting that physicians had a moral obligation to dispense anesthesia, many nevertheless embraced the notion that childbearing was a painful, even pathological condition. Historian Sylvia Hoffert has argued that they did so in part because such a view fit their "preconceived notions about the process" and in part because displays of "delicacy" testified to their family's class status.[15] At the same time, the emphasis on maternal suffering appears to have afforded some affluent women a means of leverage within the family circle.[16] Whereas the colonial husband had been "presented" with his newborn—a term that underscored his superior "legal and moral right to the child"—the Victorian father tended to be depicted as a humble and grateful witness to his wife's agonizing ordeal.[17] The greater deference that nineteenth-century men displayed for maternal suffering helped women to control their fertility while also allowing them to assume a more proprietary stance toward their children. Of course, the ideology of moral motherhood left women with no recourse, save further martyrdom, when husbands refused to follow the approved cultural script. But given the reality of women's subordinate status and the real risks associated with childbearing in the nineteenth century, it is hardly surprising that many middle-class and elite women not only accepted the association between motherhood and physical suffering but also attempted to use it to their advantage.

Accolades to maternal suffering assumed a more political cast in the late nineteenth and early twentieth centuries, as conservatives and progressives alike increasingly portrayed motherhood as a civic obligation that women rendered unto the state. In 1903, President Theodore Roosevelt declared, "The woman who has had a child has that claim to regard which we give to the soldier . . . who does a great and indispensable service which involves pain and discomfort, self-abnegation, and the incurring of risk of life."[18] When Governor Marion E. Hay of Washington proclaimed Mother's Day a state holiday in 1910, he struck a similar tone, urging every citizen to wear a white flower "in acknowledgment and honor of the one who went down into the valley of the shadow of death for us."[19] At the same time, progressive reformers emphasized maternal pain and suffering to advocate such causes as mothers' pensions, funding for maternal health initiatives, birth control, and even suffrage. Whether expressed by traditionalists who hoped to shore up sentimental ideals of motherhood, or by progressives who sought to advance women's status, an appreciation of the pain and peril of maternity formed the emotional core of maternalist ideology.

Of course, this is not to suggest that Americans accepted the inevitability of maternal suffering and death. During the twentieth century, agonizing labor pain and maternal mortality increasingly came to be viewed as inexcusable travesties rather than inescapable tragedies. In 1914, a group of middle- and upper-class clubwomen founded the National Twilight Sleep Association to assert women's right to experience "painless childbirth" through the use of a new obstetrical technique pioneered in Germany.[20] According to its proponents, twilight sleep, induced by combination of morphine and the amnesiac scopolamine, obliterated all memory of childbirth and allowed women to awaken from the experience feeling refreshed and vigorous. Although the movement quickly unraveled after one of its leaders died during a twilight sleep birth, it nevertheless helped to promote the idea that women had a right to demand—and physicians the obligation to provide—pain relief during childbirth, as well as the notion that an ideal birth was a wholly unconscious one.

In the interwar period, medical literature and the popular press grew more emphatic in urging physicians who attended childbearing women to intervene to alleviate pain. The extent to which childbearing women actually received anesthesia and analgesia is difficult to determine, but contemporary accounts suggest that, as late as the 1930s, a majority of American women still delivered their babies with no pain relief at all.[21] This helps to explain the crusading tone that informed much writing on the topic. "Modern obstetrics not only includes but demands analgesia and anesthesia," the obstetrician C. O. McCormick argued in a 1933 article in the *American Journal of Nursing*. "Shock prevention and surgical asepsis make it imperative, and with the mental and physical ordeal of childbirth increasing as civilization advances, the humanitarian demand can no longer be ignored."[22] In 1935, an article in the same journal observed that experiences over the past decade had proven conclusively that pain relief could be provided without risk to either mother or baby "and in fact with beneficial results to both." Noting the wide range of anesthetic options, the authors advocated techniques that rendered women wholly unconscious, resulting in "complete relief of suffering from the very onset of labor, throughout its entire course, and for several hours following delivery."[23] Articles in popular women's magazines during the 1930s echoed this view; for instance, the childbirth reformer Constance Todd, writing for *Good Housekeeping* in 1937, praised techniques that allowed women to deliver in a state of "complete oblivion," with "the whole period of labor . . . wiped out of consciousness."[24] Although many physicians objected to such heavy reliance on medication, medical literature and the popular press alike increasingly depicted the "complete relief of suffering" during childbirth as a realistic and desirable ideal.

Physicians who promoted such techniques during the interwar period tended to regard childbirth as a pathological process, comparable to a surgical operation. One of the nation's most prominent obstetricians, Joseph B. DeLee, famously described childbirth as a "pathologic process" that left "only a small minority of women" undamaged. "So frequent are these bad effects," he wrote in 1920, "that I have often wondered whether Nature did not deliberately intend women should be used up in the process of reproduction, in a manner analogous to that of salmon which dies after spawning."[25] Similarly, a Yale physiology professor explained to listeners of a 1931 radio address, "Child-bearing is an illness of nine months, requiring constant care and supervision; then an episode as grave as a surgical operation, needing as excellent medical care; and finally a period of convalescence, as from an operation, lasting several weeks."[26] Popular writers frequently admonished women that, if they failed to appreciate the medical risks associated childbirth, they could face the most dire of consequences. "While motherhood is a natural event in the life of a woman, it may not be normal; many abnormalities and complications may arise that demand expert medical care," an article in the journal *Hygeia* warned in 1937. "The public must realize that death may be the price for negligence."[27]

Indeed, the maternal death rate remained alarmingly high in the 1920s and 1930s, even as the medical profession succeeded in combating death and disease from a wide range of other causes. Maternal mortality gained widespread recognition as a public health problem beginning in 1917, when Grace Meigs of the Children's Bureau published a study demonstrating maternity to be the second leading cause of death for American women between the ages of fifteen and forty-five. (Only tuberculosis claimed more victims.)[28] In 1915, 61 women died per 10,000 live births; throughout the 1920s, the rate fluctuated between 65 to 70 deaths per 10,000 live births.[29] This meant that roughly one woman died for every 150 births, amounting to about 15,000 deaths per year nationwide. (By way of comparison, the maternal death rate today is one per 10,000 births.)[30] Moreover, official statistics almost certainly underestimated the extent of the problem, since physicians tended to attribute maternal death to other causes when the victim had suffered from preexisting conditions.[31] Although maternal mortality began to decline incrementally in the early 1930s and rapidly in the late 1930s, experts remained unsure as to whether they were witnessing a permanent downward trend. "Is this temporary good luck or is childbirth actually becoming safer in the United States?" pondered obstetrician Alan Guttmacher in 1937. "We do not know; the next ten years will tell."[32]

Throughout the 1920s and 1930s, government agencies, nonprofit organizations, and the press worked to draw public attention to the problem of maternal mortality. Articles in leading newspapers and women's magazines routinely decried the fact that the United States had one of the highest maternal mortality rates among industrialized nations. At times, discussions of the issue assumed a melodramatic and alarmist tone. For instance, in 1936, the *Ladies' Home Journal* ran a high-profile series, entitled "Why Should Women Die?" that relied on somewhat misleading statistics to portray the "profession of motherhood" as "more dangerous than that of soldiering." "In the past twenty-five years, 375,000 of our women have died from pregnancy and childbirth, while in all our country's wars since the Declaration of Independence, only 244,000 men were killed in battle," asserted the author, popular science writer Paul de Kruif.[33] (In fact, some 620,000 men died in the Civil War alone, though the majority had succumbed due to disease.) In 1940, the U.S. Film Service released a docudrama about childbirth, *The Fight for Life*, that opened with a harrowing scene of childbirth death; one reviewer found the film so "grueling ... to watch" that he suggested, "possibly women should not see it at all."[34]

This pervasive fear of maternal death led both physicians and the broader public to view childbirth as a debilitating medical event that required a lengthy convalescence. From the nineteenth century through the 1940s, obstetrics textbooks advised a minimum of nine days complete bed rest after delivery, based on the mistaken belief that early ambulation increased the risk of thromboembolism (blot clots) and uterine prolapse.[35] In the 1920s and 1930s, women who gave birth in hospitals typically remained hospitalized for fourteen days, with private patients often staying even longer.[36] Maternity wards adhered to a rigid protocol, according to historian Judith Walzer Leavitt: "Women stayed in bed exactly 10 days following the delivery, they dangled their legs on the 11th day, they sat in a chair on the 12th day, they walked on the 13th, and went home on the 14th."[37] The obstetrician Alan Guttmacher, writing in 1937, reported that some doctors allowed "completely normal patients" to sit in a chair on the eighth day postpartum, whereas more conservative practitioners kept all patients confined to bed for a minimum of two weeks. Upon release from the hospital, he noted, new mothers were advised to avoid climbing stairs for another week, to remain housebound for at least a full month, and to refrain from driving for six weeks.[38]

The same guidelines that structured hospital procedures also helped to determine the care of women who experienced home deliveries. Throughout the first third of the twentieth century, many prosperous families hired live-in nurses or domestic servants to assist after childbirth, absolving women of household duties for several weeks or even longer. Consider the case of Violet D'Arcy Muriel, the wife of a New England businessman who gave birth to her third child in 1908. On October 29, Muriel's labor commenced with "*very bad pains*" at 2 a.m. and progressed so quickly that the doctor and nurse barely arrived in time for the delivery. Though she suffered "after-pains" and sore nipples in the following days, within a week she could record in her diary, "Things began to settle down although its still hurts me to nurse

Baby." Nevertheless, it would be another full week before Muriel "sat up out of bed." On November 20, she recorded feeling "very glad" that her husband John had arranged for a Miss Johnson—presumably a nurse—to stay for an additional three weeks. Two days later, she wrote, "John carried me down to the drawing room: we had a fine time."[39] In other words, a full three weeks after an uncomplicated birth, neither Muriel nor her husband believed her capable of descending the stairs, let alone resuming her domestic responsibilities.

Similarly, Gladys Whitney Neil, a resident of Pittsford, Vermont, was still being attentively nursed two weeks after giving birth to her first child on January 10, 1921. Within three days, she felt wonderful; the entry that she later recorded in her diary for January 13 reads: "Our nurse takes good care of my little angel and me, we are living in the only heaven there is on earth." Four days after the birth, she sat up in bed and did some writing; on the fifth day, she had her hair combed; on the sixth day, she ate her dinner at a little table. On the tenth day postpartum, she dressed, played cards, and held her baby "quite a lot," and on the eleventh day, she ventured downstairs for the first time. At two weeks, she washed and dressed the baby herself and took her midday meal downstairs. But that evening, the nurse dissuaded Neil from returning downstairs for supper; instead, she bathed her, gave her an enema, and put her to bed. Though Neil appeared physically well and in the best of spirits, she continued to be treated as a patient who required rest and attentive care.[40]

Nor were such lengthy confinements limited to the elite. In 1931, Helen Berklich, a working-class Minnesotan who gave birth to her first child at home, attended by both a doctor and a midwife, recalled: "And then you had to stay in bed 10 days you know. You couldn't even breathe for 10 days, you had to stay in bed."[41] African-American midwives who practiced in Virginia during the 1920s and 1930s insisted that new mothers spend between nine days and three weeks confined to bed in a darkened room, as anthropologist Gertrude Jacinta Fraser has shown, followed by another two to four weeks during which they adhered to special dietary restrictions and limited their activities to the house and yard.[42] Similarly, Mexican-American midwives followed the tradition of *dietá*, in which newly delivered mothers stayed in bed for eight days, remained in the house for two weeks, and for forty days avoided certain foods and slept separately from their husbands.[43] Of course, many poor and working-class women had no choice but to resume work soon after giving birth. But across the lines of class and race, interwar Americans viewed childbirth as a debilitating affair that should ideally be followed by a period of extended convalescence.[44]

Such attitudes came to be widely challenged in the 1940s, as numerous experts, writers, and childbearing women themselves began to portray childbirth as a wholly "normal" and "natural" experience. This transitional moment, when the tendency to view childbirth as inherently pathological began to wane, can be glimpsed in an article that appeared in *Parents' Magazine* in 1940. Like many prior articles, "New Techniques in Childbirth" described childbirth pain as "unendurable" and lauded the "infinitely kinder" hospital methods that rendered women completely unconscious during delivery. Yet while this depiction of modern medicine as the solution to childbirth agony sounded familiar themes, the article concluded in a manner that suggested newer tendencies on the horizon: "Looking back, you may not be able to say, as does a friend of mine, 'I'd much rather have a baby than a bad cold!' But with science on your side and confidence in your heart, you are certain to find it an interesting, not-too-uncomfortable experience that proves to be 100 percent worth while."[45] All of these assertions—that a woman could remain dispassionate enough to deem her labor "interesting," that childbirth could entail mere discomfort rather than pain, and that the experience of giving birth might be favorably compared to that of suffering a bad cold—would have seemed quite novel in 1940. But within a decade, such claims would be ubiquitous.

Normalizing Childbirth

In the late 1930s, and increasingly in the 1940s and 1950s, a variety of critics, acting from very different motives, began to dispute the notion that childbearing entailed immense suffering and sacrifice. On the one hand, a small number of women downplayed the pain of "normal" or "natural" childbirth because they objected to the growing reliance on anesthesia, which they regarded as both physically and emotionally harmful. On the other hand, antimaternalist commentators like Philip Wylie pointed to the increasing availability of anesthesia in order to challenge widely shared views of childbirth. The idea that childbearing women risked their lives and braved extraordinary pain, they argued, no longer reflected social and medical realties, but had instead become a weapon in the battle of the sexes. These critics did not seek to improve women's birthing experiences; on the contrary, they sought to liberate *men*, whom they saw as vulnerable to guilt and manipulation. Around the same time, many obstetricians discarded prior notions of childbearing as an inherently pathological process. Particularly after World War II, they portrayed childbirth as a wholly "natural" event that neither exacted a heavy physical toll nor necessitated a prolonged confinement. Thus, as with the broader assault on moral motherhood, the repudiation of maternal suffering included protofeminist, deeply misogynist, and medical strains, which over-lapped and intersected in complicated ways.

In the mid to late 1930s, a few individuals began to criticize medicalized birthing practices in ways that anticipated the postwar natural childbirth movement. For instance, Dr. Gertrude Nielsen, a middle-aged mother of three—all delivered "without the use of modern painless methods"—pas-sionately denounced "painless childbirth" during a session of the American Medical Association's 1936 convention. The session featured several presen-tations on new techniques in obstetrical anesthesia and analgesia. In one, the presenters reported on their use of a mixture of paraldehyde and benzyl alcohol, which had successfully eradicated all memory of childbirth in 90 percent of their cases. Appalled by this complete erasure of the birth event, Nielsen spoke out during the discussion period that followed. "Childbearing is so essential an experience for a woman that the thwarting of its normal course through the excessive use of analgesics may cause great damage to her personality," she argued. Obstetricians could better assist women by striving to allay fears instilled by "sensational magazine articles" that grossly exag-gerated the pain of childbirth. Nielsen's comments clearly struck a nerve, for they received extensive coverage in the mainstream press; the *New York Times* carried a front-page story about the controversy she ignited, and *Time* quoted her at length in a cover story entitled "Nature v. Drugs."[46]

Soon thereafter, a few women began to publish testimonials in which they portrayed unmedicated childbirth as a wholly bearable and profoundly meaningful experience. In 1939, the *American Mercury* ran an article by a mother of four who criticized "'painless' methods" as "often dangerous and cowardly." "Normal birth can be a relatively easy process—if you can learn how to take it," she argued. "Women can enjoy the birth of their children to the full, physically, mentally, and emotionally. It is their right to participate in the greatest thing that happens in their lives." The writer did not deny that childbirth hurt, but she favorably compared the pain of labor to that of a bad toothache or headache. "There is even (and I am prepared for sneers)," she added, "a certain ecstasy in it."[47] That same year, a woman named Lenore Friedrich published an account of her experience with "natural birth" in the *Atlantic Monthly*. Unable to locate an obstetrician in the United States willing to deliver her baby without recourse to anesthesia, Friedrich had traveled to Switzerland to bear her fourth child. While she labored, her physician related tales of his formative years as a country doctor, when he had had to "toil on foot through the snow, hour after hour up the mountainsides." "To such a man a little 'suffering' does not seem very important," Friedrich wrote, "and with him you find yourself being brave."[48] While these women celebrated birth as an "exhilarating" and "ecstatic" moment, they also normalized the physical experience of labor by comparing it to more mundane types of bodily suffering—suffering endured by men as well as women.

Many women who encountered such views in newspapers and magazine articles responded with outrage. Invoking long-standing analogies that likened birthing women to wounded soldiers or Christ on the cross, they argued that maternal suffering should at the very least be acknowledged and respected. One "Old-Fashioned Mother," who noted that her own "agony" would always "bring a shudder," allowed that it might be preferable to refrain from using pain-relieving medications for reasons of safety. "But for heaven's sake, don't minimize the mother's pain," she insisted. "Let that, at least, stand to her credit."[49] Another woman wrote that Nielsen's claims were "enough to infuriate a woman who has spent fifty hours in child-birth" and known "pain that is a crucifixion."[50] Yet another respondent argued, "Medical history tells us more than I can read without a shudder about childbirth in the days before anaesthetics. It is comparable to the sufferings of wounded men in the same period."[51] In the 1930s, the assertion that childbearing women could forgo medication without suffering extraordinary pain struck many American women as not just ludicrous but downright offensive.

Prior to the 1940s, even hard-core motherhood debunkers often paused to acknowledge the reality of maternal suffering. For instance, when a writer mocked the tradition of Mothers' Day in a 1932 *Literary Digest* article, he opened with the caveat: "It should be said at the outset, however, that one important feature of Mothers' Day, often forgotten, is to call attention to those thousands of mothers who annually die in childbirth for lack of proper care and attention."[52] Likewise, in *The Influence of Women and Its Cure*, an acerbic account of American social life published in 1936, John Erskine grudgingly allowed that "the danger and agony of child-bearing, especially in those regions which lack proper medical care, are still so great that no man can withhold his respect for the woman who by intention has a second child."[53] So long as maternal mortality remained a pressing problem, and many women continued to give birth without anesthesia, very few Americans questioned the assumption that childbearing women braved great pain and danger.

The 1940s and 1950s, however, witnessed dramatic improvements in maternal health that helped to alter Americans' attitudes toward childbearing. Over the course of the 1940s, the maternal mortality rate fell more rapidly than ever before or since, declining from 37.6 deaths per 10,000 births in 1940 to 8.3 deaths per 10,000 births in 1950.[54] At the same time, the percentage of hospital births rose sharply: whereas only 55 percent of all American births took place in hospitals in 1940, hospital births accounted for 88 percent of total births in 1950. By 1960, only a small percentage of women living in rural areas continued to give birth in their own homes.[55] The trend toward hospital births also meant that an increasing percentage of women received some form of anesthesia or analgesia. After World War II, the general sentiment, expressed in both medical journals and the popular press, was that modern medicine had finally conquered the age-old problem of childbed suffering and death.

As childbirth became notably safer, and as the medical profession consolidated its control over the process, obstetricians increasingly rejected the notion that pregnancy and childbirth constituted pathological states. "The first thing that should be particularly impressed upon a patient is that she is undergoing a purely physiologic and not a pathologic condition," Clifford B. Lull and Robert A. Hingson argued in *Control of Pain in Childbirth*, a leading obstetrical textbook reissued in 1948. "Too many women think that when they become pregnant they have been stricken down by disease, whereas the chief role of womanhood is to bear children."[56] Some physicians, influenced by the rise of psychosomatic medicine and the growing prestige of psychoanalysis, even began to attribute labor pain to psychological factors. As early as 1936, the *American Journal of Obstetrics and Gynecology* carried an article by the psychiatrist F. W. Dershimer that traced the suffering of "civilized" women to their "emotional attitudes." "Society in general," he complained, made "every possible effort to prevent the pregnant woman from accepting pregnancy and labor as a natural physiologic function"; as a result, women tended to view of pregnancy and birth as a "martyrdom" for which "both their husbands and children would be eternally indebted to them."[57] Though many obstetricians remained skeptical of the psychosomatic paradigm, such arguments became commonplace in both medical journals and the popular press during the 1940s and 1950s. According to numerous experts, a woman's unconscious rejection of femininity could easily disrupt her sexual and reproductive life, resulting in disorders ranging from "frigidity" to infertility.[58]

The normalization of childbirth and the rise of psychosomatic medicine emboldened antimaternalist critics like Wylie, who increasingly attributed women's pain and suffering to either unconscious conflict or conscious manipulation. In *Generation of Vipers*, Wylie argued that American women perpetuated an obsolete view of childbearing as an "unnatural and hideous ordeal" to gain "respite from all other physical and social responsibility," despite the fact that "modern medical practice" could usually transform the experience into "no more of a hardship than, say, a few months of benign tumor plus a couple of hours in a dental chair."[59] The journalist Ferdinand

Lundberg and psychiatrist Marynia Farnham went even further in their 1946 polemic *Modern Woman: The Lost Sex*, dismissing the notion of " 'agony in childbirth' " as a "pet fantasy" promoted by man-hating feminists. "Today, of course, the free use of anesthesia has made the actual delivery often into a bagatelle from the point of view of pain felt," they wrote. Even without anesthesia, "Many women in their twenties and thirties, healthy physically and psychologically, effect delivery . . . with minimum pain and discomfort."[60] No longer constrained by the indisputable reality of maternal suffering, some extremists questioned whether pregnancy and childbirth exacted *any* sort of physical toll.

As perceptions of childbirth itself evolved, so, too, did practices and attitudes surrounding postpartum recovery. As late as 1940, articles in women's magazines emphasized that hospital births had the advantage of assuring new mothers "two weeks free from domestic cares."[61] But during World War II, overcrowding and a severe nursing shortage forced hospitals to curtail postpartum stays, sometimes to a mere two or three days.[62] Medical research soon validated protocols adopted for reasons of expediency; in 1944, the *Journal of the American Medical Association* published a study that showed that women who walked within three to four days of birth fared *better* than those who remained bedridden the standard ten to twelve days.[63] Although the average hospital stay lengthened again to about five or six days after World War II (roughly half that of the prewar norm), maternity wards never reinstituted the severe restrictions on mobility. After decades of counseling prolonged bed rest, obstetricians reversed course and began to portray childbirth as a normal biological process that, barring complications, required a recovery period of only a few days.[64]

Physicians and popular writers also increasingly rejected the notion that middle-class and elite women required particularly attentive and indulgent care, given their presumably more delicate and refined nature. In 1914, a physician quoted in *Good Housekeeping* had argued that, though "some leather-nerved and slow-witted woman" might resume work soon after childbirth, most women—and certainly "those of the more intelligent and highly developed types"—needed a minimum of ten to fifteen days of complete bed rest.[65] In contrast, at the 1947 annual Congress of Obstetrics and Gynecology, William F. Mengert, chief of obstetrics at the Southwestern Medical Foundation, urged his fellow practitioners to abandon "the practice of making [new] mothers feel they're ill and need lots of attention" by having their patients rise from bed soon after giving birth. As Mengert explained, his experience working on a segregated maternity ward, where he had observed African-American women "sneaking out of bed to do the family wash" a day or two after giving birth, had convinced him that new mothers did not need an extended period of recovery.[66] Thus, whereas physicians in the nineteenth and early twentieth centuries had maintained that the needs of "civilized" women could *not* be compared to those of working-class women or women of color, many experts in the 1940s and 1950s suggested that the birth experiences of racial and cultural "others" held important lessons that could be applied to white, middle-class American women. Though such arguments reflected the discrediting of scientific racism within medicine and the social sciences during the 1940s and 1950s—in the sense that they assumed all women experienced childbirth similarly—they nonetheless perpetuated noxious racial assumptions. Mengert, for instance, evoked a stereotypical image of African-American women that thoroughly effaced their own experiences of pain and suffering.

As these sources suggest, changing attitudes toward childbirth reflected not only actual improvements in maternal health but also broader shifts in gender and racial ideologies that undermined the image of white women as frail victims in need of chivalrous male protection. Indeed, in the 1940s and 1950s, some experts and commentators even began suggesting that husbands could become the real victims of childbirth. "Many women, after giving birth to a child, feel as though they have done their bit for the rest of their lives," Drs. Edward Weiss and O. Spurgeon English cautioned in *Psychosomatic Medicine*. "They 'never get their strength back' because they never wanted to assume very much responsibility in the first place," and they used their alleged weakness to "live a thoroughly self-centered life," avoiding "marital responsibilities such as sexual intercourse."[67] In 1950, one physician conveyed similar ideas directly to his patient, who recorded his comments in a lengthy diary that she kept during her pregnancy. "He said many women like to use the pain of labor as a weapon for beating their husbands;" she wrote, "that for some men this is such a terrible experience that it may be said that the father has been lost, since it is something he can never forget, or remember with peace of mind; and since it makes some men dread intercourse and even abjure it."[68] Clearly, these physicians feared that women who assumed the role of invalid or maternal martyr might effeminize their husbands, reducing them solicitous caregivers deprived of their sexual prerogatives.[69]

To avoid such threats to masculinity and paternal authority, experts cautioned husbands not to treat their pregnant wives in an overly solicitous manner. In their 1951 book, *Fathers are People, Too*, O. Spurgeon English and coauthor Constance Foster warned readers that some women believed "they were making an extraordinary contribution to society—doing it a favor—in giving birth to a child." The authors counseled husbands to prevent their wives from developing such unreasonable views by adopting and enforcing a matter-of-fact attitude toward childbearing. "The prospective father can be thoroughly considerate of his wife during her pregnancy and still not encourage her in any such unsound attitude," they wrote. "He is justified in taking for granted the normality of the processes of pregnancy and childbirth, and expecting her to do likewise."[70] Foster and English thus explicitly rejected the claims of early twentieth-century maternalists who had argued that childbearing *did* constitute "an extraordinary contribution to society." More insidiously, they encouraged men to view their wives' health complaints with skepticism, as potentially manipulative attempts to gain attention or shirk responsibilities.

Remarkably, some women adopted virtually the same language in seeking to dispel widely held assumptions about childbirth suffering. In 1937, the *American Mercury* published an article by a woman who, after giving birth to her first child, had come to believe that "all this talk about what women 'go through' to bear children is just so much bunk." As if seeking to bust up a corrupt political machine, she proclaimed it high time "that someone exposed this motherhood racket." Women played the victim card so convincingly, she argued, that most men had been completely "taken in" by their act. As a case in point, she noted that her own husband had heard such terrible stories from his mother and sister that he expected the entire nine months of her pregnancy to be period of "horrible agony." Yet she did not suffer from morning sickness, continued to work during the first trimester, and experienced no labor pains "severe enough to make me cry out." "After all the hysterical talk I had heard from women about having babies," she concluded, "I could hardly believe that this was all there was to it." While this woman disputed the notion that childbirth reduced women to afflicted invalids, her critique clearly had an antimaternalist rather than a feminist inflection, for she did not address the fact that employers routinely fired pregnant women, nor did she criticize men who treated childbearing women in a paternalistic manner. Instead, she positioned herself as men's ally and defender: "If anyone gets the worst of it in child-birth, it is the father," she asserted, noting that her husband now had "to struggle from daylight till dark" to support her and the baby. For those women who fashioned themselves maternal martyrs, she had only contempt. "The next time I hear a mother telling a son about 'all I have gone through for your sake,'" she wrote, "I am going to laugh in her face."[71]

A number of Philip Wylie's fans spurned the role of the suffering mother in equally emphatic terms. Writing in 1946, one woman avidly embraced his momism critique, even though doing so compelled her to acknowledge that she felt "utterly and completely useless." "Unless I sit and tell myself I 'gave the best years of my life to my husband' and 'went down into the valley of the shadow of death' for my sons, I can't see what earthly use they have for me," she confessed. "But—my husband gave me the best years of my life, and I had deliveries as safe and practically as quickly as any alley cat's. And I've never been one to kid myself."[72] Another fan of *Generation of Vipers*, who wrote in 1945, debunked popular notions of childbed suffering in even more acerbic terms. Expanding on Wylie's harsh denunciation of middle-aged moms, she added:

> We don't expect whelps to adore the bitch that produced them. Why, then, expect human young to adore the—I almost said "bitches"—that brought them forth? (And that goes for me, too.) Why assume that because a woman has had a child, said child must spend the rest of its mother's days circumspectly bowing to her every whim, supplying her needs and being labeled "unfilial" if, because of some streak of individualism, it doesn't?[73]

This woman presumably advocated a healthier, more natural view of childbirth as a way of liberating children from the clutches of their unreasonable mothers. Yet the intensely hostile nature of her remarks suggests a deeply personal investment in the issue. While she appeared to be disavowing any expectation of "adulation" from her own child, her parenthetical comment could also be read a different way—as an assertion that she, too, should be free of her own mother's excessive demands. Indeed, the fact that this passage appears in a letter originally addressed to her mother, which on second thought she sent to Wylie instead, suggests that she harbored repressed hostility toward her mother, which found expression in a more general anti-maternalist diatribe.

The growing suspicion of maternal suffering expressed by commentators, experts, and even some women themselves should not be taken as evidence that people suddenly began to treat pregnant and childbearing wives less kindly. But such sources do underscore the fact that American culture shifted away from depicting childbearing women as suffering victims during the 1940s and 1950s, while displaying greater concern for the role of the expectant father.[74] This is best illustrated in what was no doubt the era's most famous depiction of a couple preparing for childbirth, Lucy and Desi Arnaz of the popular television show, *I Love Lucy*. The 1953 episode "Lucy Goes to the Hospital," which drew an estimated 44 million viewers—the largest in the history of the new medium—won praise from reviewers for portraying childbirth as "one of the most natural and normal things in the world."[75] In truth, the episode focuses much more on Desi's emotional journey toward fatherhood than on Lucy's physical and emotional journey toward mother-hood. When it is time to head to the hospital, Lucy remains serenely calm, while Desi falls into a state of panic. By the time they arrive at the reception desk, Lucy is carrying her own bag, while her hapless husband, having fainted, is being pushed in a wheelchair. The message seemed clear: now that science had conquered the age-old fear of maternal death, mothers could face childbirth without anxiety, even if their husbands could not. The final shot of Lucy, which occurs midway through the episode, shows her taking leave of Desi after imploring a nurse to "take care of him."[76] Of course, the humor of the scene is premised on the audience's faith in what will happen next—on its confidence that modern medicine now virtually guaranteed Lucy a safe and humane delivery. Ironically, it was this very assumption that thousands of middle-class women had already begun to question.

Natural Childbirth in Postwar America

In 1952, a woman from Bakersfield, California, wrote to Philip Wylie, detailing how her obstetrician—"a doctor of excellent reputation and one whom I trusted"—had ignored her expressed desires concerning her labor and delivery. As she explained:

> I had talked with him on a number of occasions about the anesthetic he planned to use. I made it clear to him that I had had my first child with some demerol . . . and some gas. The first birth was an exciting and thrilling experience and I hoped to have even less anesthetic the second time. I was very emphatic with the doctor about this. . . . I also told him I wanted a conscious delivery. He assured me I would be conscious. There could have been no opportunity for him to misunderstand.

Nevertheless, toward the end of her labor, the doctor ordered an injection—which the nurse described as "only something to relax me"—that caused her to lose consciousness. She awoke six hours later feeling sore, with no recollection of birth. Only through "insistent questioning" did she and her husband learn that the injection contained Demerol and scopolamine, the amnesiac used to produce twilight sleep. The scopolamine had caused her to become so agitated that she had proven impossible to control in the delivery room. "If I had been deprived only of the conscious delivery of my baby and the first show of my husband's pride, it would not have been so tragic, although still unfortunate," she concluded, "but the physical injuries I received, the details of which I will spare you, have caused me extreme discomfort and mental anguish. I have had to limit the size of my family because of them." By conveying her story, this woman hoped to encourage Wylie to investigate and expose the continued use of scopolamine, for she suspected that many obstetricians dispensed the drug without their patients' knowledge or consent.[77]

Four years after this woman's traumatic birth experience, a young woman named Maria Elena Ortega gave birth under similarly appalling yet radically different circumstances. Ortega, who would later work as an organizer for the United Farm Workers in California, was born in Brownsville, Texas, and grew up in the Rio Grande valley. Married at age fourteen, she delivered her first child the following year in a small hospital in Post, Texas. As Ortega recounted in an oral interview, she experienced a "natural childbirth." But she did not use this term in the way that it had come to be defined by the dominant culture—as a birthing technique in which women chose to forgo anesthetics (or rely only drugs that did not dramatically dull consciousness) in order to experience the thrill of childbirth. Rather, Ortega described her birth as "natural" because the doctor had cruelly withheld pain relief to teach his adolescent patient "what motherhood was": "[H]e said that he knew I could have a normal childbirth and that he was not going to give me any medication because he wanted me to experience what it was so next time I would think, whenever I wanted a child." As she recalled, the birth was "painful, very, very painful."[78] In an era when middle-class women could not rest assured that physicians would heed their requests for minimal medication during childbirth, poor and nonwhite women could not assume that doctors would dispense the pain relief they needed or desired.[79]

While the first story points to the experiences that lay behind the emergence of the natural childbirth movement of the 1940s and 1950s, the second helps to explain the movement's limited appeal outside of the white middle class. Beginning in the early 1950s, small groups of well-educated, middle-class women began to found organizations in cities throughout the nation to promote natural childbirth and "family-centered maternity care."[80] Such groups condemned standard birthing practices, including what they regarded as physicians' excessive reliance on anesthesia, while also calling for a more central role for husbands in the birthing process. One such organization, the Boston Association of Childbirth Education (BACE), founded in 1953, defined its mission as preparing the prospective mother for "a birth in which she is a conscious participant, a birth which is a genuinely satisfying physical, emotional and spiritual experience, and one in which her husband also shares."[81] To achieve this end, BACE and similar groups designed and ran childbirth courses, often out of private homes, that taught women the basic physiology of pregnancy and childbirth as well as exercises to prepare for labor. Although instructors did not dogmatically insist that childbearing women renounce all forms of pain relief, they stressed the importance of remaining active and conscious throughout the birthing process.

Until the early 1960s, the individual who exerted by far the greatest influence over the natural childbirth movement was the charismatic and iconoclastic Grantly Dick-Read. Read began to advocate natural childbirth in the 1930s, but his influence within the United States remained minimal until after World War II, when his 1944 book, *Childbirth without Fear*, became a bestseller, and his ideas began to circulate widely in popular women's magazines.[82] Read waxed lyrical about motherhood, calling for a return to the "Victorian mothers of seven and ten children" who might restore "the quiet but irresistible goodness of true motherhood." But whereas Victorians had interpreted childbirth as physical and spiritual trial, Read portrayed it as "a normal, natural function" that "should cause no more distress than any other function of the body."[83] Women experienced labor as painful, he argued, because they had been taught to fear childbirth: fear caused their bodies to become tense, which in turn produced pain. As he put it, "fear, pain and tension are the three evils which are not normal to the natural design."[84] To reconcile this belief with Christian theology, Read went so far as to retranslate Genesis 3:16 to read, "In *hard work* shall thou bring forth children." Although his moralism, sentimentality, and religiosity set him apart from other leading commentators on motherhood, who tended to be more secular and psychoanalytically oriented, Read fully shared his contemporaries' desire to sever the long-standing association between motherhood and suffering.

In *Childbirth without Fear*, Read argued that success in natural childbirth depended on the doctor's ability to command his patient's complete trust. For he believed that the same phenomenon that lay at the root of childbearing women's troubles—the power of suggestion—also held the key to alleviating labor pain. Characterizing suggestion as "the greatest and most harmless anesthetising agent that we have," Read urged physicians to exploit its potential by "firmly but quietly offering to the subconscious the required instruction." Labor progressed most smoothly, he argued, when "the conscious, reasoning, inhibiting brain is put out of action." "It is the 'subconscious' woman . . . at whose fortitude we marvel," he effused. "Her violence is reflex, without reason; her language may not be discriminating and her behavior not always discreet, but how susceptible to suggestion, if she is well and properly controlled!"[85] Not coincidentally, Read viewed women's social networks—which in the past had proven so crucial in sustaining women during pregnancy and birth—as negative influences to be defused and counteracted. Only by lessening the patient's emotional dependence on others and redirecting it toward the obstetrician, Read argued, would a doctor gain his patient's "complete confidence."[86]

Like the childrearing experts discussed in the previous chapter, postwar natural childbirth advocates invested enormous hopes in the restoration of a more "natural" mother-child bond, viewing it as the key to both individual happiness and social stability. In addition to critiquing standard obstetrical procedures, they championed breastfeeding and the new practice of rooming-in, which allowed newborns to remain with their mothers rather than being carted off to a centralized nursery.[87] One mother of five, who wrote to Wylie in 1950, predicted that momism and other social problems would be resolved when natural childbirth and rooming-in came to be widely adopted. The fact that hospitals had begun to institute such practices, she believed, "will have a greater effect in helping those mothers become good mothers instead of moms, and on the future mental and emotional stability of the nation than anything else possibly could."[88] Others portrayed natural childbirth as a kind prophylactic that would prevent pathological attachments from taking root by allowing women to sate their maternal instincts. For instance, a woman who wrote to Read in 1952 compared the overwhelming love she felt for her older two children, whose births had been heavily medicalized, to her more tempered feelings for her newest addition, a natural birth baby. "I just simply love him—not so desperately as I love the others, but naturally and better for him and myself I feel," she explained. "I think that having a child naturally uses up enough mother instinct or whatever it is so that one does not dote upon the baby or be too possessive."[89] According to these women, natural childbirth fostered a healthy attachment between mother and child—a bond wholly unlike cloying mother love.

Scholars and activists differ widely in their interpretation of the early natural childbirth movement. Margot Edwards and Mary Waldorf have portrayed the childbirth reformers of the 1940s and 1950s as pioneers who laid the foundation for subsequent feminist critiques of medicalized childbirth.[90] In contrast, Margarete Sandelowski has depicted the movement as "distinctly nonfeminist, if not antifeminist, and promedical in control of the childbirth arena."[91] Either interpretation can seem convincing, depending on whether one emphasizes the movement's basic ideology or its grassroots organization and practical effects. Childbirth education groups in the 1950s and early 1960s did not directly challenge medical authority, nor did they advance a feminist critique of motherhood or gender roles.[92] Yet the movement did embolden individual women to assume a more proactive stance in regard to their own medical care, sometimes to the point of questioning or defying medical authorities.

Rather than assessing the natural childbirth movement of the 1940s and 1950s in relation to subsequent developments, an alternative approach is to compare it to earlier movements that addressed the issue of maternity. As we have seen, reformers who campaigned for twilight sleep, birth control, and improvement in maternal and infant health during the Progressive and interwar eras generally viewed unmedicated childbirth as quite harrowing. They also portrayed childbearing as a kind of duty or service that female citizens rendered unto the state. Though marred by elitist and sometimes overtly racist assumptions, these campaigns often drew support from working-class and minority women, no doubt because they addressed the material realities of motherhood and childbearing. In contrast, the women who spearheaded the natural childbirth movement of the 1940s and 1950s rejected the association between maternity and suffering, dispensed with the notion that childbearing had a civic component, and repudiated the idea that affluent white women were fated to suffer in childbirth more than nonwhite or so-called primitive women. Yet because the natural childbirth movement focused so narrowly on the biological and psychological experience of birth, it attracted a less diverse constituency than its predecessors. Neither the critique of medicalized childbirth nor the celebration of "natural motherhood" held much appeal for women struggling to obtain basic medical care.[93]

Moreover, while postwar childbirth reformers rejected the scientific racism of the pre–World War II era, their depictions of non-Western women who gave birth with ease would surely have been off-putting to many women of color. Just as postwar writers and experts often idealized the childrearing practices of so-called primitive women, Read and other proponents of natural childbirth urged white, middle-class women to embrace their "primitive" maternal instincts. For instance, in a 1943 article in *Parents' Magazine*, one woman described how well-wishers reacted when they heard about her remarkably easy birth, which had lasted a mere three and a half hours. As they regarded her with "an amused twinkle in their eyes," she knew they were mentally comparing her to "Indian squaws, Eskimos, buxom peasants, or perhaps just with Mother Rabbit." Yet she took no offense, for she "much preferred" to be grouped with "Mrs. Rabbit and Co." than to "go back to . . . the group that finds childbirth unimaginable torture and utterly terrifying." The article went on to quote the psychiatrist F. W. Dershimer, who argued that the comparative ease with which "primitive" women gave birth could be attributed to their "mental attitude toward childbirth." Here again, by sharply distinguishing white women from their racial or cultural "others," experts suggested that they, too, could recover their "primitive" maternal selves and give birth with relative ease. In the process, they reinforced the racist assumption that nonwhite women delivered babies without notable pain or suffering.

For all the problematic aspects of Read's theory and method—his paternalistic conception of the doctor-patient relationship, his mystical and romantic view of motherhood, his embrace of primitivism—it nevertheless represented the most "woman-friendly" critique of medicalized childbirth widely available within the United States during the 1940s and 1950s. Thousands of women wrote to Read after reading *Childbirth without Fear*—a remarkable response that testifies to the dehumanizing character of most established obstetrical practice.[94] Women respondents especially appreciated his insistence that physicians should be attuned to their patients' emotional as well as physical needs. Read urged obstetricians to show a level of compassion that few medical men at the time (or today) would have been comfortable displaying. "Your patient may wish to hold your hand," he wrote, "she may wish to lie with her head in your arm; she may call for you to be beside her, but most certainly she desires the unwavering strength of the confidence that you share with her in the successful issue of her trial."[95] In an era when laboring women were routinely strapped down in uncomfortable positions and left alone for long periods of time, it is easy to understand why so many readers found Read's ideas appealing.

Along with Read's correspondence, the records of the Boston Association of Childbirth Education shed light on women's responses to the postwar natural childbirth movement. Beginning in the late 1950s, Justine Kelliher, a founding member of BACE and its first instructor, encouraged former students to send letters detailing their childbirth experiences.[96] These reports, which women typically wrote within a month or two of giving birth, reveal how those who attempted natural childbirth understood and narrated their experiences. Unlike women's diaries from the early twentieth century, which typically refer in very general terms to falling "ill" or suffering "pains," most BACE reports draw heavily on medical terminology; many respondents discuss the stages of labor, the timing of contractions, the dilation of the cervix, as well as what type of medication, if any, the doctor used. This ability to conceptualize their labor and delivery in medical terms seems to have afforded women a greater feeling of control over the process, while also allowing them to regard their experiences with a certain degree of distance, as if viewing themselves as a "case."

The BACE reports also reveal why it is difficult to generalize about the kind of agency exercised by women who attempted natural childbirth in 1950s and early 1960s. Many students felt exhilarated and empowered by their experiences, which they portrayed as far superior to heavily medicalized childbirth.[97] As one woman exclaimed, "The discomfort is nothing compared with the satisfaction of cooperating consciously in the birth of the baby, being fully aware of the birth, and feeling so wonderful afterwards!"[98] Even when the birth did not proceed as they had expected or hoped, the vast majority of respondents clearly appreciated the instruction they had received. "Knowing more about what to expect, both of myself and of a normal delivery, helped a tremendous amount," another woman explained.[99] Yet while numerous reports suggest that natural childbirth offered women a genuine alternative to mainstream obstetrics, other letters point toward a less positive assessment. For instance, one respondent, who made it through labor and delivery without pain relief, emphasized the praise that her performance elicited from medical professionals. "Everyone said I had done a wonderful job—even a doctor who wasn't there! They couldn't get over the fact that I hadn't made a sound (except breathing)."[100] Another woman, who described the birth of her third child as "completely natural" and "*so* satisfying," claimed that her powerful contractions, "instead of being painful," had proven "somehow very satisfying."[101] Reports like these, which reveal a strong desire for the physician's approval, or seem to parrot Read's rhetoric, present a more ambiguous picture of the early natural childbirth movement. While many BACE students felt wonderful because they had relied on their own physical strength and emotional resources, others appear to have derived satisfaction from measuring up to a certain ideal of "natural" womanhood.

Moreover, many BACE students betrayed extreme self-consciousness, which at times seems to have bordered on self-censorship, when discussing pain or discomfort. The frank confession of one woman—"I'm afraid I'll never make it all the way with nat. childbirth. I find hard labor unbearable"—was a virtual anomaly.[102] Far more typically, BACE students referred to pain in highly qualified terms or skirted the issue entirely. For instance, a woman who found massage helpful when the "going seemed particularly rough" placed the word "pain" in quotation marks, thereby defusing its impact: "It was one more thing to do and to think about rather than the 'pain' of the contraction."[103] Describing the importance of her husband's support, another woman changed course midsentence, as if suddenly recalling the need to tailor her story to fit the standard natural birth narrative. "I hung onto him for dear life," she wrote, "and I know his close presence minimized my discomfort (I hesitate to use the word *pain*—I think a visit to the dentist's office would mean pain but not this)."[104] Even a woman who acknowledged that she "definitely felt pain" made a point of clarifying, "it was always a bearable pain—I suppose because it is such a different kind of thing than the usual pains of sickness."[105] Whether or not these women ultimately resorted to anesthesia, the vast majority did not portray pain as a central feature of their birthing experiences.

Even when BACE students had faced complications that forced them to abandon their hopes for a natural birth, many continued to endorse the theory and method. For instance, a woman who "started to holler for a pain killer" after four hours of laboring with a baby in the breech position later reflected, "In all fairness, I should say the natural childbirth techniques worked for me as far as I could apply them. I felt rather like a sissy for weakening, but maybe I had an excuse. Hope to behave better with next one."[106] Similarly, a woman who had to be put under for a forceps delivery—the baby presented in the posterior position, and her cervix never fully dilated—expressed her desire to try again, "this time carrying through with it naturally." Curiously, she even cited her trying experience as proof that natural childbirth was both feasible and desirable: "Now that I've had one child and know what labor is (and probably in about its worst form), I am convinced that natural labor is possible and well within a person's limit of ability to endure. The reward which I was denied I think is well worth the discomfort."[107]

Other sources also indicate that natural childbirth enthusiasts proved reluctant to relinquish their views when their own experiences did not wholly accord with their ideal of a pain-free, drug-free labor and delivery. For instance, in 1947, the husband of a Mrs. O typed up a four-page report that reveals how much the couple struggled to reconcile her actual labor with their belief in natural childbirth. As Mr. O recounted, six to twelve hours before the expected time of delivery, his wife appeared "in real distress" and complained of a "terrible feeling" in her back. At the time, he explained, "I believe we both felt as though our whole experiment was wrong, though Mrs. O denies it now." Yet Mrs. O's distress wholly "vanished" just fifteen minutes later, when the doctor examined her and reported that she would soon be moved to the delivery room. Looking back on the episode, Mr. O explained, the couple had come to believe that, "the distress was probably more from worry that the system was failing than from physical discomfort." They now suspected that, if she had fully understood the progress of her labor and felt free to bear down, "there would not have been even the small amount of discomfort there was." "We should have known from Mrs. O's feelings that the baby was on his way," he concluded, "and that knowledge alone would have eased the psychological discomfort."[108]

What is striking about this account, especially in light of prior views of childbirth, is Mr. O's reluctance to accept even short-lived pain or suffering as an inevitable consequence of the birthing process. Though he reported that his wife had spoken of a "terrible feeling" in her back and appeared desperate for relief, in the end he acknowledged only a "small amount of discomfort." There is no reason to doubt Mr. O's claim that his wife regained her composure upon learning that her labor had progressed further than she expected. But someone less committed to the ideology of natural childbirth might well have interpreted her recovery in more commonsensical terms, as evidence that she could bear the pain or discomfort more stoically with the end in sight. Instead, Mr. O questioned his wife's earlier distress, first attributing it to an imperfect understanding and performance of labor, and then going so far as to suggest that its origin might have been "psychological." Clearly, this was no simple case of a callous brute denying female suffering: Mr. and Mrs. O appear to have constructed the labor narrative collaboratively, and in her own version of events, she may well have downplayed her "discomfort" to a still greater extent.[109] It would seem that both husband and wife needed to explain away her labor pain, because both believed that childbirth should be a pleasurable experience that, from start to finish, remained well within a couple's comprehension and control.

Why did a significant number of middle-class women feel compelled to achieve a "successful," painless natural birth? And if they "failed," why did many continue to believe such a birth was possible? There is, of course, something intrinsically appealing about the notion that the "natural" is fundamentally "good"—that the problem resides not with the physiology of human birth, but rather with the ways that humans have perverted the experience. But if the basic idea of natural childbirth was (and remains) compelling in and of itself, the postwar natural childbirth movement also reflected larger historical trends. Fueled by an aversion to medicalized birthing practices, it equipped many women with the knowledge and training they needed to transform a potentially harrowing medical event into a joyful experience—one that they could understand and at least partially control. Yet at the same time, it incorporated and promoted a new ideal of "natural" motherhood that had a pernicious tendency to turn a woman's performance of pregnancy and labor into a gauge of her mental health or a test that revealed the degree of her adjustment to femininity. Because postwar natural childbirth advocates deemed severe labor pain unnatural, women who struggled with the technique at times felt compelled to diminish whatever suffering they did endure, lest they be judged somehow insufficiently "feminine."

In the 1960s, as the influence of Grantly Dick-Read declined and that of the French obstetrician Fernand Lamaze ascended, the natural childbirth movement evolved in ways that would made it more compatible with the emerging feminist critique of postwar gender ideology.[110] Lamaze, who developed his technique after studying the Soviet "psychoprophylactic" method, did not portray childbirth as the pinnacle of feminine fulfillment, nor did he exhort women to relax and embrace their primitive, womanly selves. Envisioning childbirth more like an athletic event, he sought to train childbearing women to control their labor both mentally and physically.[111] One young woman, who wrote to Betty Friedan in 1965, articulated the crucial distinction that she and many other women perceived between the two methods. Lamaze, she insisted, did not perpetuate the pernicious "feminine mystique" that Friedan decried: he urged the childbearing woman "to respond to labor, not passively, but actively, controlling labor, not submitting to it." As a result, the woman who employed his method emerged from childbirth with "a strong feeling of her own competence" that strengthened "her ego and her determination to mold her own life."[112] In the late 1960s and 1970s, increasing numbers of women would come to view natural childbirth in similar terms—as a way of standing up to the male medical establishment and asserting their right to control their own bodily experiences. But in the 1950s and the early 1960s, such a feminist perspective still lay on the horizon. In these years, natural birth advocates, intent on challenging the old associations between childbearing and perilous suffering, focused primarily on transforming childbirth into a "satisfying," "fulfilling," or "enjoyable" experience—not an empowering one.

In the nineteenth and early twentieth centuries, women had every reason to stress the physical toll of maternity, whether trying to exert greater control over their own lives or promoting policy measures designed to improve maternal health. But as the maternal death rate declined and anesthesia became more widely available, the association between childbearing and self-sacrifice grew more tenuous, and claims to maternal authority premised on pain and suffering lost credibility. One can easily imagine Philip Wylie's exasperated reaction to the following letter, written in 1950 by a mother of two teenage boys:

> You have never been pregnant and therefore have never spent nine miserable months carrying a baby, neither have you ever gone thru a delivery which is the most agonizing pain imaginable. Did you know that a mother loves her baby before it is born and will do everything in her power to protect her baby before it is born? You cannot possibly know or feel any of this, just like I can never know what it means to be a famous author.[113]

Having given birth in the 1930s, this woman may well have delivered her babies at home, with little or no anesthesia. To her, it seemed utterly self-evident that mothers suffered to bring children into the world, and that the reality of their suffering helped to explain the powerful and enduring character of maternal love.

Such views might still have been widely held in 1950, especially by older Americans, but they were no longer countenanced within the dominant culture. After World War II, young women did not speak of pregnancy as "nine miserable months," nor did they refer to childbirth as "the most agonizing pain imaginable"—at least not without risking censure. In popular culture, the woman who viewed childbearing as a trial or act of self-sacrifice tended to be portrayed as an unappealing narcissist, as in the 1955 film, *Rebel without a Cause*. This classic portrait of postwar familial pathology includes a pivotal scene in which Jim, the troubled teenage protagonist, desperately appeals to his parents for guidance in a moment of crisis; in response, his mother begins to prattle—infuriatingly and irrelevantly—about how she nearly died giving birth to him. In the Victorian past, a wayward youth who recalled his mother's suffering might have been led to right his course. But in postwar suburbia, maternal self-sacrifice had lost its power to redeem.

Most American women no doubt welcomed the normalization of childbirth as a badly needed corrective to what one feminist writer called the "concept of woman as semi-invalid."[114] They embraced the notion that childbirth—whether medicated or natural—could be viewed as predictable and even satisfying rather than dangerous and incapacitating. Still, the postwar celebration of childbearing as "natural" and "normal" carried troubling implications all its own. Prior to the 1940s, white, middle-class women who suffered during pregnancy and childbirth could at least feel that the broader culture acknowledged and honored their experience, even if it often did so in an overwrought and sentimental manner. But after World War II, those who experienced more than "discomfort" received little validation from the culture at large; still worse, they might find themselves subjected to an unflattering psychological diagnosis. Now, the woman who suffered *least*—who thrived during pregnancy and experienced little if any pain during childbirth and its aftermath—came to be deemed most worthy of that increasingly coveted adjective, "feminine." Yet as society shifted from valorizing to denying maternal suffering, one thing remained constant: the cultural ideal of motherhood subtly influenced attitudes and practices surrounding childbirth in ways that made it difficult to acknowledge and accommodate the full range of birthing women's experiences.

Mother-Blaming and *The Feminine Mystique*: Betty Friedan and Her Readers

I think of my own uneasiness, being called "mother" of the women's movement—not because of modesty, but because of the way I felt about being a mother altogether. An uneasiness, an unsureness, a fear about being a mother because I certainly didn't want to be like my mother. How many generations of American women have felt like that?

BETTY FRIEDAN, 1981

In February 1963, a young mother wrote to the popular women's magazine *McCall's* to voice her objections to an article entitled "The Fraud of Feminity," a preview of Betty Freidan's forthcoming bestseller, *The Feminine Mystique*.[1] "I suspect Mrs. Friedan has been reading too many books by Philip Wylie," she wrote:

I guess I used to believe it too, because I recall how I used to refer to "those women" who never seemed to think about anything but home and family, who didn't really have much to say, I thought. Only every time I thought I had someone "pegged" in this category, I turned out to be wrong, until I realized that there is a great deal more to most women than meets the eye.[2]

The notion that any reader would associate Betty Friedan with Philip Wylie is confounding, for her book has long been viewed as the first sustained feminist critique of the oppressive cultural climate that Wylie and like-minded commentators helped to create. As the oft-told story goes, by giving voice to the inchoate frustrations of countless middle-class women, Friedan helped to spark the feminist movement of the 1960s and 1970s. Less well known is the fact that Friedan also alienated countless other middle-class women by portraying American mothers as parasitical and pathological. To these full-time homemakers, her exposé of suburban domesticity read less like a groundbreaking feminist manifesto than a discouragingly familiar assault on mothers and housewives.

In essence, *The Feminine Mystique* reproduced the antimaternalist critique that figured so prominently in postwar psychological literature and popular culture. Citing numerous social scientific and psychiatric studies, Friedan reiterated many of the specious charges that experts and commentators like Wylie had leveled at American moms. She blamed them for the mental problems of World War II servicemen, the traitorous behavior of Korean War POWs, the difficulties of children suffering from severe mental illnesses like autism and schizophrenia, and "the homosexuality that is spreading like a murky fog over the American scene."[3] In terms of sheer hyperbole, her analogies rivaled those of confirmed misogynists: she compared suburban housewives to "male patients with portions of their brain shot away" and dehumanized concentration camp victims who had "surrendered their human identity."[4] What Friedan did that mom-bashers like Wylie did not, however, was to draw out the logical implications of momism in a forceful and systematic way. If suburban mothers had become mired in psychopathology, then for everyone's sake, she argued, they needed to be liberated from the confines of domesticity.

Although scholars have offered numerous revisionist interpretations of *The Feminine Mystique*, its debts to postwar mother-blaming have so far attracted relatively little attention.[5] Yet the fact that Friedan portrayed full-time mothers and homemakers in such a negative light goes a long way toward explaining both the appeal and the political limitations of her critique.[6] As legend would have it, the vast majority (roughly 90 percent) of readers who wrote in response to *The Feminine Mystique* avidly embraced its message.[7] These women found Friedan's critique of suburban motherhood both practically useful and emotionally invigorating, for most were already seeking to define themselves in ways that went beyond the mother-homemaker role. But the vast majority (more than 80 percent) of those who responded to the excerpt that appeared in *McCall's* rejected Friedan's arguments on the grounds that she devalued motherhood and homemaking.[8] These women, who hoped to command respect and maintain self-esteem as mothers and homemakers, found Friedan's article either infuriating or demoralizing.

In many ways, the controversy surrounding Friedan's critique of motherhood and domesticity brings us full circle, for it exposed the same basic fault line that surfaced in 1937, when numerous Americans reacted to Smith College president William Neilson's controversial debunking of "mother love." Like Neilson's defenders, Friedan's fans portrayed motherhood as a familial role and a single component of a more multifaceted identity. Her critics, like Neilson's detractors, depicted it as their central life purpose—a purpose they imbued with both spiritual and civic meaning.[9] Yet if Friedan's correspondence reveals important continuities in the ongoing debate over motherhood, it also illuminates how much had changed. For by the early 1960s, the assault on mother love had affected even those women who continued to defend "traditional motherhood." Friedan's critics argued that mothers performed an important civic duty, but they did not envision "organized mother love" as a moral and political force, nor did they believe the state owed them recognition or compensation for their maternal efforts. They insisted that only a full-time mother could provide the love and guidance that children needed, yet they avoided highly sentimental language when discussing the mother-child bond. And while they lauded the ideal of maternal selflessness, they did not portray childbearing itself as a heroic act of self-sacrifice. Finally, the very tone of their letters conveys the cultural distance traversed since the interwar period. When Neilson derided "mother love" in 1938, and when Wylie attacked moms in 1942, both men received letters from readers who were genuinely shocked that a respected cultural figure would launch such an attack on the nation's mothers. In contrast, Friedan's critics discerned nothing new, let alone shocking, about her message, save perhaps for the fact that it had been published in a women's magazine—the housewife's literary refuge. The feelings of exasperation, weariness, and defensiveness that so many of these women expressed are perhaps the most powerful testament to how far the American Mother had fallen since her elevation in the nineteenth century.

By the 1960s, many middle-class mothers, regardless of their employment status, felt condemned by a culture that subjected them to unremitting criticism. Since World War II, the ranks of working mothers had increased significantly: whereas only 28 percent of mothers with children under age eighteen had worked outside the home in 1940, 37 percent did so in 1960, and by 1970, that number would rise to 43 percent.[10] Yet many of the working mothers who wrote to Friedan still felt marginalized by a culture that lauded homemaking as the ultimate source of feminine fulfillment. In their letters, they related encounters with disapproving relatives, neighbors, teachers, and counselors who firmly believed in the adverse psychological and social effects of maternal employment. Such resistance to maternal employment is hardly surprising; it is what the established historical narrative would lead one to expect. But the letters from Friedan's critics point to a countervailing trend that historical scholarship has not adequately explained—the growing resistance to the notion that middle-class women should expect to devote their entire adult lives to motherhood and homemaking. Indeed, if anything, the homemakers who took umbrage at Friedan's critique appeared to feel even more besieged than their employed counterparts. Many believed that the "pendulum has swung in the opposite direction," as one respondent put it, and that society now applauded only working women, while reducing housewives to objects of ridicule, pity, or contempt.[11]

Critics have often condemned second-wave feminism for being "antimotherhood" or "antifamily"—an accusation that denies the complexity of the movement's multiple competing strains.[12] What Friedan's correspondence demonstrates is that this charge also obscures the role that antimaternalism played in diminishing respect for motherhood and homemaking *prior* to the resurgence of feminism. Friedan's critics did not feel devalued because of a feminist assault on traditional definitions of womanhood; they felt devalued because of the hostile attacks on maternal figures that, for several decades, had been a commonplace feature of American popular culture and professional literature. In fact, many women who responded to Friedan's *McCall's* article did not interpret it as a "feminist" critique at all, but rather as yet another negative commentary on the state of American womanhood. (It is instructive to recall that, in 1963, most Americans still viewed "feminism" as a relic of the early twentieth century, so readers lacked a framework for readily classifying Friedan's argument as such.) However much "The Fraud of Femininity" demeaned or antagonized full-time mothers—and it clearly did both—the article touched a nerve in large part because it exacerbated preexisting feelings of frustration over the lack of respect for motherhood and homemaking within the broader culture.

The fact that both full-time homemakers and working mothers felt unfairly attacked, however, did not result in a mutual sense of grievance that could translate into political or even social unity. On the contrary, whereas Progressive Era maternalism helped to unify white, middle-class women, often by masking over serious differences between fairly conservative homemakers and progressive reformers, postwar antimaternalism proved to be a profoundly divisive force within this same demographic group. In hindsight, the responses to Friedan's critique allow us to glimpse the ambiguous legacy of antimaternalism in the years to come, as it helped to propel liberal feminism while simultaneously generating a backlash among conservative women, who would ultimately rally to defend the embattled American mother and housewife.

Friedan's Critique of Suburban Motherhood

Scholars continue to debate the intellectual, cultural, and political origins of *The Feminine Mystique*. In 1998, historian Daniel Horowitz published a groundbreaking biographical study that called attention to Friedan's student radicalism and her subsequent work as a labor journalist in the 1940s and 1950s. According to Horowitz, Friedan's feminism owed much to a radical past that she later tried to downplay or obscure. Whereas Friedan claimed that she had not given serious thought to women's issues prior to 1957, Horowitz shows that she had in fact written about sexual discrimination for the labor press during the early 1950s—a revelation that makes her neglect of working-class and nonwhite women in *The Feminine Mystique* all the more striking. These are fascinating and important discoveries, yet how they should alter our understanding of the book and the movement it helped to inspire remains less clear. Horowitz contends that Friedan's earlier radicalism fundamentally informed her critique of postwar domesticity, but such influence is hard to discern in a work that stops short of urging any sort of collective action to redress women's grievances, and one that promotes solutions (advanced education and self-realization) that tended to be feasible only for middle-class and upper-middle-class women.[13]

Whatever role Friedan's connections to political radicalism played in shaping her work as a whole, the antimaternalist component of her argument must be traced to other sources.[14] Its origins lay not in the legacy of popular front radicalism but rather in the 1920s cultural rebellion against the late Victorian matriarch and the concomitant rise of a therapeutic culture. As Friedan recollected in her autobiography, "When Philip Wylie's book attacking the American 'mom' came out, and I started studying Freud in college, I would say things like: All mothers should be drowned at birth."[15] In the social and cultural milieu in which she came of age, such a vehement pronouncement may not have seemed all that extraordinary. Friedan enrolled in Smith College in 1938, just a year after Neilson delivered his much-publicized speech. She graduated in 1942, the same year that *Generation of Vipers* appeared.[16] When privileged youth of her generation attacked the all-American mom, they were not simply airing their views about childrearing techniques; they felt themselves to be doing something far more subversive. Mother-blaming allowed them to signal a rejection of Victorian moral strictures and a commitment to a more secular, psychologically oriented approach to sexuality and the self. It could also be a way of mocking a middlebrow popular culture that seemed hopelessly sentimental, or a means of repudiating nativist patriotism in favor of a more democratic notion of American identity. And for an ambitious young woman like Friedan, it could be a way of conveying a fervent desire for a different kind of life than that which her mother led.

If the cultural climate of Friedan's youth sanctioned a generalized hostility toward mothers, her attraction to *Generation of Vipers* also had deeply personal origins. Friedan grew up in the 1920s and 1930s in Peoria, Illinois, the daughter of Harry Goldstein, a Jewish immigrant from Kiev, and Miriam Goldstein, an American-born Jew. During the 1920s, Harry ran a successful jewelry store that supported the lavish lifestyle of his beautiful and much younger wife. With a nursemaid to tend the three children and a maid to cook and clean, Miriam was free to spend her time shopping, playing bridge and tennis, and pursuing desultory voluntary activities. Nevertheless, to her first-born, she often seemed angry and malcontent; according to Friedan, she badgered her children, belittled her husband, and suffered from periodic bouts of colitis that left her bedridden and "screaming in pain." Familial relations grew still more strained during the Depression, when Miriam refused to curb her spending and even resorted to gambling. Eventually, Harry's heart began to fail, and Miriam assumed responsibility for running the store, at which point her physical problems abated and her incessant nagging lessened. But by then, Friedan's resentment toward her mother had hardened into implacable hostility. In 1943, after her father died, she began suffering severe asthma attacks and entered psychoanalysis (or what she called "Freudian therapy"). Reflecting on the experience many years later, what she recalled was "lying on a couch and talking endlessly about how I hated my mother and how she had killed my father."[17]

A socially ambitious wife who drives her husband to an early grave and her children to a psychiatrist, an economic parasite who consumes with abandon, a neurotic who conspicuously suffers from psychosomatic ailments—these are, of course, the classic images of midcentury antimaternalism. As Friedan recounted in *The Feminine Mystique*, two negative images of womanhood haunted her throughout early adulthood. While she "dreaded" becoming like the women she knew who had remained single and childless—"the old-maid high-school teachers; the librarian; the one woman doctor in our town, who cut her hair like a man; and a few of my college professors"—she also recoiled from the model presented by her own mother and her friends' mothers. "In my generation, many of us knew that we did not want to be like our mothers, even when we loved them," she explained. "Did we understand, or only resent, the sadness, the emptiness, that made them hold too fast to us, try to live our lives, run our fathers' lives, spend their days shopping or yearning for things that never seemed to satisfy them, no matter how much money they cost?"[18] To Friedan, Wylie's mom—the woman who bossed her husband, dominated her children, engaged in rampant consumption, and whiled away her time with bridge games and charity work—was not simply a misogynist caricature. She was a real, all-too-prevalent social type, and she represented a potential threat to young women who desired a life beyond the home.[19]

Still, if Friedan portrayed Miriam Goldstein as a Wyliesque mom, she also implied (inadvertently, it would seem) that her mother had played a crucial role in her success as a writer and feminist critic. In 1973, when she attempted to explain the genesis of *The Feminine Mystique*, she began with her mother:

> There was my mother, and her discontent, which I never understood. I didn't want to be like my mother. Nothing my father did, nothing he bought her, nothing we did ever seemed to satisfy her. When she married my father, she'd had to give up her job editing the woman's page of the newspaper in Peoria. She could hardly wait until I got to junior high to put the idea into my head to try out for the school newspaper, to start a literary magazine in high school. She could hardly wait for me to go to the college she had no chance to go to, to edit the newspaper there.

Friedan believed that her mother had pushed her to excel as a student and a writer to compensate for her own disappointments—the missed opportunity to attend a prestigious college, the reluctantly relinquished newspaper job. If one accepts this narrative, then one must conclude that it was at least partially because of Miriam's attempts to live vicariously through her daughter that Friedan came to possess the requisite skills and drive to write such a damning indictment of domesticity. Years later, when Friedan sent her mother a copy of *The Feminine Mystique*, she seemed to acknowledge as much. "With all the troubles we have had, you gave me the power to break through the feminine mystique," she wrote in an enclosed note. "I hope you accept the book for what it is, an affirmation of the values of your life and mine."[20]

Despite the ambivalence Friedan harbored toward her own mother, she enthusiastically embraced the experience of motherhood. Her children, she would later write in her autobiography, "seemed like a *bonus* in my life, an unexpected, maybe undeserved, marvelous bonus."[21] In certain respects, Friedan was fairly typical of highly educated mothers of the late 1940s and 1950s. She bore three children (in 1948, 1952, and 1956), avidly read Dr. Spock, and chose to breastfeed, despite a lack of support from hospital personnel.[22] But unlike the vast majority of her peers, Friedan also worked outside the home, even when her children were quite young.[23] Following the birth of her first child, Daniel, she took an eleven-month leave from her job with the *UE News*, the official publication of the left-wing United Electrical, Radio, and Machine Workers of America. Three years later, when she was pregnant with her second child, Jonathan, she lost her job.[24] Friedan later claimed that she felt angry but also relieved, "because all those negative books and magazine articles about 'career women' were beginning to get to me." She had been "too indoctrinated in psychology, Freudian psychology and its derivatives sweeping America in the years after World War II," she explained, to easily dismiss the notion that professional women "were losing their femininity, undermining their husband's masculinity, and destroying or stunting their children."[25] But soon after Friedan had "dispensed with the nursemaid," she grew depressed and experienced a recurrence of severe asthma, driving her back into therapy. Before Jonathan had reached his first birthday, she had employed a maid to come three days a week, allowing her to embark on a new career as a freelance journalist.[26]

If Friedan's own life failed to fit the contours of the "feminine mystique," neither did the messages that she received about motherhood from her doctors and therapists. When she returned to work at the *UE News* in 1949, her "wonderful" pediatrician repeatedly assured her that "despite what Dr. Spock said, it did not have to hurt my baby that I went back to work."[27] Similarly, the psychoanalyst William Menaker, whom she began to see after Jonathan's birth, questioned why she tried to confine herself to "'playing the role' of suburban housewife." During one of her sessions, he interpreted a dream that centered on the journalist John Hersey not as evidence of "penis envy" but rather "as a message to take my own writing more seriously." In fact, Friedan's experience with Menaker proved so positive that she sought him out again in 1958 after signing the contract for what would become *The Feminine Mystique*. No longer a patient, she asked Menaker whether he would be interested in collaborating with her, for she believed that his expertise would lend the book "more authority."[28]

Thus, had Friedan's editor not nixed the idea, the name of an "eminent male psychoanalyst" might have graced the cover of *The Feminine Mystique*. The notion is mind-boggling, for it is so thoroughly at odds with Friedan's well-established reputation as an ardent foe of psychoanalysis.[29] In her book, she argued unequivocally that the oppressive "feminine mystique" "derived its power from Freudian thought," and she devoted an entire chapter to portraying Freud as a "prisoner of his time" when it came to women.[30] Yet Friedan always differentiated between Freudian theory and its clinical application, and her disdain for popularized Freudianism never translated into a wholesale rejection of the psychoanalytic establishment. As she explained:

> No one can question the basic genius of Freud's discoveries, nor the contribution he has made to our culture. Nor do I question the effectiveness of psychoanalysis as it is practiced today by Freudian or anti-Freudian. But I do question, from my own experience as a woman, and from my reporter's knowledge of other women, the application of the Freudian theory of femininity to women today. I question its use, not in therapy, but as it has filtered into the lives of American women through the popular magazines and the opinions and interpretations of so-called experts.[31]

This surprising defense of psychoanalytic therapy seems to have reflected Friedan's positive experiences as an analytic patient in the 1940s and 1950s. At two crucial points in her life, psychoanalysis allowed her to affirm an independent identity that felt threatened by familial ties—specifically, by the intensity of the mother-child relationship. As a young single woman struggling to make her way in the 1940s, psychoanalysis helped her separate from her own mother and renounce her mother's bourgeois values and expectations. As a depressed and newly unemployed mother in the early 1950s, psychoanalysis helped her to affirm her ambitions as a writer and thereby retain a sense of self amid the relentless demands of rearing young children. In both cases, therapy provided Friedan with a means of addressing and resolving the difficulties that motherhood posed to individualism.

Friedan's critique of suburban motherhood in *The Feminine Mystique* strongly reflected her commitment to a psychotherapeutic notion of self-realization. She argued that full-time motherhood and homemaking could not serve as the basis of a mature identity, and that women who confined their energies to the mother-housewife role ultimately harmed both themselves and their loved ones.[32] "If an able American woman does not use her human energy and ability in some meaningful pursuit," she insisted, "she will fritter away her energy in neurotic symptoms, or unproductive exercise, or destructive 'love.'"[33] Until women learned to "carry more of the burden of the battle with the world, instead of being a burden themselves," she warned, their "wasted energy" would "continue to be destructive to their husbands, to their children, and to themselves."[34] Friedan's (rather cursory) proposals for combating the "feminine mystique" therefore focused on freeing women from the all-consuming demands of motherhood and homemaking: she called for maternity leaves; greater access to childcare; and a "GI Bill" for mothers and housewives so that women could further their education.[35] "The only way for a woman, as for a man, to find herself, to know herself as a person, is by creative work of her own," she asserted. "There is no other way."[36]

In advancing her argument that women needed to move beyond the confines of domesticity, Friedan appropriated and perpetuated psychiatrists' specious allegations regarding maternal pathology. For instance, she quoted at length from Edward Strecker's *Their Mothers' Sons*, the 1946 best-selling book (discussed in chap. 3) that blamed American mothers for the high rates of neuropsychiatric rejections and casualties during World War II. Interestingly, Friedan mischaracterized Strecker as "oddly enough, one of the psychiatric experts most frequently cited in the spate of postwar articles condemning women for their loss of femininity—and bidding them to rush back home again." The real moral to be learned from his case histories, she argued, was that the nation's immature draftees and soldiers had been reared by "mothers who devoted *too* much of their lives to their children."[37] But as we have seen, this *was* the lesson that most people drew at the time; very few commentators cited Strecker's work in order to argue women should confine themselves to motherhood and homemaking. In other words, Friedan downplayed or denied the genuine concerns about overmothering that existed in the 1940s, while exaggerating the extent to which Strecker and other postwar commentators had been preoccupied with women's workforce participation. Moreover, she reproduced rather than questioned the anxieties about male effeminacy and homosexuality that informed such critiques.[38] In these important respects, the distance separating Friedan from a figure like Strecker or Wylie was simply not as great as she (and historians) have suggested.[39]

Similarly, Friedan opened her discussion of David Levy's famous study, *Maternal Overprotection*, by attempting to differentiate her own interpretation of the psychiatrist's findings from his work's popular impact in 1943. "No headlines marked the growing concern of psychiatrists with the problem of 'dependence' in American children," she insisted. But here again, the popular press had in fact addressed such concerns; for instance, *Time* carried a review of Levy's work, headlined "Too Much Mother," that described "the overly protective mother who . . . turns her child into a sissy or a tyrant" as one of the "greatest problems" that psychiatrists faced.[40] Friedan also quickly brushed past Levy's offensive biologism in rushing to appropriate his claim that strongly "maternal" women could seriously impede their children's psychological development. Summarizing his findings, she wrote, "All these [overprotective] mothers—according to physiological indexes such as menstrual flow, breast milk, and early indications of a 'maternal type of behavior'— were unusually strong in their feminine or maternal instinctual base, if it can be described that way."[41] Only with the afterthought—"if it can be described that way"—did Friedan register any discomfort with Levy's attempt to correlate a woman's maternal behavior directly to her reproductive physiology. In sum, when referencing studies like *Maternal Overprotection* that helped to advance her feminist argument, Friedan failed to question some of their most misogynist or objectionable components.

Yet Friedan also drew two strikingly new conclusions from psychiatric studies of maternal pathology. Experts like Strecker generally assured women they could avoid the dangers of momism so long as they enjoyed a healthy marital sex life and cultivated other interests as their children grew older. In contrast, Friedan insisted that women needed to pursue a lifelong commitment to a career or some kind of work outside the home. Second, psychological authorities viewed the threat of momism in very gender-specific terms; in regard to daughters, their concerns were typically limited to the fear that moms might undermine girls' prospects for healthy sexual adjustment and marital happiness. In marked contrast, Friedan insisted that momism had precisely the same effects on girls that it had on boys. Because Americans did not expect women to display "independence, firmness of purpose, aggressiveness, self-assertion," she argued, they failed to perceive a lack of such traits in girls as a serious problem. "The insult, the real reflection on our culture's definition of the role of women," she concluded, "is that as a nation we only noticed that something was wrong with women when we saw its effects on our sons."[42]

In the end, Friedan's largely uncritical appropriation of the momism critique remains puzzling, for there is evidence she did recognize the pernicious character of mother-blaming. In a remarkable passage that appears in an earlier draft of *The Feminine Mystique*, but not in the final version, she strongly condemned the pervasive attacks on American mothers by drawing on ideas about scapegoating developed by the psychologist Kurt Lewin (with whom she had studied in college). Commentators and experts, she argued, had made a scapegoat of the American mother, just as the Nazis had done to the Jews:

> The Jews made a good scapegoat in Germany because there weren't very many, and they were "different," and enough were rich and brilliant to blame them for your troubles. You could pretend you were solving everything by burning them in furnaces, and getting rid of all that helpless anger, and feel important again. . . .
>
> Mothers made better scapegoats in America . . . but Americans wouldn't do anything as mean as furnaces. What did it hurt to write those nasty words about the women?[43]

Here, Friedan leveled the most damning indictment of mother-blaming conceivable. It seems highly doubtful that she cut the passage from the published version because she came to view the analogy as too hyperbolic or objectionable, given that she employed similar analogies elsewhere in the book. More likely, she excised the passage because she sensed that it undermined her own use of mother-blaming as a tool for critiquing domesticity.

Similar contradictory impulses can be glimpsed in a passage that appears in the published version of *The Feminine Mystique*, in which Friedan appeared to be embarking on an analysis of psychiatric mother-blaming, only to shift abruptly toward employing such works as unproblematic evidence. In the chapter "The Mistaken Choice," she described how American mothers had found themselves "singled out for special attention" during the postwar period, when enthusiasm for psychoanalysis gripped the nation:

It was suddenly discovered that the mother could be blamed for almost everything. In every case history of a troubled child; alcoholic, suicidal, schizophrenic, psychopathic, neurotic adult; impotent, homosexual male; frigid, promiscuous female; ulcerous, asthmatic, and otherwise disturbed American, could be found a mother. A frustrated, repressed, disturbed, martyred, never satisfied, unhappy woman. A demanding, nagging, shrewish wife. A rejecting, overprotecting, dominating mother.[44]

While this passage reads like a powerful lead-in to a critical discussion of experts' tendency to trace every conceivable manifestation of psychopathology back to the mother, no such discussion follows. Instead, Friedan proceeded to quote from such studies to illustrate the negative consequences of women's confinement to full-time motherhood and domesticity.

How could Friedan so astutely analyze the pressure placed on women to become "feminine" homemakers and mothers, yet not the pressure placed on them to constantly police their maternal behavior, lest they irreparably harm their children? Some scholars have suggested that Friedan chose to suspend her critical judgment, since the prevalent attacks on housewives and mothers could so readily be turned to support her central claim.[45] There is no doubt a strategic element in Friedan's appropriation of antimaternalist critiques. But in light of her own familial and intellectual history, it also seems likely that she had so thoroughly imbibed an antimaternalist and therapeutic perspective that she did not always perceive how psychiatric mother-blaming could negatively affect women.

If Friedan's appropriation of psychiatric mother-blaming is largely derivative, however, her discussion of the cultural climate of postwar pronatalism is more original and discerning. For instance, she criticized the natural childbirth movement and related movements like La Leche League for their tendency to transform procreation into a "cult, a career to the exclusion of every other kind of creative endeavor." According to Friedan, this impulse was symptomatic of the broader "feminine mystique."[46] Yet Friedan also noted that the natural childbirth movement appealed to "the independent, educated, spirited American woman," who hoped to "experience childbirth not as a mindless female animal, an object to be manipulated by the obstetrician, but as a whole person, able to control her own body with her aware mind." In short, Friedan supported the notion that women should reclaim greater control over the birthing process, even as she remained legitimately skeptical of the glorification of "natural motherhood" within the natural childbirth movement—a tendency that Lamaze had only recently begun to challenge.

Similarly, Friedan commented astutely on maternalist politics when discussing the antinuclear group Women Strike for Peace, an organization founded in 1961 by left-leaning, middle-class women who had devoted much of their lives to motherhood and homemaking.[47] Friedan approved of the organization's goals, and she recognized that its members had actually shown restraint in their use of maternalist rhetoric. (They could, after all, have called themselves "Mothers Strike for Peace.") "It is, perhaps, a step in the right direction when a woman protests nuclear testing under the banner 'Women Strike for Peace,'" she conceded. "But why does the professional illustrator who heads the movement [Dagmar Wilson] say she is 'just a housewife,' and her followers insist that once the [nuclear] testing stops, they will stay happily home with their children?" she demanded.[48] Friedan believed that women should entirely abandon maternalist rhetoric and ideology, regardless of its potential value as a political tactic. "Even in politics," she insisted, "women must make their contributions not as 'housewives' but as citizens."[49]

Thus, The Feminine Mystique did not simply lambaste maternal influence; it also urged women to cultivate personal, professional, and political identities not defined or restricted by sex. But in her McCall's article, "The Fraud of Femininity," Friedan failed to adequately differentiate her critique from earlier attacks on suburban housewives and mothers—a failure that would seriously antagonize her audience. The article consists mainly of sentences drawn, more or less unchanged, from The Feminine Mystique. The fact that McCall's readers responded so much more negatively than did readers of the book must therefore be attributed largely to important differences between the two self-selected groups. However, it is also crucial to note that, in the process of condensing her argument for an article-length piece, Friedan enhanced its polemical character in ways virtually guaranteed to alienate her intended audience.

This is particularly evident in the opening paragraphs of the two different works. In The Feminine Mystique, Friedan appealed to middle-class readers by fostering a feeling of identification or self-recognition:

> The problem lay buried, unspoken, for many years in the minds of American women. It was a strange stirring, a sense of dissatisfaction, a yearning that women suffered in the middle of the twentieth century in the United States. Each suburban wife struggled with it alone. As she made the beds, shopped for groceries, matched slipcover material, ate peanut butter sandwiches with her children, chauffeured Cub Scouts and Brownies, lay beside her husband at night—she was afraid to even ask herself the silent question—"Is this all?"[50]

Here, Friedan posited a vague feeling of dissatisfaction and desire—something that all readers had doubtless experienced at one point or another—and then knowingly detailed the moments that filled a typical suburban homemaker's day. Only at the chapter's end did she identify the "problem with no name"—"that voice within women that says, 'I want something more than my husband and my children and my home.'"[51]

This same passage also appears in the *McCall's* article, but it is preceded by a very different introductory paragraph that set the stage for a much more fraught relationship between the author and her readers:

> For women of ability, in America today, there is something about the housewife state itself that is dangerous. The women who "adjust" as housewives are actually in peril. This may seem absurd to the American suburban housewife, who leads such a comfortable life; but isn't her house in reality a comfortable concentration camp? Haven't women who live in the image of the feminine mystique—the cult of housewifery—trapped themselves within the narrow walls of their homes? Haven't they become dependent, passive, childlike? Given up their adult frame of reference merely to live at the level of food and housekeeping? What they do generally does not require mature capabilities; it is endless, monotonous, unrewarding. So many millions of American women are suffering a slow deterioration of mind and spirit.[52]

Instead of attempting to draw her readers in, Friedan immediately confronted them with the assertion that housewives are trapped and infantilized. Moreover, she advanced her argument in wholly negative terms, referring only to the debilitating character of the housewife role rather than to women's longing for something more. Finally, Friedan immediately introduced her "comfortable concentration camp" analogy—an extremely provocative rhetorical device that did not surface in the book until the twelfth chapter. A few paragraphs later, she set forth her inflammatory thesis, also drawn from the book's controversial twelfth chapter: "By adjusting to her prescribed circumstances, a woman becomes a biological robot, preyed upon by outside pressures, and herself preying upon her husband and children."[53] By foregrounding her most extreme claims, decontextualized from much of the supporting evidence she mustered in the book, the *McCall's* article presented a particularly severe version of Friedan's critique.

Nevertheless, Friedan was taken aback by readers' negative reactions. Her notes for a subsequent *McCall's* article about the massive response that "The Fraud of Femininity" elicited suggest that she agonized over these "Angry Letters." On legal page after legal page, she hand-copied excerpts from readers' letters, while attempting to summarize and explain their objections:

Shaken by letters—hundreds, thousands, a great many of which are outraged at the very suggestion that the duty of wife and mother is *not* the end-all, the be-all of any woman's life—and others who have been struggling, against odds, with guilt and doubts . . . often alone, to find a personal goal with a purpose for their own lives. . . .

Many of these letters attack the very possibility of a good wife and mother needing any further identity. . . .

Are there two distinctly different kinds of American women, or merely different stages in our growth as women? And if the latter is the case, isn't it possible for women at these different stages to help one another?[54]

The fact that Friedan could speculate with apparent wonder that there might be "two distinctly different kinds of American women" speaks volumes to the myopia that prevented her from appreciating the diversity of American women's experiences. As bell hooks has observed, Friedan wrote as if working-class women and women of color "did not exist"; she "made her plight and the plight of white women like herself synonymous with a condition affecting all American women."[55] The class and race biases embedded within Friedan's critique are mirrored in her correspondence, for she received hardly any letters from women who articulated a sense of working-class identity or described themselves as belonging to a racial minority group.

However, within Friedan's overwhelmingly white, middle-class readership, the broad contours of "two distinctly different kinds of American women" did in fact emerge. Yet these women were not, as Friedan speculated, at "different stages" of "growth" according to some shared standard of development. Instead, they viewed their basic identities as homemakers and mothers in profoundly different ways. For one group, the mother-homemaker role was incidental to—and often perceived as an impinging upon—a more fundamental sense of self as a distinct individual. For the other group, it constituted the very foundation of identity. In retrospect, Friedan's tentative hope that these two constituencies could "help one another" appears sadly naive, for in the years that followed, the fault line that divided them would only widen.

Motherhood and the Search for Self-Realization: Friedan's Fans

The familiar story told about *The Feminine Mystique*—a story promulgated by Friedan herself—is that her book served as a catalyst, awakening suburban housewives to their plight and prompting them to take steps to improve their situation. Many women sent Friedan compelling letters that support this narrative, such as the following, from a resident of Pomona, California:

My dear, wonderful, Mrs. Friedan,

I have just finished devouring your "Emancipation Proclamation," "The Feminine Mystique," and I owe you a debt of eternal gratitude!

You have freed me from such a mass of subconscious and conscious guilt feelings, that I feel, today, as though I had been filled with helium and turned loose! To feel like a "misfit" for long years; to feel like a wretched ingrate and an abnormal mother for so long, and then to find out that perhaps the mold was made wrong, has done me more good than years of analysis could have done.

Do you know that I have four children, ranging from 5 years to 12 years, and I have never once experienced a deep sense of serenity or joy, or an all-encompassing wave of maternalism at the news that I was pregnant! Also, I have never been able to convince myself that there was any satisfaction to be derived from housework!

I have attained the Mount Everest of American womanhood! The Goal! I have a husband, four children, and a nice home in a nice neighborhood. I am 31 years old. What do I do now? Retire? At least, you have put me back on the road to "somewhere."[56]

To this woman and many others who felt chronically dissatisfied as mothers and homemakers, Friedan's message was like a badly needed tonic: it validated their frustration, assuaged their guilt, and encouraged them to envision new ways of structuring their future.

Friedan's fans conceptualized motherhood in highly individualistic terms, drawing few if any connections between their maternal responsibilities and the broader social and political world. They did not describe motherhood as the basis of female citizenship or as a religious duty. Instead, they portrayed it as a component of their personal identity and a private, familial role. These women did not take offense at Friedan's unflattering portrait of the typical suburban housewife, for most already viewed themselves as deviating in some fashion from that norm. For them, the fundamental maternal dilemma was the problem of reconciling the demands of motherhood and homemaking with the imperative to cultivate an independent identity.

Predictably, women who had already decided to pursue careers welcomed Friedan's claim that motherhood and paid employment could be successfully combined. A young married woman about to embark on a graduate program in literature confessed that, prior to reading *The Feminine Mystique*, she had seriously doubted whether she was "worthy to be a mother," since she "could never bear to completely abandon" her career.[57] Similarly, a government employee who had suffered from "gnawing guilt feelings" thanked Friedan for giving her "the courage of my convictions" that her four children (ages nine through seventeen) did not "need Mama sitting at home waiting . . . [for] their return from school."[58] While some respondents clearly relished Friedan's negative portrait of "suburban matriarchs who stayed home and tended the children and dabbled in bridge and golf," others were simply grateful to be told they need not "feel guilty about not being a full time housewife."[59] Long weary of the barrage of criticism directed toward working mothers, these readers viewed *The Feminine Mystique* as offering women a fundamentally helpful and positive message.

Friedan's fans questioned the notion that a "good mother" was a selfless nurturer, always available to meet her children's physical and emotional needs. Some even argued that the imperatives of full-time homemaking—the trivial yet relentless nature of housework, along with the constant focus on satisfying others' needs—actually prevented women from cultivating the healthy individualism that effective mothering required. "I just keep telling [my husband] I cannot fully love him or the children if I do not in some way love myself and I cannot love myself if my mind stagnate [*sic*]," wrote a mother of five small children who had recently become active in local Republican politics. "I cannot make him happy or the children happy if I am not happy and I have never equated housework with happiness."[60] Another respondent explained how she had begun to see her children as "something more than voracious birds with their mouths open" after embarking on studies to become an English teacher. "I like my children now and think I am a better mother since I have learned how important it is to feed their spirits as well as their bodies," she wrote. "Becoming a person one's self [*sic*] is a big step in recognizing the uniqueness in others."[61] According to these women, everyone suffered when mothers felt trapped; to be a truly good mother, they argued, a woman first had to be a happy individual.

At the heart of this conception of motherhood lay an emphasis on personal fulfillment, coupled with the rejection of maternal self-sacrifice as an admirable ideal—both central components of the maternal ideal promoted by postwar psychological experts. Mothers who strove to be wholly selfless, Friedan and her fans believed, incurred psychological damage that inevitably redounded on their loved ones. "No one is created an altruist, and the conflicts, the resentment, and disillusion in trying to be one . . . is exactly what has made so many women—perhaps most women—incapable of . . . objectivity and empathy," wrote one young unmarried woman.[62] Another woman, who had gone on to pursue a successful career after her husband left her, argued, "If your only reason for living is that 'somebody needs me' this can be pretty dreadful in the family setting. You have to shift over to 'I need me,' if you want to stop swallowing others in your need to be needed."[63] Typically, postwar experts resolved the threat that such beliefs posed to traditional views of maternal obligation by stressing the significance of biologically based differences between the sexes: women, they argued, achieved happiness and fulfillment when they embraced their biological destiny as mothers. Friedan's fans appropriated the emphasis on happiness and fulfillment but left the biological determinism behind.

Some respondents argued that mothers had not only a right but also a familial obligation to pursue happiness and personal fulfillment. For instance, one young mother of four (all under the age of five) described her decision to return to a graduate program in philosophy as follows: "I have been telling myself that when the kids are in school I will take up something seriously, but that's not soon enough. For the sake of my husband, my children, for my own sake, I'm going to get my Phd and I'm going to teach."[64] Similarly, a part-time nurse and mother of three, who had been deferring her dream of returning to school until her children were older, decided upon reading *The Feminine Mystique* that "it would be unfair to them and to me not to try right now." Although her husband and therapist both objected to her decision, she felt confident that she would be "a better wife and mother" once she began "using my capabilities to their fullest."[65] Significantly, these women did not attempt to banish feelings of maternal duty or even guilt; rather, by redefining maternal failure to include such shortcomings as a lack of courage or complacency, they tried to infuse their extradomestic goals with a sense of maternal (as well as individual) purpose.

Such sources provide compelling evidence of the ways in which the proliferation of a therapeutic culture after World War II helped pave the way for liberal feminism in the 1960s and 1970s. Although second-wave feminists identified psychology and especially psychoanalysis as primary sources of women's oppression, their own ideas and political practices (such as consciousness-raising) often drew heavily on psychological concepts, as historians Ellen Herman and Eva Moskowitz have both shown.[66] Similarly, the letters from Friedan's fans indicate that, despite the patently sexist character of much midcentury psychological theory, the relationship between feminism and the psychological professions cannot be described as a wholly antagonistic one. In fact, counterintuitive as it may seem, respondents who expressed a general receptivity to psychological expertise tended to be much more likely to embrace Friedan's feminist message than those who derided it.[67] To be sure, some women described deeply unsatisfying therapeutic encounters, in which their psychiatrist or therapist seemed unsympathetic or made blatantly reactionary pronouncements about woman's proper role.[68] Yet many other women related how therapy had granted them license to

question the "feminine mystique."[69] The crucial point is that the very willingness to pursue a therapeutic solution reflected an attitude toward the self
and one's own desires that made a woman more likely to question traditional
notions of maternal obligation.

Consider, for example, how a former journalist and mother of two young
children described her experience of "coping with 'the problem that has no
name'":

> I had even resorted to a psychiatrist, who kept asking me if I was sure there
> wasn't "Another Man" involved, and whether I really loved my children! All I
> knew was that I had to be ME . . . but when I took time off to be myself—writ-
> ing occasional feature articles or going to New York by myself for a weekend,
> I was enough brain-washed by the wretched feminine mystique to feel rather
> defiant and guilty about it.
>
> Reading your book has given me a whole new zest for life. I know now that
> I must get back to taking my writing seriously, instead of reconciling myself
> to being an amateur. I'm lucky enough to have an intelligent, perceptive hus-
> band who is delighted with my decision.
>
> Also, since reading "The Feminine Mystique" I have hired a baby-sitter
> for a few hours every day, as well as my regular cleaning woman one day a
> week, and I spend that time being me, which is enormously refreshing men-
> tally and physically, and is also bringing in money. Hooray for you![70]

This woman reacted positively to Friedan's message in part because of the
various resources she possessed: a set of skills that allowed her to attain satisfaction and financial compensation for work outside the home; a husband
who supported her career aspirations; the financial ability to hire both a
housecleaner and babysitter. But what is also striking about her letter is the
extent to which she defined "being me" in opposition to motherhood and
homemaking. For her, the fundamental problem with full-time caretaking
was that it made her feel alienated from herself. Though she received no help
from her clueless psychiatrist, the fact that the culture encouraged her to view
her unhappiness as a problem worthy of psychiatric attention was essential.
She clearly needed Friedan's feminist message to distance herself further from
domesticity, but the therapeutic ethos had played a crucial role in preparing
her to act on that message.

Some respondents demonstrated a particularly high level of engagement
with psychological and social scientific expertise; like Friedan, they selectively
deployed scientific claims to buttress their arguments. For instance, a Cornell
graduate and mother of two, who had encountered many "extremely anx-

ious" mothers as the director of a girls' camp, disputed the notion that young children required uninterrupted maternal care. "'Thou shalt not leave thy child' seemed to be the unwritten eleventh commandment," she complained. "And it is this commandment that has been written by the modern psychologists and psychoanalysts." Yet even as she assumed a highly skeptical stance toward one body of psychological expertise, she uncritically endorsed equally questionable findings concerning the dangers of momism and mother-child symbiosis. Specifically, she applauded Friedan for citing works that held mothers accountable for severe childhood mental illnesses as well as a sociological article that portrayed maternal overprotection as more hazardous than physical abuse. Despite her evident concern with mothers' emotional well-being, she seemed insensible to the misogynist character of much of this literature. To her mind, studies of maternal pathology apparently represented the most effective—or perhaps the only effective—means of countering the still-prevalent belief that maternal employment harmed young children.[71]

Indeed, for women who hoped to justify pursuits that took them away from their homes and children, the language of maternal pathology could be highly useful, even liberating. One woman, having just signed a contract to return to teaching full-time, insisted that her four children (ages eight months to five years) would be "better off" once they no longer had "such a frustrated and nagging mother with them all day." "I know this," she added, "because I so 'enjoyed' the children when I returned home after substituting by the day this past year."[72] Another mother of four (ages seven through nineteen) reported that her husband had accused her of "running away from home" when she began taking courses at a community college. In fact, she wrote, she was really "running away from doing too much for my children." Her two younger children, she predicted, would be "much more self-sufficient" than their elder siblings, since she was now "too busy to wait on them hand and foot" and "somewhat happier myself."[73] Yet another correspondent, fearful that she had devolved into the "typical suburban housewife you picture so truthfully," explained her urgent desire to return to school: "I want to be a real wife and mother, not just a vampirish shell drawing the life's blood from the very ones I really want to give it to."[74]

But in general, only well-educated women—those who could rest assured that they would be rewarded for their efforts outside the home—could harness antimaternalism to the credo of self-development in a manner that affirmed their basic personhood. A final letter, written in 1969, tells a story that suggests, albeit unwittingly, why so many full-time homemakers felt blindsided rather than empowered by Friedan's critique. "Blindly eager for marriage," Mrs. B. had dropped out of college to marry at age eighteen, abandoning a full-tuition scholarship so she could put her husband through graduate school by working as a cocktail waitress. Over the next six years, she bore four children. "Those were happy years for me," she recalled. "I really felt creative when I made curtains for the living room, waxed the kitchen floor, and tucked the babies into fresh, clean cribs. . . . I truly loved to cook and sew and make scrap books of each child's babyhood." But her husband, now a university professor, did not share her feelings of domestic contentment, and a few years later their marriage "threatened to split wide open." Horrified, she "dragged" them first to a marriage counselor and then to a psychiatrist, who helped her to "see things more clearly." Her epiphany came when she found herself explaining to the psychiatrist, "when I try to look at my self, the real me, THERE'S ABSOLUTELY NOTHING THERE!" Convinced that she needed "a new identity other than housewife" in order to "rebuild a worn out marriage structure" and "create a more complete individual who in turn would be a better wife and mother," Mrs. B. acted on her husband's suggestion that she return to school. "It isn't easy and many times I feel guilty because the beds aren't made and the children have to fix their own lunch while I'm in the middle of a term paper," she concluded. "But I don't feel guilty enough to stop my own growth and I can't tell you how ALIVE I feel."

Though Mrs. B. wrote to Friedan as an ardent fan who "recognized herself on every page" of *The Feminine Mystique,* hers was not the standard narrative of feminist awakening.[75] As a mother and housewife, she had not suffered from feelings of futility, boredom, or emptiness; only when her husband threatened to leave did she conclude that she had a serious problem. Moreover, her psychiatrist did not urge her to "adjust" to her proper feminine role; he encouraged her to cultivate a more independent and autonomous identity. In other words, Mrs. B. came to appreciate Friedan's message after having been pushed beyond the home by two men, her husband and psychiatrist, who seem to have held a dismissive view of full-time housewives. From their perspective, Mrs. B.'s exclusive focus on her family—which most Americans would no doubt still have regarded as laudable—had ultimately resulted in a *lack* of self.

Mrs. B.'s story ended well. Her marriage survived (at least for the time being) and she felt more "alive" once she began to pursue her own, independent goals. Still, it is easy to imagine how a different woman—especially one who had never won a scholarship nor attended college for at least a year—might have proven far less resilient in the same situation. To many women who had devoted years of their lives to meeting others' needs, the growing imperative to cultivate an identity outside the home did not just feel, as Friedan would later allege, like a "threat." It felt more like a slap in the face.

In Defense of Homemaking: Friedan's Critics

If Friedan's critique led many women to voice feelings of relief, vindication, and even exhilaration, it prompted others to express a very different range of emotions. "Sigh. What is there about the American housewife that makes her an irresistible target?" asked a mother of four who had dropped out of college to marry and raise a family. "Am I dependent? I think rather that I am depended upon. Am I grasping? Without being in the least resentful, I think rather that I give more than I get."[76] Another woman penned an indignant letter after her closest friend—"a magna cum laude graduate, a devoted and loving wife, an excellent mother of four, an outstanding asset and contributor to her community's life"—confided that Friedan's article had left her feeling terribly "inadequate."[77] Likewise, a thirty-nine-year-old mother of four, who had done well in high school but lacked a college degree, described how demoralized she felt upon discovering that her husband concurred with Friedan's views. "Never have I felt useless or unneeded until now," she wrote. "Knowing my husband agreed so wholeheartedly with the article has knocked all the wind out of my sails, it was so unexpected. . . . I never felt like he begrudged my staying at home while he earned the living. I am crushed."[78] Obviously, these women did not feel validated and inspired after reading Friedan's article; they felt belittled, angry, or depressed.

Reading the letters from Friedan's critics alongside those from her fans, it almost seems as if the two groups of women inhabited alternate universes. Whereas many of the latter thought that American society denigrated career women while celebrating full-time homemakers, many of the former believed the reverse to be true. As one woman complained:

> I was brought up to believe that a woman was herself when she made a home for her husband and children. That was considered quite an achievement and women were looked up to because they were Mothers and wives not scientists, chemists, doctors, lawyers or astronauts. Please, won't someone come to the defense of the women who put in twelve hours a day trying to be good Mothers and wives, so they won't feel that in years to come they too may be replaced by another time saving appliance.[79]

Other *McCall's* readers also looked back wistfully to a time when the role of mother and homemaker had been held in higher regard. "I wish I had lived in my grandmother's time when a woman could proudly answer the question

'Who am I' with 'I'm a housewife and mother,'" wrote one respondent. "Please *no more degrading the housewife*."[80] To women who felt "besieged by magazine articles that say that [a woman's] life is wasted, worthless unless she finds a career to benefit society outside the home," Friedan's article did not read like a critique of social norms so much as an articulation of them.[81] Convinced that a transformation in women's roles was already well underway, they viewed the article as part of a broader trend toward devaluing homemaking and encouraging women to pursue careers.

Determined to resist this trend, the *McCall's* respondents promoted a vision of the maternal role that echoed the long-standing ideals of Republican and moral motherhood, while also subtly registering the cultural assault upon those ideals that this book has traced. Friedan's critics continued to define motherhood in fundamentally social terms, insisting that mothers and homemakers served not only their families, but also their God, country, and local communities. They also disputed the notion that motherhood and homemaking thwarted a woman's self-development, for they believed that women realized their deepest selves when they fulfilled their duties as wives and mothers. The fundamental dilemma that these women perceived was not the problem of reconciling the demands of motherhood with the imperatives of individualism; it was the problem of commanding respect and maintaining self-esteem in a culture that often demeaned their social role.

Friedan's critics were not of a single mind, however. Some were uncompromising traditionalists who perceived any change in women's roles as a threat to Christian values.[82] "Marriage *is* a vocation, instituted by God for the primary purpose of having children, which obviously involves sacrifices," wrote a college graduate from Galveston, Texas. "He never intended that a mother should leave her children and home to work, unless by necessity, which does not fall under the category of your own selfish ambitions."[83] In contrast, other respondents appropriated the more contemporary language of "feminine fulfillment" that Friedan excoriated. One woman, for instance, insisted that full-time homemakers were the "happiest, most contented women" she knew:

> These delightful, feminine women are vitally interested in their husbands' work, and show it by reading the Wall Street Journal, the Automotive News, or some such and converse intelligently at superb dinner parties for which they have cleaned and cooked and emerged radiantly confident that the evening will be a success. Their unselfishness does not erupt because they are supposed to be martyrs, but rather as a natural outgrowth of a peaceful, contented, love-filled heart.[84]

Rejecting older notions of maternal self-sacrifice, this woman portrayed the selflessness of the modern wife as a natural manifestation of her femininity, as effortless as her seemingly magical transformation from domestic worker to refined hostess.

Finally, yet another group of respondents concurred with Friedan's diagnosis of the "problem with no name," while adamantly rejecting the solutions she proposed. These women felt obliged to remain at home while their children were young, but they tended to view motherhood as a "job" and a particular life stage rather than an all-encompassing identity. For instance, the mother of an infant and a toddler, who had previously enjoyed working as a bookkeeper, acknowledged that she found homemaking "boring" and felt "trapped, frustrated and guilty." But whereas some of her friends had gone back to work after having children, she remained "very much against" the idea, believing that children were "entitled" to a full-time mother. "My children are much too precious to me that I'd leave them with another woman," she explained. "It is in their early years that their characters are formed, and this is a big job for a mother and it takes all the intelligence, patience and love I have to do it."[85] A former nurse, who likewise admitted to feelings of discontent, argued forthrightly that her child's development was simply "more important" than her own happiness.[86] These women did not laud maternal self-sacrifice, nor did they wax lyrical about the joys of feminine fulfillment. They simply resigned themselves to suppressing their personal desires, at least temporarily, because they accepted the proposition that young children had a profound need for intensive maternal care.

Regardless of how they framed the issue, however, nearly all of Friedan's critics believed that she radically undervalued women's daily efforts on behalf of their families, while overemphasizing the importance of achievements that required a significant degree of freedom from domestic responsibilities. "Who would dare say that doing a good job of raising my four children, being a good wife, and obeying my Lord, could count less in the eternal scheme of things than painting a picture that expresses my 'self'[?]" inquired one incredulous reader. Another woman, fearful of the impact Friedan's article might have on young mothers, wrote angrily, "It would be a fine thing if all the Mothers in America decided to follow her advice to 'Self Realization.' I would like Miss or Mrs. Friedan to tell me what would happen to the future generations of children deprived of having just a plain ordinary 'Mom.'"[87] According to these women, the "plain" and "ordinary" mother should be lauded at least as much as the "exceptional" woman who distinguished herself through professional or artistic accomplishments.

As these remarks suggest, most of Friedan's critics regarded the pursuit of self-realization as a shallow and unworthy goal that conflicted with the fulfillment of civic and familial duties. In language reminiscent of John F. Kennedy's 1961 inaugural address, which famously revived the rhetoric of civic republicanism ("Ask not what your country can do for you . . ."), they challenged the prevailing therapeutic ethos. "Many women regard the upbringing of children and the concomitant housework as a service to society and a duty to their husbands," explained one woman. "Our happiness comes unsought as the fruit of unselfish work. Fulfillment is a gift, not a goal."[88] The "frustrated neurotic . . . usually has no one but herself to blame," another woman wrote. "She feeds her discontent by asking, 'Who am I?' and 'What shall I do with my life?' Never wondering, 'What can I do for my husband, family, community?' or 'How can I serve my God?' "[89] When these women felt discouraged or frustrated, they did not typically seek out psychological counseling (or at least they did not own up to doing so in their letters). Rather, they sought sustenance in God or tried to summon a sense of duty. "It seems to me that if these trapped, frustrated women would put as much faith in God as they put in their psychoanalyst, their problems would be greatly reduced," ventured one woman.[90] "Ego is a relatively new word," wrote another. "Has [Friedan] ever heard of these relics?—Patience, Fortitude, Faith, Will-Power?"[91]

The skepticism with which Friedan's critics regarded her call for self-realization is also evident in their view of the mother-child relationship. Compared to Friedan's fans, they referred more frequently to maternal "responsibilities," "duties," and "obligations," while placing somewhat less emphasis on the importance of "enjoying" their children. They were more willing to accept the notion that a child's deepest needs might sometimes conflict with his or her mother's deepest desires. Indeed, these women would have scoffed at the notion that children benefited most from a mother who was happy and fulfilled, even if the mother's happiness and fulfillment required her to be away from home for much of the day. As one young mother—a college graduate who hoped to resume to her career eventually—explained, she would be "ashamed" to ask herself such questions as "Who am I? What Should I Do with My Life?":

> I cannot be so selfish when I see my three precious children in front of me with their lives in my hands. A child cannot live on all this great education from his mother or appreciate her great talents. He cannot survive without warmth, love, understanding and a secure home life. And no one can convince me that with a mother home only a few hours of the day she can provide this love and secure home.[92]

What children most needed, these women firmly believed, was their mother's presence.

Thus, even as Friedan's critics rejected the therapeutic emphasis on self-development, they reiterated the claims of postwar psychological authorities regarding the importance of the mother-child bond. Many buttressed their defense of full-time motherhood by referencing experts who drew an association between maternal employment and juvenile delinquency or disputed the idea that group care could adequately meet the emotional needs of young children.[93] One woman, for instance, rebuked Friedan for promoting nursery schools when "the modern studies of psychology point more and more to the importance of the early years."[94] Another reader flatly asserted, "Only the unprofessional love and care of a mother can prepare a child properly to face life."[95] Because these women viewed full-time maternal care as so indispensable to children's mental health, they judged middle-class mothers who placed their children in day care quite harshly. "I personally do not believe we can place [our children] in a professional nursery for the sake of a career . . . as one would place a dog in a reputable kennel while you go on vacation," a mother of three preschool-aged children opined.

Yet while Friedan's critics perceived intensive maternal care as essential for children's development, their responses nevertheless reveal the extent to which they had been influenced by the transformation of motherhood. Rather than stressing the role that mothers played in promoting children's moral and spiritual development, some respondents defined the mother's primary responsibility in more psychological terms, as that of equipping the child with a sense of emotional security. One woman argued that mothers of young children "should be home, keeping their families together, raising children who are happy and secure."[96] Another demanded, "What is more rewarding than meeting the emotional needs of a child as they arise?"[97] Still other respondents echoed the noninterventionist approach promoted by experts wary of pernicious maternal influence. For instance, one woman argued that mothers could best "guide our families along" by "being available when small people feel like talking or asking questions," while another went out of her way to clarify, "I do not try to live through anyone. Such possession of another's soul is the worst perversion of love."[98] To be sure, many of Friedan's critics continued to argue that mothers played a crucial role in educating children and overseeing their moral, spiritual, and social development. But even the most conservative women refrained from using effusive language when discussing the benefits of maternal care, and none subscribed to the view that mothers should attempt to bind children to the home through "silver cords" of love.

Moreover, while Friedan's critics insisted that no one could care for a child as well as his or her own mother, the very fact that they felt compelled to articulate and defend this claim is itself notable. In the past, a white, middle-class mother could take for granted that society would view her as uniquely equipped to care for her own children. Yet many of Friedan's respondents sounded defensive and anxious when emphasizing the importance of their maternal labor, presumably because they no longer felt the same degree of societal support for their role. As one woman wrote:

> I know that it has become fashionable to depreciate the role of the housewife, and that to suggest that homemaking is a career in itself is to invite sneers and snickers; but, please, Betty Friedan, can't we poor, misguided souls cling to the belief that the welfare of our children is still of some importance and that they perhaps benefit just a wee bit from the tender, loving care of a mother? I have the outmoded idea that my talents and education enable me to bring up my children more capably than any "substitute mother" or day nursery.[99]

Like this woman, many of Friedan's critics favorably contrasted their own mothering to the inferior care that a paid "substitute mother" would presumably provide. Yet, their remarks often betray a kind of status anxiety arising from the prospect of commercialized caregiving: if large numbers of middle-class and upper-middle-class families began paying other women low wages to perform such work, what would it imply about a full-time homemaker's worth? "I see in all articles written about women working outside the home, [no] mention is made of babysitters and household life," wrote one woman. "If the care of a house and children is so degrading and unrewarding and unfulfilling to a wife and mother, why isn't it so to other women, and why should other women do such work?"[100] Another woman wondered, "Are the children so unimportant? Am I so unimportant to them that just anybody we could afford to pay would have been good enough to bring them up?"[101] To many of Friedan's critics, the suggestion that childcare could be purchased in the marketplace was itself demeaning. However, because the culture strongly prohibited mothers from overidentifying with their children or taking credit for their children's successes, these women were somewhat constrained in their ability to assert the importance of their maternal efforts.

Finally, the broader transformation of maternal ideals is also apparent in the ways that Friedan's respondents referred to pregnancy and childbirth. As we have seen, a deep appreciation of the perils of childbirth persisted through the 1930s and into the 1940s; recall that both Neilson and Wylie received letters from respondents who protested that mothers should be shown proper deference and respect because of the pain and suffering they endured. Friedan did not receive similar responses. In fact, very few respondents referred to childbirth at all, and those who did generally downplayed its significance. "It takes a lot more than bringing a child into this world to be worthy of the name 'mother' in its full meaning," asserted one woman.[102] "The act of childbirth does not create a real mother," wrote another. "The years spent, not in momism, but in *real* motherhood develop one facet of self-fulfillment."[103] In the past, the act of childbirth had often been imagined as a perilous passage that did, at least in part, "create a mother." Yet by the 1960s, respect for the physical act of childbearing had diminished, and women no longer tried to stake claims on the basis of maternal pain and suffering.

In defending motherhood and homemaking as a serious and "responsible undertaking," Friedan's critics were fighting a rearguard action against the forces of historical change. From the Revolutionary through the Progressive eras, such a defense of the mother-homemaker role had been a key strategy for American women who sought to enhance their status within the home and gain great influence within society at large. But Friedan's critics did not champion motherhood as a way of claiming new rights or responsibilities; on the contrary, they did so either to criticize other women who were branching out in new directions or to assert their own value and importance in the face of social change. The arguments they used were strikingly similar to those of their foremothers, but the context lent them a different political valence: as historian Linda Kerber has observed, "the language of Republican motherhood, once a progressive language (if ambivalently so), increasingly became a conservative one."[104]

By the time *The Feminine Mystique* appeared, a fundamental division had already begun to emerge among white, middle-class women. Some women felt prepared to minimize, even jettison the traditionally defined roles of "housewife" and "mother" (though not necessarily the experience of being a wife or mother) in order to cultivate greater autonomy and to compete on equal terms with men. But for other women, those roles did not represent oppression or constraint but rather the basis of a meaningful identity. In 1963, the political significance of this division remained incipient. But as Friedan's correspondence reveals, the intense emotions that women on both sides harbored about their roles as mothers and homemakers—their feelings of love and resentment, pride and guilt, purposefulness and futility—had already been compounded by a sense of grievance in relation to the broader culture. When feminists and antifeminists built movements that allowed those feelings to acquire political meaning and direction, the result would be explosive and transformative.

It is hard not to feel a sense of regret. Was it essential to attack the mother-homemaker role in order to challenge gender discrimination and fight for sexual equality? Considering the cultural images, social norms, laws, and economic constraints that determined women's status and opportunities in the 1950s and early 1960s, one must conclude that, yes, it was absolutely essential. But was it necessary to launch a full-scale assault on the notion that motherhood and homemaking could be the basis of a fulfilling and productive life? In retrospect, Friedan's appropriation of antimaternalism appears both ironic and counterproductive, since it played an important role in generating the widespread demoralization of suburban women that she decried.

If readers conclude that the crucial lesson to be learned here is that liberal feminism was "antimotherhood," however, then I have failed in my task. It is indeed regrettable that the leading spokeswoman of the movement's initial phase appropriated the momism critique so uncritically, but the larger historical point is that the antimaternalist dimension of *The Feminine Mystique* was among its *least* original components. A significant presence within American culture since the 1920s, antimaternalism emerged as a notable force during the very period renowned for its glorification of motherhood and homemaking. By portraying her own appropriation of antimaternalism as a new departure, wholly at odds with the dominant culture's depiction of motherhood, Friedan helped to establish a somewhat misleading and confusing historical account of the 1940s and 1950s that sank deep roots. In the process, she obscured the extent to which antimaternalist critiques had already transformed and diminished the maternal role prior to the emergence of second-wave feminism.[105]

Reading Friedan's correspondence today, it is easy to discern the passionate beliefs and emotions that would fuel not only liberal feminism but also the subsequent mobilization of conservative women. But few feminists in the 1960s and 1970s foresaw the coming reaction, in part because they did not fully grasp how deeply committed many women remained to the mother-homemaker role. Even Betty Friedan, initially "shaken" by all those letters from angry *McCall's* readers, ended up explaining away the evidence before her. Reflecting on the reception of *The Feminine Mystique* in 1973, she noted that the "strange hostility" she had met with from some women at first "amazed and puzzled" her, until she realized that, "if you were afraid to face your real feelings about the husband and children you were presumably living for, then someone like me opening up the can of worms was a menace."[106] In other words, Friedan concluded that women who felt offended by her critique were living in a state of denial that prevented them from acknowledging how unhappy they truly felt.

By 1981, Friedan had changed her tune. That year, soon after the New Right swept to power following Ronald Reagan's election, she published another book, *The Second Stage*. Written in part as a last-ditch attempt to rally support for the Equal Rights Amendment, the book addressed head-on a troubling development for feminism—the rise of a grassroots women's movement determined to stymie progress toward feminist goals. Mobilized by Phyllis Schlafly's STOP-ERA campaign, conservative housewives played a central role in halting progress toward passage of the Equal Rights Amendment.[107] They also formed the main constituency of a new anti-abortion movement that emerged in the wake of the 1973 Supreme Court decision, *Roe v. Wade*.[108] Confronted with this resurgent conservatism and its valorization of traditional motherhood, Friedan reassessed the relationship between feminism and the family. The "first stage" of the feminist movement—the fight for equal opportunities in the workplace—had basically been won, she argued. "But the liberation that began with the women's movement isn't finished. The equality we fought for isn't livable, isn't workable, isn't comfortable in the terms that structured our battle."[109] Now, men and women needed to move to a "second stage" that would address the difficulties that sexual equality posed to familial life.

If Friedan's proposal for a "second stage" represented a response to the New Right, it can also be seen as a reaction to younger, more radical feminists whose critiques of motherhood and the family went far beyond her own. In *The Second Stage*, Friedan voiced regret over the ways in which her earlier work had contributed to an antimaternalist strain within the feminist movement. As she explained, the feminists of her own generation had never really rejected motherhood or the family; they had been "locked in violent reaction against their own identity—in those days when a woman was defined not as a person in herself, but as someone else's wife or mother." Yet ironically, even as Friedan recanted her relentlessly negative depiction of domesticity and motherhood, she continued to reproduce Wylie's momism critique—this time as a way of dismissing the views of radical feminists. Quoting Shulamith Firestone, who characterized motherhood as "a condition of terminal psychological and social decay, total self-abnegation and physical deterioration," Friedan argued that such "rhetorical extremes" could only be understood as a manifestation of the "personal rage smoldering under the excessive, self-denying 'smotherlove' of countless women who took Dr. Spock literally in that era."[110] Even in the 1980s, Friedan remained so enmeshed in the momism paradigm that she could critique antimaternalist views only by reviving her own, less extreme version of antimaternalism.

There is much to criticize in *The Second Stage*. Because Friedan conceded ground to the movement's critics, because she prematurely declared victory in areas where much work remained to be done, and because she continued to employ a universalizing "we," most feminists dismissed the book as a contemptible retreat. (Sarah Stage, referencing Booker T. Washington, called it Friedan's "Atlanta Compromise.")[111] Still, there is also something admirable in Friedan's belated attempt to understand the viewpoint of women who strongly identified as full-time homemakers. In one crucial passage, she wrote:

> The women's movement did not fail in the battle for equality. Our failure was our blind spot about the family. It was our own extreme reaction against the wife-mother role: that devotional dependence on men and nurture of children and housewife service which has been and still is the source of power and identity, purpose and self-worth and economic security for so many women—even if it is not all that secure any more. . . .
>
> Something very complex is involved here. Is there a real polarization between the feminist who wants equality and "choice," and the woman for whom "the family" is security? Aren't those feminists who most stridently deny the family trying to deny that woman's vulnerability in themselves? Do women who want equal rights really threaten that clean, pure, sacred family morality that once made her feel secure? Or are ERA advocates threatening because they make her aware of her real insecurity, and her buried wish for independence and autonomy?[112]

Here, Friedan put her finger on the crucial question: was it inevitable that feminists who hoped to transcend the roles of wife and mother should find themselves at odds with women who continued to construct their identities primarily in these terms? Friedan clearly wanted to believe that both groups of women could be united in their interests and concerns. But surely this was wishful thinking. Though feminists supported a whole host of measures designed to make housewives less economically vulnerable, committed traditionalists would never believe that feminism represented their true interests.[113] For in truth, the two groups held fundamentally different and irreconcilable views of womanhood and motherhood.

By the 1960s, middle-class women, whether liberal-leaning or traditionalist, confronted a situation not of their own making—a transformation and diminution of motherhood and homemaking. The mother-homemaker role commanded less respect than it had in the past, and it could no longer be assumed to be the stable core around which the majority of women would build their entire adult lives. For many women, this represented an opening or opportunity; for others, it felt like a loss or a threat. But to focus narrowly on the conflicts that emerged in the 1970s—as if traditionalists rose up simply because a feminist movement threatened their self-conception as mothers and homemakers—is to fail to grasp the larger historical dynamics that paved the way for such confrontations. In this sense, both liberal feminism and the conservative women's movements of the 1970s and 1980s can be viewed as reactions to the decline of maternalism and the transformation of mother-hood that it entailed.

Notes

Introduction

1. Transcript of the Twentieth Anniversary Dinner in honor of President William A. Neilson, p. 59, November 16, 1937, Smith College Club of New York City records, Acc. 03A-094, box 3, Smith College Archives, Northampton, MA. Throughout, the transcript parenthetically makes note of "laughter" or "applause." The "mother love" remark was one of only two times during Neilson's lengthy speech when the audience both laughed and applauded. I am extremely grateful to archivist Nanci Young for tracking down the transcript of this speech.

2. "Dr. Neilson Finds Mother Love Is Only Self-Love," *New York Herald Tribune,* November 17, 1937, 1; "Dr. Neilson Warns on Mother Love," *New York Times,* November 17, 1937, 25; and "Mother-Love Talk Stirs Up a Storm," *New York Times,* November 18, 1937, 25, folder 797, box 38, series V, William A. Neilson Personal Papers, Smith College Archives, Northampton, MA (hereafter WANPP).

3. Alumna-Parent, "Letters to the Times," *New York Times,* November 19, 1937, 18.

4. Sara Jordan to the editor, *Boston Traveler,* November 26, 1937, folder 823, box 39, series V, WANPP.

5. Important works include Ruth H. Bloch, "American Feminine Ideals in Transition: The Rise of the Moral Mother, 1790–1815," *Feminist Studies* 4 (June 1978): 100–26; Nancy F. Cott, *The Bonds of Womanhood: "Woman's Sphere" in New England, 1780–1835* (New Haven, CT: Yale University Press, 1977); Ann Douglas, *The Feminization of American Culture* (New York: Alfred A. Knopf, 1979); Sylvia D. Hoffert, *Private Matters: American Attitudes toward Childbearing and Infant Nurture in the Urban North, 1800–60* (Urbana: University of Illinois Press, 1989); Amy Kaplan, "Manifest Domesticity," *American Literature* 70, no. 3 (September 1998): 581–606; Anne L. Kuhn, *The Mother's Role in Childhood Education: New England Concepts, 1830–1860* (New Haven, CT: Yale University Press, 1947); Jan Lewis, "Mother's Love: The Construction of an Emotion in Nineteenth-Century America," in *Social History and Issues in Human Consciousness: Some Interdisciplinary Connections,* ed. Andrew E. Barnes and Peter N. Stearns (New York: New York University Press, 1989), 209–29; Mary P. Ryan, *Cradle of the Middle Class: The Family in Oneida County, New York, 1790–1865* (Cambridge: Cambridge University Press, 1981); and idem, *The Empire of the Mother: American Writing about Domesticity* (New York: Harrington Park Press, 1982).

6. The literature on the rise of scientific motherhood is vast. Important works include Rima D. Apple, *Perfect Motherhood: Science and Childrearing in America* (New Brunswick, NJ: Rutgers University Press, 2006); Julia Grant, *Raising Baby by the Book: The Education of American Mothers* (New Haven, CT: Yale University Press, 1998); Kathleen W. Jones, *Taming the Troublesome Child: American Families, Child Guidance, and the Limits of Psychiatric Authority* (Cambridge, MA: Harvard University Press, 1999), Molly Ladd-Taylor, *Mother-Work: Women, Child Welfare, and the State, 1890–1930* (Urbana: University of Illinois Press, 1994); idem, *Raising a Baby the Government Way: Mothers' Letters to the Children's Bureau, 1915–1932* (New Brunswick, NJ: Rutgers University Press, 1986), 1–46; Alice Boardman Smuts, *Science in the Service of Children, 1893–1935* (New Haven, CT: Yale University Press, 2006); Susan Contratto, "Mother: Social Sculptor and Trustee of the Faith," in Miriam Lewin, ed., *In the Shadow of the Past: Psychology Portrays the Sexes: A Social and Intellectual History* (New York: Columbia University Press, 1984), 226–55; and Barbara Ehrenreich and Deirdre English, *For Her Own Good: 150 Years of Experts' Advice to Women* (Garden City, NY: Anchor Press, 1978), chap. 6.

7. Ann Douglas, *Terrible Honesty: Mongrel Manhattan in the 1920s* (New York: Farrar, Straus, and Giroux, 1995). See esp. chap. 6. Christine Stansell has described how an earlier generation of female modernists vehemently refused identification with their mothers. "The psychology of disaffiliation spread through feminism, so much so that the disavowal of the mother came to be almost a trademark of female modernism. . . . The very stuff of the daughterly self, the 'I' so different from the woman her late nineteenth-century mother thought she should be, could represent defiant recantation." Christine Stansell, *American Moderns: Bohemian New York and the Creation of a New Century* (New York: Metropolitan Books, 2000), 247.

8. William A. Neilson to "Grania" [Mrs. Harold B. Hoskins], November 23, 1937, folder 823, box 39, series V, WANPP.

9. [N.p., n.d.], folder 823, box 39, series V, WANPP.

10. [New York, NY] to William A. Neilson, November 17, 1937, folder 823, box 39, series V, WANPP.

11. [Somerville, MA, n.d.], folder 823, box 39, series V, WANPP.

12. [Houston, TX], December 3, 1937, folder 823, box 39, series V, WANPP.

13. [New York, NY], November 8, 1937, folder 823, box 39, series V, WANPP.

14. Dorothy Dix, "Life Lines: 'Mother Love' That Shuts Door of Opportunity Is the Worst Type of Self Love," clipping, folder 823, box 39, series V, WANPP.

15. [New York, NY], November 12, 1937, folder 823, box 39, series V, WANPP.

16. [New York, NY], February 2, 1937, folder 823, box 39, series V, WANPP.

17. See, e.g., Jennifer Terry, "'Momism' and the Making of Treasonous Homosexuals," in *"Bad" Mothers: The Politics of Blame in Twentieth-Century America*, ed. Molly Ladd-Taylor and Lauri Umansky (New York: New York University Press, 1998), 169–90; and Michael Paul Rogin, "Kiss Me Deadly: Communism, Motherhood, and Cold War Movies," *Representations* 6 (Spring 1984): 1–36. Ruth Feldstein uses the term "gender conservatism" in *Motherhood in Black and White: Race and Sex in American Liberalism, 1930–1965* (Ithaca, NY: Cornell University Press, 2000), 40, 2–3.

18. Ann Douglas has written, "It is easy, I think, to underestimate cultural power, particularly cultural power like the Victorian matriarch's, that is grounded largely in religious organizations, beliefs and practices. The matriarch's authority, however the moderns exaggerated it, was the ascendant cultural force in late-Victorian America, and it did not disappear after the Great War." Similarly, I argue that, although female moral authority was in steep decline by the

1940s, many Americans still perceived it as a significant cultural force—and reacted accordingly. Douglas, *Terrible Honesty*, 7.

19. My argument both builds upon and departs from Feldstein's analysis. Focusing on the period from 1930 through 1965, Feldstein shows how mother-blaming proved central to the emergence of racial liberalism in the midcentury United States: the same psychologists and social scientists who sought to discredit biological theories of racial difference, she demonstrates, often implicated mothers in the perpetuation of racial prejudice. Whereas experts accused white "moms" of rearing sons susceptible to authoritarian attitudes and prejudicial thinking, they blamed black "matriarchs" for raising sons incapable of withstanding racial prejudice without severe personality distortion. Noting how these harsh critiques of mothers helped to promote a new liberal paradigm that defined racism as "un-American," Feldstein cautions, "Mother-blaming cannot be explained as simply a conservative backlash, or only as an expression of reactionary misogyny." These are crucial insights that I draw on in the chapters that follow. Yet, to my mind, her term "gender conservatism" does not adequately capture the thrust of much midcentury mother-blaming, since many critics sought to undermine *traditional* forms of female authority. Although I view midcentury mother-blaming as deeply misogynist and at times explicitly antifeminist, I do not see it as a "conservative" force in regard to gender ideology. Feldstein, *Motherhood in Black and White*, 40, 2–3.

20. Elizabeth Dilling, *The Red Network: A Who's Who and Handbook of Radicalism for Patriots* (Chicago: Ayer, 1935), 310. During World War II, Dilling would play a leading role in the far-right Mothers' Movement. See Glen Jeansonne, *Women of the Far Right: The Mothers' Movement and World War II* (Chicago: University of Chicago Press, 1996).

21. Maria Leonard to Neilson, December 25, 1937, folder 823, box 39, series V, WANPP.

22. Violet Allyn Storet, "Letters to the Times," *New York Times*, November 19, 1937, 18.

23. Seth Koven and Sonya Michel, "Womanly Duties: Maternalist Politics and the Origins of Welfare States in France, Germany, Great Britain, and the United States, 1880–1920," *American Historical Review* 95, no. 4 (1990): 1076–108. Idem eds., *Mothers of a New World: Maternalist Politics and the Origins of Welfare States* (New York: Routledge, 1993), 4, 6. Important works that focus on maternalist reformers in the United States include Ladd-Taylor, *Mother-Work*; Theda Skocpol, *Protecting Soldiers and Mothers: The Political Origins of Social Policy in the United States* (Cambridge, MA: Belknap Press, 1992); Gwendolyn Mink, *The Wages of Motherhood: Inequality in the Welfare State, 1917–1942* (Ithaca, NY: Cornell University Press, 1995); Lynne Curry, *Modern Mothers in the Heartland: Gender, Health and Progress in Illinois, 1990–1930* (Columbus: University of Ohio Press, 1999); and Linda Gordon, *Pitied But Not Entitled: Single Mothers and the History of Welfare* (Cambridge, MA: Harvard University Press, 1994). See also Robyn Muncy, *Creating a Dominion in American Female Reform, 1890–1935* (New York: Oxford University Press, 1991), a work that does not use the concept of maternalism but that addresses many of the same historical developments.

24. The term "social feminism" was used by J. Stanley Lemons in *The Woman Citizen: Social Feminism in the 1920s* (Urbana: University of Illinois Press, 1973). Nancy F. Cott advocated a more narrow use of "feminism" in "What's in a Name? The Limits of 'Social Feminism'; or, Expanding the Vocabulary of Women's History," *Journal of American History* 76, no. 3 (December 1989): 809–29. For an opposing view, see Karen Offen, "Defining Feminism: A Comparative Historical Approach," *Signs* 14, no. 1 (1988): 119–57.

25. Christine Kimberly Erickson, "Conservative Women and Patriotic Maternalism: The Beginnings of a Gendered Conservative Tradition in the 1920s and 1930s" (PhD diss., University

of Santa Barbara, 1999); and Laura McEnaney, *Civil Defense Begins at Home: Militarization Meets Everyday Life in the Fifties* (Princeton, NJ: Princeton University Press, 2001), chap. 4.

26. For an astute discussion of the concept of "sensibility" as an object of historical inquiry, see Daniel Wickberg, "What Is the History of Sensibilities? On Cultural Histories, Old and New," *American Historical Review* 112, no. 3 (June 2007): 661–84. Wickberg claims that a focus on sensibilities can allow historians to move away from an exclusive concern with representations, toward an analysis of "the perceptual, emotive, and conceptual frameworks" that allow objects or phenomena to be represented in a particular manner. The concept's value, he argues, is that "by bringing together the elements of sense perception, cognition, emotion, aesthetic form, moral judgment, and cultural difference, it provides a way of talking about an object of historical study that is both ubiquitous and yet strangely invisible" (quotation, 669).

27. I am not arguing that this is the "right" way to define "maternalist" or "maternalism." Because these terms were hardly ever used in the past, the question of historical accuracy—an issue in debates concerning how to define the term "feminism"—is not at stake. While the basic idea that motherhood is central to women's public or civic identities must figure in any definition of maternalism, I believe that scholars should define the term in whatever manner provides the maximum analytical payoff in relation to the particular phenomena and context that they hope to explain. Other scholars, however, have argued for a more narrow definition. For discussions of the issue, see Lynn Weiner, Ann Taylor Allen, Eileen Boris, and Molly Ladd-Taylor, "Maternalism as Paradigm: Defining the Issues," *Journal of Women's History* 5 (Fall 1993): 96–130; Geoff Eley and Atina Grossman, "Maternalism and Citizenship in Weimar Germany: The Gendered Politics of Welfare," *Central European History* 30, no. 1 (1997): 67–75; and Eileen Boris, "On the Importance of Naming: Gender, Race, and the Writing of Policy History," *Journal of Policy History* 17, no. 1 (2005): 72–92.

28. Holly Stovall, "Resisting Regimentation: The Committee to Oppose the Conscription of Women," *Peace and Change* 23 (October 1998): 483–99.

29. For works on the emergence of modern feminism and the "New Woman," see Nancy F. Cott, *The Grounding of Modern Feminism* (New Haven: Yale University Press, 1987); Stansell, *American Moderns*; and Jean V. Matthews, *The Rise of the New Woman: The Women's Movement in America, 1875–1930* (New York: Ivan R. Dee, 2003).

30. According to historian Ian Tyrrell, the temperance reformer Hannah Whitall Smith coined the phrase "organized mother-love" in 1890 to describe the efforts of the World's WCTU (Woman's Christian Temperance Union). Ian Tyrrell, *Woman's World, Woman's Empire: The Woman's Christian Temperance Union in International Perspective, 1880–1930* (Chapel Hill: University of North Carolina Press, 1991), 125.

31. On sentimental emotional culture and intimate same-sex friendships in the nineteenth century, see Carroll Smith-Rosenberg, "The Female World of Love and Ritual: Relations Between Women in Nineteen Century America," *Signs* 1, no. 1 (1975): 1–29; Donald Yacovone, "Abolitionists and the 'Language of Fraternal Love,'" in *Meanings for Manhood*, ed. Carnes and Griffen, 85–95. Changes in cultural and medical views of same-sex friendships are discussed in Lillian Faderman, *Surpassing the Love of Men: Romantic Friendship and Love Between Women from the Renaissance to the Present* (1981; New York: HarperCollins, 2001); Martha Vicinus, *Intimate Friends: Women Who Loved Women, 1778–1928* (Chicago: University of Chicago Press, 2004); Linda W. Rosenzweig, *Another Self: Middle-Class American Women and Their Friends in the Twentieth Century* (New York: New York University Press, 1999). Other important works that discuss the rise of new attitudes toward sexuality and homosexuality include Christina Sim-

mons, "Modern Sexuality and the Myth of Victorian Repression," in *Passion and Power: Sexuality in History*, ed. Kathy Peiss and Christina Simmons (Philadelphia: Temple University Press, 1989), 157–77; John D'Emilio and Estelle B. Freedman, *Intimate Matters: A History of Sexuality in America* (New York: Harper & Row, 1988); and George Chauncey, *Gay New York: Gender, Urban Culture, and the Making of the Gay Male World, 1890–1940* (New York: Basic Books, 1994).

32. For discussions of sentimental affectivity between mothers and their children in the nineteenth and early twentieth centuries, and the growing concerns about maternal pathology that emerged thereafter, see Peter N. Stearns, *American Cool: Constructing a Twentieth-Century Emotional Style* (New York: New York University Press, 1994), 34–8, 79–80, 164–71; John C. Spurlock and Cynthia A. Magistro, *New and Improved: The Transformation of American Women's Emotional Culture* (New York: New York University Press, 1998), chap. 5; Nancy M. Theriot, *Mothers and Daughters in Nineteenth-Century America: The Biosocial Construction of Femininity*, rev. ed. (Lexington: University of Kentucky, 1996); and Linda W. Rosenzweig, *The Anchor of My Life: Middle-Class American Mothers and Daughters, 1880–1920* (New York: New York University Press, 1993). See also Michael Roper, "Maternal Relations: Moral Manliness and Emotional Survival in Letters Home during the First World War," in *Masculinity in Politics and War: Rewritings of Modern History*, ed. Stefan Dudink, Karen Hagermann, and John Tosh (Manchester: Manchester University Press, 2004), 295–315.

33. John B. Watson, *Psychological Care of Infant and Child* (New York: W.W. Norton, 1928), 80.

34. As Julia Grant has shown, concerns about overprotective mothers who reared effeminate sons date back to the late nineteenth century and emerged as a constant refrain in psychological literature of the 1920s. Julia Grant, "'A Real Boy' and Not a Sissy: Gender, Childhood and Masculinity, 1890–1940," *Journal of Social History* 37, no. 4 (2004): 82–41. On the connections between maternal pathology, male effeminacy and homosexuality, and political subversion, see Susan Zeiger, "She Didn't Raise Her Boy To Be a Slacker: Motherhood, Conscription, and the Culture of the First World War," *Feminist Studies* 22, no. 1 (1996): 7–39; Rogin, "Kiss Me Deadly"; and Terry, "'Momism' and the Making of Treasonous Homosexuals."

35. For works on the history of fatherhood in the twentieth-century United States, see Robert Griswold, *Fatherhood in America: A History* (New York: Basic Books, 1993); Rachel Devlin, *Relative Intimacy: Fathers, Adolescent Daughters and Postwar American Culture* (Chapel Hill: University of North Carolina Press, 2005); Jessica Weiss, "Making Room for Fathers: Men, Women, and Parenting in the United States, 1945–1980," in *A Shared Experience: Men, Women and the History of Gender*, ed. Laura McCall and Donald Yacovone (New York: New York University Press, 1998), 349–68; Ralph LaRossa, *The Modernization of Fatherhood: A Social and Political History* (Chicago: University of Chicago Press, 1997); and James Gilbert, *Men in the Middle: Searching for Masculinity in the 1950s* (Chicago: University of Chicago Press, 2005), chap. 7.

36. For discussions of nineteenth-century views of manhood, see Mark C. Carnes and Clyde Griffen, eds., *Meanings for Manhood: Constructions of Masculinity in Victorian America* (Chicago: University of Chicago Press, 1990); Mary Chapman and Glenn Hendler, eds., *Sentimental Men: Masculinity and the Politics of Affect in American Culture* (Berkeley: University of California Press, 1999); Frances Clarke, *Sentimental Bonds: Suffering, Sacrifice and Benevolence in the Civil War North* (Chicago: University of Chicago Press, forthcoming); and E. Anthony Rotundo, *American Manhood: Transformations in Masculinity from the Revolution to the Modern Era* (New York: Basic Books, 1993). For works that focus specifically on fatherhood, see Shawn Johansen, *Family Men: Middle-Class Fatherhood*

in Early Industrializing America (New York: Routledge University Press, 2001); and Stephen Frank, *Life with Father: Parenthood and Masculinity in the Nineteenth-Century American North* (Baltimore: Johns Hopkins University Press, 1998).

37. Arnaldo Testi, "The Gender of Reform Politics: Theodore Roosevelt and the Culture of Masculinity," *Journal of American History* 81, no. 4 (March 1995): 1509–33 (quotation, 1523). See also Julia Grant, "A 'Real Boy' and Not a Sissy"; and Gail Bederman, *Manliness and Civilization: A Cultural History of Gender and Race in the United States, 1880–1917* (Chicago: University of Chicago Press, 1995). For a study that argues for greater continuity between Victorian and modern conceptions of manhood, see Ben Jordan, "'A Modest Manliness': The Boy Scouts of America and the Making of Modern Masculinity, 1910–1930" (PhD diss., University of California, San Diego, 2009).

38. This literature is too vast to cite comprehensively. Important works include John C. Burnham, *Paths into American Culture: Psychology, Medicine, and Morals* (Philadelphia: Temple University Press, 1988); Ellen Herman, *The Romance of American Psychology: Political Culture in the Age of Experts* (Berkeley: University of California Press, 1995); Gerald Grob, *From Asylum to Community: Mental Health Policy in Modern America* (Princeton, NJ: Princeton University Press, 1991), chap. 1; Nathan G. Hale, Jr., *The Rise and Crisis of Psychoanalysis in the United States: Freud and the Americans, 1917–1985* (Oxford: Oxford University Press, 1995); Elizabeth Lunbeck, *The Psychiatric Persuasion: Knowledge, Gender, and Power in Modern America* (Princeton, NJ: Princeton University Press, 1994); Eva S. Moskowitz, *In Therapy We Trust: America's Obsession with Self-Fulfillment* (Baltimore: Johns Hopkins University Press, 2001); Mari Jo Buhle, *Feminism and Its Discontents: A Century of Struggle with Psychoanalysis* (Cambridge, MA: Harvard University Press, 1998); Eli Zaretsky, *Secrets of the Soul: A Social and Cultural History of Psychoanalysis* (New York: Knopf, 2004); T. J. Jackson Lears, *No Place of Grace: Antimodernism and the Transformation of American Culture, 1880–1920* (Chicago: University of Chicago Press, 1994); and idem, "From Salvation to Self-Realization: Advertising and the Therapeutic Roots of the Consumer Culture, 1880–1930," in *The Culture of Consumption: Critical Essays in American History, 1880–1930*, ed. Richard Wightman Fox and T. J. Jackson Lears (New York: Pantheon Books, 1983); Warren I. Susman, "Personality and the Making of Twentieth-Century Culture," in *Culture as History: The Transformation of American Society in the Twentieth Century* (New York: Pantheon, 1984): 271–85; and Sonya Michel, "American Conscience and the Unconscious: Psychoanalysis and the Rise of Personal Religion, 1906–1963," *Psychoanalysis and Contemporary Thought* 7 (1983): 387–421.

39. "Mother-Love Talk Stirs Up a Storm," 25. Karl A. Menninger to Neilson, March 12, 1938, folder 832, box 39, series V, WANPP.

40. Karl A. Menninger to Neilson, March 12, 1938, folder 832, box 39, series V, WANPP. In his 1942 bestseller, *Love against Hate*, Menninger referred to the Neilson episode when describing how some of his own remarks, "to the effect that we should study 'mother hate' as well as 'mother love,'" had prompted newspapers across the country to run editorials lauding "the great sacrifices that mothers make" and condemning "the callousness of modern scientific opinion." Karl A. Menninger, *Love against Hate* (New York: Harcourt, Brace & World, 1942), 29.

41. Helen A. Schadd, "Letters to the Times," *New York Times*, November 19, 1937, 18.

42. William C. Lengel to Neilson, December 9, 1937, folder 832, box 39, series V, WANPP; Wainwright Evans, "Memorandum," December 16, 1937, folder 832, box 39, series V, WANPP; and Jo H. Chamberlin to Neilson, November 18, 1937, folder 832, box 39, series V, WANPP.

43. For an excellent study that traces changing scientific conceptions of maternal instinct, see Marga Vicedo, "The Maternal Instinct: Mother Love and the Search for Human Nature" (PhD diss., Harvard University, 2005).

44. Elaine Tyler May has argued that the postwar family was not, "as common wisdom tell us, the last gasp of 'traditional' family life with roots deep in the past. Rather, it was the first wholehearted effort to create a home that would fulfill virtually all its members' personal needs through an energized and expressive personal life." Elaine Tyler May, *Homeward Bound: American Families in the Cold War Era* (New York: Basic Books, 1988), 11.

45. The Merriam-Webster dictionary dates the word "mom" to circa 1894 (http://www .merriam-webster.com/dictionary/mom), as does the *Oxford English Dictionary*, which identifies it as primarily a North American colloquialism (http://dictionary.oed.com/)(both accessed April 20, 2009).

46. Significantly, neither theory enjoyed much credibility outside of the United States. The child psychiatrist Leo Kanner, an Austrian who emigrated to the United States in 1921, first used the term "refrigerator mother" in 1943. The psychoanalyst Bruno Bettelheim developed what was probably the most devastating critique of mothers of autistic children in his well-known book, *The Empty Fortress: Infantile Autism and the Birth of the Self* (New York: Free Press, 1967). On the history of autism and mother-blaming, see Laura Ellen Schreibman, *The Science and Fiction of Autism* (Cambridge, MA: Harvard University Press, 2005), chap. 4; Roy Richard Grinker, *Unstrange Minds: Remapping the World of Autism* (New York: Basic Books, 2007), chap. 4; and Richard Pollack, *The Creation of Dr. B: A Biography of Bruno Bettelheim* (New York: Simon and Schuster, 1997), chap. 11. See also the compelling documentary by David E. Simpson, J. J. Hanley, and Gordon Quinn, "Refrigerator Mothers," Katemquin Films, 2003. For background on the concept of the schizophrenogenic mother, see Deborah Fran Weinstein, "The Pathological Family: A Cultural History of Family Therapy in Post-World War II America" (PhD diss., Harvard University, 2002); and Carol Eadie Hartwell, "The Schizophrenogenic Mother Concept in American Psychiatry," *Psychiatry* 59 (Fall 1996): 274–97.

47. As one African-American mother explained, "According to my doctors, my son could not be autistic. I was not white and it was assumed that I was not educated. Therefore he was labeled emotionally disturbed. Here your child has a disability that you recognize and they said, 'No, you can't be that.' You can't even be a 'refrigerator mother.' The irony of it all." *Refrigerator Mothers*.

48. On the history of Jewish and immigrant mothers, see Joyce Antler, *You Never Call! You Never Write! A History of the Jewish Mother* (New York: Oxford University Press, 2007); Katrina Irving, *Immigrant Mothers: Narratives of Race and Maternity* (Urbana: University of Illinois Press, 2000); and Elizabeth Ewen, *Immigrant Women in the Land of Dollars: Life and Culture on the Lower East Side, 1890–1925* (New York: Monthly Review Press, 1985). On working-class women's experiences of motherhood and labor, see Eileen Boris, *Home to Work: Motherhood and the Politics of Industrial Homework in the United States* (New York: Cambridge University Press, 1994). On African-American motherhood, see Feldstein, *Motherhood in Black and White*; and Carol Stack, *All Our Kin: Strategies for Survival in a Black Community* (1975; New York: Basic Books, 1997). For an excellent study of poor single mothers in the contemporary United States, see Kathryn Edin and Maria Kefalas, *Promises I Can Keep: Why Poor Women Put Motherhood before Marriage* (Berkeley: University of California, 2005).

49. Feldstein, *Motherhood in Black and White*; and Mink, *The Wages of Motherhood*. On the concept of black "matriarchy," see also Daryl Michael Scott, *Contempt and Pity: Social Policy*

and the Image of the Damaged Black Psyche (Chapel Hill: University of North Carolina Press, 1997).

50. For instance, historian Elizabeth Rose has shown how day care providers devalued both working- and middle-class mothers, though in different ways. Whereas the directors of Progressive Era day nurseries that served employed, working-class mothers blamed them for not providing adequate care, directors of nursery schools that served affluent mothers, which emerged in the 1920s, emphasized the problem of maternal overprotection. "The help that both kinds of child care programs offered to mothers came at the cost of women's confidence in their ability to rear their children;" she writes, "Yet many mothers welcomed their new dependence on experts, even finding in it a measure of class status and modernity." Elizabeth Rose, *A Mother's Job: The History of Day Care, 1890–1960* (New York: Oxford University Press, 1999), 100.

51. Ann Taylor Allen, *Feminism and Motherhood in Western Europe, 1890–1970: The Maternal Dilemma* (New York: Palgrave MacMillan, 2005), 15. Marilyn Lake has made similar arguments in regard to Australia. She notes how, in the aftermath of World War II, a growing emphasis on the "mutuality of women's and men's interests" gradually supplanted the older maternalist paradigm. Thus, whereas the 1943 Australian Women's Charter included a separate section on "Woman as Mother and/or Home Maker," by 1946, this section had been subsumed under a section entitled "The Family, the Home and the Community." Marilyn Lake, "Female Desires: The Meanings of World War II," in *Gender and War: Australians at War in the Twentieth Century*, ed. Joy Damousi and Marilyn Lake (Cambridge: Cambridge University Press, 1995), 60–80 (quotation, 75).

52. Skocpol argues that the relative strength of maternalist movements within the United States can be attributed to three factors: women's groups could more easily forge transdenominational and autonomous women's associations, because the United States was an overwhelmingly Protestant nation with no established church; American women as a whole achieved higher levels of education earlier than their European counterparts; and "American women reacted more intensely, both ideologically and organizationally, against their relatively sharper exclusion from a fully democratized male polity." Theda Skocpol, *Protecting Soldiers and Mothers: The Political Origins of Social Policy in the United States* (Cambridge, MA: Belknap Press, 1992), 51–52.

53. Frieda Fromm-Reichmann, "Notes on the Mother Role in the Family Group," *Bulletin of the Menninger Clinic* 4 (1940): 132–48.

54. This literature is too large to cite in a single note. For a broad overview that focuses on prescriptive literature and women's economic roles, see Maxine Margolis, *Mothers and Such: Views of American Women and Why They Changed* (Berkeley: University of California Press, 1984), and Glenna Matthews, *"Just a Housewife": The Rise and Fall of Domesticity in America* (New York: Oxfor University Press, 1987). Important edited collections include Rima D. Apple and Janet Golden, eds., *Mothers and Motherhood: Readings in American History* (Columbus: Ohio State University Press, 1997); Molly Ladd-Taylor and Lauri Umansky, eds., *"Bad" Mothers: The Politics of Blame in Twentieth-Century America* (New York: New York University Press, 1998); Evelyn Nakano Glenn, Grace Chang, and Linda Rennie Forcey, eds., *Mothering: Ideology, Experience, and Agency* (New York: Routledge, 1994); and Donna Bassin, Margaret Honey, and Meryle Mahrer Kaplan, eds., *Representations of Motherhood* (New Haven, CT: Yale University Press, 1996).

55. That said, there are important issues related to the transformation of motherhood this book does not explore, such as changes in workplace policies related to maternity and the evolu-

tion of welfare policies. Some scholars who have addressed these issues, however, have developed interpretations that appear roughly congruent with the basic narrative and chronology presented here. For instance, Allison Hepler has identified the 1940s as a crucial turning point in the history of occupational health policies: in contrast to the broadly conceived protective legislation enacted in the Progressive Era, post–World War II policies defined motherhood in narrowly biological terms, emphasizing the need to protect women's reproductive organs from dangerous chemicals. Allison L. Hepler, *Women in Labor: Mothers, Medicine, and Occupational Health in the United States, 1890–1980* (Columbus: Ohio State University Press, 2000), 8. Also, Jennifer Mittelstadt, who has analyzed the effects of postwar welfare reform, sees the 1940s as a pivotal moment, when liberal reformers began to redefine the purpose of welfare from "supporting stay-at-home motherhood to encouraging economic independence"—a fateful move that unintentionally paved the way for coercive work requirements. Jennifer Mittelstadt, *From Welfare to Workfare: The Unintended Consequences of Liberal Reform, 1945–1965* (Chapel Hill: University of North Carolina Press, 2005), 170. Another issue not addressed here is the rise of eugenics and its impact on the construction motherhood and maternal experiences. Important works that deal with this subject include Wendy Kline, *Building a Better Race: Gender, Sexuality, and Eugenics from the Turn of the Century to the Baby Boom* (2001; Berkeley: University of California Press, 2005); Laura L. Lovett, *Conceiving the Future: Pronatalism, Reproduction, and the Family in the United States, 1890–1938* (Chapel Hill: University of North Carolina Press, 2007); Alexandra Minna Stern, *Eugenic Nation: Faults and Frontiers of Better Breeding in Modern America* (Berkeley: University of California Press, 2005); and Johanna Schoen, *Choice and Coercion: Birth Control, Sterilization, and Abortion in Public Health* (Chapel Hill: University of North Carolina Press, 2005).

56. Betty Friedan, *The Feminine Mystique* (New York: W. W. Norton, 1963), 44.

57. Joanne Meyerowitz, "Beyond the Feminine Mystique: A Reassessment of Postwar Mass Culture, 1946–1958," *Journal of American History* 79, no. 4 (March 1993): 1458.

58. Jessica Weiss has shown that "magazines with national readerships affirmed the growing consensus of the 1950s that once a woman's children reached a certain age it was permissible, in fact desirable, that she go to work." Jessica Weiss, *To Have and To Hold: Marriage, the Baby Boom, and Social Change* (Chicago: University of Chicago Press, 2000), 60. Susan Hartmann has argued that the postwar era should be viewed as one of "transition" rather than "paradox" in regard to women's employment. In her study, which focuses on the National Manpower Council, the Commission on the Education of Women, and changes to the 1954 tax code that established child care as a deductible expense, she demonstrates that historians have tended to overlook "the support for women's employment expressed by leading decision makers and opinion shapers." Hartmann, "Women's Employment and the Domestic Ideal in the Early Cold War Years," in *Not June Cleaver: Women and Gender in Postwar America, 1945–1960*, ed. Joanne Meyerowitz (Philadelphia: Temple University Press, 1994), 86.

59. Joan W. Scott, "The Evidence of Experience," *Critical Inquiry* 17, no. 4 (Summer 1991): 773–97.

60. [Nashville, TN], December 2, 1937, folder 832, box 39, series V, WANPP.

Chapter One

1. Stanley Rinehart to Philip Wylie, [n.d.], enclosed with a letter from Farrar to Wylie, July 27, 1942, folder 4, box 183, Philip Wylie Papers, Firestone Library, Princeton University, Princeton, NJ (hereafter PWP). In 1944, Wylie confided to one fan, "When I wrote GENERATION OF

NOTES TO PAGES 19–21

VIPERS I had an idea that about 1,000 copies would be sold." Wylie to H.S., December 26, 1944, folder 1, box 233, PWP. Used with permission of Princeton University Library.

2. Philip Wylie to John Farrar, July 2, 1942, folder 4, box 183, PWP.

3. The most widely read review of *Generation of Vipers* was "Amateur Messiah," *Time* 41 (January 18, 1943): 100. For a more critical review, see Paul Stringer, "But Nothing That Hitler Can Fix," *Saturday Review of Literature* 26 (February 6, 1943): 11. The book also received a mention in Malcolm Cowley's column, "Briefly Noted," *New Yorker* 18 (January 2, 1943): 8. To Wylie's chagrin, the *New York Times* did not review *Generation of Vipers*. For sales figures up to 1945, see "Postscript, 1945," folder 8, box 48, PWP.

4. Wylie, *Generation of Vipers*, annotated ed. (New York: Rinehart, 1955), xi. In fact, *Generation of Vipers* continued to sell so well in hardback that Wylie held off releasing a paperback until 1959. In paperback, the book sold thousands more copies and went through ten additional printings, remaining in print until 1968. Wylie, *Generation of Vipers* (New York: Pocket Books, 1968). The book has been back in print since 1996, when Dalkey Archive Press—a small press devoted to restoring neglected American classics—reissued the 1955 edition.

5. Cowley, "Briefly Noted," 8.

6. "Postscript, 1945," folder 8, box 48, PWP. This addendum appears only in the 1946 edition of the book. Wylie, *Generation of Vipers* (New York: Rinehart, 1946).

7. Philip Wylie, "Is Mother a Failure? Yes," *Look* 9 (December 11, 1945): 28–29. The first professional to adopt Wylie's terminology was the psychiatrist Edward A. Strecker. See his "Psychiatry Speaks to Democracy," *Mental Hygiene* 20 (October 1945): 591–605; and idem, *Their Mothers' Sons: The Psychiatrist Examines an American Problem* (Philadelphia: J. B. Lippincott, 1946). Subsequent appropriations or references include Arnold Green, "The Middle Class Male Child and Neurosis," *American Sociological Review* 11 (February 1946): 31–41; Ferdinand Lunberg and Marynia F. Farnham, *Modern Woman: The Lost Sex* (New York: Harper and Brothers, 1947), 298–321; Geoffrey Gorer, *The American People: A Study in National Character* (New York: W. W. Norton, 1948), 50–51; Erik Erikson, *Childhood and Society* (New York: W. W. Norton, 1950), 288–306, 368; Edward A. Strecker and Vincent T. Lathbury, *Their Mothers' Daughters* (Philadelphia: J. B. Lippincott, 1956); Wolfgang Lederer, *The Fear of Women* (New York: Harcourt Brace Jovanovich, 1968), 76–81; and Hans Sebald, *Momism: The Silent Disease* (Chicago: Nelson Hall, 1976).

8. Wylie, *Generation of Vipers* (1955 rev. ed.), 194.

9. Lewis Nichols, "Talk with Philip Wylie," *New York Times Book Review*, February 21, 1954, 12.

10. Martin Arnold, "Philip Wylie, Author, Dies; Noted for 'Mom' Attack," *New York Times*, October 27, 1971, 44; J. Y. Smith, "Philip Wylie Dies; Assailed 'Momism,'" *Washington Post*, October 26, 1971, C6. *Time* reported, "In fact, Wylie was an early supporter of women's rights. But his description of Mom as a 'puerile, rusting, raging creature' did little to dispel the notion that he was indeed a confirmed misogynist." "Milestones," *Time* 69 (November 8, 1971): 98.

11. Wylie, *Generation of Vipers* (1955 rev. ed.), 194.

12. Susan Ware, "American Women in the 1950s: Nonpartisan Politics and Women's Politicization," in *Women, Politics, and Change*, ed. Louise A. Tilly and Patricia Gurin (New York: Russell Sage Foundation, 1990), 289.

13. For example, in describing Wylie's critique, historian Elaine Tyler May has argued that, "'Momism' . . . was the result of frustrated women who smothered their children with overprotection and overaffection, making their sons in particular weak and passive." Elaine Tyler

May, *Homeward Bound: American Families in the Cold War Era* (New York: Basic Books, 1988), 74. Important works that have situated Wylie within the context of developments in the psychological and social sciences include Mari Jo Buhle, *Feminism and Its Discontents: A Century of Struggle with Psychoanalysis* (Cambridge, MA: Harvard University Press, 1998), chap. 4; Ruth Feldstein, *Motherhood in Black and White: Race and Sex in American Liberalism, 1930–1965* (Ithaca, NY: Cornell University Press, 2000); Jennifer Terry, "'Momism' and the Making of Treasonous Homosexuals," in *"Bad" Mothers: The Politics of Blame in Twentieth-Century America*, ed. Molly Ladd-Taylor and Lauri Umansky (New York: New York University Press, 1998), and Marga Vicedo, "The Maternal Instinct: Mother Love and the Search for Human Nature" (PhD diss., Harvard University, 2005), chap. 5.

14. *Oxford English Dictionary*, 2nd ed., s.v. "momism." *Webster's* conveys something of the social and cultural flavor that inhered in Wylie's use of "momism," while still emphasizing its psychological meaning: "An excessive popular adoration and oversentimentalizing of mothers that is held to be oedipal in nature and that is thought to allow overprotective or clinging mothers unconsciously to deny their offspring emotional emancipation and thus to set up psychoneuroses." *Webster's Third New International Dictionary*, s.v. "momism."

15. In a particularly ingenious essay, political theorist Michael Rogin showed how Wylie's momism critique, and subsequent representations of moms in Cold War films, conflated maternal pathology and political subversion: the inappropriately intimate mother-son dyad signified both the source of psychosexual maladjustment and the locus of communist infiltration. Michael Paul Rogin, "Kiss Me Deadly: Communism, Motherhood, and Cold War Movies," *Representations* 6 (Spring 1984): 1–36. Literary critic Jacqueline Rose built upon this formulation by exploring Wylie's preoccupation with mass culture as an effeminizing and homogenizing force. Jacqueline Rose, *The Haunting of Sylvia Plath* (London: Virago Press, 1991), chap. 5. Jennifer Terry and K. A. Cuordileone have both called attention to the homophobic nature of the momism critique. Terry, "'Momism' and the Making of Treasonous Homosexuals"; and K. A. Cuordileone, *Manhood and American Political Culture in the Cold War* (New York: Routledge, 2005), chap. 3. E. Ann Kaplan sees the momism critique as reaction to women's wartime employment. E. Ann Kaplan, *Motherhood and Representation: The Mother in Popular Culture and Melodrama* (London: Routledge, 1991). Similarly, Wini Breines has argued that the scapegoating of mothers reveals how "women were blamed or punished for gender changes in the post-war period." Breines, "Domineering Mothers in the 1950s: Image and Reality," *Women's Studies International Forum* 8, no. 6(1985): 601–8; quotation, 602.

16. One approving reader, for example, referred to the momism chapter as "that delicious hit-center of yours!" [N.p.], December 13, 1943, folder 10, box 231, PWP.

17. For other works that locate the sources of Wylie's critique in the interwar period, see Buhle, *Feminism and Its Discontents*; and Feldstein, *Motherhood in Black and White*.

18. Ann Douglas has analyzed the militantly antimaternalist ethos of 1920s modernism. Her book evocatively portrays the cultural milieu in which Philip Wylie—who worked briefly at *The New Yorker* as a young man—came of age. Ann Douglas, *Terrible Honesty: Mongrel Manhattan in the 1920s* (New York: Farrar, Straus, and Giroux, 1995). See esp. chap. 6.

19. In an introductory section of *Generation of Vipers* called "Directions for Reading This Book," Wylie mockingly challenged his audience: "If you enjoy this book, I would be glad if you wrote and told me so. . . . And if you do not enjoy this book, the devil take you!" Though he hardly expected to be taken seriously, fan mail "of every sort" soon began "pouring in." Wylie to Farrar and Rinehart, January 22, 1943, and April 3, 1943, folder 12, box 183, PWP. In

the introduction to the 1955 edition, Wylie claimed to have received between 50,000 to 60,000 letters. However, in the voluminous Philip Wylie Papers, by far the highest concentration of mail regarding *Generation of Vipers* dates from 1943 through 1946, and in a 1945 postscript to the book, Wylie reported that he had received only 5,000 responses. Thus, unless he began to discard letters after 1945, his 1955 claim must have been seriously exaggerated. In fact, although Wylie insisted that the 1945 estimate of 5,000 was "conservative," his correspondence suggests that even this lower number may have been substantially inflated. For example, in July 1944, he wrote that he had received "about twelve hundred" letters, and in November 1944, he placed the total at 1,500. Wylie to Harry Salpeter, July 21, 1944, folder 12, box 183, PWP; Wylie to an unidentified fan, November 29, 1944, folder 3, box 233, PWP. For a draft of the 1945 postscript, see folder 8, box 160, PWP.

20. Of the 1,019 letters regarding *Generation of Vipers* in Wylie's Fan Mail files from 1943 to 1946, 606 were written by men and 379 by women. Three letters were jointly written by husbands and wives, and 31 letters do not indicate the writer's sex. Sixty-six additional letters appear in a scrapbook that Wylie compiled (box 285). Many others letters concerning the book are scattered throughout Fan Mail files from 1947through 1971 (boxes 237–251), Unsorted Correspondence (boxes 252–257), and the alphabetized correspondence files (boxes 169–230). Although I quote from letters drawn from all of these files, I have based my calculations on the material in boxes 231–236 only, which contain the bulk of correspondence regarding *Generation of Vipers*.

21. As shown below, when excerpts of or references to the momism chapter appeared in popular magazines, published letters-to-the-editor in response tended to be more critical than those sent to Wylie himself.

22. Many respondents identified themselves as doctors, professors, teachers, students, ministers, or individuals employed in the advertising, publishing, film, and radio industries. In contrast, relatively few writers indicated that they held blue-collar jobs or discussed economic hardship. Wylie's correspondents also appear to have been strikingly homogenous in terms of race: not a single writer identified him- or herself as African-American or Hispanic. Of those who discussed religion, a large majority indicated that they had been raised as Protestants, though a notable minority identified themselves as Jews.

23. As a young child, Wylie related, his sexually deprived mother had provided them both with satisfaction by inserting suppositories and enema tubes in his anus: "She enjoyed my enjoyment and pleasured me up in many ways, including digital manipulation. If a few faint semi-recollections which accompanied these real memories are correct, she also pleasured herself while I lay across her knees with this or that in my anus, tenderly working in and out. She did to me, that is to say, what pappy wasn't doing to her—but did it anally, with God only knows what excuses to her conscience if any, or what frank fun, or what obliviousness." Wylie to Robert Lindner, April 7, 1948, folder 3, box 198, PWP.

24. Philip Wylie, "Notes on Alcoholism," [n.d.], folder 3, box 156, PWP.

25. The fact that Wylie's animosity toward women stemmed from a hatred of his effeminized self suggests why it is problematic to use a single term, like "sexism," to encompass all attitudes that are somehow anti-woman. Wylie was a far cry from, say, the powerful male executive who regarded women with unreflective condescension. When it came to women, he was the opposite of dismissive; to him, they loomed larger than life.

26. [Covington, KY], July 10, 1945, folder 2, box 236, PWP; [Charleston, SC], January 25, 1945, folder 2, box 233, PWP; and [Clinton, NY], April 18, 1946, folder 6, box 236, PWP.

27. One of the classic works to explore the complexities of reader response is Janice A. Radway's *Reading the Romance: Women, Patriarchy, and Popular Literature* (Chapel Hill: Uni-

versity of North Carolina Press, 1984). For another illuminating analysis of women's responses to popular fiction, see Regina Kunzel, "Pulp Fiction and Problem Girls: Reading and Rewriting Single Pregnancy in the Postwar United States," *American Historical Review* 100 (December 1995): 1465–87.

28. Wylie, *Generation of Vipers*, 190–91.

29. The following passage reveals Wylie's contempt for feminists, while also underscoring the fact that they were not the focus of his critique: "In a preliminary test of strength, [mom] also got herself the vote and, although politics never interested her (unless she was exceptionally naïve, a hairy foghorn, or a size forty scorpion), the damage she forthwith did to society was so enormous and so rapid that even the best men lost track of things." Ibid., 188.

30. After his wife fell ill with undulant fever, Wylie explained, "I got a gaggle of these creatures behind a move toward a pasteurization law, only to find, within a few weeks, that there was a large, alarmed and earnest committee at work in my wake to prevent the passage of any such law." Ibid., 191–92. Milk pasteurization campaigns in other U.S. cities did in fact lead to controversy among politically active women. For background, see Jennifer Koslow, "Putting It to a Vote: The Provision of Pure Milk in Progressive Era Los Angeles," *Journal of the Gilded Age and Progressive Era* 3, no. 2 (2004): 111–44.

31. For Wylie's derisive remarks on women's antivice activities, see *Generation of Vipers*, 190.

32. On the history of women's clubs, see Karen Blair, *The Clubwoman as Feminist: True Womanhood Redefined, 1868–1914* (New York: Holmes and Meier, 1980); Janice C. Steinschneider, *An Improved Woman: The Wisconsin Federation of Women's Clubs, 1895–1920* (Brooklyn, NY: Carlson, 1994); and Joan Marie Johnson, *Southern Ladies, New Women: Race, Region, and Clubwomen in South Carolina, 1890–1930* (Gainesville: University Press of Florida, 2004). See also Anne Firor Scott, *Natural Allies: Women's Associations in American History* (Urbana: University of Illinois Press, 1991).

33. [Wheeling, WV], February 6, 1948, folder 6, box 239, PWP. For an illuminating discussion of the tensions that emerged between an older generation of evangelical women who viewed illegitimacy as a moral problem and a younger generation of professionally trained social workers who perceived it in psychological terms, see Regina G. Kunzel, *Fallen Women: Unmarried Mothers and the Professionalization of Social Work* (New Haven, CT: Yale University Press, 1993).

34. [Maxwell Field, AL], August 29, 1945, folder 5, box 234, PWP.

35. Mrs. Raymond Clapper, "Is Mother a Failure? No," *Look* 9 (December 11, 1945): 28–29.

36. Characterizations of Wylie as an anticommunist crusader are wholly accurate, but they have tended to obscure the fact that he was resolutely liberal in his political views throughout the 1940s and 1950s. In 1944, he condemned the right-wing journalist Westbrook Pegler for denying the existence of anti-Semitism in the United States; in 1952, he supported Adlai Stevenson for the presidency; in 1955, he chatted with Eleanor Roosevelt at a luncheon sponsored by the Florida Association for the United Nations. And for all his anticommunist fervor, Wylie strongly condemned Senator Joseph McCarthy: in the 1955 edition of *Generation of Vipers*, he associated momism not with communism but McCarthyism. Only in the 1960s did the cultural and political climate shift in such a way that Philip Wylie, the daring iconoclast, came to be dismissed as Philip Wylie, the outdated and curmudgeonly reactionary. Philip Wylie, "An Answer to Westbrook Pegler," first appeared in the *Miami Daily News* on January 20, 1944, and was reprinted in *P.M.* and numerous Jewish papers. Wylie noted his support for Adlai Stevenson in Wylie to R.F., October 30, 1952, folder 4, box 243, PWP. Eleanor Roosevelt mentions her

conversation with Wylie in "My Day," October 6, 1955, http://www.gwu.edu/~erpapers/ [accessed May 27, 2008].

37. Wylie, *Generation of Vipers*, 193. For instance, a woman who "wholeheartedly" concurred with his remarks on "the worship of 'moms'" parenthetically noted, "The DARs are a good example," while a lieutenant in the Armed Services reported that he had delighted in Wylie's "sundry attacks on such as DAR moms." [TN], December 15, 1943, folder 9, box 231, PWP; and [Miami Beach, FL], August 21, 1945, folder 4, box 233, PWP. In an earlier chapter, Wylie did refer briefly to the DAR. Wylie, *Generation of Vipers*, 90.

38. Founded in 1890 and incorporated in 1896, the DAR defined its mission as the preservation of national heritage and the fostering of patriotic spirit. Applicants were (and still are) required to show proof of lineal blood descent from an ancestor who helped to achieve American independence.

39. Although the DAR initially lent support to some progressive causes, such as the Sheppard-Towner Act, its politics had become unequivocally reactionary by the mid-1920s. Moreover, according to historian Francesca Morgan, the DAR's "explicit, statutory ban on black women," which dated from 1894, was "unique among white-led women's organizations with large, national memberships." Francesca Morgan, *Women and Patriotism in Jim Crow America* (Chapel Hill: University of North Carolina Press, 2005), 12. See also Christine Kimberly Erickson, "Conservative Women and Patriotic Maternalism: The Beginnings of a Gendered Conservative Tradition in the 1920s and 1930s" (PhD diss., University of Santa Barbara, 1999); and Kirsten Delegard, "Women Patriots: Female Activism and the Politics of American Anti-Radicalism, 1919–1935" (PhD diss., Duke University, 1999).

40. John Erskine, *The Influence of Women and Its Cure* (Indianapolis: Bobbs-Merrill, 1936), 82–83.

41. The story behind the painting, including Wood's earlier clashes with the local DAR chapter in Cedar Rapids, Iowa, is detailed in Wanda M. Corn, *Grant Wood: The Regionalist Vision* (New Haven, CT: Yale University Press, 1983), 98–101; quotation, 100. See also Morgan, *Women and Patriotism in Jim Crow America*, 159.

42. See Carl Jung, *C. G. Jung Letters*, vol. 2, *1951–1961*, ed. Gerhard Adler and Aniela Jaffé, trans. R. F. C. Hull (Princeton, NJ: Princeton University Press, 1975), xxxviii.

43. Roosevelt explained her decision in a "My Day" column that appeared on the front page of more than four hundred newspapers across the country. Although she refrained from actually naming the organization, it was well understood that she was referring to the DAR. See "Eleanor Roosevelt and Civil Rights," http://www.nps.gov/archive/elro/teach-er-vk/lesson-plans/notes-er-and-civil-rights.htm [accessed July 20, 2008].

44. For a discussion of the concert, see Scott A. Sandage, "A Marble House Divided: The Lincoln Memorial, the Civil Rights Movement, and the Politics of Memory," *Journal of American History* 80 (June 1993): 143–51; and Morgan, *Women and Patriotism in Jim Crow America*, 153–63.

45. Harold Ickes to Wylie, March 25, 1943, scrapbook, box 285, PWP. One of the nation's most prominent New Dealers, Ickes was an impassioned civil rights advocate who, by the time he wrote to Wylie, had become an outspoken critic of the government's policy of Japanese internment. As Francesca Morgan has noted, he had been "lavishly and repeatedly red-baited in publications endorsed and circulated by DAR leaders." Morgan, *Women and Patriotism in Jim Crow America*, 155.

46. Though Wylie referred at one point to "our half slaves, the Negroes," *Generation of Vipers* includes virtually no discussion of African Americans or race relations—a silence that

is striking in a book that otherwise provides a sweeping survey of the national scene. Wylie, *Generation of Vipers*, 101. See also 170.

47. Wylie, *Generation of Vipers*, 193.

48. Ibid., 194.

49. [San Francisco, CA], September 25, 1945, folder 2, box 234, PWP.

50. [Hollywood, CA], March 12, 1945, folder 1, box 235, PWP.

51. In an earlier chapter on Americans' attitudes toward sexuality, Wylie wrote, "our national attitude toward sex . . . is so disoriented, so unreal, so prejudiced, and so wishful that it is not an attitude at all," he declared, "but a hallucination." Wylie, *Generation of Vipers*, 76.

52. Philip Stoughton to Wylie, June 15, 1943, scrapbook, box 285, PWP.

53. For a discussion of the rumors regarding sexual activity and immorality that plagued the WAC throughout the war, see Leisa D. Meyer, *Creating GI Jane: Sexuality and Power in the Women's Army Corp during World War II* (New York: Columbia University Press, 1996), chap. 2. For Wylie's criticism of the government's ineptitude in dealing with venereal disease, see *Generation of Vipers*, 73–75.

54. The couple first learned of *Generation of Vipers* through Walter Wanger, a Hollywood executive, and Florence Mahoney, a well-connected Democrat who also played a key role in lobbying for federal funding to support medical research. Albert Lasker to Farrar and Rinehart, August 18, 1943, folder 2, box 232, PWP.

55. Mary W. Lasker to Wylie, April 2, 1943, scrapbook, box 285, PWP.

56. There is a large literature on the history of the birth control movement. Important overviews include Linda Gordon, *The Moral Property of Women: A History of Birth Control Politics in America* (Urbana: University of Illinois Press, 2007); Carole R. McCann, *Birth Control Politics in the United States, 1916–1945* (Ithaca, NY: Cornell University Press, 1994); and James Reed, *The Birth Control Movement and American Society: From Private Vice to Public Virtue* (1978; Princeton, NJ: Princeton University Press, 1983).

57. Wylie, *Generation of Vipers*, 236–37. According to historian David K. Johnson, Wylie was one of the first commentators to publish such charges. David K. Johnson, *The Lavender Scare: The Cold War Persecution of Gays and Lesbians in the Federal Government* (Chicago: Chicago University Press, 2004), 75.

58. Wylie, *Generation of Vipers*, 61.

59. In 1949, one young woman even appealed to Wylie for advice on "what a common citizen can do to further the cause" of "sex tolerance." Writing after a friend and fellow teacher had been fired for homosexuality, she reflected, "One would like to . . . tramp around the country preaching the gospel of sex tolerance, or issue a decree to the government that all arresting of homosexuals must cease. But all these things are too fantastically impossible." [Waco, TX], November 11, 1949, folder 1, box 240, PWP.

60. Wylie to Charles Fenton, November 25, 1956, folder 1, box 183, PWP. Similarly, the painter Hilaire Hiler described the book as having a "concealed fascist viewpoint." Hilaire Hiler to Wylie, May 22, 1943, folder 4, box 232, PWP.

61. This respondent was probably referring to Ewald Banse's 1932 book, *Raum und Volk im Weltkrieg*, which was published in English as *Germany Prepares for War: A Nazi Theory of "National Defense"* (New York: Harcourt, Brace, 1934). Banse argued that, in the United States, "ideals go to the wall or at most serve to maintain the exalted position of woman in American life in a sentimentalized and debased form" (292).

62. [Miami, FL], September 26, 1944, folder 2, box 233, PWP.

63. [Pittsburgh, PA], January 23, 1943, folder 1, box 232, PWP.

64. For instance, in 1952, a successful lawyer who strongly supported the Equal Rights Amendment reported to Wylie that she had been quoting *Generation of Vipers* for years. Assuming that he shared her commitment to "legal civil equality" as at least a partial "solution of the age-old battle of the sexes," she urged him to be more forthright in his promotion of feminist goals. [Los Angeles, CA], February 25, 1952, folder 9, box 199, PWP.

65. In a book-in-progress that focuses on transatlantic debates surrounding *The Second Sex*, the historian Judith Coffin writes, "It is astonishing to see how often and how approvingly Beauvoir quoted Wylie. Sometimes she referred her readers to Wylie's 'Mom' as a good 'portrait' of an American type, sometimes she called Mom a 'myth,' but in no instance did she treat Mom as an example of the male myth-making that she otherwise set out to deflate." Coffin also notes that Beauvoir published translated excerpts of the momism chapter in *Les Temps Modernes* in 1946. See also Judith G. Coffin, "Historicizing *The Second Sex*," *French Politics, Culture and Society* 25, no. 3 (Winter 2007): 123–48.

66. Friedan did refer to Wylie (approvingly) in her later work, *The Second Stage*. Betty Friedan, *The Feminine Mystique* (New York: W. W. Norton, 1963), 189–205; idem, *The Second Stage* (New York: Summit Books, 1981), 91.

67. For Wylie's references to Dorothy Thompson, whom he called one of the "greatest she-sachems of the intellectuals," see *Generation of Vipers*, 86, 93, 98; quotation, 86.

68. [Lafayette, IN], June 29, 1943, folder 4, box 232.

69. [Charlotte, NC], February 4, 1947, folder 2, box 237, PWP.

70. Referring to this letter, historian Nancy Cott has noted that, although Beard often "seemed to take at face value popular claims that middle-class American women were leisured, even lazy," she still "retained confidence in the possibility that women could sustain a socially valuable and uplifting role differing from men's occupational emphasis." Mary Ritter Beard, *A Woman Making History: Mary Ritter Beard through Her Letters*, ed. Nancy F. Cott (New Haven, CT: Yale University Press, 1991), 268–69. See also Mary Beard, *Women as a Force in History* (New York: Macmillan, 1946), 18–19.

71. This passage appears not in the momism chapter but rather in an earlier chapter of the book. Wylie, *Generation of Vipers*, 49.

72. Rogin, "Kiss Me Deadly," 7. Similarly, E. Ann Kaplan has speculated that women's wartime employment "must have represented an unconscious threat that could be displaced" onto "the greedy, stay-at-home moms." Kaplan, *Motherhood and Representation*, 116. In contrast, Barbara Ehrenreich has correctly pointed out that the "towering figure of 'Mom' reflected no change in the social and occupational position of women, which, if anything, had reached a nadir for the twentieth century. Behind the hatred and fear of the mother was a growing sense that men had somehow lost power—that they were no longer 'real men.'" Barbara Ehrenreich, *For Her Own Good: Two Centuries of the Experts' Advice to Women*, rev. ed. (1978; repr., New York: Anchor Books, 2005), 261.

73. [Newton Highlands, MA], December 4, 1945, folder 1, box 234, PWP.

74. Barbara Ehrenreich has called attention to a "male rebellion" against the pressures of providing in the 1950s, but the attitudes that she uncovers predate the post–World War II era. Barbara Ehrenreich, *Hearts of Men: American Dreams and the Flight from Commitment* (New York: Anchor Books, 1983). Pamela S. Haag discusses contempt for the "calculating woman" in "In Search of 'The Real Thing': Ideologies of Love, Modern Romance, and Women's Sexual Subjectivity in the United States, 1920–40," *Journal of the History of Sexuality* 2 (April 1992): 547–77. See also Peter N. Stearns and Mark Knapp, "Men and Romantic Love: Pinpointing a Twentieth-Century Change," *Journal of Social History* 26 (Summer 1993): 769–95.

75. In 1900, the average life expectancy rates for men and women, respectively, stood at 46.3 and 48.3—a difference of only two years. By 1930, life expectancy had increased to 58.1 years for men and 61.6 years for women—a difference of three years. This differential increased considerably in the 1930s and 1940s; by 1945, women outlived men by an average of 4.6 years. U.S. Department of Commerce, *Historical Statistics of the United States, Colonial Times to 1970*, pt. 1 (Washington, D.C., 1975), 55. In 1920, the total average fertility rate for white women was 3.17 children, and for black women, 3.64. The birth rate bottomed out during the Depression but had risen slightly by 1940; that year, the total average fertility rate was 2.22 and 2.87 for white and black women, respectively; see http://www.answers.com/topic/birthrate-and-mortality [accessed July 25, 2008]. These crude statistics do not capture the full significance of the demographic trends that troubled Wylie, since he was concerned primarily with white, middle- and upper-middle-class women, who generally lived longer and had fewer children than less affluent and minority women. The claim that women had been freed from domestic drudgery starkly reveals the class dimensions of Wylie's critique. For millions of American women, housekeeping remained a laborious and time-consuming job. As Ruth Schwartz Cowan has noted, in 1940 a third of American households still cooked with wood and coal, and roughly the same percentage lacked indoor plumbing. In 1941, only 52 percent of families owned or had access to a washing machine in their apartment buildings, and only 53 percent had mechanical refrigerators. See Ruth Schwartz Cowan, *More Work for Mother: The Ironies of Household Technology from Open Hearth to Microwave* (New York: Basic Books, 1983); and Susan Strasser, *Never Done: A History of American Housework* (New York: Pantheon Books, 1982). For a fascinating history of the concept of the "unproductive housewife," see Nancy Folbre, "The Unproductive Housewife: Her Evolution in Nineteenth-Century Economic Thought," *Signs* 16, no. 3 (1991): 463–84.

76. This passage appears in a chapter titled "Businessmen." Wylie, *Generation of Vipers*, 205. Commentators of the era repeatedly asserted that women made 80 percent of all consumer purchases—a claim that historian Mark A. Swiencicki has convincingly challenged in "Consuming Brotherhood: Men's Culture, Style and Recreation as Consumer Culture," *Journal of Social History* 31 (Summer 1998): 773–808.

77. T. J. Jackson Lears, "Sherwood Anderson: Looking for the White Spot," in *The Power of Culture: Critical Essays in American History*, ed. Richard W. Fox and T. J. Jackson Lears (Chicago: University of Chicago Press, 1993), 13–38.

78. Beginning in the 1890s, the department store emerged as a potent symbol of women's increasing power as consumers. See William Leach, "Transformations in a Culture of Consumption: Women and Department Stores, 1890–1925," *Journal of American History* 71, no. 2 (1984): 319–42; Susan Porter Benson, *Counter Cultures: Saleswomen, Managers, and Customers in American Department Stores, 1890–1940* (Urbana: University of Illinois Press, 1986); and Elaine Abelson, *When Ladies Go A-Thieving: Middle-Class Shoplifters in the Victorian Department Store* (New York: Oxford University Press, 1989).

79. Wylie, *Generation of Vipers*, 201.

80. Sherwood Anderson, *Perhaps Women* (New York: Horace Liverwright, 1931), 48.

81. Charlotte Perkins Gilman, *Women and Economics* (1898; New York: Cosimo Classics, 2006); and Olive Schreiner, *Woman and Labour* (Leipzig: Bernhard Tauchnitz, 1911). For a discussion of how feminists deployed stereotypes of female idleness in the late nineteenth and early twentieth centuries, and how the emphasis on work served to obscure more radical feminist goals and ideals, see Daniel Rogers, *The Work Ethic in Industrial America, 1850–1920* (Chicago: University of Chicago Press, 1977), chap. 7. See also Margaret Morganroth Gullette, "Inventing the 'Postmaternal' Woman, 1898–1927: Idle, Unwanted, and Out of a Job," *Feminist Studies* 21

(Summer 1995): 221–53. For a comprehensive study of feminist ideas between 1910 and 1930, see Nancy Cott, *The Grounding of Modern Feminism* (New Haven, CT: Yale University Press, 1987).

82. Lorine Pruette, *Women and Leisure: A Study of Social Waste* (New York: E. P. Dutton, 1924), xi–xiii.

83. Dorothy Canfield Fisher, "A Challenge to American Women," in Sidonie Matsner Gruenberg, ed., *The Family in a World at War* (New York: Harper & Brothers, 1942), 192–205 (quotation, 194).

84. Talcott Parsons, "Age and Sex in the Social Structure" (1942), in *Essays in Sociological Theory* (Glencoe, IL: Free Press, 1954), 190.

85. Anna W. Wolf, *The Parents' Manual: A Guide to the Emotional Development of Young Children* (New York: Simon and Schuster, 1941), 302–3.

86. Sara M. Evans, *Born for Liberty: A History of Women in America* (New York: Free Press, 1989), 202. See also May, *Homeward Bound*, chap. 1; and Lois Scharf, *To Work and To Wed: Female Employment, Feminism, and the Great Depression* (Westport, CT: Greenwood Press, 1980).

87. Quoted in Leila J. Rupp, *Mobilizing Women for War: German and American Propaganda* (Princeton, NJ: Princeton University Press, 1978), 97.

88. Quoted in Evans, *Born for Liberty*, 221.

89. Industrial and military leaders backed the proposal, as did Eleanor Roosevelt. And despite strong public resistance, polls indicated the majority of Americans (61 percent) were prepared to comply with such a measure if the need could be shown to be truly imperative. Interestingly, polls showed that Americans preferred to draft single women before fathers to fill noncombat military jobs, indicating that they were more anxious to preserve the family unit than to safeguard women per se from compulsory employment. Holly Stovall, "Resisting Regimentation: The Committee to Oppose the Conscription of Women," *Peace and Change* 23 (October 1998): 483–99. See also Eleanor F. Straub, "United States Government Policy toward Civilian Women during World War II," *Prologue* 5 (Winter 1973): 248.

90. A bill to draft nurses had passed the House and come within one vote of passing in the Senate when Germany surrendered. In the meantime, however, the enrollment of more than 10,000 nurses in the Army Nurse Corps had rendered such a measure superfluous. For a discussion of the debate, see Barbara Brooks Tomlin, *G.I. Nightingales: The Army Nurses Corps in World War II* (Lexington: University of Kentucky Press, 2004), 199–204.

91. Certain passages of this editorial read like antifeminist rant: the writer not only depicted women as idle parasites but also dismissed the Equal Rights Amendment as "largely nonsense." Yet other passages read like a feminist manifesto: the writer attributed female idleness to "the fact that women's emancipation is incomplete" and asserted, "There is no reason why more social equality between the sexes should threaten the family, the birth rate, or any other vital institution." "American Women: Draft Them? Too Bad We Can't Draft Their Grandmothers," *Life* 18 (January 29, 1945): 28. For a similar argument, see J. C. Furnas, "Are Women Doing Their Share in the War?" *Saturday Evening Post* 216 (April 29, 1944): 12–13, 40–44.

92. In response to the editorial, *Life* printed twenty letters to the editor—an unusually high number. Of these, eleven were decidedly negative and seven decidedly positive. Nine women wrote negative letters, as compared to two men; only two women wrote positive letters, as compared to five men. "Letters to the Editor," *Life* 18 (February 19, 1945): 2–4.

93. Ibid.

94. [Oklahoma City, OK], November 27, 1945, folder 1, box 184, PWP. *Look* did not print this letter; it was forwarded to Wylie by Janet Clapper, who had written the defense of American women that appeared alongside the excerpt from *Generation of Vipers*. Even though Clapper criticized Wylie's attack on moms, her private remarks to him suggest that she did not want to be associated with such a traditional defense of "American Womanhood." "Here is the letter I spoke of at the party yesterday," she wrote. "I have no doubt that you have more interesting things to read, but I feel if I don't send it along I might be accused of tampering with the mails." Clapper to Wylie, December 11, 1945, folder 1, box 184, PWP.

95. [Los Angeles, CA], June 11, 1943, folder 1, box 232, PWP.

96. [Lafayette, IN], May 14, 1947, folder 3, box 237, PWP.

97. "The American Woman's Dilemma," *Life* 22 (June 16, 1947): 116.

98. Ibid., 108–9.

99. George Gallup and Evan Hill, "The American Woman," *Saturday Evening Post* 235, no. 46 (December 22–29, 1962): 32.

100. [Plymouth, MI], November 11, 1950, folder 2, box 241, PWP. This letter was written in response to an article that Wylie published in *Look* magazine.

101. As scholars have long noted, this increase was greatest among those women who historically had been least likely to seek paid employment—middle-class, middle-aged wives and mothers. William H. Chafe portrayed women's rising employment in the postwar era as a "paradox" in his groundbreaking book, *The American Woman: Her Changing Social, Economic, and Political Roles, 1920–1970* (London: Oxford University Press, 1972), 201.

102. Jessica Weiss, *To Have and To Hold: Marriage, the Baby Boom and Social Change* (Chicago: University of Chicago Press, 2000), chap. 2; and Susan Hartmann, "Women's Employment and the Domestic Ideal in the Early Cold War Years," in *Not June Cleaver: Women and Gender in Postwar America, 1945–1960*, ed. Joanne Meyerowitz (Philadelphia: Temple University Press, 1994), 84–100.

103. Wylie, *Generation of Vipers*, 202–3.

104. Wylie described mom's educational background as follows: "She was graduated from high school or a 'finishing' school or even a college in her distant past and made up for the unhappiness of compulsory education by sloughing all that she learned so completely that she could not pass the final examinations of a fifth grade." Ibid.

105. Literary critic Jacqueline Rose has astutely analyzed the ways in which Wylie drew "an association between femininity and those components of the culture that can be designated as cheap." Jacqueline Rose, *The Haunting of Sylvia Plath*, (Cambridge, MA: Harvard University Press, 1992), 166.

106. Kathryn Kish Sklar, *Catherine Beecher: A Study in American Domesticity* (New York: W. W. Norton, 1976).

107. Rachel Klein, "Gentility and Distinction: Art and Artists in Sentimental Culture" in *Culture Wars: Art, Authority and the Transformation of Taste in Nineteenth-Century New York* (forthcoming).

108. Ann Douglas, *The Feminization of American Culture* (New York: Alfred A. Knopf, 1977), 76. The feminization of the teaching profession is described in Joel Perlman and Robert A. Margo, *Women's Work? American Schoolteachers, 1650–1920* (Chicago: University of Chicago Press, 2001). By 1910, 78.5 percent of all library workers in the United States were women. Dee Garrison, "The Tender Technicians: The Feminization of Public Librarianship, 1876–1905," *Journal of Social History* 6 (Winter 1972): 131–59.

109. Alison M. Parker, *Purifying America: Women, Cultural Reform, and Pro-Censorship Activism, 1873–1933* (Urbana: University of Illinois Press, 1997); and Leigh Ann Wheeler, *Against Obscenity: Reform and the Politics of Womanhood in America, 1873–1935* (Baltimore: Johns Hopkins University Press, 2004).

110. The first radio soap opera aired in 1930, and the last one went off the air in 1960. The heyday of the daytime serial was from the mid-1930s to the mid-1950s. For historical accounts, see Kathy M. Newman, *Radio Active: Advertising and Consumer Activism, 1935–1947* (Berkeley: University of California Press, 2004), chap. 4; and Gerd Horton, *Radio Goes to War: The Cultural Politics of Propaganda during World War II* (Berkeley: University of California Press, 2002), chap. 6. For studies of soap opera as a genre, see Tania Modleski, *Loving with a Vengeance: Mass-Produced Fantasies for Women* (New York: Methuen, 1984), chap. 4; and Robert C. Allen, *Speaking of Soap Operas* (Chapel Hill: University of North Carolina Press, 1985). For an overview of the various types of radio programs directed toward homemakers, see Morleen Getz Rouse, "Daytime Radio Programming for the Homemaker, 1926–1956," *Journal of Popular Culture* 12 (Fall 1979): 315–72. For a fascinating account of how radios came to be feminized and incorporated into domestic space, see Louis Carlat, "'A Cleanser for the Mind': Marketing Radio Receivers for the American Home, 1922–1932," in *His and Hers: Gender, Consumption, and Technology*, ed. Roger Horowitz and Arwen Mohun (Charlottesville: University Press of Virginia, 1998), 115–37.

111. According to one study, the typical fan listened daily to 5.8 serials. Newman, *Radio Active*, 110.

112. Ibid.

113. Berg's first pamphlet, titled "Preliminary Report: A Study of Certain Radio Programs and Their Effects upon the Audience, Especially Adolescents and Women at the Climacterium," was based on a talk delivered at the Buffalo Advertising Club. See "Suppurating Serials," *Time* (March 23, 1942), http://www.time.com/time/magazine/article/0,9171,802311,00.html [accessed July 28, 2008].

114. Quoted in Max Wylie, "Dusting off Dr. Berg," *Printer's Ink* (January 12, 1943): 19–20, 42–45.

115. Ibid. Berg's most effective critic was none other than Philip Wylie's brother, Max Wylie. Max Wylie served as vice-president of Blacket-Sample-Hummert, an advertising agency that produced some of the nation's most successful soap operas. See also his defense of daytime serials: Max Wylie, "Washboard Weepers: A Small Case for Radio," *Harper's Magazine* 185, no. 110 (November 1942): 633–38.

116. James Thurber, "Soapland," reprinted in *The Beast in Me and Other Animals* (New York: Harcourt Brace, 1948), 191–260; quotation, 216.

117. In a preliminary report, the committee (composed of editor of the *Journal of the American Medical Association* Morris Fishbein, neurologist Henry R. Viets, and psychiatrist Winifred Overholser) concluded, "The listeners identify themselves and their own major and minor crises with the characters of these dramas. Since, however, the tendency of all the dramas studied is toward solutions that are generally accepted as ethical in our social existence, the effects of the dramas tend toward helpfulness rather than harm." Quoted in Wylie, "Dusting Off Dr. Berg," 20.

118. Katherine Best, "'Literature' of the Air: Radio's Perpetual Emotion," *Saturday Review of Literature* 23 (April 20, 1940): 11–13, 16; quotation, 12.

119. By March 1940, one of the movement's leaders claimed that it had spread to thirty-nine states. See Newman, *Radio Active*, 133.

120. [Albany, NY], August 26, 1945, folder 5, box 234, PWP.

121. [Buffalo, NY], October 16, 1945, folder 3, box 234, PWP.

122. Only a few scholars have analyzed the content of radio soap operas. See Horton, *Radio Goes to War*, chap. 6; and Timothy Shuker-Harris, "Home Is the Hunter: Representations of Returning World War II Veterans and the Reconstruction of Masculinity, 1944–1951" (PhD diss., University of Michigan, 1994), chap 4.

123. According to historian Gerd Horton, the prolific serial writer Irna Phillips resisted incorporating positive images of working women into her shows during World War II. "The image of 'Rosie the Riveter' did not successfully reach into Phillips's soap operas," he writes. "Instead, her serials reconfirmed her listeners' choice of adhering to a traditional gender ideology." Horton, *Radio Goes to War*, 176.

124. Susan M. Hartmann, *Beyond the Homefront: American Women in the 1940s* (Boston: Twayne, 1982), 196–97.

125. While not a soap opera, another extremely popular radio show, *The Goldbergs*, also centered on a middle-aged matriarchal character. For a thoughtful analysis of Molly Goldberg's depiction as an Old World Jewish mother who was nevertheless receptive to certain modern ideas about childrearing, see Joyce Antler, *You Never Call! You Never Write! A History of the Jewish Mother* (New York: Oxford University Press, 2007), chap. 2.

126. James Thurber, "Soapland," 216. Thurber's report on radio soap operas originally appeared as a series of articles in the *New Yorker*. The mother in the show is also singled out for derision in "Soap Opera," *Fortune* 33 (March 1946): 119–23, 146–51.

127. Whitfield Cook, " 'Be Sure To Listen in!' " *American Mercury* 52 (March 1940): 318.

128. Ibid., 319.

129. Kate Lacey, *Feminine Frequencies: Gender, German Radio, and the Public Sphere, 1923–1945* (Ann Arbor: University of Michigan Press, 1996), 242.

130. Literary critic Jacqueline Rose has shown how Wylie echoed Frankfurt School theorists who similarly associated mass culture with both femininity and the political threats of fascism and communism. As she notes, Wylie suggested that "the popular, the mass, the consumer, were—like Nazism and then like the Communism to which all these increasingly became associated—destroying the American mind." Rose, *The Haunting of Sylvia Plath*, 166.

131. [Longmeadow, MA], March 20, 1945, folder 1, box 235, PWP.

132. [FL, n.d.], folder 11, box 11, box 220, PWP. The quotations are from a review that appeared in the magazine *Florida Police Office* sometime in 1951, which a fan clipped and sent to Wylie.

133. [Nahant, MA], November 16, 1950, folder 4, box 240, PWP.

134. [Lufkin, TX], July 9, 1947, folder 3, box, 237, PWP.

135. [Massillon, OH], June 11, 1945, folder 4, box 234, PWP.

136. Wini Breines has identified a similar dynamic, in which young white women in 1950s expressed feelings of alienation from mainstream society by allying themselves with Beat subculture, despite its pervasive sexism. She argues that, "Middle-class white girls who rejected dominant values had little choice but to utilize and adapt male versions of rebellion and disaffection." Wini Breines, *Young, White, and Miserable: Growing Up Female in the Fifties* (Chicago: University of Chicago Press, 1992), 130.

137. Wylie, *Generation of Vipers*, 196. The phrase "barbaric period" likely refers to G. Stanley Hall's views of childhood. Around the turn of the twentieth century, Hall developed his theory of racial recapitulation, which held that a white boy's progress toward manhood mirrored the

race's progress from savagery to civilization. Hall argued that schoolteachers and mothers too often repressed boys' natural "savagery," leading to effeminacy and neurasthenia in later life. For background on Hall, see Dorothy Ross, *G. Stanley Hall: The Psychologist as Prophet* (Chicago: University of Chicago Press, 1972); and Gail Bederman, *Manliness and Civilization: A Cultural History of Gender and Race in the United States, 1880–1917* (Chicago: University of Chicago Press, 1995), chap 3.

138. As Mari Jo Buhle has put it, "*Generation of Vipers* stood out . . . only for its lack of scholarly dispassion." Buhle, *Feminism and Its Discontents*, 129. See also Feldstein, *Motherhood in Black and White*; Terry, "'Momism' and the Making of Treasonous Homosexuals;" and Vicedo, "The Maternal Instinct."

139. This reading differs from Michael Rogin's influential depiction of the momism critique as the "demonic version" of postwar domestic ideology. According to Rogin, by encouraging "maternal surveillance," domestic ideology heightened anxieties about "boundary invasion, loss of autonomy and maternal power"—anxieties that became manifest in monstrous depictions of mothers. The problem with this interpretation is that it posits postwar domestic ideology as a continuation or extension of Victorian domesticity, which centered on the moral mother who "entered the self, formed it, understood its feelings, and thereby at once produced it and protected it from corruption." But in fact, in marked contrast to their Victorian forebears, midcentury psychological experts strongly discouraged "maternal surveillance" and repeatedly insisted on the need for psychological boundaries between mothers and their children, especially sons. The momism critique was not a byproduct of, nor a counterreaction to, the maternal ideal that achieved dominance in the 1940s and 1950s: it informed and helped to produce that ideal. Rogin, "Kiss Me Deadly," 6–7, 21.

140. [Birmingham, AL], March 23, 1946, folder 6, box 236, PWP.

141. [San Francisco, CA], June 25, 1945, folder 4, box 234, PWP.

142. [Oak Ridge, TN] February 26, 1946, folder 2, box 236, PWP.

143. [Detroit, MI, n.d.], folder 7, box 245, PWP.

144. Buhle, *Feminism and Its Discontents*, 127.

145. [N.p.], October 19, 1943, folder 1, box 232, PWP.

146. O. Spurgeon English and Constance Foster, *Fathers Are Parents, Too* (New York: G. P. Putnam, 1951). In his letter, English discussed the unexpected popular success of a textbook on psychosomatic medicine that he had recently coauthored, Edward Weiss and O. Spurgeon English, *Psychosomatic Medicine: The Clinical Application of Psychopathology to General Medicine* (Philadelphia: W. B. Saunders, 1943). O. Spurgeon English to Wylie, May 18, 1943, folder 9, box 231, PWP.

147. Karl Menninger to Wylie, March 12, 1943, scrapbook, box 285, PWP. Menninger was so enthusiastic about *Generation of Vipers* that he had copies sent to all staff members who were away from the clinic serving in the military. Karl Menninger to Wylie, April 9, 1943, folder 2, box 232, PWP. For background on Menninger, see Lawrence J. Friedman, *Menninger: The Family and the Clinic* (New York: Alfred A. Knopf, 1990). See also the articles in "Special Issue: The Menninger School of Psychiatry," *Psychohistory Review* 19 (Fall 1990). Selections from Menninger's advice column in *Ladies' Home Journal*, "Mental Hygiene in the Home," which appeared from 1930 to 1932, have been published in *Dear Dr. Menninger: Women's Voices from the Thirties*, ed. Howard J. Faulkner and Virginia D. Pruitt (Columbia: University of Missouri Press, 1997).

148. On the relationship between popularized psychoanalysis and Christianity, see Sonya Michel, "American Conscience and the Unconscious: Psychoanalysis and the Rise of Personal

Religion, 1906–1963," *Psychoanalysis and Contemporary Thought* 7 (1983): 387–421; and Donald Meyer, *The Positive Thinkers: Popular Religious Psychology from Mary Baker Eddy to Norman Vincent Peale and Ronald Reagan*, rev. ed. (Middleton, CT: Wesleyan University Press, 1988).

149. Karl Menninger, *Love against Hate* (New York: Harcourt, Brace & World, 1942), 55.

150. Ibid., 33.

151. Historians Kathleen Jones and Elizabeth Rose have both found that mother-blaming could prove surprisingly useful to mothers. In tracing the history of childcare in the late nineteenth and early twentieth centuries, Rose argues that ideas about maternal incompetence sometimes served the interests of mothers and children, for they justified women's need for a break from full-time mothering and helped lay the groundwork for broader claims about the need for publicly supported childcare. Elizabeth Rose, *A Mother's Job: A History of Day Care, 1890–1960* (New York: Oxford University Press, 1999). Similarly, Jones, who has examined the history of the child guidance movement in the pre–World War II era, has explored the ambiguous effects of mother-blaming at the level of the clinic, where it sometimes "provided an outlet for frustrations unrelated to the troublesome child." Kathleen W. Jones, *Taming the Troublesome Child: American Families, Child Guidance, and the Limits of Psychiatric Authority* (Cambridge, MA: Harvard University Press, 1999), 9.

152. [Bemidji, MN], January 31, 1958, folder 11, box 199, PWP. Interestingly, this postscript followed the writer's account of her struggle with "schizophrenia or severe neurosis," as if, on some level, she recognized that Wylie's hostile critique and the psychological problems that she suffered were connected. Wylie replied to this reader; he expressed doubts that she suffered from schizophrenia, noted that he was glad she had not submitted to electroshock therapy, and encouraged her to read the works of Karen Horney. Wylie to S.J.M., February 8, 1958, folder 11, box 199, PWP.

153. [Montepelier, VT], March 16, 1945, folder 2, box 234, PWP.

154. [N.p.], March 31, 1945, folder 1, box 235, PWP.

155. [Union, TN], July 7, 1949, folder 5, box 240, PWP.

156. [Cincinnati, OH], January 14, 1951, folder 1, box 242, PWP.

157. [Oklahoma City, OK], December 9, 1944, folder 1, box 233, PWP. Wylie replied, "You are obviously one of the non-vipers, and I suspect your children have picked the right mother after all." Wylie to B.I., December 26, 1944, folder 1, box 233, PWP.

158. [Los Angeles, CA], January 11, 1945, folder 2, box 235, PWP.

159. [Portland, OR], September 1, 1943, folder 4, box 232, PWP.

160. [Highland Park, MI], September 9, 1945, folder 5, box 234, PWP.

161. [N.p.] to Wylie, [1958], folder 2, box 156, PWP.

162. Nina C. Leibman, who has analyzed popular shows like *Leave It to Beaver*, has argued that 1950s television programs relegate mothers to the periphery of the family circle and "'solve' the 'problem' of mothers' all powerful and harmful influence . . . by decisively reconfiguring the father as the crucial molder of his children's psyches." See "Leave Mother Out: The 50s Family in American Film and Television," *Wide Angle* 10 (1988): 24–41, and *Living Room Lectures: The Fifties Family in Film and Television* (Austin: University of Texas Press, 1995), chap. 6. For discussions of the television show *Mama*, which was set in pre–World War I San Francisco and centered on Mama Hansen, the matriarch of a Norwegian immigrant family, see George Lipsitz, *Time Passages: Collective Memory and American Popular Culture* (Minneapolis: University of Minnesota Press, 2001), 77–96; and Judith Smith, *Visions of Belonging: Family Stories, Popular Culture, and Postwar Democracy, 1940–1960* (New York: Columbia University Press, 2004), 73–106. This fantastically popular show, which aired from 1949 through 1957, was based on Kathryn

Forbes's book, *Mama's Bank Account* (New York: Harcourt, Brace and Co., 1943). The book had previously inspired a play (1944) and a film (1948), both entitled *I Remember Mama*.

163. [Killeen, TX], May 10, 1962, folder 2, box 183, PWP.

Chapter Two

1. Philip Wylie, "More Musings on Mom," *Saturday Review* 29 (December 7, 1946): 21.

2. Discussions concerning sentimental representations of mothers and sons in the Civil War North appear in Frances Clarke, "Sentimental Bonds: Suffering, Sacrifice and Benevolence in the Civil War North," (PhD diss., Johns Hopkins University, 2001); Alice Fahs, "The Feminized Civil War: Gender, Northern Popular Literature, and the Memory of the War, 1861–1900," *Journal of American History* 86 (March 1999): 1461–94 and idem, "The Sentimental Soldier in Popular Civil War Literature, 1861–65," *Civil War History* 46 (June 2000): 107–31; and Reid Mitchell, *The Vacant Chair: The Northern Soldier Leaves Home* (New York: Oxford University Press, 1993). Susan Zeiger provides an astute analysis of the relationship between motherhood, militarism, and pacifism in "She Didn't Raise Her Boy To Be a Slacker: Motherhood, Conscription, and the Culture of the First World War," *Feminist Studies* 22 (Spring 1996): 6–39. The cultural construction of motherhood is also discussed in Michael Coventry, "'God, Country, Home, and Mother'": Soldiers, Gender, and Nationalism in Great War America (PhD diss., Georgetown University, 2004).

3. Quoted in Zeiger, "She Didn't Raise Her Boy to Be a Slacker," 6.

4. Robert Westbrook has explored how the ubiquitous "pin-up" girl came to symbolize men's private obligations as protectors (and possessors) of American women. He acknowledges, however, that he "ignores the cultural construction of an important group of women as icons of obligation: mothers." Robert Westbrook, "'I Want a Girl, Just Like the Girl That Married Harry James': American Women and the Problem of Political Obligation in World War II," *American Quarterly* 42 (December 1990): 587–614.

5. The concept of "Republican motherhood" was introduced by Linda K. Kerber in "The Republican Mother: Women and the Enlightenment—An Historical Perspective," *American Quarterly* 28 (Summer 1976): 187–205 and idem, *Women of the Republic: Intellect and Ideology in Revolutionary America* (Chapel Hill: University of North Carolina Press, 1980). Works that seek to revise or challenge Kerber's concept of Republican motherhood include Jan Lewis, "The Republican Wife: Virtue and Seduction in the Early Republic," *William and Mary Quarterly* 44 (October 1987): 689–721; Margaret Nash, "Rethinking Republican Motherhood: Benjamin Rush and the Young Ladies' Academy of Philadelphia," *Journal of the Early Republic* 17 (Summer 1997): 171–91; Rosemarie Zagarri, "Morals, Manners, and the Republican Mother," *American Quarterly* 44 (June 1992): 192–215; and Caroline Winterer, *The Mirror of Antiquity: American Women and the Classical Tradition* (Ithaca, NY: Cornell University Press, 2007).

6. For discussions of female voluntarism in the antebellum era, see Nancy F. Cott, *The Bonds of Womanhood: "Woman's Sphere" in New England, 1780–1835* (New Haven, CT: Yale University Press, 1977), chaps. 3 and 4; Barbara Leslie Epstein, *The Politics of Domesticity: Women, Evangelism and Temperance in Nineteenth-Century America* (Middletown, CT: Wesleyan University Press); Lori Ginzberg, *Women and the Work of Benevolence: Morality, Politics and Class in the Nineteenth-Century United States* (New Haven, CT: Yale University Press, 1990); Mary P. Ryan, *Cradle of the Middle Class: The Family in Oneida County, New York, 1790–1865* (Cambridge: Cambridge University Press, 1981), chap. 3; and Larry Whiteaker, *Seduction, Prostitution, and Moral Reform in New York, 1830–1860* (New York: Garland, 1997).

7. By the late nineteenth century, "almost every town had at least one women's club." Suzanne Lebsock, "Women and American Politics, 1880–1920" in *Women, Politics, and Change*, ed. Louise A. Tilly and Patricia Gurin (New York: Russell Sage Foundation, 1990), 41–42.

8. In 1890, a national organization, the General Federation of Women's Clubs, was formed as an umbrella organization. Ibid., 42.

9. For studies focusing on the club movement, see Karen Blair, *The Clubwoman as Feminist: True Womanhood Redefined, 1868–1914* (New York: Holmes and Meier, 1980), and Janice C. Steinschneider, *An Improved Woman: The Wisconsin Federation of Women's Clubs, 1895–1920* (Brooklyn, NY: Carlson, 1994). See also Anne Firor Scott, *Natural Allies: Women's Associations in American History* (Urbana: University of Illinois Press, 1991).

10. Works that discuss the relationship between maternalism and social welfare legislation include Linda Gordon, *Pitied But Not Entitled: Single Mothers and the History of Welfare* (Cambridge, MA: Harvard University Press, 1994); Seth Koven and Sonya Michel, eds., *Mothers of a New World: Maternalist Politics and the Origins of Welfare States* (New York: Routledge, 1993); Molly Ladd-Taylor, *Mother-Work: Women, Child Welfare, and the State, 1890–1930* (Urbana: University of Illinois Press, 1994); Gwendolyn Mink, *The Wages of Motherhood: Inequality in the Welfare State, 1917–1942* (Ithaca, NY: Cornell University Press, 1995); Robyn Muncy, *Creating a Dominion in American Female Reform, 1890–1935* (New York: Oxford University Press, 1991)and Theda Skocpol, *Protecting Soldiers and Mothers: The Political Origins of Social Policy in the United States* (Cambridge, MA: Belknap Press, 1992).

11. Estelle Freedman, "Separatism as Strategy: Female Institution Building and American Feminism, 1870–1930," *Feminist Studies* 5 (Fall 1979): 514.

12. Paula Baker, "The Domestication of Politics: Women and American Political Society, 1780–1920," *American Historical Review* 89 (June 1984): 644.

13. "From recent histories one might gain the impression that women's voluntary organizations waned after 1920," Nancy Cott has noted, "but nothing is further from the truth." Nancy F. Cott, "Across the Great Divide: Women in Politics before and after 1920," in *Women, Politics, and Change*, ed. Tilly and Gurin, 161.

14. Perhaps the most striking challenge to the notion that women formed a unified voting bloc was the founding of the Women's Organization for National Prohibition Reform (WONPR), a group that supported the repeal of prohibition. See Caryn Neumann, "The End of Gender Solidarity: The History of the Women's Organization for National Prohibition Reform in the United States, 1929–1933," *Journal of Women's History* 9 (Summer 1997): 31–51; and Kenneth D. Rose, *American Women and the Repeal of Prohibition* (New York: New York University Press, 1996).

15. Nancy F. Cott, *The Grounding of Modern Feminism* (New Haven, CT: Yale University Press, 1987), 14.

16. Women's ambivalence toward party politics is discussed in Kristi Anderson, "Women and Citizenship in the 1920s," in *Women, Politics and Change*, ed. Tilly and Gurin, 177–98.

17. Recently, a number of studies have emphasized the endurance of women's political traditions in the interwar era. Landon R. Y. Storrs, for example, has called attention to the activities of the National Consumers' League in the 1930s, noting, "The early view that enfranchisement killed white women's separate, autonomous reform networks has given way to an emphasis on persistence. . . . The NCL story suggests that we have underestimated the longevity of progressive women's networks." Storrs, *Civilizing Capitalism: The National Consumers' League, Women's Activism, and Labor Standards in the New Deal Era* (Chapel Hill: University of North Carolina Press, 2000), 5. Similarly, Kenneth Rose has argued that, after attaining the

vote, "large numbers of women . . . continued to cleave to women's organizations to make their political presence felt—just as they had done during the nineteenth century—and continued to believe in the antebellum notion that women wielded a decisive moral authority on issues dealing with home and family." Rose, *American Women and the Repeal of Prohibition*, 3. Finally, Estelle Freedman has revised her previously quoted views in her biography of prison reformer Miriam Van Waters, *Maternal Justice: Miriam Van Waters and the Female Reform Tradition* (Chicago: Chicago University Press, 1996). She argues that Van Waters's career demonstrates how, in the interwar period, women combined older traditions of female voluntarism with newer political strategies made possible by suffrage. Freedman now depicts the female reform tradition as a casualty of anticommunism and the reactionary sexual politics of the post–World War II era.

18. For discussions concerning the use of maternalist ideology in the temperance and anti-obscenity movements, respectively, see Suzanne M. Marilley, "Frances Willard and the Feminism of Fear," *Feminist Studies* 19 (Spring 1993): 123–46; and Alison M. Parker, *Purifying America: Women, Cultural Reform, and Pro-Censorship Activism, 1873–1933* (Urbana: University of Illinois Press, 1997).

19. Scholars have not analyzed the gold star mothers' pilgrimages specifically in relation to women's history, but a number of works have explored their significance in regard to the memory and commemoration of World War I. See G. Kurt Piehler, "The War Dead and the Gold Star: American Commemoration of the First World War," in *Commemorations: The Politics of National Identity*, ed. John R. Gillis (Princeton, NJ: Princeton University Press, 1994), 168–85 and idem, *Remembering War the American Way* (Washington, D.C.: Smithsonian Institution Press, 1995), chap. 3; Lisa M. Budreau, "The Politics of Remembrance: The Gold Star Mothers' Pilgrimage and America's Fading Memory of the Great War," *Journal of Military History* 72, no. 2 (2008): 371–411; Lotte Larsen Meyer, "Mourning in a Distant Land: Gold Star Pilgrimages to American Military Cemeteries in Europe, 1930–33," *Markers* 20 (2003): 31–75. The most comprehensive account of the pilgrimages appears in John W. Graham, *The Gold Star Mother Pilgrimages of the 1930s* (Jefferson, NC: McFarland, 2005).

20. Invitations were extended to more than 16,000 women, but approximately 9,800 women declined. Graham, *The Gold Star Mother Pilgrimages of the 1930s*, 11–12.

21. Private organizations in Europe, the United States, Canada, and Australia arranged for similar pilgrimages to World War I battlefields and cemeteries in the 1920s, but in no other instance did a government assume the responsibility of organizing and financing such trips. Two notable precedents were the American Legion's "Second AEF," in which 16,000 Americans, mostly veterans, journeyed to Paris in 1927 for the Legion's tenth annual convention, and the British Legion's pilgrimage the following year, in which 10,000 pilgrims traveled to France and Flanders. See Graham, *The Gold Star Mother Pilgrimages of the 1930s*, chap. 3; David W. Lloyd, *Battlefield Tourism: Pilgrimage and the Commemoration of the Great War in Britain, Australia and Canada, 1919–1939* (Oxford: Berg, 1998); and Tony Walter, "War Grave Pilgrimage," in *Pilgrimage in Popular Culture*, ed. Ian Reader and Tony Walter (Houndmills: MacMillan Press, 1993), 63–91.

22. Christine Kimberly Erickson has defined "patriotic maternalism" as a "fusion between a militant patriotism that defended American values and institutions against subversive forces and a sense that motherhood provided women with the unique ability to safeguard American ideals" ("Conservative Women and Patriotic Maternalism: The Beginnings of a Gendered Conservative Tradition in the 1920s and 1930s" [PhD diss., University of Santa Barbara, 1999], viii).

23. In terms of cost, the two programs were roughly comparable. Congress appropriated $5.38 million for the four-year pilgrimage program, whereas allocations for the first four years of the Sheppard Towner Act (1921–25) totaled $5.23 million. Ladd-Taylor, *Mother-Work*, 175.

24. For background on the right-wing Mothers' Movement, see Laura McEnaney, "He-Men and Christian Mothers: The America First Movement and the Gendered Meanings of Patriotism and Isolationism," *Diplomatic History* 18 (Winter 1994): 47–57; Kari Frederickson, "Catherine Curtis and Conservative Isolationist Women, 1939–1941," *Historian* 58 (Summer 1996): 825–39; Glen Jeansonne, *Women of the Far Right: The Mothers' Movement and World War II* (Chicago: University of Chicago Press, 1996); and June Melby Benowitz, *Days of Discontent: American Women and Right-Wing Politics, 1933–1945* (DeKalb: Northern Illinois University Press, 2002).

25. Works on women's contributions to the interwar peace movement include Harriet Hyman Alonso, *Peace as a Women's Issue: A History of the U.S. Movement for World Peace and Women's Rights* (Syracuse, NY: Syracuse University Press, 1993); Harriet Hyman Alonso, *The Women's Peace Union and the Outlawry of War, 1921–1942* (Knoxville: University of Tennessee Press, 1989); Carrie A. Foster, *The Women and the Warriors: The U.S. Section of the Women's International League for Peace and Freedom, 1914–1940* (Syracuse, NY: Syracuse University Press, 1995); Nitza Berkovitch, *From Motherhood to Citizenship: Women's Rights and International Organizations* (Baltimore: Johns Hopkins University Press, 1999), 58–74; Linda K. Schott, *Reconstructing Women's Thoughts: The Women's International League for Peace and Freedom before World War II* (Stanford, CA: Stanford University Press, 1997); and Susan Zeiger, "Finding a Cure for War: Women's Politics and the Peace Movement in the 1920s," *Journal of Social History* 24 (Fall 1990): 69–86. For the use of maternal imagery in 1930s antiwar art and drama, see Barbara Melosh, *Engendering Culture: Manhood and Womanhood in New Deal Public Art and Theater* (Washington, D.C.: Smithsonian Institution Press, 1991), chap. 6.

26. For discussions of sentimental representations of mothers in the Civil War North, see Clarke, "Sentimental Bonds"; Fahs, "Feminized Civil War" and "Sentimental Soldier"; and Mitchell, *Vacant Chair*.

27. In point of fact, only two of Lydia Bixby's sons died in the war, and she herself sympathized with the Confederate cause. Nevertheless, the letter has remained a part of national mythology, as when it is read in the 1998 Steven Spielberg film, *Saving Private Ryan*. Michael Burlingame, "The Trouble with the Bixby Letter," *American Heritage* 50, no. 4 (1999): 64–67.

28. The name "Gold Star Mothers" reflected the practice, first adopted during World War I, of wearing or displaying a gold star to signal the loss of a loved one who died while serving the nation. Citizens hung service flags in their homes and businesses, as many military families still do today, with blue stars indicating the number of family members in military service. If a serviceman died, a gold star would be superimposed over the blue one.

29. Piehler, "The War Dead and the Gold Star," 176–77.

30. I am grateful to Christine Erickson for sharing information about the American Gold Star Mothers' participation in the Women's Patriotic Conference on National Defense (WPCND) conferences in the 1930s. For background on the WPCND, see Erickson, "Conservative Women and Patriotic Maternalism." According to Kirsten Delegard, the WPCND, along with the standing "national defense" and "loyalty" committees of its affiliates, "became the driving institutional force behind female anti-radicalism" in the interwar period. Kirsten Delegard, "Women Patriots: Female Activism and the Politics of American Anti-Radicalism, 1919–1935" (PhD diss., Duke University, 1999), 98.

31. For an instructive discussion of the founding of the WPCND, see Delegard, "Women Patriots," chap. 2.

32. House Committee on Military Affairs, *To Authorize Mothers and Unmarried Widows of Deceased World War Veterans Buried in Europe to Visit the Graves: Hearing before Committee on Military Affairs*, 70th Cong., 1st sess., January 27, 1928, 27. At the war's end, more than 70,000 American servicemen were buried in Europe. The U.S. government urged servicemen's next-of-kin to grant permission to have the bodies interred in U.S. cemeteries in Europe, but it covered the expense of exhuming and returning bodies to the United States for those who chose not to do so. Most families had the bodies repatriated: the Graves Registration Service returned 45,588 bodies to the United States, whereas some 30,000 remained buried in Europe. Mark Meigs, *Optimism at Armageddon: Voices of American Participants in the First World War* (New York: New York University Press, 1997), chap. 5.

33. Graham, *The Gold Star Mother Pilgrimages of the 1930s*, 69. Graham provides a detailed discussion of the pilgrimage program's legislative history.

34. Senate Subcommittee on Military Affairs, *To Authorize Mothers and Unmarried Widows of Deceased World War Veterans Buried in Europe to Visit the Graves: Hearing before a Subcommittee of the Committee on Military Affairs*, 70th Cong., 1st sess., May 14, 1928, 4.

35. 1928 Senate Hearing, 29.

36. House Subcommittee on Military Affairs, *To Authorize Mothers of Deceased War Veterans Buried in Europe to Visit the Graves*, 68th Cong., 1st sess., February 19, 1924, 15.

37. 1928 Senate Hearing, 7.

38. 1928 House Hearing, 22. Burling later read the same statement in her testimony before the Senate. 1928 Senate Hearing, 4.

39. Quoted in Graham, *The Gold Star Mother Pilgrimages of the 1930s*, 52–53.

40. Kipling's much-cited poem reads as follows:

> If I were hanged on the highest hill,
> *Mother o' mine, O mother o' mine!*
> I know whose love would follow me still,
> *Mother o' mine, O mother o' mine!*
> If I were drowned in the deepest sea,
> *Mother o' mine, O mother o' mine!*
> I know whose tears would come down to me,
> *Mother o' mine, O mother o' mine!*
> If I were damned of body and soul,
> I know whose prayers would make me whole,
> *Mother o' mine, O mother o' mine!*

41. 1928 Senate Hearing, 10.

42. Ibid., 27.

43. In February 1930, Sen. Henry Allen introduced a bill that would have provided funds for fathers to make pilgrimages, but nothing came of the measure. "Asks Trips for Fathers," *New York Times*, February 14, 1930, 15. Several men who accompanied their wives at their own expense found themselves relegated to the background; one account reported that eight fathers who had made the journey "were almost lost in the excitement of the reception." "Gold Star Group Arrives in London," *New York Times*, May 25, 1930, 9.

44. For histories of fatherhood that cover the interwar period, see Robert Griswold, *Fatherhood in America: A History* (New York: Basic Books, 1993); and Ralph LaRossa, *The*

Modernization of Fatherhood: A Social and Political History (Chicago: University of Chicago Press, 1997).

45. 1928 Senate Hearing, 21–22.

46. Ibid., 18.

47. Quoted in Graham, *The Gold Star Mother Pilgrimages of the 1930s*, 71.

48. 1924 House Hearing, 12–13.

49. Senate Committee on Military Affairs, *To Authorize Mothers and Unmarried Widows of Deceased World War Veterans Buried in Europe to Visit the Graves: Hearing Before Committee on Military Affairs*, 70th Cong., 2nd sess., February 12, 1929, 7.

50. House Committee on Military Affairs, *To Authorize Mothers and Unmarried Widows of Deceased World War Veterans Buried in Europe to Visit the Graves: Hearing Before Committee on Military Affairs*, 71st Cong., 2nd sess., December 17, 1929, 18.

51. Piehler, "The War Dead and the Gold Star," 377.

52. 1928 Senate Hearing, 19.

53. For background on the Tomb of Unknown Soldier, see Piehler, *Remembering War the American Way*, 116–25, and Ken Inglis, "Entombing Unknown Soldiers: From London and Paris to Baghdad," *History and Memory* 5 (Fall/Winter 1993): 7–31.

54. A report prepared on the constitutionality of the proposed legislation clarified these dual justifications by pointing to two types of legal precedents, those which established the government's power to "grant relief to soldiers and their dependents," and those which recognized the government's power to enact legislation that would "further patriotic sentiment." "Memorandum upon Constitutionality of Use of Federal Funds for Gold Star Mothers' Pilgrimages," 1929 Senate Hearing, 11–15.

55. 1928 House Hearing, 3.

56. 1928 Senate Hearing, 14.

57. Moreover, beginning in World War I, the American Red Cross defined itself in explicitly maternalist terms, adopting the slogan "The Greatest Mother on Earth." Foster Rhea Dulles, *The American Red Cross: A History* (New York: Harper and Brothers, 1950), 150. The organization appears to have dropped this slogan during World War II; the last usage I have located dates from 1943.

58. 1928 House Hearing, 2.

59. "Gold Star Ship Sails with 235 on Pilgrimage," *Chicago Daily Tribune*, May 18, 1930, 5.

60. 1924 House Hearing, 4.

61. Ibid., 16, 19.

62. Maj. Louis C. Wilson, "The War Mother Goes 'Over There,'" *Quartermaster Review* (May–June 1930): 21–25.

63. "Capital Rebuffs Gold Star Negroes," *New York Times*, May 30, 1930, 12; "Gold Star Mothers Balk at Jim Crow Move," *Chicago Defender*, June 7, 1930, 2.

64. "Capital Rebuffs Gold Star Negroes," 12.

65. The most complete account of the African-American pilgrimages appears in Graham, *The Gold Star Mother Pilgrimages of the 1930s*, chap. 6. A total of 279 black women—out of some 650 who were eligible to participate in the program—ultimately decided to make the pilgrimage. In the end, despite the boycott, the rate of overall participation did not differ significantly according to race. However, it should be noted that more than a quarter of the black pilgrims (as compared to only 10 percent of the white pilgrims) waited until the very last year of the program to make the trip. See also Budreau, "The Politics of Remembrance," 400–403. The experiences of Katherine

Bell Holley, an African-American widow who made the pilgrimage, are described in Constance Potter, "World War I Gold Star Mothers Pilgrimages, Parts I and II," *Prologue* 31 (Spring 1999): 140–45 and *Prologue* 31 (Summer 1999): 210–15. The decision to segregate the pilgrims helped to fuel African Americans' growing alienation from the Republican Party. George Garcia, "Black Disaffection from the Republican Party during the Presidency of Herbert Hoover, 1928–1932," *Annals of Iowa* 45 (Fall 1980): 469–70; and Donald J. Lisio, *Hoover, Blacks, and Lily-Whites: A Study of Southern Strategies* (Chapel Hill: University of North Carolina Press, 1985), 235–36.

66. "Gold Star Mothers Wildly Greeted on Arrival in Paris," *Chicago Defender*, July 26, 1930, 4; and "Paris Fetes War Mothers: France Seeks to Make up for U.S. Jim Crow," *Afro-American*, July 26, 1930, 1. For background on African-Americans' travel abroad and its implications for black citizenship, see Elizabeth Stordeur Pryor, "'Jim Crow' Cars, Passport Denials and Atlantic Crossings: African-American Travel, Protest and Citizenship at Home and Abroad, 1827–1865" (PhD diss., University of California, Santa Barbara, 2008).

67. Michele Paige McElya, *Clinging to Mammy: The Faithful Slave in Twentieth-Century America* (Cambridge, MA: Harvard University Press, 2007); and Joan Marie Johnson, "'Ye Gave Them a Stone': African American Women's Clubs, the Frederick Douglass Home, and the Black Mammy Monument," *Journal of Women's History* 17, no. 1 (2005): 62–86.

68. K. Walter Hickel, "War, Region, and Social Welfare: Federal Aid to Servicemen's Dependents in the South, 1917–1921," *Journal of American History* 87, no. 4 (2000): 1363–91.

69. Linda K. Kerber, *No Constitutional Right To Be Ladies: Women and the Obligations of Citizenship* (New York: Hill and Wang, 1998).

70. "Gold Star Black Mothers: Stay Out of France if Forced to Sail on Jim Crow Ships!" *Chicago Defender*, April 19, 1930, 1.

71. "Gold Star War Mothers Talk for the *Afro*," *Afro-American*, August 9, 1930, 1, 17.

72. J. A. Rogers, "Second Group of Gold Star Mothers Will Sail for France August 16," *Afro-American*, August 16, 1930, 7.

73. Several scholars have explored black women reformers' relationship to maternalism. See in particular Linda Gordon, *Pitied but Not Entitled*, chap. 5; and Eileen Boris, "The Power of Motherhood: Black and White Activist Women Redefine the 'Political,'" in Koven and Michel, eds., *Mothers of a New World*, 213–45.

74. These attacks on the black pilgrims resemble critiques of black mothers discussed by Ruth Feldstein, who has shown how mother-blaming came to be aligned with the cause of racial liberalism (*Motherhood in Black and White: Race and Sex in American Liberalism, 1930–1965* [Ithaca, NY: Cornell University Press, 2000]).

75. "Gold Star Mothers Sail for France on Freight Steamer," *Chicago Defender*, July 19, 1930, 1.

76. Frank A. Young, "The Gold Star Turns Out To Be One of Brass," *Chicago Defender*, July 19, 1930, 13.

77. "Many Gold Star Mothers Cancel Jim Crow Trip," *Afro-American*, July 19, 1930, 1.

78. Ibid., 19.

79. "Black and Gold Stars," *Nation* 131 (July 23, 1930): 86.

80. As Francesca Morgan notes, "decrying the DAR did not amount to opposing Jim Crow." Francesca Morgan, *Women and Patriotism in Jim Crow America* (Chapel Hill: University of North Carolina Press, 2005), 153.

81. Mrs. C. D. BuDois to President Herbert Hoover, March 3, 1930, President's Personal Files, box 131, Gold Star Mothers, Herbert Hoover Presidential Library, West Branch, Iowa (hereafter HHPL).

82. "The Other War Mothers," *Los Angeles Record*, June 24, 1930, sent to President Herbert Hoover by Richard P. Yockisch, June 25, 1930, President's Subject Files, box 165, Gold Star Mothers, HHPL.

83. The average cost of a pilgrimage is cited in Graham, *The Gold Star Mother Pilgrimages of the 1930s*, 55. For historian Jennifer Keene's computation of the average bonus, see http://www .worldwar1.com/dbc/bonusm.htm [accessed May 15, 2009].

84. The most comprehensive account of these events appears in Roger Daniels, *The Bonus March: An Episode of the Great Depression* (Westport, CT: Greenwood Publishing Corporation, 1971). See also Jennifer D. Keene, *Doughboys, the Great War, and the Remaking of America* (Baltimore: Johns Hopkins University Press, 2001), chap. 8.

85. Graham, *The Gold Star Mother Pilgrimages of the 1930s*, 140.

86. Letter to the Editor, "War Mothers Pilgrimage," *New York Times*, January 17, 1933, 18.

87. Louis F. Henry, "Letters to the Editor," *New York Times*, April 15, 1932, 18.

88. Quoted in "Editorial Paragraphs," *Nation* 134 (March 23, 1932): 327. The book in question, which included forwards by Harry Emerson Fosdick and the prominent peace activist and feminist Carrie Chapman Catt, attempted to challenge the stereotypical image of peace activists as "soft-hearted idealists" by portraying war in starkly "realistic" terms. "This book says in effect that if the militarists want realism we will give it to them," wrote Fosdick. Frederick Barber, *The Horror of It: Camera Records of War's Gruesome Glories* (New York: Brewer, Warren & Putnam, 1932).

89. Scrapbook, Box 7, American Gold Star Mothers Collection, Manuscript Division, Library of Congress, Washington, DC.

90. " 'Future Veterans' Seek a Bonus Now," *New York Times*, March 17, 1936, 24; "Future Veterans," *Time* 27, no. 13 (March 30, 1936): 38. Vassar president Henry N. MacCracken vigorously rebutted claims that a Future Gold Star Mothers chapter existed at Vassar, arguing that the college had not chartered the organization. "Vassar Head Protests," *New York Times*, March 27, 1936, 46.

91. For background on the group, see Donald W. Whisenhunt, "The Veterans of Future Wars in the Pacific Northwest," *Pacific Northwest Quarterly* 85, no. 4 (1994): 134–36; and Joseph P. Lash and James A. Wechsler, *War: Our Heritage* (New York: *International* Publishers, 1936), 135–42. See also the group's manifesto: Lewis J. Gorin, Jr., *Patriotism Prepaid* (Philadelphia: J. B. Lippincott, 1936).

92. Villard came from a distinguished line of radical activists: his mother, Fanny Garrison Villard, was a member of the Women's Peace Party and helped to found the Women's International League for Peace and Freedom. His grandfather was the famous abolitionist, William Lloyd Garrison.

93. Oswald Garrison Villard, "Issues and Men," *Nation* 142 (April 8, 1936): 450.

94. "Future Veterans," *Time* 27, no. 13 (March 30, 1936): 38.

95. Lewis Gorin to Marys Austin Converse, March 21, 1936, box 6, folder "Gold Star Mothers/Home Fires Division," Veterans of Future Wars Collection, Seeley G. Mudd Manuscript Library, Princeton University, Princeton, NJ (hereafter VFW). Used with permission of Princeton University Library.

96. "Future Veterans Bow to Criticism," *New York Times*, March 21, 1936, 19.

97. Gorin to Marys Austin Converse, March 21,1936, VFW.

98. The film is based on a short story that portrays the generational conflict between mother and son in more ambiguous terms. I. R. A. Wylie, "Pilgrimage: A Story," *American Magazine* 114 (November 1932): 44–47, 90–96. According to one of Ford's biographers, *The Pilgrimage* departs

from his "usual tendency to idealize motherhood." Joseph McBride, *Searching for John Ford: A Life* (New York: St. Martin's Press, 2001), 194–98.

99. When the American Gold Star Mothers learned that a film about the pilgrimages was in the works, the vice president wrote to Twentieth Century Fox to urge the production company to consult with the organization, noting "The pilgrimage was very sacred to us and we may not wish it to be commercialized." There is no evidence that Fox responded.

100. For discussions of the magazine's contemptuous attitude toward women, see Kenon Breazeale, "In Spite of Women: *Esquire* Magazine and the Construction of the Male Consumer," *Signs* 20 (Autumn 1994): 1–22; and Peter N. Stearns and Mark Knapp, "Men and Romantic Love: Pinpointing a Twentieth-Century Change," *Journal of Social History* 26 (Summer 1993): 769–95.

101. Philip Stevenson, "Gold Star Mother," *Esquire* 3 (December 1935): 205.

102. Philip Wylie, *Generation of Vipers* (New York: Farrar and Rinehart, 1942), 192–93.

103. [N.p.], June 5, 1943, scrapbook, box 285, Philip Wylie Papers, Firestone Library, Princeton University, Princeton, NJ (hereafter PWP).

104. [Lafayette, IN], June 29, 1943, folder 4, box 232, PWP.

105. [Akron, OH, n.d.], folder 4, box 235, PWP.

106. However, the racial and political meaning of the war mother identity was never uniform or stable, as evidenced by the case of "Mom Chung." As historian Judy Tzu-Chun Wu has detailed, Margaret Chung—an unmarried, Chinese-American doctor in her fifties—gained fame by acting as a surrogate mother to hundreds of (mainly white) American servicemen who passed through San Francisco. Donning a gingham apron, Chung cooked huge meals for U.S. servicemen who flocked to the weekly parties she threw at her home. Letters to and from her "sons" testify to the emotional bonds that she forged with the young men whom she ceremonially "adopted." According to Wu, Chung became a wartime celebrity because she put a comforting face on the nation's wartime alliance with China, and because she helped Americans to conceptualize the ideal of democratic pluralism in nonthreatening, familial terms. Her story would have been impossible during World War I, but the rise of racial liberalism allowed nonwhite women to contest the racial construction of "American motherhood" more successfully during World War II. Judy Tzu-Chun Wu, *Doctor Mom Chung of the Fair-Haired Bastards: The Life of a Wartime Celebrity* (Berkeley: University of California Press, 2005), 138.

107. Another aerial photograph taken at an army training school in Enid, Oklahoma, showed cadets' parachute packs spelling out "Hi Mom." "Mother's Day," *Life* 12 (May 25, 1942): 28–29.

108. Captions inform readers that Covington had lost four brothers in the Civil War and call attention to a miniature of her deceased husband on her collar. In other words, Covington's special status resided in her connection to a long history of male sacrifice and female suffering in wartime. "Mother's Day," 28.

109. A separate commemoration ceremony staged by the American Women's Voluntary Services on the Lower East Side drew an audience of three thousand. "War Sets Keynote for Mother's Day," *New York Times*, May 11, 1942, 10.

110. Rachel K. McDowell, "Churches to Mark Mother's Day Here," *New York Times*, May 8, 1943, 9.

111. "War Hero Marches with His Mother," *New York Times*, May 11, 1942, 10.

112. "War Sets Keynote for Mother's Day," 10. Similarly, Mrs. Eisenhower, mother of General Dwight Eisenhower, was named the Kansas Mother of 1945.

113. It should be noted that, of the eleven Van Coutren children who joined the military, three were daughters who served with the WACs. "Outstanding Mother," *New York Times*, May 7, 1944, 8.

114. Jean Bethke Elshtain, *Women and War* (New York: Basic Books, 1987), 189.

115. "5 Sullivans Died, Survivor Writes," *New York Times*, January 15, 1943, 7.

116. "Sullivans to Tour War Work Plants," *New York Times*, February 3, 1943, 12.

117. Mrs. Thomas F. Sullivan, "I Lost Five Sons," *American Magazine* 137 (March 1944): 17, 92–95. Aletta Sullivan also appealed to Americans to buy war bonds. See Mrs. Sullivan, "Instead of Our Thanksgiving Message," *Good Housekeeping* 121 (November 1945): 21.

118. "Speed Up Production, the Sullivans Plead," *New York Times*, February 9, 1943, 2.

119. Mrs. Sullivan, "I Lost Five Sons," 17.

120. *The Fighting Sullivans*, directed by Lloyd Bacon (Twentieth Century-Fox Film, 1944). Aletta Sullivan later explained that she had hesitated to allow the film to be made, insisting that "our lives weren't particularly interesting. We've always been just a typical American family." Navy officials, however, had reassured her, "That's just it. The picture could show the American way of life. By showing the kind of life for which our boys are fighting, it could be an inspiration to all Americans." Mrs. Sullivan, "I Lost Five Sons," 95. Indeed, the film was deemed such an exemplary representation of American values that it was shown to German prisoners of war as part of a political reeducation program. Ron Robin, *The Barbed Wire College: Reeducating German POWs in the United States during World War II* (Princeton, NJ: Princeton University Press, 1995), 117.

121. *So Proudly We Hail!* directed by Mark Sandrich (Paramount Pictures, 1943). The story of the film's production, which involved intensive collaboration with the Office of War Information, appears in Clayton R. Koppes and Gregory D. Black, *Hollywood Goes to War: How Politics, Profits and Propaganda Shaped World War II Movies* (New York: Free Press, 1987), 98–104.

122. James Agee, "So Proudly We Fail," in *Reporting World War II*, pt. 1: *American Journalism, 1938–1944* (New York: Library of America, 1995), 658–61.

123. *Hail, the Conquering Hero*, directed by Preston Sturges (Paramount Pictures, 1944). One psychiatrist approvingly noted the "delicate sarcasm" with which *Hail, the Conquering Hero* portrayed the national penchant for glorifying mothers. "The adoration which one of the Marines feels for the elderly lady [Woodrow's mother] is the highlight of the picture: any fancied slight to her—from her son or anyone else—is met with prompt physical violence from this worshipping admirer." Herbert I. Kupper, *Back to Life: The Emotional Adjustment of Our Veterans* (New York: L. B. Fischer, 1945), 83.

124. The enormously successful campaign raised $39 million. Robert Merton, *Mass Persuasion: The Social Psychology of a War Bond Drive* (New York: Harper & Brothers Publishers, 1946), 2. For a broader discussion of role that the bond program played in the American war effort, see Lawrence Samuel, *Pledging Allegiance: American Identity and the Bond Drive of World War II* (Washington, D.C.: Smithsonian Press, 1997).

125. Philip Furia recounts Smith's debut of the song "God Bless America" on Armistice Day, 1938, in *As Thousands Cheer: The Life of Irving Berlin* (New York: Viking Penguin, 1990), 368–72.

126. Elizabeth-R. Valentine, "Singing Lady Who Likes People," *New York Times Magazine*, January 16, 1944, sec. VI, 20.

127. The Blue Star Mothers made Smith an honorary lifetime member of their organization. Merton, *Mass Persuasion*, 151.

128. Ibid., 101, 177.

129. Ibid., 59, 49.

130. McEnaney, "He-Men and Christian Mothers," 48–49. For other accounts of the right-wing mothers' movement, see Frederickson, "Catherine Curtis and Conservative Isolationist Women, 1939–1941"; Jeansonne, *Women of the Far Right*; and Melby, *Days of Discontent.*

131. Dilling was charged along with twenty-five other extremists in *U.S. v. Winrod*, which later evolved into *U.S. v. McWilliams.* The case was eventually dismissed. See Christine K. Erickson, "'I Have Not Had One Fact Disproven': Elizabeth Dilling's Crusade against Communism in the 1930s," *Journal of American Studies* 36 (2002): 473–89.

132. Russell Whelan and Thomas M. Johnson, "The Menace of the 'Mothers,'" *Liberty* 137 (July 26, 1944): 18–19, 72–73.

133. Patricia Lochridge, "The Mother Racket," *Woman's Home Companion* 71 (July 1944): 20–21, 71–74. The notion that seemingly innocuous mothers' groups might harbor subversives was convincing enough to serve as a plot device in Fritz Lang's 1944 film *Ministry of Fear* (Paramount Pictures, 1944), in which Nazi spies infiltrate the British defense system, using an organization of "dear old dowagers" called the "Mothers of Free Nations" as their front.

134. Whelan and Johnson, "The Menace of the 'Mothers,'" 73.

135. Lochridge, "The Mother Racket," 20–21.

136. John Roy Carlson, *Under Cover: My Four Years in the Nazi Underworld of America* (New York: E. P. Dutton, 1943), 226. Relying on the same kind of masculine bravado and sensationalism that Wylie employed, Carlson also attracted some of the same fans. Six months after championing *Generation of Vipers* on the air, the radio announcer Walter Winchell promoted *Under Cover* while railing against the fascist mothers' movement. As with *Generation of Vipers*, Winchell's plug helped to turn *Under Cover* into a bestseller. Ed Weiner, *Let's Go to Press: A Biography of Walter Winchell* (New York: G. P. Putnam's Sons, 1955), 203–4.

137. Howard Mumford Jones, "Mother Love Is Not Enough," *Saturday Review of Literature* 27 (October 28, 1944): 16.

138. Sylvie Murray, *The Progressive Housewife: Community Activism in Suburban Queens, 1945–1965* (Philadelphia: University of Pennsylvania Press, 2003), 11.

139. Jennifer Audrey Stevens, "Feminizing the Urban West: Green Cities and Open Space in the Postwar Era, 1950–2000" (PhD diss., University of California, Davis, 2008), 37.

140. Michelle Nickerson, "'The Power of a Morally Indignant Woman': Republican Women and the Making of California Conservatism," *Journal of the West* 42, no. 3 (2003): 35–43 (quotation, 36). As Nickerson notes, the National Federation of Republican Women was both one of the most effective and one of the most conservative constituencies within the Republican Party. See also idem, "Moral Mothers and Goldwater Girls," in *The Conservative Sixties*, eds. David Farber and Jeff Roche (New York: Peter Lang, 2003), 51–62.

141. See, for example, the following studies of the welfare rights movement: Felicia Kornbluh, *The Battle for Welfare Rights: Politics and Poverty in Modern America* (Philadelphia: University of Pennsylvania Press, 2007); Premilla Nadasen, *Welfare Warriors: The Welfare Rights Movement in the United States* (New York: Routledge, 2004); Annelise Orleck, *Storming Caesar's Palace: How Black Mothers Fought Their Own War on Poverty* (Boston, Beacon Press, 2006); Kazuyo Tsuchiya, "The Contested Terrains of Welfare: Race, Class, and Gender in Community Action in Los Angeles and Kawasaki City, 1964–1982" (PhD diss, University of California, San Diego, 2008); and Ann M. Valk, "'Mother Power': The Movement for Welfare Rights in Washington, D.C., 1966–1972," *Journal of Women's History* 11, no. 4 (Winter 2000): 34–58.

142. It should be noted that women continued to emphasize their maternal role when lobbying for certain causes, particularly those aimed at protecting human life, such as peace, the abolition of drunk driving, and gun control. Still, it is revealing that, in these cases, women activists often frame their demands by insisting on children's needs or rights instead of asserting their own rights as mothers. See Amy Swerdlow, *Women Strike for Peace: Traditional Motherhood and Radical Politics in the 1960s* (Chicago: Chicago University Press, 1993). For discussions of women's recent maternalist activism in regard to gun control, see Kristin Goss, *Disarmed: The Missing Movement for Gun Control in America* (Princeton, NJ: Princeton University Press, 2006); and Patrice di Quinzio, "Love and Reason in the Public Sphere: Maternalist Civic Engagement and the Dilemma of Difference," in Sharon M. Meagher and Patrice di Quinzio, eds., *Women and Children First: Feminism, Rhetoric, and Public Policy* (Albany: State University of New York Press, 2005), chap. 12. In recent years, the rise of internet-based groups like MomsRising and the Mothers Movement Online suggest that, as women have continued to experience motherhood as a barrier to full economic and political equity, many have found it necessary to construct a new form of maternalist politics. See Kara Jesella, "Mom's Mad. And She's Organized," *New York Times*, February 22, 2007, sec. 2, 22. Significantly, this article appeared in the Fashion and Style section, suggesting that maternalist activism still carries some of the same political risks that it has in the past.

Chapter Three

1. [Napa, CA], May 16, 1957, folder 7, box 245, Philip Wylie Papers, Firestone Library, Princeton University, Princeton, NJ (hereafter PWP).

2. Quoted in Linda A. Pollock, *Forgotten Children: Parent-Child Relations from 1500 to 1900* (Cambridge: Cambridge University Press, 1983), 117.

3. Peter Stearns portrays the decline of sentimental mother love as part of a much broader shift toward a "cooler," more restrained emotional culture that took shape in the United States in the 1920s. He traces the rise of a culture characterized by a "growing aversion to emotional intensity" and the imposition of new forms of emotional restraint in Peter Stearns, *American Cool: Constructing a Twentieth-Century Emotional Style* (New York: New York University Press, 1994), 34–38, 79–80, 164–71. Other important works on the history of emotions include Peter N. Stearns and Carol Z. Stearns, "Emotionology: Clarifying the History of Emotions and Emotional Standards," *American Historical Review* 90, no. 4 (October 1985): 813–36; quotation, 813; William R. Reddy, *The Navigation of Feeling: A Framework for the History of Emotions* (New York: Cambridge University Press, 2001); and Barbara Rosenwein, "Worrying about Emotions in History," *American Historical Review* 107, no. 3 (June 2002): 821–45. Sociologist Arlie Hochschild's concept of "feeling rules" is also useful for thinking about the history of mother love and maternal affect (*The Managed Heart: The Commercialization of Human Feeling* [Berkeley: University of California Press, 1983]).

4. For instance, in her history of the concept of maternal bonding, Diane Eyer argues that the Victorian "hearth angel" ideal "reemerged" in a new guise after World War II, transformed by Freudian psychology into the "feminine mystique." Diane E. Eyer, *Mother-Infant Bonding: A Scientific Fiction* (New Haven, CT: Yale University Press, 1992), 9. Likewise, Wendy Kline argues that the "reproductive morality" promoted by experts in the postwar period can be viewed as "little more than a nineteenth-century notion of gender dressed in the garb of science." Wendy Kline, *Building a Better Race: Gender, Sexuality, and Eugenics from the Turn of the Century to the Baby Boom* (2001; Berkeley: University of California Press, 2005), 156.

5. Nancy Pottisham Weiss, "Mother, the Invention of Necessity: Dr. Benjamin Spock's *Baby and Child Care*," *American Quarterly* 29 (Winter 1977): 519–46. Benjamin Spock's *The Common Sense Book of Baby and Child Care* (New York: Duell, Sloan and Pearce, 1946) revised and reissued in 1957, was by far the most influential child-rearing manual in the postwar era. For other insightful discussions of Spock and his influence, see: Julia Grant, *Raising Baby by the Book: The Education of American Mothers* (New Haven: Yale University Press, 1998); chap 7; Rima D. Apple, *Perfect Motherhood: Science and Childrearing in America* (New Brunswick, NJ: Rutgers University Press, 2006), chap. 5; Michael Zuckerman, "Dr. Spock: The Confidence Man," in *The Family in History*, ed. Charles E. Rosenberg (Philadelphia: University of Pennsylvania Press, 1975), 179–207; Thomas Maier, *Dr. Spock: An American Life* (New York: Harcourt Brace, 1998); Ann Hulbert, *Raising America: Experts, Parents, and a Century of Advice about Children* (New York: Vintage Books, 2003), chap. 8; William Graebner, "The Unstable World of Benjamin Spock: Social Engineering in a Democratic Culture, 1917–1950," *Journal of American History* 67 (December 1980): 612–29; Henry Jenkins, "The Sensuous Child: Benjamin Spock and the Sexual Revolution," in *The Children's Culture Reader* (New York: New York University Press, 1998), 209–30; Fred Matthews, "In Defense of Common Sense: Mental Hygiene as Ideology and Mentality in Twentieth-Century America," in *Prospects*, vol. 4, ed. Jack Salzman (New York: Burt Franklin, 1979): 459–516; and idem, "The Utopia of Human Relations: The Conflict-Free Family in American Social Thought, 1930–1960," *Journal of the History of the Behavioral Sciences* 24 (October 1988): 343–62.

6. Of course, mothers rarely imbibed experts' prescriptions in a wholesale or uncritical manner, as Rima Apple and Julia Grant have shown. "Most mothers," Grant notes, "are discriminating consumers who evaluate professional expertise as one body of knowledge to be considered along with existing maternal practices and familial, religious, and community values." Grant, *Raising Baby by the Book*, 6. See also Apple, *Perfect Motherhood*; and Jay Mechling, "Advice to Historians on Advice to Mothers," *Journal of Social History* 9 (1975): 44–63. Still, even when mothers rejected particular childrearing prescriptions, they did not remain untouched by the broader cultural rejection of sentimental affectivity.

7. Booklet commemorating the twentieth anniversary of the Mother's Club of Cambridge, folder 2, box 1, Papers of the Mother's Club of Cambridge, Schlesinger Library, Harvard University, Cambridge, MA.

8. Michael Paul Rogin, "Kiss Me Deadly: Communism, Motherhood, and Cold War Movies," *Representations* 6 (Spring 1984): 5.

9. Ryan, *The Empire of the Mother*, 57–58, 45–46.

10. Margaret Johnston Grafflin, "Like Mother, Like Son," in *Best Loved Poems of the American People*, selected by Hazel Fellman (Garden City, NY: Doubleday, 1936), 370. Pinky MacArthur had also included the following postscript: "Never tattle, never lie"—advice that, given the circumstances, placed her son in something of a double-bind. As William Manchester has noted, "Like Franklin Delano Roosevelt at Harvard and Adlai Stevenson at Princeton, Douglas MacArthur would share much of his collegiate experience with an alert mother-in-residence." William Manchester, *American Caesar* (Boston: Little, Brown, 1978), 48–52.

11. Burton Rascoe, "On a Hickory Limb," *Newsweek* 12 (July 25, 1938): 30.

12. "The Army's Poets," *Stars and Stripes* 1, no. 14 (May 10, 1918): 5.

13. Gordon Shipman, "How to Make Your Son a Misfit," *American Mercury* 43 (January 1938): 283–88.

14. Although contemporaries viewed Murphy's attachment to his mother as unusually strong, many apparently regarded it as admirable rather than deviant. For instance, a newspaper reporter who interviewed Murphy when he was a thirty-one-year-old bachelor (he never married) described the mother-son relationship as "a thing so beautifully sacred that any attempt to describe . . . that tender bond of rare understanding, would be nothing short of profane." Quoted in Sidney Fine, *Frank Murphy: The Detroit Years* (Ann Arbor: University of Michigan Press, 1975), 6–7.

15. Annie Kilburn Kilmer, *Leaves from My Life* (New York: Fry Publishing, 1925), 121. A review described the book as "a fascinating chronicle of fine American family life and a testimonial of the enduring love which abides between mothers and sons." "Mrs. Kilmer Pens Loving Book on Son," *Washington Post*, August 2, 1925, S13.

16. This letter is reprinted in Annie Kilburn Kilmer, *Memories of My Son, Sergeant Joyce Kilmer* (New York: Brentano's, 1920), 140.

17. An exception to this is Grant, "A 'Real Boy' and not a Sissy."

18. Again, though it is very difficult to assess the pervasiveness of such changes, there is evidence that middle-class women did gradually internalize a new emotional stance toward their children. For instance, a sociological study published in 1959 found working-class mothers to be far more protective than their middle-class counterparts. Though there would seem to be obvious reasons why less affluent women might be more fearful for their children's safety, the study's authors portrayed their subjects' "almost phobic concern" as evidence of psychopathology. (They speculated that it could be understood as overcompensation for repressed hostility.) In contrast, the authors approvingly noted that middle-class mothers tended to adopt a far more "matter-of-fact attitude toward sheltering their children from danger." The authors also claimed that working-class mothers "want to be needed and loved by their children in a way which middle class women do not." Obviously, this study cannot be accepted as unbiased "truth," but it is still possible that it successfully identified significant class differences in maternal attitudes and approaches. Lee Rainwater, Richard P. Coleman, and Gerald Handel, *Workingman's Wife: Her Personality, World and Life Style* (New York: Oceana Publications, 1959), 89–91, 97. See also Gerald R. Leslie and Kathryn P. Johnsen, "Changed Perceptions of the Maternal Role," *American Sociological Review* 28, no. 6 (December 1963), 919–28.

19. John C. Spurlock and Cynthia A. Magistro, *New and Improved: The Transformation of American Women's Emotional Culture* (New York: New York University Press, 1998), 121. Likewise, Peter Stearns has argued that, "Victorian motherlove died in American emotionology during the 1920s and 1930s." Stearns, *American Cool*, 165.

20. According to historian Maxine Margolis, "The major tenet of child-rearing literature in the 1920s and 1930s was that mothers are dangerous, dangerous to the health and well being of their children and ultimately to society at large" (*Mothers and Such: Views of American Women and Why They Changed* [Berkeley: University of California Press, 1984], 56). Historian Kathleen Jones traces the "professional history" of mother-blaming by highlighting its functions within child guidance clinics, where clients were overwhelmingly mothers and children. She argues, "Mother-blaming came to dominate the field of child mental health because, along with its availability in the research literature, its appeal to psychoanalytically oriented practitioners, and its 'fit' with larger cultural concerns, it seemed to work in the clinic" (Kathleen W. Jones, *Taming the Troublesome Child: American Families, Child Guidance, and the Limits of Psychiatric Authority* [Cambridge, MA: Harvard University Press, 1999], chap. 7; quotations, 175, 186–87).

21. Julia Grant, "A 'Real Boy' and Not a Sissy: Gender, Childhood, and Masculinity, 1890–1940," *Journal of Social History* 37, no. 4 (2004): 829–41.

22. Although childrearing advice from the Progressive Era had also advocated strict schedules and repression of behavior such as thumb-sucking and genital touching, behaviorists in the 1920s and 1930s viewed the figure of the mother in a more antagonistic manner, as "an impediment to the scientific upbringing of the young, and even worse, a potential threat." Weiss, "Mother, the Invention of Necessity," 530.

23. John B. Watson, *Psychological Care of Infant and Child* (New York: W. W. Norton, 1928), chap. 3. An insightful discussion of Watson's book appears in Weiss, "Mother, the Invention of Necessity."

24. Watson, *Psychological Care of Infant and Child*, 81–82.

25. Quoted in Jenkins, "The Sensuous Child," 213–14.

26. *Life Begins*, directed by James Flood (First National Pictures, 1932).

27. "The New Pictures," *Time* (February 21, 1938).

28. William A. White, *The Mental Hygiene of Childhood* (Boston: Little, Brown, 1919), 135–36.

29. Lorine Pruette, "Mother's Job," *Parents' Magazine* 7 (November 1932): 19.

30. *A Holiday Affair*, directed by Don Hartman (RKO Radio Pictures, 1949).

31. Julie Berebitsky, *Like Our Very Own: Adoption and the Changing Culture of Motherhood, 1851–1950* (Lawrence: University of Kansas Press, 2000), chap. 4; quotation, 116–17. See also Barbara Melosh, *Strangers and Kin: The American Way of Adoption* (Cambridge, MA: Harvard University Press, 2002). Melosh notes that, "Single women, accepted as adopters before 1940, had been pushed aside as postwar ideals touted the heterosexual nuclear family. By the 1980s, agencies were again placing children with single women" (288).

32. *Blossoms in the Dust*, directed by Mervyn LeRoy (Metro-Goldwyn-Mayer, 1941). Writer Anita Loos explained that she constructed the screenplay for *Blossoms in the Dust* around Edna Gladney's precept that, "even the most perfect orphanage creates traumas that can harm children for life; they should be gotten into real homes as soon as possible." Quoted in Michael Troyan, *A Rose for Mrs. Miniver* (Louisville: University of Kentucky Press, 1998), 112. This emphasis reflected the trend in psychological literature in the 1940s, spearheaded by figures like René Spitz and Anna Freud, toward emphasizing the harm suffered by children in institutional settings. For background on this literature, see Eyer, *Mother-Infant Bonding*, chap. 3; and Marga Vicedo, "The Maternal Instinct: Mother Love and the Search for Human Nature," (PhD diss., Harvard University, 2005), chap. 4.

33. Regina G. Kunzel, *Fallen Women, Problem Girls: Unmarried Mothers and the Professionalization of Social Work* (New Haven, CT: Yale University Press, 1993), 32–33. See also Rickie Solinger, *Wake Up Little Susie: Single Pregnancy and Race before Roe v. Wade* (New York: Routledge, 1992). As both Kunzel and Solinger have shown, attitudes and policies toward African-American unwed mothers differed radically. Whereas postwar experts drew on psychiatric concepts to explain cases involving white women, they turned to sociological explanations that emphasized the allegedly matriarchal character of the black family to account for cases involving African-American women.

34. The vast majority (85 percent) of unmarried white girls and women who gave birth in maternity homes in the 1950s and 1960s gave up their children for adoption. For an informative and affecting account of their experiences, see Ann Fessler, *The Girls Who Went Away: The Hidden History of Women Who Surrendered Children for Adoption in the Decades before Roe v. Wade* (New York: Penguin Press, 2006).

35. As Mari Jo Buhle has shown, many social scientists associated with the "national character" school of anthropology in the 1940s and 1950s argued that certain familial formations promoted democracy, while others hindered its development. Focusing intensively on parental attitudes and behavior, these scholars drew a close association between psychological and political disorder. Buhle, *Feminism and Its Discontents*, chap. 4.

36. [Burlingame, CA], February 19, 1947, folder 1, box 239, PWP.

37. Arlie Hochschild defines "feeling rules" as "standards used in emotional conversation to determine what is rightly owed and owing in the currency of feeling. Through them, we tell what is 'due' in each relation, each role" (*The Managed Heart*, 18).

38. According to Alice Fahs, popular literature during the Civil War era generally represented younger women as more "astringent than nurturing." Alice Fahs, "The Feminized Civil War: Gender, Northern Popular Literature, and the Memory of the War, 1861–1900," *Journal of American History* 85 (March 1999): 1468. See also her book *The Imagined Civil War: Popular Literature of the North and South* (Chapel Hill: University of North Carolina Press, 2001). Susan Zeiger argues that, during World War I, "the middle-aged American 'Mom' was the predominant image of womanhood" in "She Didn't Raise Her Boy To Be a Slacker: Motherhood, Conscription, and the Culture of the First World War," *Feminist Studies* 22 (Spring 1996): 6–39.

39. For a broader discussion of marriage during World War II and its aftermath, see Nancy F. Cott, *Public Vows: A History of Marriage and the Nation* (Cambridge, MA: Harvard University Press, 2000), chap. 8.

40. See also Rebecca Jo Plant, "The Veteran, His Wife, and Their Mothers: Prescriptions for Psychological Rehabilitation after World War II," in *Tales of the Great American Victory: World War II in Politics and Poetics*, ed. Diederik Oostdijk and Markha G. Valenta (Amsterdam: Vrije University Press, 2006), 95–105.

41. While 163,000 men were dishonorably discharged for reasons such as drug addiction, alcoholism, homosexuality, and psychopathic personality traits, 386,000 received honorable discharges under a variety of diagnoses, the most common being "psychoneurotic." For a more detailed discussion of statistics regarding neuropsychiatric rejections and casualties, see Ellen Herman, *The Romance of American Psychology: Political Culture in the Age of Experts* (Berkeley: University of California Press, 1995), 88–99. The most comprehensive study of psychiatry in World War II is Rebecca Schwartz Greene, "The Role of the Psychiatrist in World War II" (PhD diss., Columbia University, 1977). Other import sources include Ben Shephard, *A War of Nerves: Soldiers and Psychiatrists in the Twentieth Century* (Cambridge, MA: Harvard University Press, 2001), chaps. 13–22; Josephine Callisen Bresnahan, "Danger in Paradise: The Battle against Combat Fatigue in the Pacific War" (PhD diss., Harvard University, 1999); Gerald Grob, *From Asylum to Community: Mental Health Policy in Modern America* (Princeton, NJ: Princeton University Press, 1991), chap. 1; Nathan G. Hale, Jr., *The Rise and Crisis of Psychoanalysis in the United States: Freud and the Americans, 1917–1985* (Oxford: Oxford University Press, 1995), chap. 11; Ruth Leys, *Trauma: A Genealogy* (Chicago: Chicago University Press, 2000), chap. 6; Eva S. Moskowitz, *In Therapy We Trust: America's Obsession with Self-Fulfillment* (Baltimore: Johns Hopkins University Press, 2001), chap. 4; Hans Pols, "War Neurosis, Adjustment Problems in Veterans, and an Ill Nation: The Disciplinary Project of American Psychiatry during and after World War II," *Osiris* 22 (2007): 72–92; Mark K. Wells, *Courage and Air Warfare: The Allied Aircrew Experiences in the Second World War* (London: Frank Cass, 1995), chaps. 1, 3, and 7. See also the official military history: Albert J. Glass, ed., *U.S. Army Medical Department, Neuropsychiatry in World War II*, 2 vols. (Washington, D.C.: Office of the Surgeon General, Department of the Army, 1966, 1973). Finally, for information on the pathologizing of homosexuality in the military,

see Alan Bérubé, *Coming Out under Fire: The History of Gay Men and Women in World War II* (New York: Free Press, 1990), 149–74.

42. "The Psychiatric Toll of Warfare," *Fortune* 28 (December 1943): 141–49. Combat exhaustion had become a serious problem for the military by the fall of 1943. In January 1944, the Security Board imposed a complete black-out on all reports concerning neuropsychiatric casualties, fearing that such information might strengthen the enemies' resolve and weaken U.S. morale. The black-out was relaxed somewhat in April 1944, but a ban on publishing statistics remained in force until the war's end. The publishing industry, however, did not always abide by these restrictions. See William Menninger, *Psychiatry in a Troubled World: Yesterday's War and Today's Challenge* (New York: Macmillan, 1948), 258.

43. S. H. Kraines, "The Adviser System—Prophylactic Psychiatry on a Mass Scale," *Mental Hygiene* 27, no. 4 (October 1943): 598–99.

44. J. L. Henderson and Merrill Moore, "The Psychoneuroses of War," *New England Journal of Medicine* 230 (March 19, 1944): 277. It is important to note, however, that many psychiatrists objected to this psychodynamic view of war trauma and instead emphasized environmental stress.

45. Henderson and Moore, "The Psychoneuroses of War," 276.

46. At least one popular commentator carried this line of reasoning to its logical conclusion. "For years we've been so busy developing self-reliance in children that we've forgotten that mothers need it too," Rachel Rubin wrote in a 1944 article that described the case of a mother "on the verge of a nervous breakdown" because her son, Bobby, anticipated a letter from the draft board. As a result, Bobby would confront the typical "problems of adjustment to army life" while "weighted down by the shackles of mother love." What he and other young Americans really needed, Rubin argued, "is a mother who is self-confident and calm, a mother whose life as an individual is full enough so that she need not become an emotional parasite on her children." Rachel Rubin, "Whose Apronstrings?" *American Home* 31 (May 1944): 28.

47. Roy R. Grinker and John P. Spiegel, *War Neuroses in North Africa: The Tunisian Campaign (January-May 1943)* (New York: Josiah Macy, Jr. Foundation, 1943), 281. For an illuminating analysis of the treatment methods that Grinker and Spiegel employed, narcosynthesis and abreaction, see Leys, *Trauma*, chap. 6.

48. Grinker and Spiegel, *War Neuroses in North Africa*, 281–82.

49. Roy R. Grinker and John P. Spiegel, *Men under Stress* (Philadelphia: Blakiston, 1945), 455–57. More worrisome still, Grinker and Spiegel believed that military service actually reinforced submissive and dependent tendencies, since it required men to relinquish their autonomy. For further analysis of their concerns, see Benjamin L. Alpers, "This is the Army: Imagining a Democratic Military in World War II," *Journal of American History* 85 (June 1998): 129–63.

50. [N.p.], June 9, 1945, folder 4, box 234, PWP.

51. [Topeka, KS], August 31, 1946, folder 5, box 235, PWP. The Menninger School of Psychiatry, which opened under the leadership of psychiatrist Karl Menninger in January 1946, operated out of Winter Hospital. By 1951, the program was training 15 percent of all psychiatric residents in the nation. The relationship between Winter Hospital and the Menninger School of Psychiatry is discussed in Lawrence J. Friedman, *Menninger: The Family and the Clinic* (New York: Alfred A. Knopf, 1990), chap. 7.

52. In 1943 and 1944, Strecker also served as president of the American Psychiatric Association. For further details about Strecker's career, see Lauren H. Smith, "Edward A. Strecker, M.D.: A Biographical Sketch," *American Journal of Psychiatry* 101 (July 1944): 9–11; and "Dr. E. A. Strecker, a Psychiatrist, 72," *New York Times*, January 3, 1959, 17. For a more detailed analysis of

Strecker's work, see Jennifer Terry, "'Momism' and the Making of Treasonous Homosexuals," in *"Bad" Mothers: The Politics of Blame in Twentieth-Century America,* ed. Molly Ladd-Taylor and Lauri Umansky (New York: New York University Press, 1998), 169–90.

53. This speech was published as Edward A. Strecker, "War Psychiatry and Its Influence upon Postwar Psychiatry and upon Civilization," *Journal of Mental Disease* 101 (May 1945): 401–13.

54. "'Moms' Denounced as Peril to Nation," *New York Times,* April 28, 1945, 11.

55. Strecker to Ellis Bacon, March 16, 1945, folder labeled "Military," Edward Strecker Papers, Institute of Pennsylvania Hospital, Philadelphia, Pennsylvania (hereafter ESP). The Edward Strecker Papers collection is not processed; the following citations are as specific as possible.

56. Lynn Carrick to Strecker, May 14, 1945, folder labeled "Publishers," ESP. Carrick subsequently revealed the depths of his own hostility toward moms, confiding to Strecker, "I think 'Mom' deserves even more drastic treatment than you are giving her in your book. Boiling in oil or melted lead seems indicated." Carrick to Strecker, November 16, 1945, folder labeled "Publishers," ESP.

57. Strecker appears to have received the first installment of a $1,500 advance from Lippincott on June 5, 1945. Folder labeled "Publishers," ESP.

58. Edward A. Strecker, "What's Wrong with American Mothers?" *Saturday Evening Post* 21 (October 26, 1946): 14–15, 83–104.

59. The *Post* not only ran a condensed version of Strecker's forthcoming book but also later carried a feature story on the psychiatrist himself. Greer Williams, "He Made Psychiatry Respectable," *Saturday Evening Post* 220 (October 18, 1947): 33.

60. Edward A. Strecker, *Their Mothers' Sons: The Psychiatrist Examines an American Problem* (Philadelphia: J. B. Lippincott, 1946), p. 13.

61. Ibid., 32, 75. Strecker included a chapter on "pops" in *Their Mothers' Sons* and published an article on the same subject in 1947, in which he denounced "intensive preoccupation with business or profession, often accompanied by restricted stag diversions, perhaps golf or poker" as a "sin against fatherhood." Edward A. Strecker, "Pops and Popism," *Saturday Evening Post* 22 (May 1947): 99.

62. Strecker, *Their Mothers' Sons,* 30.

63. For a discussion regarding the postwar cult of maturity, see William Graebner, "Coming of Age in Buffalo: The Ideology of Maturity in Postwar America," *Radical History Review* 34 (January 1986): 53–74. Graebner illustrates how "maturity" carried different prescriptions for working- and middle-class youth, but he does not discuss the concept's gendered meanings. For men, the term tended to imply the ability to function cooperatively within hierarchical settings such as the military and bureaucratic work environments. For women, it generally meant a willingness to embrace their "biological destiny" and assume the responsibilities of marriage and motherhood.

64. According to Strecker, maturity was defined as "independence of thought and action. Maturity represents the capacity to cooperate, to work with others, to work in an organization, and to work under authority. The mature person is pliable and can alter his own desires according to time, persons, and circumstances." Strecker, *Their Mothers' Sons,* 21–22.

65. Ibid., 177.

66. James S. Plant, "Book Reviews," *Mental Hygiene* 31 (July 1947): 487.

67. E. B. Garside, "The Habit of 'Momism,'" *New York Times,* December 8, 1946, 54.

68. Philip Wylie, "More Musings on Mom," *Saturday Review of Literature* 30 (December 7, 1946): 21–22.

69. Walter A. Adams, "You Can't Talk That Way about Mother!" *Better Homes & Gardens* 25 (June 1947): 45.

70. "Changing Roles in Modern Marriage," *Life* 41 (December 25, 1956): 114.

71. For a full transcript of the speech, see Anne Edwards, *The Reagans: Portrait of a Marriage* (New York: Macmillan, 2004), app. 2, 367–69. See also Haynes Johnson, *Sleepwalking through History: America in the Reagan Years* (New York: W. W. Norton, 1991), 59–60. Thanks to Robert Lane Fenrich for sharing his unpublished paper, "Their Mothers' Sons: Maternal Pathology and the Problem of Defection, 1953–63," which first called my attention to this speech.

72. Adam J. Zweiback, "The 21 'Turncoat GIs': Nonrepatriations and the Political Culture of the Korean War," *The Historian* 60, no. 2 (1998): 345–62. The figure of the overbearing or overly possessive mother would also inform discussions of American POWs during the Vietnam War. In this later conflict, however, the focus shifted to the wives and children of POWs. As Natasha Zaretsky has shown, various studies suggested that husbands' prolonged absence led to disturbed relations between mothers and children, particularly sons. Natasha Zaretsky, *No Direction Home: The American Family and the Fear of National Decline, 1968–1980* (Chapel Hill: University of North Carolina Press, 2007), 52–60.

73. For analyses of the advice literature on returning veterans, see Susan M. Hartmann, "Prescriptions for Penelope: Literature on Women's Obligations to Returning World War II Veterans," *Women's Studies* 5, no. 3 (1978): 223–39; and Robert B. Townsend, " 'Home Fears Burning': Manhood, Family, and the Returning GI Problem," unpublished paper in the author's possession. For discussions of popular representations of returning veterans, see Sonya Michel, "Danger on the Home Front: Motherhood, Sexuality, and Disabled Veterans in American Postwar Films," *Journal of the History of Sexuality* 3 (July 1992): 109–28; James I. Deutsch, "Coming Home from 'The Good War': World War II Veterans as Depicted in American Film and Fiction" (PhD diss., George Washington University, 1991); David A. Gerber, "Heroes and Misfits: The Troubled Social Reintegration of Disabled Veterans in *The Best Years of Our Lives*," *American Quarterly* 46 (December 1994): 545–74; and Timothy Shuker-Haines, "Home Is the Hunter: Representations of Returning World War II Veterans and the Reconstruction of Masculinity, 1944–1951" (PhD diss., University of Michigan, 1994).

74. David A. Gerber, "Heroes and Misfits: The Troubled Social Reintegration of Disabled Veterans in *The Best Years of Our Lives*," *American Quarterly* 46 (December 1994): 549.

75. William Lynch, "Strictly Personal: Home Fears Burning," *Saturday Review of Literature* 28 (April 28, 1945): 8.

76. In nations that had suffered much greater devastation during World War II, such as the Soviet Union and East and West Germany, discussions of veterans' dilemmas assumed very different forms. See Frank Biess, *Homecomings: Returning POWs and the Legacies of Defeat in Postwar Germany* (Princeton, NJ: Princeton University Press, 2006); and Anna Krylova, " 'Healers of Wounded Souls': The Crisis of Private Life in Soviet Literature, 1944–1946," *Journal of Modern History* 73 (June 2001): 307–31.

77. A cartoon expressed this message succinctly. Beneath an image of a young woman, surrounded by four tea-sipping matrons, ran the caption: "They're no substitute for the doctor." Alexander G. Dumas and Grace Keen, *A Psychiatric Primer for the Veteran's Family and Friends* (Minneapolis: University of Minnesota Press, 1945), 143.

78. Jere Daniel, "The Whys of War Divorces," *New York Times Magazine*, February 3, 1946, 48.

79. "Kilroy Was Here," *Time* 48 (August 19, 1946): 68.

80. George K. Pratt, *Soldier to Civilian: Problems of Readjustment* (New York: McGraw- Hill, 1944), 181.

81. Arline Britton Boucher, "They Learn to Live Again," *Saturday Evening Post* 216 (May 27, 1944): 105.

82. [New York, NY], October 26, 1947, folder 4, box 238, PWP.

83. Dumas and Keen, *A Psychiatric Primer for the Veteran's Family and Friends*, 210.

84. George K. Pratt, *Soldier to Civilian: Problems of Readjustment* (New York: McGraw Hill, 1944), 3-6.

85. Willard Waller, "What You Can Do To Help the Returning Veteran," *Ladies' Home Journal* 62 (February 1945): 94.

86. Ibid., 95-96.

87. *Not Wanted*, directed by Elmer Clifton (Emerald Productions, 1949). Although Clifton is credited as the director, Ida Lupino took over after he suffered a heart attack.

88. *The Enchanted Cottage*, directed by John Cromwell (RKO Radio Pictures, 1945). *The Enchanted Cottage* was a remake of a 1924 film by the same name. In the earlier version, the veteran's overbearing sister drives him to take refuge in the cottage, whereas in the 1945 version, it is his domineering mother whom he seeks to elude. Thanks to James Deutsch for calling my attention to the earlier version.

89. [N.p.], January 31, 1947, folder 3, box 237, PWP.

90. Sibylle Escalona, "A Commentary upon Some Recent Changes in Child Rearing Practices," *Child Development* 20 (September 1949): 159.

91. Anna Freud and Dorothy Burlingham, *Infants without Families* (New York: International Universities Press, 1944). For another important work that stressed the importance of early mother-child attachment, see John Bowlby, *Maternal Care and Mental Health* (Geneva: World Health Organization Monograph Series no. 2, 1951).

92. Ribble, *The Rights of Infants*, 14.

93. Spock, *The Common Sense Book of Baby and Child Care*, 263-64.

94. John Bowlby, *Maternal Care and Mental Health* (Geneva: World Health Organization, 1952), 158. Originally published in the *Bulletin of the World Health Organization*, no. 3, 1951, 355-534.

95. For an excellent study that traces changing scientific conceptions of maternal instinct, see Vicedo, "The Maternal Instinct."

96. Margaret Ribble, *The Rights of Infants: Early Psychological Needs and Their Satisfaction* (New York: Columbia University Press, 1943), 14.

97. Albert Q. Maisel, "Relax, You May Not Be Nuts!" *Collier's* 119 (August 16, 1947): 18-19.

98. Harry F. Harlow, "The Nature of Love," *The American Psychologist* 13 (1958): 673-85. For background on Harlow, see Deborah Blum, *Love at Goon Park: Harry Harlow and the Science of Affection* (New York: Perseus Press, 2002). For a fascinating account of Harlow's monkey experiments and the varied ways in which they came to be interpreted within the context of Cold War America, see Vicedo, "The Maternal Instinct," chap. 9.

99. As Vicedo explains, "According to his detractors, [Harlow] was simply a mouthpiece for the cultural assumption of his time that motherhood is a woman's natural role." But in fact his views on mother love were complex from the outset. Based on his early experiments, Harlow concluded that infant monkeys reared by their own biological mothers displayed no greater attachment than did the monkeys "raised" by cloth surrogates, nor did they derive a greater "sense of security" from the relationship. Later, when the monkeys raised by surrogates began

to display signs of severe emotional disturbance, Harlow would revise his views, though not in the direction of stressing the importance of the biological mother. Instead, he emphasized the importance of peer groups. Vicedo, "The Maternal Instinct," chap. 9; quotation, 454.

100. Ribble, *The Rights of Infants*, 39.

101. "Mother's Career Should Come after Child Is 10, Students Told," *Washington Post*, March 8, 1949, B5. Interestingly, the headline of this article appears at odds with the passages that directly quote Rep. St. George, in which she suggested that women needed to devote only "a few short years" to intensive, full-time mothering.

102. Ferdinand Lundberg and Marynia F. Farnham, *Modern Woman: The Lost Sex* (New York: Harper Brothers, 1947), 320.

103. Martha Wolfenstein, "Fun Morality: An Analysis of Recent American Child-training Literature," in Margaret Mead and Martha Wolfenstein, eds., *Childhood in Contemporary Cultures* (Chicago: University of Chicago Press, 1955), 168–79.

104. Walter C. Adams, "You Can't Talk That Way about Mother!" *Better Homes & Gardens* 25 (June 1947): 44–66, 148, 171–73.

105. David M. Levy, "Clinical Evidence of Changing Parenthood," [n.d.], folder 10, box 6, David M. Levy Papers, Oskar Diethelm Library, Institute for the History of Psychiatry, Department of Psychiatry, Weill Medical College of Cornell University, New York, NY.

106. Strecker, *Their Mothers' Sons*, 160.

107. The psychiatrist also stressed that the father had been "pushed to the background" and had "accepted the passive position assigned him." The solution in such cases, he argued, was to lessen maternal influence by keeping the child busy with school or neighborhood activities or, if necessary, sending him to camp or boarding school. Herman N. Bundesen, "The Overprotective Mother," *Ladies' Home Journal* 67 (March 1950): 243–44.

108. Kathryn Keller has identified three versions of this justification for mothers working outside the home: "Children are more independent as a result of the mother working; mothers who are satisfied with their jobs are happy and raise happy children; and children need the companionship of other children, which they could attain if they went to day care." Kathryn Keller, *Mothers and Work in Popular American Magazines* (Westport, CT: Greenwood Press, 1994), 21.

109. Anna W. Wolf, *The Parent's Manual: A Guide to the Emotional Development of Young Children* (New York: Simon and Schuster, 1941), 285.

110. Zuma Steele, "Love and Let Me Go," *Good Housekeeping* 120 (February 1945): 37, 76–79.

111. Maurice Zolotow, *American Weekly* (September 2, 1956), 10.

112. "The American Woman's Dilemma," *Life* 22 (June 16, 1947): 105.

113. Kuhn, *The Mother's Role in Childhood Education*, 189–99.

Chapter Four

1. Marjorie Karmel, *Thank You, Dr. Lamaze: A Mother's Experience in Painless Childbirth* (Philadelphia: J. B. Lippincott, 1959), 106–7.

2. In her study of childbearing in Weimar Germany, Patricia Stokes argues that, although women and physicians both perceived childbearing as potentially risky, their attitudes differed markedly. Whereas doctors regarded the danger of pregnancy and childbearing as contingent on a range of potentially complicating factors, women of all social classes viewed the process as inherently fraught. "Most expectant mothers continued to regard the dangers of childbearing

as diffuse and largely unpredictable during the 1920s and indeed for some decades to come," she writes. Patricia Stokes, "Pathology, Danger, and Power: Women's and Physicians' Views of Pregnancy and Childbirth in Weimar Germany," *Social History of Medicine* 13, no. 3 (2000): 359–80; quotation, 363.

3. Quoted in Victoria De Grazia, *How Fascism Ruled Women: Italy, 1922–1945* (Berkeley: University of California Press, 1992), 281; and Grantly Dick-Read, *Childbirth without Fear: The Principles and Practices of Natural Childbirth* (New York: Harper & Brothers, 1944), 130.

4. Judith Walzer Leavitt, *Brought to Bed: Child-Bearing in America, 1750–1950* (New York: Oxford University Press, 1986). Other important works on the history of childbirth include Richard W. Wertz and Dorothy C. Wertz, *Lying-in: A History of Childbirth in America*, rev. ed. (New Haven, CT: Yale University Press, 1989); Catherine M. Scholten, *Childbearing in American Society, 1650–1850* (New York: New York University Press, 1985); Jan Lewis and Kenneth Lockridge, "'Sally Has Been Sick': Pregnancy and Family Limitation among Virginia Gentry Women, 1780–1830," *Journal of Social History* 22 (1988): 5–20; Sylvia D. Hoffert, *Private Matters: American Attitudes toward Childbearing and Infant Nurture in the Urban North, 1800–1860* (Urbana: University of Illinois Press, 1989) and idem, "Childbearing on the Trans-Mississippi Frontier, 1839–1900," *Western Historical Quarterly* 22, no. 3 (August 1991): 272–88; Sally G. McMillen, *Motherhood in the Old South: Pregnancy, Childbirth, and Infant Rearing* (Baton Rouge: Louisiana State University Press, 1990); Judy Barrett Litoff, *American Midwives, 1860 to the Present* (Westport, CT: Greenwood Press, 1978); Charlotte G. Borst, *Catching Babies: The Professionalization of Childbirth, 1870–1920* (Cambridge, MA: Harvard University Press, 1995); Margarete Sandelowski, *Pain, Pleasure, and American Childbirth: From the Twilight Sleep to the Read Method, 1914–1960* (Westport, CT: Greenwood Press, 1984); William Ray Arney, *Power and the Profession of Obstetrics* (Chicago: University of Chicago Press, 1982); and Margot Edwards and Mary Waldorf, *Reclaiming Birth: History and Heroines of American Childbirth Reform* (New York: Crossing Press, 1984).

5. Leavitt, *Brought to Bed*, 12, 267; and Litoff, *American Midwives*, 141. As Natalia Molina has noted, public health officials often turned a blind eye to the persistence of unlicensed midwifery within Mexican-American and African-American communities. See Natalia Molina, *Fit To Be Citizens? Public Health and Race in Los Angeles, 1879–1939* (Berkeley: University of California Press, 2006), 100–105.

6. In 1933, a study of maternal deaths by the New York Academy of Medicine in New York City revealed that hospital deliveries had a death rate more than twice that of home deliveries. Joyce Antler and Daniel M. Fox, "The Movement toward Safe Maternity: Physician Accountability in New York City, 1915–1940," *Bulletin of the History of Medicine* 50 (1976): 381.

7. "Childbirth: Nature v. Drugs," *Time* 27, no. 21 (May 25, 1936): 32.

8. For discussions of Euro-Americans' perceptions of the childbearing experiences of Native Americans and slaves, see Patricia Jasen, "Race, Culture, and the Colonization of Childbirth in Northern Canada," *Social History of Medicine* 10, no. 3 (1997): 383–400; Jennifer Morgan, *Laboring Women: Reproduction and Gender in New World Slavery* (Philadelphia: University of Pennsylvania Press, 2004); and Marie Jenkins Schwartz, *Birth a Slave: Motherhood and Medicine in the Antebellum South* (Cambridge, MA: Harvard University Press, 2006), 166–68. Antebellum health reformers, as Regina Morantz-Sanchez has shown, opposed pain relief and other medication for birthing women, regarding pregnancy and childbirth as wholly natural functions. "They rejected the notion that pain in childbirth was inevitable," she writes, "labelling such a belief 'an insult to Providence.'" Regina Markell Morantz-Sanchez,

Sympathy and Science: Women Physicians in American Medicine (New York: Oxford University Press, 1985), 40.

9. Lorine Livingston Pruette, "The Evolution of Disenchantment" (1926–27), reprinted in *These Modern Women*, ed. Elaine Showalter, rev. ed. (1979; New York: Feminist Press, 1989), 70.

10. Martin S. Pernick, *A Calculus of Suffering: Pain, Professionalism, and Anesthesia in Nineteenth-Century America* (New York: Columbia University Press, 1985), 46.

11. Laurel Thatcher Ulrich, *Goodwives: Image and Reality in the Lives of Northern New England, 1650–1750* (New York: Oxford University Press, 1980), 144.

12. For discussions of antebellum views of childbirth as illness, see McMillen, *Motherhood in the Old South*, 74; Hoffert, *Private Matters*, chap. 2; and Lewis and Lockridge, " 'Sally Has Been Sick,' " 11–12.

13. For instance, after witnessing the birth of his first child, Richard Henry Dana, Jr., recorded in his diary, "There is surely no pain like it in the world. . . . It is the rending asunder of all but body & soul." Quoted in Shawn Johansen, "Before the Waiting Room: Northern Middle-Class Men, Pregnancy and Birth in Antebellum America," *Gender and History* 7, no. 2 (1995): 183–200.

14. Quoted in Hoffert, *Private Matters*, 88.

15. Ibid., 68.

16. Historians Jan Lewis and Kenneth Lockridge have suggested that Virginia gentrymen were "more susceptible to a feminine reason for birth control, fear of maternal death in childbirth, than to the more 'masculine' one of economic necessity." However, they caution against celebrating women's achievement of family limitation as evidence of what Daniel Scott Smith has called "domestic feminism." In order to secure male cooperation, Lewis and Lockridge argue, women may well have been compelled to "depict themselves as weak, frail, and too delicate to endure the rigors of repeated pregnancies. . . . Such a view perhaps gave them leverage over their husbands, in a sort of 'domestic feminism,' but it was possibly as 'the weaker vessel' and not as autonomous equals that Virginia gentry women finally prevailed on their husbands to liberate them from the pain of childbirth." Lewis and Lockridge, " 'Sally Has Been Sick,' " 11, 13. For Smith's argument, see "Family Limitation, Sexual Control, and Domestic Feminism in Victorian America," *Feminist Studies* 1, nos. 3–4 (Winter–Spring 1973): 40–57.

17. Johansen, "Before the Waiting Room," 186.

18. Quoted in Linda K. Kerber, "A Constitutional Right To Be Treated Like American Ladies: Women and the Obligations of Citizenship," in *U.S. History As Women's History: New Feminist Essays*, ed. Linda K. Kerber, Alice Kessler-Harris, and Kathryn Kish Sklar (Chapel Hill: University of North Carolina Press, 1995), 33.

19. Quoted in Eugene Pharo, "This Mother's Day Business," *American Mercury* 41 (May 1937): 62.

20. The National Twilight Sleep Association promoted the procedure as a potential boon to all womankind, but it still reflected the sensibilities of the elite; some members even claimed that twilight sleep could help to counter the alleged problem of "race suicide," or comparatively low birth rates among affluent, native-born Americans. The history of twilight sleep and the movement it inspired is discussed in Leavitt, *Brought to Bed*, chap. 5; Sandelowski, *Pain, Pleasure, and American Childbirth*, chap. 1; and Lawrence G. Miller, "Pain, Parturition, and the Profession: Twilight Sleep in America," in *Health Care in America: Essays in Social History*, ed. Susan Reverby and David Rosner (Philadelphia: Temple University Press, 1979), 19–44.

21. For instance, in 1936, *Time* reported that two-thirds of all "normal births" occurred without "any form of pain-killer" ("Childbirth: Nature v. Drugs," *Time*, 35). Similarly, in 1937, the obstetrician Roy P. Finney claimed that "of the two million women who yearly come to confinement one and a quarter million [62.5 percent] will have no deadening drug of any kind." Roy P. Finney, *The Story of Motherhood* (New York: Liverwright, 1937), 189. Moreover, according to historian Jacqueline Wolf, the pain relief that women did receive was rarely given during transition, the most difficult phase of labor. Instead, male physicians typically dispensed medication during the delivery itself, which they mistakenly assumed to be the most painful phase. Jacqueline H. Wolf, " 'Mighty glad to gasp the gas': Perceptions of Pain and the Traditional Timing of Obstetric Anesthesia," *Health* 6, no. 3 (2002): 365–87.

22. C. O. McCormick, "Rectal Ether Analgesia in Obstetrics," *American Journal of Nursing* 33, no. 5 (May 1933): 15–20.

23. Harold H. Rosenfield and Catherine Yeo, "Analgesia in Obstetrics," *American Journal of Nursing* 35, no. 5 (May 1935): 437.

24. Constance L. Todd, "Babies without Pain," *Good Housekeeping* 105, no. 5 (November 1937): 78.

25. Quoted in Leavitt, *Brought to Bed*, 179. For a nuanced and extensive discussion of DeLee's views, see Judith Walzer Leavitt, "Joseph B. DeLee and the Practice of Preventive Obstetrics," *American Journal of Public Health* 78, no. 10 (1988): 1353–59.

26. "Asks Nation To Curb Maternity Deaths," *New York Times*, May 4, 1931, 19.

27. "Mother's Day and Maternal Care," *Hygeia* 15 (May 1937): 476.

28. Grace L. Meigs, *Maternal Mortality—from All Conditions Connected with Childbirth in the United States and Certain Other Countries*, U.S. Children's Bureau Pub. 19 (Washington, D.C.: Government Printing Office, 1917).

29. U.S. Department of Commerce, *Historical Statistics of the United States, Colonial Times to 1970*, pt. 1 (Washington, D.C., 1975), 57.

30. In her study of the midwife Martha Ballard, who practiced in the late eighteenth and early nineteenth centuries, Laurel Thatcher Ulrich has assessed maternal mortality in broad historical terms. "By our standards, mortality was high," she writes. "Martha saw one maternal death for every 198 living births. Today that rate is one per 10,000. But as late as 1930, there was one maternal death for every 150 births in the United States; the major gains in obstetrical safety have come in the past fifty years. In fact, many historians believe that the routine employment of physicians in the nineteenth century probably increased rather than decreased mortality." Laurel Thatcher Ulrich, *A Midwife's Tale: The Life of Martha Ballard, Based on Her Diary, 1785–1812* (New York: Vintage Books, 1990).

31. Antler and Fox, "The Movement toward Safe Maternity," 375.

32. Alan Frank Guttmacher, *Into This Universe: The Story of Human Birth* (New York: Viking Press, 1937), 330.

33. Paul De Kruif, "Why Should Mothers Die?" *Ladies' Home Journal* 58 (March 1936): 8.

34. *The Fight for Life*, directed by Pare Lorentz (U.S. Film Service, 1940); "The New Pictures," *Time* 35, no. 13 (March 25, 1940).

35. Elizabeth Temkin, "Rooming-In: Redesigning Hospitals and Motherhood in Cold War America," *Bulletin of the History of Medicine* 76 (2002): 275–76.

36. For an account of how two different ethnic groups experienced the transition from home to hospital births, see Susan Cotts Watkins and Angela D. Danzi, "Women's Gossip and

Social Change: Childbirth and Fertility Control among Italian and Jewish Women in the United States, 1920–1940," *Gender and Society* 9, no. 4 (August 1995): 469–90.

37. Judith Walzer Leavitt, " 'Strange Young Women on Errands': Obstetric Nursing between Two Worlds," *Nursing History Review* 6 (1988): 10.

38. Guttmacher, *Into This Universe*, 282–83.

39. Muriel Violet d'Arcy, diaries, 1902–1909, Schlesinger Library, Harvard University, Cambridge, MA. See entries from October 29 through November 23, 1908.

40. Gladys Whitney Neil, diaries, 1915–1923, Schlesinger Library, Harvard University, Cambridge, MA. See entries from January 10 through January 22, 1921.

41. Transcript of interview with Helen Berklich, conducted on March 31, 1980, in Work and Family: Low Income and Minority Women Talk about Their Lives, ca. 1930 to 1990 collection, creator Fran Leeper Buss, Schlesinger Library, Harvard University, Cambridge, MA, pt. 1, p. 19, folder 16, box 2 (hereafter Work and Family). Berklich went on to explain that, after the births of her other children, she did not remain in bed for as long: "I didn't do heavy work but I was up and around which was much better for a woman than staying in bed." Ibid., April 1, 1980, pt. 3, p. 91.

42. Gertrude Jacinta Fraser, *African American Midwifery in the South: Dialogues of Birth, Race and Memory* (Cambridge, MA: Harvard University Press, 1998), chap 11.

43. Fran Leeper Buss, *La Partera: Story of a Midwife* (Ann Arbor: University of Michigan Press, 1980), 65–66.

44. Maria Elena Ortega, whose parents worked as farm laborers in Texas in the 1940s and 1950s, recalled that her mother would get up three days after giving birth: "Mom would get up on the third day and she'd start housework and recuperate real fast." After a month, her mother would be working in the fields again. Transcript of interview with Maria Elena Ortega, September 24, 1981, in Work and Family, creator Buss, pt. 12, p. 231.

45. Constance Foster, "New Techniques in Childbirth," *Parents' Magazine* 15 (May 1940): 24–25, 41, 83–84.

46. William L. Laurence, "Doctors Assail 'Twilight' Birth as Perilous to Mother and Child," *New York Times*, May 15, 1936, 1; and "Childbirth: Nature v. Drugs," *Time* 27, no. 21 (May 25, 1936): 32–36.

47. Anon., " 'Painless' Childbirth: A Mother Protests" *American Mercury* 47 (June 1939): 220–22. Accompanying this article was a rejoinder by an obstetrician who criticized mothers for presuming to be "experts on the subject of childbirth." He identified two groups of would-be "maternal experts": young women who thought that modern medicine should eliminate all discomfort, and older women who believed that childbirth should be "a grim and spartan affair" because maternal suffering promoted "a closer connection between mother and child." Joseph T. Boltin, " 'Painless Childbirth': A Doctor Comments," *American Mercury* 47 (June 1939): 222–24.

48. Lenore Pelham Friedrich, "I Had a Baby," *Atlantic Monthly* 163 (April 1939): 461–65.

49. "A Mother Protests," *New York Times*, May 15, 1936, 16.

50. "Favoring Twilight Sleep," *New York Times*, May 19, 1936, 22.

51. "I Had a Baby, Too: A Symposium," *Atlantic Monthly* 163 (June 1939): 764–72.

52. "The 'Gush' of Mothers' Day," *Literary Digest* 113 (May 21, 1932): 20. Another anti–Mother's Day editorial, published sixteen years later, reveals how much had changed: while the author argued that the holiday should serve to generate support for research on infant mortality, sterility, stillbirths and miscarriages, she said nothing about maternal mortality, for it was

no longer viewed as a serious problem. Sylvia R. Lyons, "I Hate Mother's Day," *Saturday Review of Literature* 31 (May 8, 1948): 29.

53. John Erskine, *The Influence of Women and Its Cure* (Indianapolis: Bobbs-Merrill, 1936), 46.

54. The maternal death rates among nonwhites, however, remained more than twice that of whites. In 1940, 77.4 nonwhite women died per every 10,000 live births; by 1950, the number had declined to 22.2. U.S. Department of Commerce, *Historical Statistics of the United States, Colonial Times to 1970*, pt. 1, 57.

55. Leavitt, *Brought to Bed*, 171.

56. Clifford B. Lull and Robert A. Hingson, *Control of Pain in Childbirth*, 3rd ed. (Philadelphia: J. B. Lippincott, 1948), 130.

57. F. W. Dershimer, "The Influence of Mental Attitudes in Childbearing," *American Journal of Obstetrics and Gynecology* 31 (1936): 444–54; quotations, 444, 450.

58. For discussions of the psychosomatic approach to female infertility, see Randi Hutter Epstein, "Emotions, Fertility and the 1940s Woman," *Journal of Public Health Policy* 24, no. 2 (2003): 195–211; Elaine Tyler May, *Barren in the Promised Land: Childless Americans and the Pursuit of Happiness* (New York: Basic Books, 1995); and Margaret Marsh and Wanda Ronner, *The Empty Cradle: Infertility in America from Colonial Times to the Present* (Baltimore: Johns Hopkins University Press, 1996). For discussions of the concept of frigidity, see Jessamyn Neuhaus, "The Importance of Being Orgasmic: Sexuality, Gender, and Marital Sex Manuals in the United States, 1920–1963," *Journal of the History of Sexuality* (2000): 447–73. For a more general discussion of the relationship between psychosomatic medicine and gynecology, see Barbara Ehrenreich and Deirdre English, *For Her Own Good: 150 Years of Experts' Advice to Women* (Garden City, NY: Anchor Press, 1978), 301–7.

59. Philip Wylie, *Generation of Vipers* (New York: Farrar and Rinehart, 1942), 50.

60. Ferdinand Lundberg and Marynia F. Farnham, *Modern Woman: The Lost Sex* (New York: Harper Brothers, 1947), 293.

61. Foster, "New Techniques in Childbirth," 24.

62. Elizabeth Temkin, "Driving Through: Postpartum Care during World War II," *American Journal of Public Health* 89 (1999): 587–95.

63. Tina Cassidy, *Birth: The Surprising History of How We Are Born* (New York: Atlantic Monthly Press, 2006),223.

64. The birthing practices of African-American midwives reflected a similar shift; by the 1940s and 1950s, they typically encouraged their patients to "stay put" for only two to three days. Fraser, *African American Midwifery in the South*, 242–43.

65. Quoted in Cassidy, *Birth*, 223.

66. Paul Dix, "Mothers Told Not To Linger in Hospital," *Washington Post*, September 10, 1947, B9. The first line of this article pronounced, "Women who insist on staying in bed after childbirth may just be looking for sympathy!"

67. Edward Weiss and O. Spurgeon English, *Psychosomatic Medicine: The Clinical Applications of Psychopathology to General Medical Problems* (Philadelphia: W. B. Saunders, 1943), 609.

68. Report of Pregnancy-Delivery Experience, "To Our First Born," July 1950, folder 60, box 3, Edith Banfield Jackson Papers, Schlesinger Library, Harvard University, Cambridge, MA (hereafter EBJ).

69. For an analysis of the very different cultural meanings of female invalidism in Victorian America, see Ann Douglas Wood, "'The Fashionable Diseases': Women's Complaints in Nineteenth-Century America," *Journal of Interdisciplinary History* 4 (Summer 1973): 25–52.

70. O. Spurgeon English and Constance Foster, *Fathers Are Parents, Too* (New York: G. P. Putnam's Sons, 1951), 7.

71. The author of this article chose to remain anonymous, claiming that she anticipated "a deluge of criticism from thousands . . . whose mothers have imbued them with the idea of Mother-Sacredness." Anon., "This Motherhood Bunk," *American Mercury* 45 (November 1938): 287–89.

72. [Columbus, OH], November 18, 1946, folder 6, box 235, Philip Wylie Papers, Firestone Library, Princeton University, Princeton, NJ (hereafter PWP).

73. [Minneapolis, MN], January 7, 1945, folder 2, box 235, PWP.

74. For discussions of fathers' role in childbirth during the twentieth century, see Judith Walzer Leavitt, "What Do Men Have to Do with It? Fathers and Mid-Twentieth-Century Childbirth," *Bulletin of the History of Medicine* 77, no. 2 (2003): 235–62; and Richard K. Reed, *Birthing Fathers: The Transformation of Men in American Rites of Birth* (New Brunswick, NJ: Rutgers University Press, 2005).

75. A reviewer for the *New York Times* approvingly noted, "the matter of approaching motherhood, although one of the oldest themes for the dramatist, seldom has been treated with the light touch." But not everyone approved; CBS and the show's sponsor, Philip Morris, both received letters of complaint from viewers who believed that pregnancy and childbirth were not suitable themes for a comedy show. Jack Gould, "Nearing Birth of (?) Arnaz Is Engendering Interest of the Fans of 'I Love Lucy,'" *New York Times*, January 16, 1953, 29. For an analysis of the episode, see Lori Landay, "*I Love Lucy*: Television and Gender in Postwar Domestic Ideology," in *The Sitcom Reader: America Viewed and Skewed*, ed. Mary M. Dalton and Laura R. Linder (Albany: State University of New York Press, 2005), 87–98.

76. The image of the lumbering yet self-possessed expectant mother, gently directing her flustered husband to the hospital, surfaced repeatedly in postwar depictions of childbirth, appearing even in medical films produced for educational purposes. See *Labor and Childbirth*, directed by D. M. Hatfield (Medical Films, 1950).

77. [Bakersfield, CA], May 28, 1952, folder 5, box 242, PWP. Although the letter writer did not elaborate on her injuries, she may have been referring to severe perineal tearing.

78. Transcript of interview with Maria Elena Lucas Ortega, June 24, 1989, in Work and Family, creator Buss, pt. 39, tape 251 B, pp. 1605–06. For background on Ortega, see Maria Elena Lucas, *Forged Under the Sun/Forjada bajo el Sol*, ed. and intro. by Fran Leeper Buss (Ann Arbor: University of Michigan Press, 1993).

79. A recent study found that racial disparities persist in U.S. hospitals in regard to the administration of pain relief. Mark J. Fletcher et al., "Trends in Opiod Prescribing by Race/Ethnicity for Patients Seeking Care in US Emergency Departments," *Journal of the American Medical Association* 229, no. 1 (2008): 70–78.

80. By the end of the 1950s, representatives from more than a dozen local organizations had begun to discuss the formation of an umbrella organization. In 1961, the International Childbirth Education Association held its first national convention. Edwards and Waldorf, *Reclaiming Birth*, 62.

81. Justine Kelliher, "Natural Childbirth in Boston," Boston Association for Childbirth Education Records (hereafter BACE), Schlesinger Library, Harvard University, Cambridge, MA,

folder 1, box 1, p. 2. The childbirth course at the Yale School of Nursing served as the model for the BACE course, which was held in six two-hour sessions. See "The Boston Association for Childbirth Education: Content of Classes for Expectant Parents," BACE folder 1, box 1. By 1956, about fifty women had completed training through BACE. Although the organization seems to have grown substantially thereafter, it is unclear exactly how many students attended.

82. Read, *Childbirth without Fear*. Read's book was first published in Britain as *Revelation of Childbirth: The Principles and Practice of Natural Childbirth* (London: Heinemann, 1943). See also his earlier work, Grantly Dick-Read, *Natural Childbirth* (London: Heinemann, 1933). For discussions of Read and his impact, see Sandelowski, *Pain, Pleasure, and American Childbirth*, chap. 4; O. Moscucci, "Holistic Obstetrics: The Origins of 'Natural Childbirth' in Britain," *Postgraduate Medical Journal* 79 (2003): 168–73; Sara Jane Williams, "Caught in the Middle: Maternity Nurses and the Natural Childbirth Movement" (M.S., Nursing, University of Wisconsin-Madison, 1987); Arney, *Power and the Profession of Obstetrics*, chap. 7; and Wertz and Wertz, *Lying-In*, chap. 6. For biographical background on Read and a selection of his extensive correspondence with women, see Mary Thomas, ed., *Post-war Mothers: Childbirth Letters to Grantly Dick-Read, 1946–1956* (Rochester, NY: University of Rochester Press, 1997).

83. Read, *Childbirth without Fear*, vii–viii, 95. Read's ideas were highly idiosyncratic; as Richard and Dorothy Wertz have observed, he "glorified motherhood as woman's true fulfillment in panegyrics that mixed Victorianism, sentimentality, mysticism, nature philosophy and religion." Wertz and Wertz, *Lying-In*, 183.

84. Read, *Childbirth without Fear*, 2–6.

85. Ibid., 117–19.

86. Ibid., 68.

87. Temkin, "Rooming-In"; and Sara Lee Silberman, "Pioneering in Family-Centered Maternity and Infant Care: Edith B. Jackson and the Yale Rooming-In Research Project," *Bulletin of the History of Medicine* 64 (1990): 262–87. As Temkin notes, "On maternity wards before World War II, rooming-in would have been unthinkable. Taking an active role in the care of their infants required that mothers be mobile and in sound health; before the war, most mothers were neither." By the late 1950s, some three hundred hospitals offered rooming-in, and favorable press coverage made the practice seem even more prevalent that it actually was. Temkin, "Rooming-In," 275. The postwar movement for natural childbirth had much in common with La Leche League, an organization founded in 1956 by suburban mothers outside Chicago that encouraged women to breastfeed their babies. As historian Lynn Weiner has observed, the women who established and participated in La Leche League strove to "dignify the physical, biological side of motherhood": "Mother and baby were not so much icons of purity as symbols of nature and simplicity. For these women, behaving in a 'natural' manner became the new moral imperative." Lynn Y. Weiner, "Reconstructing Motherhood: The La Leche League in Postwar America," *Journal of American History* 80, no. 4 (March 1994): 1357–81.

88. [Carlisle, PA] to Wylie, [1950], folder 6, box 241, PWP.

89. [Anon.] to Read, November 10, 1952, quoted in Thomas, ed., *Post-war Mothers*, 178–80.

90. Edwards and Waldorf, *Reclaiming Birth*.

91. Sandelowski, *Pain, Pleasure, and American Childbirth*, 136.

92. For instance, although BACE leader Justine Kelliher recognized that "some mothers are apparently deterred" from participating in the childbirth course "by the indifference or hostility of their doctor," the group still required women to receive their physician's permission in order to attend the course. Despite strong opposition to heavily medicalized births, BACE and similar

groups maintained a deferential stance toward the medical profession in the 1950s and early 1960s. Kelliher, "Natural Childbirth in Boston," BACE, folder 1, box 1, 2.

93. A fascinating study conducted in Vermont by sociologist Margaret K. Nelson indicated that, by the late 1970s and early 1980s, middle-class women had internalized the messages and adopted the language of the natural childbirth movement, whereas working-class women had not. Nelson found that working-class women placed less emphasis on childbirth as an important stage in becoming a mother and were less likely to believe that the birth experience could affect the quality of the mother-child relationship. They generally favored medical intervention and often expressed the desire for faster, easier, and less painful deliveries. In contrast, middle-class women tended to value personal participation and sought to avoid medical intervention; they rarely complained either about the intensity of the pain or the length of labor. Margaret K. Nelson, "Working-Class Women, Middle-Class Women, and Models of Childbirth," *Social Problems* 30, no. 3 (February 1983): 284–97. Given the increasing popularity of C-sections and epidurals since the 1980s, a similar study would no doubt yield different results today.

94. According to Mary Thomas, who edited a volume of Read's correspondence, his papers include over 3,400 letters from women, covering a period ranging from 1933 to 1959. Approximately 18 percent of these letters are from the United States. For a more detailed description of the collection, see Thomas, *Post-war Mothers*, x.

95. Ibid., 90.

96. Through at least 1962, BACE instruction appears to have been based on the Read method, for a number of letter writers refer explicitly to Read or discuss "abdominal" or "deep" breathing (whereas Lamaze emphasized shallow, rapid breathing). Moreover, while one respondent parenthetically referred to Marjorie Karmel and Pierre Vellay—both advocates of the Lamaze method—she wrote as if to inform Kelliher of their works ("The two best books about this are . . ."), suggesting that she learned of them elsewhere. [Redacted], November 6, 1960, BACE, folder 2, box 8. Because the natural childbirth movement changed markedly in the second half of the 1960s, I have relied exclusively on birth reports from the late 1950s and early 1960s, though the BACE records contain additional reports and questionnaires dating through the 1970s. Although the records include no demographic information about the students, the vast majority who wrote birth reports were highly literate and appear to have been middle or upper-middle class.

97. Women who attended BACE courses learned that "most women have to expect some pain," but "never more than they can reasonably bear." They also learned that a woman attempting natural childbirth could request "the same medications normally used . . . to relieve discomfort," though she would "probably . . . never want any of the types which will dim her awareness of participation in this vital experience." In other words, BACE instructors downplayed but did not deny the pain of childbirth; while they emphasized the importance of remaining conscious, they did not pressure women to forgo anesthesia entirely. Most BACE students, however, appear to have regarded an entirely drug-free childbirth as the ideal.

98. [Redacted] to Justine Kelliher, September 2, 1960, BACE, folder 2, box 8.

99. [Redacted] to Justine Kelliher, November 6, 1960, BACE, folder 3, box 8.

100. [Redacted] to Justine Kelliher, [n.d.], BACE, folder 3, box 8.

101. [Redacted] to Justine Kelliher, January 7, 1960, BACE, folder 3, box 8.

102. [Redacted] to Justine Kelliher, [n.d.], BACE, folder 3, box 8.

103. [Redacted] to Justine Kelliher, November 6, 1960, BACE, folder 3, box 8.

104. [Redacted] to Justine Kelliher, October 17, 1959, BACE, folder 1, box 8.

105. [Redacted] to Justine Kelliher, July 27, 1964, BACE, folder 4, box 8.

106. [Redacted] to Justine Kelliher, June 11, 1956, BACE, folder 1, box 8.

107. [Redacted] to Justine Kelliher, May 19, [1960], BACE, folder 2, box 8.

108. [Husband's Report], May 7, 1947, folder 52, box 3, EBJ. It is not clear to whom this report was addressed, or how it came into the possession of Edith Jackson, a child psychiatrist and pediatrician who promoted natural childbirth, breastfeeding, and rooming-in.

109. Mr. O. opened his report by noting, "Mrs O. has written a more-or-less continuous account of her labor with which I agree in every detail." However, I was unable to locate this document. Ibid.

110. Later, however, some feminists would criticize the Lamaze method on the grounds that it alienated women from childbirth by placing too great an emphasis on exerting control over bodily sensations and experience. See, e.g., Suzanne Arms, *Immaculate Deception: A New Look at Women and Childbirth in America* (Boston: Houghton Mifflin, 1975), 145–46.

111. Paula Michaels discusses the technical and theoretical differences between Read and Lamaze in her forthcoming study, a transnational history of the childbirth preparation movement, *Good Girls and Their Helpful Husbands: A History of Childbirth Preparation in the USSR, France and the US*. See also Wertz and Wertz, *Lying-In*, chap. 6.

112. [N.p.], March 16, 1965, folder 686, box 19, Betty Friedan Papers, Schlesinger Library, Cambridge, MA.

113. [N.p.], November 1950, folder 2, box 241, PWP.

114. "Invalids?" *Equal Rights* 11 (June 7, 1947), 132. See Kathryn Kish Sklar, "Who Won the Debate over the Equal Rights Amendments in the 1920s?" document 7, Women and Social Movements in the United States, 1600–2000, http://womhist.alexanderstreet.com/projectmap .htm.

Chapter Five

1. Betty Friedan, "The Fraud of Femininity," *McCall's* 90 (March 1963): 81, 130–32. In 1963, *McCall's* boasted a circulation of over 8 million. *The Feminine Mystique* was released in hardback by W. W. Norton on February 19, 1963. The following year, Dell published a paperback edition that sold 1.3 million copies, making it the top-selling nonfiction paperback of 1964. By 1970, there were 1.5 million paperback copies in print. Judith Hennessee, *Betty Friedan: Her Life* (New York: Random House, 1999), 77–78.

2. [N.p.], February 22, 1963, folder 741, box 21, Betty Friedan Papers, Schlesinger Library, Harvard University, Cambridge, MA (hereafter BFP).

3. Friedan, *The Feminine Mystique*, chaps. 11–12; quotation, 276. Unless otherwise indicated, all citations are from the original 1963 edition.

4. Ibid., 312, 305.

5. Historians Joanne Meyerowitz, Jessica Weiss, and Eva Moskowitz have all questioned Friedan's portrait of a hegemonic postwar "feminine mystique" by demonstrating that the cultural messages concerning women in postwar America were in fact much more varied than she allowed. Joanne Meyerowitz, "Beyond the Feminine Mystique: A Reassessment of Postwar Mass Culture, 1946–1958," *Journal of American History* 79 (March 1993); Jessica Weiss, *To Have and To Hold: Marriage, the Baby Boom and Social Change* (Chicago: University of Chicago Press, 2000), chap. 2; and Eva Moskowitz, "'It's Good to Blow Your Top': Women's Magazines and a Discourse of Discontent," *Journal of Women's History* 8, no. 3 (1996): 66–98, and idem, *In Therapy We Trust: America's Obsession with Self-Fulfillment* (Baltimore: Johns Hopkins

University Press, 2001). Sylvie Murray has analyzed Friedan's experiences as a volunteer engaged in community work in the 1950s and the ways in which her attitude toward such activities changed in *The Progressive Housewife: Community Activism in Suburban Queens, 1945–1965* (Philadelphia: University of Pennsylvania Press, 2003).

6. Jessica Weiss has written the most extensive analysis of Friedan's negative portrait of domesticity and the responses that it evoked from readers. " 'Comrade Betty': Anticommunism, Domesticity and Antifeminism in Response to *The Feminine Mystique*," unpublished paper in the author's possession, 2. Elizabeth More analyzes Friedan's appropriation of psychological and social scientific critiques of motherhood in "Social Scientists, Feminists and the Reassessment of Working Mothers" (PhD diss., Harvard University, forthcoming). Other important works that discuss Friedan's appropriation of the momism critique or her critical portrait of domesticity include Glenna Mathews, " 'Just a Housewife': The Rise and Fall of Domesticity in America* (New York: Oxford University Press, 1987), chap. 8; Ruth Feldstein, *Motherhood in Black and White: Race and Sex in American Liberalism, 1930–1965* (Ithaca, NY: Cornell University Press, 2000), 152–55; and K. A. Cuordileone, *Manhood and American Political Culture in the Cold War* (New York: Routledge, 2005), 131–32. For an analysis of Friedan's discussion of housewifery, see Alexandra Harwin, " 'Occupation: Houseworker': Second Wave Feminist Evaluations of Housewifery, 1963–1981" (honors thesis, Harvard University, 2007), chap. 1.

7. My survey of 100 letters that Friedan received in response to *The Feminine Mystique* found that 90 were positive, 7 negative, and 3 neutral or equivocal. These findings are in line with those Jessica Weiss, who has conducted a thorough analysis of all Friedan's fan mail from 1963 through 1965. Weiss has concluded that 92 percent of the book readers wrote positive letters. Weiss, " 'Comrade Betty,' " 7.

8. My survey of 100 letters sent to *McCall's* in response to "The Fraud of Femininity" found that 86 were wholly critical of Friedan's critique, while 14 were positive. Again, this accords with Jessica Weiss's findings. Weiss, who has analyzed all 511 letters sent to *McCall's*, concluded that 87 percent were negative. See Weiss, " 'Comrade Betty,' " 7.

9. This chapter contrasts favorable letters from fans who read Friedan's book with negative letters from critics who responded to her *McCall's* article. I have adopted this approach to highlight the broad differences that characterized the two groups of readers as a whole. Moreover, since the magazine article differed from the book in ways detailed below, I hoped to avoid the cumbersome problem of contrasting four different groups of her readers. Thus, when I refer to "Friedan's fans," I mean fans of her book, and when I refer to "Friedan's critics," I mean critics of the *McCall's* article. However, it is important to stress that Friedan also received a relatively small numbers of letters from readers who either criticized the book (less than 10 percent of all respondents) or who praised the magazine article (less than 15 percent of all respondents).

10. The increase in employment among mothers of children under the age of six was particularly notable: whereas only 10.8 percent had worked in 1948, that number had risen to 18.6 by 1960 and would reach 30.3 by 1970. Lynn Y. Weiner, *From Working Girl to Working Mother: The Female Labor Force in the United States, 1820–1980* (Chapel Hill: University of North Carolina Press, 1985), 6, 93.

11. [Westmont, NJ, n.d.], folder 752, box 21, BFP.

12. As Lauri Umansky has shown, whereas second-wave feminists addressed the issue of motherhood from a wide range of perspectives, only a small minority portrayed motherhood in unequivocally negative terms. Lauri Umansky, *Motherhood Reconceived: Feminism and the Legacies of the Sixties* (New York: New York University Press, 1996). In contrast, Yen-Chuan Yu

has argued that the manner in which second-wave feminists dealt with "the problem of mother-hood" proved to be one of the movement's "greatest ideological weaknesses." Yen-Chuan Yu, "Both Mother and Feminist: The Problem of Motherhood in the Second Women's Movement in America" (PhD diss., Indiana University, 2001). See also Ann Snitow, "Feminism and Mother-hood: An American Reading," *Feminist Review* 40 (Spring 1992): 32–51.

13. Daniel Horowitz, *Betty Friedan and the Making of "The Feminine Mystique": The Ameri-can Left, the Cold War and Liberal Feminism* (Amherst: University of Massachusetts Press, 1998).

14. While mother-blaming often went hand-in-hand with politically progressive views on race and other social issues, as Ruth Feldstein has shown, it appealed more to liberals who em-braced psychological concepts of the self than radicals who privileged class-based approaches to social problems. This was not a hard and fast division; some leading intellectuals who sought to combine psychoanalytic and Marxist approaches were influenced by the momism critique. (For instance, T. W. Adorno's *The Authoritarian Personality*, which Friedan cited as a major influence, briefly refers to "Wylie's theory of momism.") Still, antimaternalism does not appear to have figured prominently in the left-wing labor or communist movements of the 1940s and 1950s. See Dorothy Sue Cobble, *The Other Women's Movement: Workplace Justice and Social Justice in Modern America* (Princeton, NJ: Princeton University Press, 2004); and Kate Weigand, *Red Feminism: American Communism and the Making of Women's Liberation* (Baltimore: Johns Hopkins University Press, 2001).

15. Betty Friedan, *Life So Far: A Memoir* (New York: Simon & Schuster, 2000), 31.

16. For a highly informative account of Friedan's college years, see Horowitz, *Betty Friedan and the Making of "The Feminine Mystique,"* chaps. 2–4.

17. Friedan, *Life So Far*, 121. According to biographer Judith Hennessee, Friedan told friends that Miriam was paying for the analysis because, after all, her mother was the reason why she needed psychoanalysis in the first place. Hennessee, *Betty Friedan: Her Life*, 38–39. For a more extensive account of Friedan's childhood and college years, see Horowitz, *Betty Friedan and the Making of "The Feminine Mystique,"* chaps. 1–5.

18. Friedan, *The Feminine Mystique*, 72–3.

19. Historian Joyce Antler, who has analyzed the cultural constructions of Jewish mothers, writes, "It was Friedan's negative perception of her mother . . . that provided the driving force of the liberation movement that younger feminists put in motion by the end of the 1960s. Young Jewish women's relationships with their own Jewish mothers served as one factor in the mix of causes that generated the energy of women's liberation. Alternatively resentful of their mothers' domination of their lives or disappointed in their weaknesses, these women scornfully rejected both their mothers' authority and their compromises and sought other models." Joyce Antler, *You Never Call! You Never Write! A History of the Jewish Mother* (New York: Oxford University Press, 2007), 151.

20. Quoted in Susan Oliver, *Betty Friedan: The Personal Is Political* (New York: Pearson Longman, 2008), 76.

21. Friedan, *Life So Far*, 77. Emphasis in the original.

22. Ibid., 74.

23. Friedan also married somewhat later, at age twenty-six, and spaced her children less closely together than most women of her generational cohort: Daniel was born in 1948; Jona-than in 1952; and Emily in 1956. For informative accounts of postwar marital and childbearing patterns, see May, *Homeward Bound*, introduction and chap. 6; and Weiss, *To Have and to Hold*, chap. 1.

24. Daniel Horowitz discusses the complicated circumstances surrounding her departure from *UE News* in *Betty Friedan and the Making of "The Feminine Mystique,"* 141–43.

25. Friedan, *Life So Far,* 79.

26. Ibid., 81–82.

27. Ibid., 75.

28. Ibid., 121–22.

29. For example, historian Mari Jo Buhle contrasts Friedan to later writers like Nancy Chodorow, who sought to reconcile the insights of feminism with those of psychoanalysis. "While Betty Friedan and Kate Millett busied themselves lambasting Freud," she writes, "a small coterie of feminists were preparing the way for a reunion with psychoanalysis." Mari Jo Buhle, *Feminism and Its Discontents: A Century of Struggle with Psychoanalysis* (Cambridge, MA: Harvard University Press, 1998), 240. Similarly, Eva Illouz writes, "Consensus grew among feminists to the effect that psychology reinforced traditional gender roles and inequality. Nowhere was this voice more strident than in Betty Friedan's *The Feminine Mystique.*" Eva Illouz, *Saving the Modern Soul: Therapy, Emotions, and the Culture of Self-Help* (Berkeley: University of California Press, 2008), 113. Such formulations, however, imply a more hostile and critical stance toward psychoanalysis than Friedan actually assumed.

30. Friedan, *The Feminine Mystique,* 103.

31. Ibid., 104.

32. According to Friedan's biographer, Judith Hennessee, such arguments "deeply hurt" and angered women neighbors and friends who had been "a support system" for Friedan during the years that she worked on *The Feminine Mystique.* These homemakers, who had "fed and cared for her children along with their own," felt "dismissed" and "used" when they learned that she had been busily writing about how "housework was something an eight-year-old could do." Hennessee, *Betty Friedan: Her Life,* 85–86.

33. Friedan, *The Feminine Mystique,* 374.

34. Ibid., 377.

35. For Friedan's practical suggestions as to how to improve women's status, see ibid., 370–78.

36. Ibid., 344. Although Friedan did not stipulate that women had to engage in remunerative labor, most of the positive models she discussed in *The Feminine Mystique* were women who pursued professional careers.

37. Ibid., 192. A year after *The Feminine Mystique* appeared, the sociologist Alice Rossi published an influential essay that similarly used claims regarding widespread maternal pathology to promote feminist ends. "It is a short-sighted view indeed to consider the immature wife, dominating mother or interfering mother-in-law as a less serious problem to the larger society than the male homosexual, psychoneurotic soldier or ineffectual worker, for it is the failure of the mother which perpetuates the cycle from one generation to the next, affecting sons and daughters alike," she wrote. "Equality between the Sexes: An Immodest Proposal," *Daedalus* 93, no. 2 (Spring 1964): 607–52; quotation, 621.

38. In a later chapter, Friedan wrote, "The role of the mother in homosexuality was pinpointed by Freud and the psychoanalysts. But the mother whose son becomes homosexual is usually not the 'emancipated' woman who competes with men in the world, but the very paradigm of the feminine mystique—a woman who lives through her sons, whose femininity is used in virtual seduction of her son, who attaches her son to her with such dependences that he

can never mature to love a woman, nor can he, often, cope as an adult with life on his own."
Friedan, *The Feminine Mystique*, 275.

39. Of course, Friedan's critique of the suburban housewife differed from Wylie's attack on
moms in crucial respects. Unlike Wylie, Friedan was not driven by a fundamentally religious
impulse to ferret out hypocrisy and foster spiritual renewal. Her unhappy housewife is not a
repressed moralist who relies on sentimental ideas of mother love to conceal her perverse nature; on the contrary, she is *over*sexed, for she tries to quell her inner emptiness by pursuing
sexual fulfillment. Thus, her fundamental flaw is not selfishness and hypocrisy but unquestion-
ing conformity. Second, *Generation of Vipers* and *The Feminine Mystique* offer polar opposite
views of women's relationship to consumer culture. Whereas Wylie portrays American women
as the monstrous force driving consumerism, Friedan portrays them as its primary victims.
Third, the generational antagonism that infused *Generation of Vipers* is not a central feature
of *The Feminine Mystique*. Although Friedan, like Wylie, blamed present-day dilemmas on the
poor decisions of a prior generation—the couples who rushed headlong into domesticity after
World War II—her trapped housewife is a relatively young mother with children still living at
home rather than a middle-aged matron. Finally, and most importantly, Friedan spoke directly
to women, albeit only a select group of them; her criticism is to a large extent self-criticism. In
contrast, Wylie spoke to men, and his critique is best understood as a projection of masculine
fears and anxieties.

40. "Too Much Mother," *Time* 39, no. 5 (February 2, 1942): 47.

41. Friedan, *The Feminine Mystique*, 198.

42. Ibid., 202–3.

43. Quoted in Kirsten Fermaglich, "'The Comfortable Concentration Camp': The Significance of Nazi Imagery in Betty Friedan's *The Feminine Mystique* (1963)," *American Jewish History* 91, no. 2 (2003): 205–32; quotation, 217. In her autobiography, Friedan confessed that she
had come to regret the concentration camp analogy. In retrospect, she believed that it not only
belittled what Nazi prisoners had endured but also "denied" her "personal truth"—the fact that
she had experienced "many happy hours with my kids, my husband, my friends and neighbors"
during her years as "a suburban housewife and mother." Friedan, *Life So Far*, 132–33.

44. Friedan, *The Feminine Mystique*, 189.

45. "Friedan's belittlement of housewives was an ingenious use of misogynist stereotyp-
ing in the cause of women's liberation," legal scholar Joan Williams has argued. "She skillfully
turned the literature attacking housewives into evidence in favor of the need to eliminate the
housewife role." Joan Williams, *Unbending Gender: Why Family and Work Conflict and What To
Do About It* (New York: Oxford University, 2000), 43.

46. Friedan wrote, "I began to see in a strange new light the American return to early marriage and the large families that are causing the population explosion; the recent movement to
natural childbirth and breastfeeding; suburban conformity, and the new neuroses, character
pathologies and sexual problems being reported by the doctors." Friedan, *The Feminine Mystique*, 147.

47. For an illuminating history of this organization, see Amy Swerdlow, *Women Strike for
Peace: Traditional Motherhood and Radical Politics in the 1960s* (Chicago: University of Chicago
Press, 1993).

48. Dagmar Wilson spoke to this question in a 1976 interview with the activist and historian
Amy Swerdlow, and the answer that she gave is a revealing one: "My idea in emphasizing the

housewife rather than the professional was that I thought the housewife was a downgraded person, and that we, as housewives, had as much right to an opinion and that we deserved as much consideration as anyone else, and I wanted to emphasize . . . this was an important role and that it was time we were heard." Quoted in Swerdlow, *Women Strike for Peace*, 55. It is difficult to imagine maternalists prior to World War II referring to the American housewife as "a downgraded person."

49. Ibid., 375.

50. Friedan, *The Feminine Mystique*, 15.

51. Ibid., 32.

52. Friedan, "The Fraud of Femininity," 81.

53. In the book, this passage reads: "The comfortable concentration camp that American women have walked into, or have been talked into by others, is just such a reality, a frame of reference that denies woman's adult human identity. By adjusting to it, a woman stunts her intelligence to become childlike, turns away from individual identity to become an anonymous biological robot in a docile mass. She becomes less than human, preyed upon by outside pressures, and herself preying upon her husband and children." Friedan, *The Feminine Mystique*, 308. For a discussion of Friedan's references to Nazism and the Holocaust, see Fermaglich, " 'The Comfortable Concentration Camp.' "

54. See material in folder 738a, box 21, BFP. In the final version of this article, which Friedan belatedly sent to *McCall's* after being sternly rebuked for submitting a draft that greatly exceeded the word limit, she does not mention feeling "shaken" by the letters. See Betty Friedan, "Angry Letters," *McCall's* 90 (August 1963): 38–40, 165. For earlier drafts, see folder 738b, box 21, BFP. For *McCall's* communication with Friedan, see Peter Wyden to Betty Friedan, April 15, 1963, folder 738b, box 21, BFP. Interestingly, when Friedan reprinted this piece in a collection of her essays, she changed the title to "Angry Letters, Relieved Letters." Friedan, *It Changed My Life: Writings on the Women's Movement* (Cambridge, MA: Harvard University Press, 1998), 22–36.

55. Moreover, Friedan never discussed "who would be called in to take care of the children and maintain the home if more women like herself were freed from their house labor and given equal access with white men to the professions," nor did she consider whether the employment opportunities available to poor and working-class women would represent any real improvement over full-time domesticity. bell hooks, *Feminist Theory: From Margin to Center* (Boston: South End Press, 1984), 1–3.

56. [Pomona, CA], June 22, 1964, folder 682, box 19, BFP.

57. [Norman, OK], September 24, 1967, folder 701, box 19, BFP.

58. [GA], July 5, 1964, folder 691, box 19, BFP.

59. [Staten Island, NY], June 24, 1964, folder 683, box 19, BFP; [N.p., n.d.], folder 706, box 19, BFP.

60. [N.p., n.d.], folder 680, box 19, BFP.

61. [N.p., n.d.], folder 687, box 19, BFP.

62. [N.p., n.d.], folder 699, box 19, BFP.

63. [Palo Alto, CA], February 22, 1963, folder 684, box 19, BFP.

64. [N.p.], April 28, 1963, folder 685, box 19, BFP.

65. [N.p.], September 3, 1963, folder 689, box 19, BFP.

66. Ellen Herman, *The Romance of American Psychology: Political Culture in the Age of Experts* (Berkeley: University of California Press, 1995), chap. 10; and Moskowitz, *In Therapy We Trust*, chap. 6. See also Illouz, *Saving the Modern Soul*.

67. Several respondents even described their encounter with Friedan's writing in explicitly therapeutic terms. For instance, a mother of four explained that, while she had found group therapy useful in helping to identify her troubles, it was only the experience of reading *The Feminine Mystique* "over and over again" that allowed her to "summon up enough courage" to enroll in college part-time. [Wayne, NJ], September 18, 1964, folder 692, box 19, BFP.

68. A successful opera singer, who had undergone ten years of psychoanalysis, related a fascinating story that suggests something of the complexity of women's relationships to their analysts and therapists. "Finally my first analyst heard a tape of a performance of mine. . . . He decided that I am an artist of exceptional merit and has since gone to really extraordinary lengths to help me start [singing again]—I stopped originally under his benign guidance to 'be a more feminine woman'—and promptly stopped functioning as a human being. Therefore I feel that he can darned well help me now. I have been timidly saying in the exalted scientific circles in which my husband moves . . . that American Freudian analysts have done a most cruel thing to American women and have induced sort of mass sickness instead of healing. I get back their patronizing 'Hostility, hostility, my dear' as they smile at their downtrodden wives pregnant with the fifth child, so you can see how deeply I feel your book." [N.p.], January 8, 1969, folder 703, box 19, BFP.

69. For instance, a mother who went to a child guidance clinic with one of her four sons was "astounded" and deeply relieved when her counselor told her that, "in many cases a mother is a better person for having an outside job." [MI], April 18, 1964, folder 690, box 19, BFP.

70. [Richmond, VA], November 22, 1963, folder 681, box 19, BFP.

71. [New York, NY], January 21, 1963, folder 683, box 19, BFP. This correspondent was referring to Arnold W. Green's "The Middle Class Male Child and Neurosis," *American Sociological Review* 11 (February 1946): 31–41. In a study based on his Massachusetts hometown, Green argues that the sons of working-class Polish immigrants, who were subjected to harsh parental discipline, suffered none of the neuroses prevalent among their middle-class counterparts. But a footnote reveals that this "finding" rested on nothing more than the author's own observations and an informant's assurance that "there is no known case of army rejection because of psychoneurosis within the local Polish community" (33). For Friedan's lengthy discussion of this article, see *The Feminine Mystique*, 199–202.

72. [South Orange, NJ], June 23, 1964, folder 683, box 19, BFP.

73. [Stockton, CA], April 17, 1964, folder 690, box 19, BFP.

74. [N.p.], April 21, 1964, folder 690, box 19, BFP.

75. [Montreal, Canada], March 10, 1969, folder 703, box 19, BFP. Although living in Montreal, this woman seems to have been American, for she strongly identified with what she referred to as Friedan's portrait of "American women." It should also be stressed that this letter was written several years later than the other letters quoted in this chapter. The respondent's experiences appear to reflect the cultural upheavals of the late 1960s; a case like hers—in which a husband and father of four small children threatened to divorce his wife in the absence of a glaringly obvious reason—would have been less common earlier in the decade.

76. [NJ], March 14, 1963, folder 748, box 21, BFP.

77. [Tulsa, OK], March 12, 1963, folder 748, box 21, BFP.

78. [Granbury, TX], March 13, 1963, folder 748, box 21, BFP.

79. [Mattapan, MA, n.d.], folder 745, box 21, BFP.

80. [Stockton, CA], March 11, 1963, folder 748, box 21, BFP.

81. [Murfreesboro, TN], March 6, 1963, folder 746, box 21, BFP.

82. As Jessica Weiss has shown, a significant minority of *McCall's* respondents (about 9 percent) also drew a direct connection between Friedan's critique of domesticity and the threat of communism. For her illuminating analysis of the relationship between anticommunism and antifeminism in the early 1960s, see Weiss, " 'Comrade Betty.' "

83. [Galveston, TX], February 20, 1963, folder 741, box 21, BFP.

84. [Farmington, MI], February 21, 1963, folder 741, box 21, BFP.

85. [N.p.], February 20, 1963, folder 741, box 21, BFP.

86. [San Diego, CA], February 27, 1963, folder 743, box 21, BFP.

87. [Torrance, CA], February 20, 1963, folder 741, box, 21, BFP.

88. [Washington, D.C.], March 14, 1963, folder 748, box 21, BFP.

89. [N.p.], February 2, 1963, folder 741, box 21, BFP.

90. [Liberal, KS], March 1, 1963, folder 745, box 21, BFP.

91. [N.p.], February 26, 1963, folder 742, box 21, BFP.

92. [Nacogdoches, TX], April 3, 1963, folder 751, box 21, BFP.

93. For studies of child care in the twentieth-century United States, see Sonya Michel, *Children's Interests/Mothers' Rights: The Shaping of American's Child Care Policy* (New Haven, CT: Yale University Press, 1999); Elizabeth Rose, *A Mother's Job: The History of Day Care, 1890–1960* (New York: Oxford University Press, 1999); and Emilie Stoltzfus, *Citizen, Mother, Worker: Debating Public Responsibility for Child Care after the Second World War* (Chapel Hill: University of North Carolina Press, 2003).

94. [Indian Head, MD], March 11, 1963, folder 748, box 21, BFP.

95. [Brooklyn, NY], March 30, 1963, folder 750, box 21, BFP.

96. [N.p.], February 19, 1963, folder 741, box 741, BFP.

97. [Sebastopol, CA], February 16, 1963, folder 741, box 21, BFP.

98. [Preston, Ontario], March 2, 1963, folder 746, box 21, BFP; and [Kenmore, NY], March 8, 1963, folder 747, box 21, BFP.

99. [Fair Lawn, NJ], March 29, 1963, folder 750, box 21, BFP.

100. [Fargo, ND], February 22, 1963, folder 744, box 21, BFP.

101. [Granbury, TX], March 13, 1963, folder 748, box 21, BFP.

102. [Johnson, KS, n.d.], folder 752, box 21, BFP.

103. [N.p.], March 18, 1963, folder 749, box 21, BFP.

104. Linda K. Kerber, *No Constitutional Right To Be Ladies: Women and the Obligations of Citizenship* (New York: Hill and Wang, 1998), 12.

105. Historian Joanne Meyerowitz has rightly argued that *The Feminine Mystique* should not be viewed as a judicious historical account. "For a journalistic exposé," she writes, "Friedan's work has had a surprisingly strong influence on historiography." Meyerowitz makes this point in regard to Friedan's claim that the postwar period saw the rise of a hegemonic "feminine mystique" that sought to confine women to domesticity, but it is equally relevant in regard to her account of psychiatric mother-blaming. Friedan's portrait of mother-blaming as an exclusively postwar phenomenon that paradoxically served to reinforce the dominant domestic ideal does not offer a sound basis for a historical understanding of antimaternalism. Meyerowitz, "Beyond the Feminine Mystique," 1456.

106. Betty Friedan, "Up from the Kitchen Floor," *New York Times Magazine*, March 4, 1973, 8–9, 28–37; quotation, 28.

107. For discussions of Phyllis Schlafly and the battle over the ERA, see Jane J. Mansbridge, *Why We Lost the ERA* (Chicago: University of Chicago Press, 1986); Donald T. Critchlow, *Phyllis*

Schlafly and Grassroots Conservatism: A Woman's Crusade (Princeton, NJ: Princeton University Press, 2005); and Catherine E. Rymph, *Republican Women: Feminism and Conservatism from Suffrage through the Rise of the New Right* (Chapel Hill: University of North Carolina Press, 2006).

108. As sociologist Kristin Luker has shown, the battle over abortion in the 1970s and early 1980s was essentially a debate about motherhood and a debate between women, who by 1974 constituted 80 percent of both prolife and prochoice activists. On the one hand, prochoice activists, who generally possessed the education and resources that allowed them to compete as professionals in the workplace, wanted motherhood "recognized as a private, discretionary choice." On the other hand, prolife activists, who had fewer resources and more limited opportunities for success in the workplace, wanted motherhood "to be recognized as the most important thing a woman can do." They viewed women's capacity for motherhood as a potential "resource" that would be diminished if pregnancies could be readily terminated. "In order for pro-choice women to achieve their goals, they must argue that motherhood is not a primary, inevitable, or 'natural' role for all women; for pro-life women to achieve their goals, they must argue that it is," Luker concludes. "In short, the debate rests on the question of whether women's fertility is to be socially recognized as a resource or as a handicap." Kristin Luker, *Abortion and the Politics of Motherhood* (Berkeley: University of California Press, 1984), 202.

109. Friedan, *The Second Stage* (New York: Summit Books, 1981), 40.

110. Ibid., 49.

111. Sarah J. Stage, "Women," *American Quarterly* 35 (1983): 169–90.

112. Friedan, *The Second Stage*, 203.

113. Harwin, "'Occupation: Houseworker.'"

Index